COSMOLOGIES OF CREDIT

COSMOLOGIES OF CREDIT

TRANSNATIONAL MOBILITY AND THE POLITICS OF DESTINATION IN CHINA

Julie Y. Chu

DUKE UNIVERSITY PRESS · *Durham and London* · 2010

© 2010 Duke University Press
All rights reserved
Printed in the United States
of America on acid-free paper ∞
Designed by Amy Ruth Buchanan
Typeset in Scala and Scala Sans
by Achorn International
Library of Congress Cataloging-
in-Publication Data appear on the
last printed page of this book.

For my mother
and my siblings
&
For MSH
In recognition
of all the debts sustained
amid grand absences

CONTENTS

ACKNOWLEDGMENTS

This work would not have been possible without the kindness and generosity of the people I met in the field, many of whom appear in this book under pseudonyms. In particular I want to thank the family with whom I resided in "Longyan," as well as the local middle school there for providing me with a secure institutional home. I owe a special debt to the more than two hundred students at the middle school, who always kept me on my toes and who led me to various, unexpected destinations throughout my fieldwork. In nearby Fuzhou City, I am extremely grateful to Lin Guoping and his wife and daughter for their unfailing support, both scholarly and otherwise. I also would not have gotten much done without my dearest friend and occasional research assistant, Zheng Xiaojuan. My Fuzhounese language teacher, Liang Yuzhang, was not only a true role model, but also another crucial anchor for me in China. Other friends, including Deng Qikai, Zhang Yan, Lan Weifang, and Liu Haiyan, made my time in Fuzhou infinitely more welcoming and enjoyable. I also thank Xie Bizhen and Cai Xiuling for their friendship and support. Finally, I am grateful to Fujian Normal University for providing me an academic base as a research fellow for 2001–2002 and for hosting me at the International College during the summer of 2000.

On the U.S. end of things, Faye Ginsburg and Eric Manheimer were instrumental in enabling me to develop my initial interests in Fuzhounese migration during the MA phase of my research. This book would also not have been possible without Angela Zito, whose timely arrival at New York University at the tail end of my MA gave me the necessary boost of confidence and intellectual inspiration to follow the Fuzhounese back to China for further PhD fieldwork. Once I turned my attention to China, I benefited tremendously from conversations with Ko-lin Chin and Michael Szonyi, both of whom were exceptionally generous in sharing knowledge and resources for getting research done in Fuzhou. Several other scholars also gave me valuable insights and advice about doing fieldwork in China, including Kenneth Dean, Leo Douw, Lisa Rofel, Murray Rubenstein, Louisa Schein, Frank Pieke, and Li Minghua. My actual fieldwork was supported by fellowships from the Chiang Ching-Kuo Foundation for International Scholarly Exchange and from the International Migration Program of the Social Science Research Council, with funds provided by the Andrew W. Mellon Foundation. Various stages of writing were given institutional support by anthropology departments at New York University, the University of California at Santa Cruz, Wellesley College, and the University of Chicago, as well as the American Anthropology Association's Minority Dissertation Fellowship, the University of California's Presidential Postdoctoral Fellowship, and the Irmgard Coninx Foundation.

Many people helped see me through the writing and rewriting of this book. During the initial dissertation phase at NYU, my thanks go out to Jessica Cattelino, Omri Elisha, Faye Ginsburg, Sherine Hamdy, Adria Imada, Jong Bum Kwon, Emily Martin, Fred Myers, Ayse Parla, Ramona Perez, Lok Siu, Elizabeth Smith, Winifred Tate, and Angela Zito. I am especially grateful to Winifred and Sherine for allowing me to subject them to various half-baked drafts of chapters over the long haul from dissertation to final book manuscript. Lisa Rofel also provided invaluable support and feedback on the entire manuscript during the post-dissertation phase of writing. I thank her not only for her sharp insights, but also for generously circulating my work-in-progress among her graduate students at UC Santa Cruz, who gave me many additional ideas for revisions. Similarly, this book benefited from feedback from graduate courses taught by Angela Zito at NYU and Kesha Fikes at the University of Chicago. I also received much needed comments for revising individual chapters and discrete parts of the book from Amahl Bishara, Summerson Carr, Jessica Cattelino, Sealing Cheng, Sara Friedman, D. J. Hatfield, Eleana Kim, John Osberg, Gilberto Rosas, Greg Ruf, and Robin Shoaps, as well as from various colloquium and workshop audiences at UC Santa Cruz, UC San Diego, Brown, the University of Chicago, the University of Texas at Austin, the New School, Tufts, Brandeis, Johns Hopkins, and the Berlin Roundtables for Transnationality. I am also grateful to the two anonymous readers from Duke University Press for their careful readings and thoughtful suggestions for revisions, as well as to my editor, Ken Wissoker, for his Zen-like patience and support for seeing this book to publication. My thanks also go out to assistant managing editor Tim Elfenbein, copy editor Bojana

Ristich, and J. Naomi Linzer Indexing Services for helping me through the final stages.

Last but not least, two people have been my most stalwart supporters throughout the research and writing of this book. First, I want to thank my mother for putting her own doubts aside to travel to China with me when I first embarked on this project. We literally took the slow boat down the Yangtze on the way to Fuzhou, and as I describe in the introduction, this project would not have gone nearly as smoothly if I had not been my mother's daughter. Finally, I thank my partner, Matthew Harris, for providing all the little things that helped make the good days great and the bad days forgettable.

• • •

An earlier version of chapter 1 appeared in *Identities* 13, no. 3 (September 2006).

This book uses the pinyin system for romanizing both Mandarin (Standard Chinese) and Fuzhounese in the text. Fuzhounese words and phrases are only distinguished from Mandarin, with the notation "Fz," when they appear in parenthetical format. While Fuzhounese has sometimes been transcribed according to the international phonetic alphabet, I have elected to use pinyin in keeping with the standardized format of the *Fuzhou Dialect Dictionary* (*Fuzhou fangyan cidian*), authored by my Fuzhounese teacher, Liang Yuzhang (Fuzhou: Fujian People's Publishing, 1995). Though Teacher Liang also taught me Fuzhounese through the more precise international phonetic system, I trust she will forgive me for sacrificing precision for simplicity's sake.

In order to protect the confidentiality of my subjects, I refer to my particular field site as well as all its members by pseudonyms. Except for known names of political figures like Mao Zedong and broad regional markers like "the rural outskirts of Fuzhou City" or Fujian Province, I have eliminated or disguised various identifying markers of my field site, to which I refer here as "Longyan." This includes a modification of the published sources I cite that include the specific name of my field site in the title, as well as the authors of such sources. In using pseudonyms consistently throughout, I have assigned one unique name to each subject cited in this book so that the reader, if he or she chooses to do so, can follow particular characters through all the chapters with the assurance that "Deng Feiyan" in the introduction is the same "Deng Feiyan" in chapter 6.

Deng Feiyan already had her bags packed when we first met in Fuzhou in the summer of 2000. In her barren living quarters, stripped of all signs of permanent residence, her bags—two bloated canvas and burlap bundles of indeterminate content—leaned against the wall between a makeshift tatami mattress and a miniscule pink plastic stool, where the sole phone, a bright red clanging unit, beckoned. The stage was already set: just one ring from her *shetou* (snakehead or human smuggler) and she was prepared to swoop from phone to bags to the door in a single choreographed move out of her house and out of China for good.

Our relationship grew out of an expectation of confluent departures: we were both bound for New York City before the first gusts of typhoon weather promised to hit the southeast coast of China at the seasonal turn of humid summer to tepid autumn. It was only a question of who would depart first: me on my open-ended return plane ticket via Guangzhou and Los Angeles to New York's John F. Kennedy Airport or Deng Feiyan on her anticipated smuggling venture via foreign ports yet unknown. If she left Fuzhou first, she promised to stay put in New York long enough to have a hearty meal with me in Chinatown. We both imagined this New York reunion was in our near future and often whiled away time on sticky summer afternoons sketching the possible scenarios of our converging itineraries and lives overseas.

Partly out of homesickness and partly out of naive optimism, I felt a deep affinity for Deng Feiyan's transient state and her sense of momentum toward a destination beyond China's borders. Like her, my bags were constantly in my purview that summer as a reminder of my temporary positioning in Fuzhou as a foreign researcher on a short, three-month stint of preliminary fieldwork. More important, I had come here precisely to figure out the imaginative trajectories that led back to New York City, the prime destination of massive migrant flows from Fuzhou's countryside over the past two decades. It was only too easy to imagine, alongside Deng Feiyan, that all roads pointed toward a convergence of transnational destinations for us in a matter of weeks and months.

By mid-June, Deng Feiyan had nailed down a timeframe for departure. Twenty or so days from now, she expected to get the phone call from her *shetou* to grab her bags and go. She did not know exactly how her trip would shape up—which route, what transport, how long in transit—but one thing was for sure: "It looks like I will leave before you do," she beamed. Two days after she firmed up her departure date, news of a smuggling disaster in Dover, England, began to circulate all through the city. Fifty-eight migrants from Fuzhou had slowly suffocated to death while hiding in the back of a sealed produce truck on a transcontinental ride from Belgium to Dover. This story made international headlines as the single worst case of smuggling deaths at the time and quickly filtered into our lives not more than a day later as we sat in Deng Feiyan's kitchen with a friend of hers on a breezy June afternoon. Deng Feiyan was in the middle of one of her typical rosy musings of life overseas when her friend abruptly thrust a newspaper clipping in front of us. "Look here!" the friend interrupted. "See how fifty-eight people just died in smuggling? Ah, it's really too terrifying!" But Deng Feiyan barely blinked at her friend's comments or at the article leaping off the kitchen table with its bold, alarmist headline and ghostly image of crooked silhouettes entombed in the truck. As her friend began to retrace the sensational details of the case, Deng Feiyan simply pushed the article aside and casually excused herself from the kitchen. She did not seem concerned about the news at all. Instead, she took a quiet afternoon nap.

Later Deng Feiyan told me she had a vivid dream that day about how she had already made it to New York. There she was, far away from Fuzhou, sitting and chatting contentedly over a cup of tea with a good friend who had successfully departed for the United States many years ago. Deng Feiyan's face lit up as she recalled this vision of herself already abroad in the long-lost comfort of good company. More than a dream, she was sure this was a divine prophecy of her upcoming trip overseas. The Dover case did not faze her, she told me, because she knew the gods would protect her. Even when her travel plans unraveled as the Chinese government initiated swift crackdowns on human smuggling amid international embarrassment over the Dover disaster, Deng Feiyan remained confident that her destiny lay overseas.

"Let me tell you, Little Sister," she confided. "I know the only road for me leads to America because Mazu resides in me and she has told me so." Mazu, the goddess of the sea and the guardian of all who braved its rough waters, not only had a devoted worshipper in Deng Feiyan, but it also turned out that Deng Feiyan served as a spirit medium for channeling the goddess's divine knowledge and powers. Over the years with Mazu present inside her, Deng Feiyan had rooted out and healed the elusive pains and illnesses of those who sought her out precisely for these divine services. Now it was also Mazu's voice from the depths of Deng Feiyan's heart-and-mind (*xinli*) that soothed and assured her as her departure date slipped out of her reach and stretched indefinitely into late summer. Perhaps she would no longer reach New York before I did, she admitted. But with Mazu on her side, she was still certain that we would keep our Chinatown date some time that year.

Deng Feiyan never did manage to leave China, though she remained constantly on the cusp of departure over the years I knew her. When I returned to Fuzhou a year later, I found her dwelling in almost the same transient state, her house still sparsely filled with just a few pieces of disposable furniture—the makeshift bed, the plastic stools, the same two bags lingering near the clunky old phone. More than four years after we first met, Deng Feiyan continued to embody a forward momentum, constantly adjusting her designs for emigration whenever previous itineraries stalled or simply dissipated. Nothing seemed to diffuse the promise of her destiny overseas, neither the ever-increasing smuggling fee for successful travel (currently averaging $60,000) nor her personal knowledge of the deadly risks in transit and exploitative labor conditions abroad. Long after she had turned from the bold headlines of the Dover disaster and taken her prophetic nap that June afternoon, the sense of imminent departure still enchanted her every move and overshadowed the mundane signs of her present and indeterminate immobility. Though her various travel plans repeatedly fell apart before she ever stepped foot out of China, Deng Feiyan remained unbowed about her fateful dream of arrival overseas, merely deferring it after each setback to a future just ever so slightly out of reach.

• • •

This book examines the pervasive sense of momentum that has taken hold of Fuzhounese subjects like Deng Feiyan with transnational destinations on their horizons. More specifically, it is an exploration of how mobility as a key trope in projects of capitalist development and modernity is currently lived in post-Mao China among a rural-coastal population situated on the mercurial edge between global flows and parochial closures. Since China initiated its policies for "economic reform and opening up" (*gaige kaifang*) in 1979, much has been written about transformations in spatial-temporal orders from the caste-like rural/urban divide of the socialist planned economy to the new, market-liberalizing regime of coastal development and inland stasis with the latter often euphemized as "socialism with Chinese characteristics." The aspiring Fuzhounese migrants I discuss here reside at a most awkward intersection of these spatial-temporal processes. As state-classified peasants for four decades, they have long lingered in the stagnant, rural backwaters of a socialist vision of modernity. But as coastal subjects, they also now find themselves at the dynamic front of global exchange and capitalist circulation in the newly revised imaginary of post-Mao modernization.[1] This is less a linear account of the passage from rural backwardness to coastal cosmopolitanism than a heterogeneous retracing of the entangled, discordant, and contested trajectories of a double-edged figure: the coastal yet peasant, mobile but errant Fuzhounese transmigrant.

Fuzhounese migration came to international attention through several tragic disasters, including the 1993 *Golden Venture* boat drownings off the shores of Queens, New York, and the aforementioned 2000 truck suffocation deaths at Dover. Over the years, repeated news of Chinese stowaways washed up on Western shores, asphyxiated in shipping containers, and exploited in overseas sweatshops and restaurants has continued to highlight the unrelenting desire of the Fuzhounese to leave China, despite the ever-increasing physical dangers and uncertain economic payoff of traveling through transnational human smuggling networks.[2] Descriptions from home villages have often suggested that an inexplicable craze had swept through the Fuzhou countryside. As the *Sing Tao Daily* reported as early as 1996, "Everybody went crazy. The area was in a frenzy. Farmers put down their tools, students discarded their books, workers quit their jobs, and everybody was talking about nothing but going to America."[3] What fueled this "frenzy" of illicit migration from Fuzhou to the United States? What kept the likes of Deng Feiyan in the perpetual pursuit of departure? This desire—its conditions of possibility, its entailments as embodied value—forms the puzzle at the heart of my research.

Cosmologies of Credit is an ethnography of the entangled calculative logics and regimes of value propelling Fuzhounese desires for mobility in the post-Mao era.[4] Specifically, I am interested in the particular cultural-historical moments when desire meets potentiality, that zone of indeterminacy where one must confront the hazards involved in translating desires into projects worth pursuing. In this sense, this book offers an exploration of the *pragmatics* of desire[5]—the cultural-historical configuration of its incitements, the social hazards of its translation into action, the political implications of its effects—among a particular group of Fuzhounese subjects situated in an emergent social field spanning China and the United States. One goal of this book is to move beyond utilitarian questions of risks and rewards, costs and benefits, to a consideration of the overflow of Fuzhounese aspirations—the productive frictions, the indeterminate remainders, and the unexpected effects entailed in the Fuzhounese pursuit of transnational mobility.[6] I do this by attending not just to the movement of migrant bodies in the following chapters, but also to the paths and diversions of related things-in-motion: shipping containers and planes, luggage and immigration papers, money and cosmic debt, food and prayers, traveling gods and the unsettled dead. In doing so, my aim is to connect Fuzhounese migration to the broader social field of circulations and transactions that make it possible to recognize and assess the differential value of various people and things entangled in webs of increasing transnational exchange. In particular, this book offers a sketch of the various confluent and disjunctive movements propelled by exchange—of which migrant bodies constitute just one flow—that support what Nancy Munn (1986) has aptly described as the "spatial-temporal extension" of persons and collectivities.

• • •

This book joins recent anthropological works that have grappled with the enchantments of state power and capitalist modernity at the turn of the twenty-first century (Comaroff and Comaroff 2000; Coronil 1997; Dorfman 1996; Klima 2002; Meyer and Pels 2003; Mueggler 2001; Ong 1987; Taussig 1993, 1997). Like many of these works, my project traces the mutual constitution of enchantment and disenchantment among unabashedly modern(izing) subjects—of divine practice alongside profound state cynicisms, of cosmic credit amid insurmountable financial debt, of prophetic destinies in the face of crushing immobility. More than oppositional resistance or ideological reflection, such enchantments, I argue, are integral to the production of modern imaginaries themselves. Far from forging a "third space" or exterior Other to capitalist modernity, ritual life among the Fuzhounese (re)constituted the grounds for the enactment of modern selves and relations; it offered yet another "staging of the modern" (Mitchell 2000). To their Fuzhounese followers, gods like Mazu, with powers to divine the future and instantaneously crisscross the oceans, were fundamentally forward-looking, cosmopolitan forces, exemplary incarnations of space-time compression, among other features, of late and post-modernity (cf. Harvey 1989). As I will show, this kind of "spirit," embraced and embodied by aspiring migrants like Deng Feiyan, propelled them toward, rather than away from, dreams of mobile and cosmopolitan destinies.

The title of this book, with its old-fashioned nod to "cosmology"—that ethnographic juggernaut of "primitive," enchanted worldviews—is an attempt to capture what Timothy Mitchell (1992) has described as the impossible unity and incomplete universal inherent in every staging of modernity. Framed here in the multiple as *Cosmologies of Credit*, this title speaks to oscillations between the one and the many of modernity, between its singularizing claims as ideology and its heterogeneous configurations as practice.[7] This lived tension is the very generative source of modernity's efficacy as a floating, master signifier of ontological difference, able to accrue value to particular people, places, practices, and things by conjuring the specter of excluded, oppositional, and inevitably vanishing others.[8] That such boundaries between the modern and nonmodern are tenuous, shifting, and constantly being remade has been aptly demonstrated by a wide and rich range of scholarship.[9] In keeping both the one and the many in my purview, however, my goal is neither to give another iteration of "alternative modernities" per se nor to displace the dominant fictional realities of capitalist modernity with the privileged Real of a "local" order of things.[10] Instead, this book seeks to illuminate the *interpenetrations* of these various regimes of value in the (re)production of power asymmetries among differentiated persons and their differentiated worlds.

More than a decade ago, Marshall Sahlins (1994) forcefully argued for recognizing such entanglements of cosmologies in intercultural encounters and exchanges between the West and its Others. Partly inspired by the imperial imaginary of the Qing court in China, Sahlins showed how *The* World System (as we know it) could be made to serve, rather than simply obliterate, alternative cultural logics and indigenous transactional orders. Sahlins entitled his article "Cosmologies of Capitalism" to emphasize the transposable and reciprocal nature of various non-Western schemas of value in both shaping and being shaped by capitalist encounters.[11] Additionally, he meant to highlight the cultural-historical specificity of capitalism as a "Western cosmology" in its own right, a cosmology that he would later trace to particular Judeo-Christian concepts of human finitude, a disenchanted nature, and the pleasure-pain principle (Sahlins 1996).

Partly by coincidence and partly by osmosis, I had been trafficking in uncannily similar conceptual terrain, circulating my own research project with the title "Cosmologies of Credit" for a good three years before Sahlins's 1994 article came into my purview.[12] Clearly some retroactive debt is in order since this book shares the broad strokes of Sahlins's analytic approach to questions of exchange and value. However, it is with a finer brush that I seek to sketch the conceptual contours of "cosmologies."[13] Specifically, this project departs from less solid conceptions of culture and locality, putting into question, rather than assuming, the durable unity of a "Chinese" order of things or, for that matter, an opposing "Western cosmology." Highlighting "credit" rather than "capitalism" as a focal point of cosmologies is another way I hope to complicate the assumed foundation or domain for producing value among the Fuzhounese. As I hope to show, credit, with its multivalent implications—as confidence or approval of an action or another, as deferred payment and flip side of debt, as the positive balance of accounting—offers a richer conceptual touchstone for exploring the calculative horizons of value production than a notion like capitalism or capital. Even in the most diversified usage, à la Pierre Bourdieu's social-cultural-economic schema, capital often retains an inherent economism of means-ends utility (Bourdieu 1977, 1986). By speaking of "cosmologies of credit" rather than "cosmologies of capitalism," I aim to move beyond an examination of value production as accumulation, growth, or surplus to a broader inquiry into credit-able practices that include such activities as the personal assumption of loss and the collective generation of karmic debt and its repayment.[14]

A starting point for this work is the suspension of conventional analytic domains and their boundaries—of "the market," "the state," or "local culture"—in favor of the discursive and material *processes* for boundary and subject making. As Jane Collier and Sylvia Yanagisako have argued for the analysis of gender and kinship, "we should seek rather than assume knowledge of the socially significant domains of relations in any particular society and what constitutes them" (1987, 34). Rather than taking for granted "the existence of a gender system based on natural differences in sexual reproduction, a kinship system based on the genealogical grid, a polity based on force, or an economy based on the production and distribution of needed resources," we should investigate what processes make certain "domains appear self-evident, and perhaps even 'natural,' as fields of activity in any society" (35).

In this book, I am interested in how such boundaries among "fields of activity" become stabilized as legible and "self-evident," as well as how they are troubled and transgressed by Fuzhounese subjects situated in a particularly active and unsettling contact zone of translocal and transnational flows. Broadly speaking, I am concerned here with Fuzhounese efforts to remake and re-world their lives in a site where the very terms of dwelling and mobility—and, by extension, locality and scale—have shifted dramatically over the years. Part I of this book sketches these various boundary-making (and -breaking) projects by analyzing shifting Fuzhounese imaginaries of place and emplacement (chapter 1) and the cross-class tensions resulting from recent Fuzhounese attempts, particularly via mass emigration, for transcending the material and discursive limitations of peasant subjectification in China (chapter 2). By attending to practices for demarcating space and time, domains and histories, I aim to provide insights about everyday struggles and political contestations over the ordering of social transactions and entanglements, and of persons and things.[15]

The Politics of Destination

Boundary making, as I will show, is as much about temporality and historical consciousness as it is about spatiality and scale. In the contemporary context of the People's Republic of China (PRC), ethnographers, like their subjects, have been faced with a dominant historical narrative of dramatic social change, "reversals and ironies" (Dirlik 1996), over China's long twentieth century: from liberation to revolution to reform; from collectivization to decollectivization; from communism to market liberalization.[16] Along the way, modernity has been a recurring and elusive figure, marking each subsequent periodization (for example, "after liberation," "after reform") as the penultimate break between "backwardness" and "progress" in a perpetually revised linear narrative of China's development. Lisa Rofel (1999) has aptly described these historicizations as a modernity continually deferred, a dominant narrative reflected as much in academic exegesis as in party-state discourse about China's positioning in the world.

By chance, I arrived in Fuzhou for my year-long stint of fieldwork in 2001 during another momentous turn in the story of China's imminent "rise" on the global stage. Between China's winning bid for the 2008 Olympics in June and its entry into the World Trade Organization (WTO) in November, I managed to land at Changle International Airport in Fuzhou on September 11, just in time for my Chinese friends to inform me of the terrible news that was being broadcast from New York City live via satellite on various Chinese television stations. No one knew what to make of the tragedies of 9/11 at the time. However, it was clear that along with China's successful Olympics bid and expected entry into the WTO, 9/11 compelled people in Fuzhou, particularly those aspiring to leave China, to fixate ever more on the future and particularly on how the things to come might alter their prospects at home and overseas. While the first decade or so of the post-Mao era was replete with accounts of Chinese subjects reflexively grappling with a past tinged with both recent political traumas (Jing 1996; Mueggler 2001) and nostalgic yearnings (Dorfman 1996; Rofel 1994, 1999), I seemed to find the Fuzhounese at a decidedly future-oriented, anticipatory moment when I embarked on my field research at the beginning of China's third decade of experiments with market liberalization. To my surprise, in both interviews and casual conversations people were much more interested in discussing their possible trajectories from the present forward than in retracing the bygone fits and starts from their pre-reform past. This is not to say that the past no longer figured in personal narratives and native exegesis of social life. What struck me, however, were the ways people conjured the past not merely as a site to dwell upon or to give meaning to the present moment. Instead, making claims on the past was crucially about activating the vectors of one's likely destiny and possible future; it both backformed and propelled the sense of momentum in people's lives (see chapter 2). As I will show, contestations over the past were often struggles over the legitimacy of Fuzhounese aspirations and prospects and particularly their claims to becoming mobile, cosmopolitan subjects.

The rural Fuzhounese, I argue, were precisely *not* the kinds of subjects authorized by the Chinese state (or for that matter, U.S. immigration agendas) to chart moral careers as Chinese cosmopolitans. In turn, what they revealed through their persistent yearnings and strategies for going overseas was not only the normativity of mobility per se in post-Mao China but also the power relations inherent in what Doreen Massey (1993) has called "differentiated mobility"—that is, the uneven and unequal positioning of different groups and persons in relation to various flows and movements (see chapters 3–4). It is no secret that since the Chinese central government began promoting a policy for "opening up" and "stepping out" (see chapter 2), the population has been redrawn along all sorts of newly mobile distinctions: the upward (a growing urban middle class) and the outward (the "new immigrants," the "old" overseas Chinese); the stagnant (rural unemployed) and the uprooted ("floating population" or internal migrants). As Xin Liu has described, "Economic reforms have set the population on the run. Everywhere in China, people are trying to leave various kinds of home spaces in order to 'get rich first.' From the point of view of ordinary people, travel and its associated imaginings are becoming an important condition of everyday life" (1997, 110). In arguing for the emergence of a new kind of valorized subjectivity in late modernity—the "flexible citizen" or transnational Chinese—Aihwa Ong has similarly noted that "flexibility, migration, and relocations, instead of being coerced or resisted, have become practices to strive for rather than stability" (1999, 19). This change did not mean that coercion and resistance to mobility no longer took place. In fact, several ethnographies continued to show that these dynamics were alive and well in contemporary China (Kipnis 1997; Mueggler 2001; Zhang 2001b; Zhou 1996). However, what both Ong and Liu illuminated was the distinctive formation of a desiring Chinese subject hinged to mobility as the principle and modus operandi for value production.

This book elaborates on these observations of mobility as a "condition of everyday life" and as "practices to strive for" in post-Mao China. But while mainstream narratives of transnational and cosmopolitan Chinese often focus only on the elite movements of jet-setting entrepreneurs and intellectuals, I turn my attention to the formation of what James Clifford loosely termed "*discrepant* cosmopolitanisms" (1997, 36, my emphasis;

see also Nyers 2003; Ong 2005).[17] In particular I draw on Clifford's notion here to highlight the disjunctures and tensions among various classed, gendered, and otherwise unequally positioned subjects with desires and claims to a cosmopolitan ideal in the post-Mao era (see chapters 2 and 6). Chinese scholars abroad, smuggled Fuzhounese migrants, and the internal "floating population" may all be mobile subjects, but certainly they do not share the same access to and mastery over their movements, not to mention over other circulatory flows such as those of money, transit, paperwork, or information. While scholarly emphasis on elite cosmopolitanism has tended to marginalize the still active forces of nation-states in constraining mobility across borders, I hope to illuminate how aspiring Fuzhounese migrants, even in their circumvention and defiance of state expectations for travel, were still profoundly entangled in the hegemonic project of Chinese modernity. As part II of this book shows, by forging unauthorized and unconventional roads to becoming mobile subjects, the Fuzhounese infused dissonant aspects of rural practice that were not valorized by the state into an existing ideal of the modern Chinese cosmopolitan, including a productive alliance with mobile, worldly gods. In this sense they complicated and even hybridized the state grounds for subject formation even if they did not dismantle the state categories of meaningful difference.

Ultimately, while mobility has typically been framed as a state of instability and dislocation, I argue that it was actually *immobility* that was experienced as the definitive form of displacement among my Fuzhounese subjects. This contention departs from much scholarship on migration and diaspora, which has led us to think of displacement as the result of a physical departure from a "home" and in turn to think of migrant articulations of belonging in terms of a "politics of return" (cf. M. Smith 1994). In contrast, this book highlights experiences of emplacement in a world where neither locality nor home could be assumed to be stable objects and points of anchorage. Drawing on Paul Gilroy's work (1991), Ien Ang has argued that "The experience of migration brings with it a shift in perspective: to paraphrase Gilroy, for the migrant it is no longer 'where you're from,' but 'where you're at' which forms the point of anchorage" (1994, 10). In the chapters that follow, I highlight yet another point of anchorage that had to do more with "where you're *going*" than either "where you're from" or "where you're at." The metric for im/mobility in this case did not just concern people's capacities for travel overseas. In fact, one did not need to physically leave China to aspire for spatial-temporal extension as a subject emplaced within a larger global and transnational social field. Likewise, one could experience displacement while remaining at "home" simply because the boundaries of locality and one's social world had shifted or come under contestation. Against normative and sometimes romanticized assumptions of the pleasures and comforts of home sites, this book highlights the dislocating effects of being stuck in place while others all around were moving to broaden their spatial-temporal horizons. As I will show, longing and belonging among the Fuzhounese were less about either place of origin or physical travel than about inhabiting the world in a particular cosmopolitan and future-oriented way—that is, as a valorized subject of a modernizing and globalizing China. Fuzhounese struggles and claims over such ways of being "modern" are what I describe in this book as "the politics of destination."

By arguing for a politics of destination, my aim is not only to invert previous formulations of migrant identities and orientations hinged to nostalgia for home and the promise of return. Here I also offer a riff on Max Weber's famous thesis in *The Protestant Ethic and the Spirit of Capitalism* (1992), where a politics of *pre*-destination became key to people's understandings and enactments of value in their daily lives.[18] As a play off Weber's thesis on the spirit of capitalism, the politics of destination is also meant to highlight a cosmology of value and value transformation among the Fuzhounese, which, like the project of the Protestants, was anchored in religious imaginations of social life. Only in this case, the gods were no longer on the sidelines and simply watching from above as the predetermined blessed and damned sorted themselves out through a display of economic rationality and the ever-expanding accumulation of capital. Rather, in this politics of destination, there were still possibilities for negotiation with divine authorities (as well as human authorities) in altering one's fate and fortune and channeling human energies (in their various material forms as labor power, capital, commodities, and so forth) beyond the hegemonic projects of the Chinese nation-state or larger global forces for capitalist development. As I will show in part III, there were other forms of credit at stake in Fuzhounese projects for mobility than the kind one gets from a credit card—for example, karmic relations of de/merit and social recognition of *renqing* (human feeling/bonds)—in a world where powerful absent presences, both human and nonhuman, continually shaped everyday life and in turn were seen as integral to the calculus of prosperity.

Mobility as a Qualisign

To remain stationary in these times of change, when all the world is on the move, would be a crime.
—Thomas Cook, *Cook's Excursionist*

How was the self to move or live in the whirlwind?
—Marshall Berman, *All That Is Solid Melts into Air*

Global flows and transnational circulation, flexible citizens and traveling cultures, acceleration and space-time compression—all these characterizations of modernity or post-modernity converge on a normative sense of mobility at the heart of contemporary social imaginations and embodiments.[19] A final aim of this book is to examine how this relationship of mobility to modernity is variously enacted and reworked through the daily encounters and transactions of heterogeneous social actors. Many scholars have turned to mobility as the key trope for thinking through the modern condition (Berman 1982; Urry 2007). Noting the critical mass of contemporary research focused on mobility across various disciplines, John Urry (2007) has even suggested that there has been a distinctive "mobility turn" recently in the social sciences and in turn has offered his own "new mobilities paradigm" for reorienting theory and empirical analysis to the centrality of movement at the turn of the twenty-first century.[20]

Yet plenty of skeptics have questioned mobility's novelty and distinction as an ontological marker of modern selves and relations. Old diasporic networks as well as imperial regimes have long revealed worlds of differentiated mobility and long-distance exchange well before such features came to be identified with modern and post-modern conditions (Abu-Lughod 1989; Ho 2006; Mintz 1998). Similarly, one could critique post-Mao claims to the newness of China's "opening up" to mobile flows and global exchanges given, on the one hand, long-standing Maoist engagements with much of the non-Western world (for example, Africa, Latin America, Asia, the former Soviet bloc) and, on the other, the persistence of enclosures and immobilizations regarding the movement of certain people, things, and information in the contemporary era.[21] In fact, one could endlessly debate the question of mobility's novelty on such empirical grounds, pointing to various metrics of historical intensity and scale to argue for or against the inextricable linkages of mobility to modernity.

My intervention here is more modest, aimed not so much at settling these far-reaching historical questions as in refining analysis of the very relationality at stake. How exactly, I ask, does mobility come into recognition as a salient index of modern life? How is this relationship articulated and made iterable in practice? In particular, here I offer a query into mobility's everyday operations and efficacies as a key sign—or rather "qualisign"—among the contemporary Fuzhounese. A qualisign, as C. S. Peirce famously defined it, is a "quality which is a sign" and which in turn "cannot actually act as a sign until it is embodied" (1998, 291). Nancy Munn (1986) later drew from Peirce's notion to analyze certain qualities that become "value signifiers" when embodied by persons and things in Gawan exchanges and encounters in Papua New Guinea. Interjecting political questions of hierarchy, value transformation, and struggles over spatial-temporal extension into the mix, Munn importantly elaborated on qualisigns as "certain embodied qualities that are components of a given intersubjective spacetime . . . whose positive or negative value they signify" (16). Drawing on these insights of Peirce and Munn, I argue that mobility is a privileged qualisign of modern selves and relations among the people I encountered in contemporary China. To think of mobility in this way is to attend to both its ideological and performative dimensions as a much-touted feature of being "modern." It necessarily recasts mobility's relationship to modernity as normative, as a claim on the world made "real" only through various social embodiments and transactions.

In the chapters that follow, I look at how mobility operates as a qualisign by analyzing the multiplicity of its materializations in various embodied forms alongside (and sometimes against) the singularity of its abstraction as an all-pervasive marker of the modern condition. As I will show, mobility is at once a worldly and world-ordering sign, legible only when it is both thoroughly enmeshed with the materiality of other things and in turn abstracted from these entanglements as a specific "component," in Munn's words, of "a given intersubjective spacetime." To put it another way, mobility can be described here as a "sensible concept" in an ever-shifting field of emergence (Massumi 2003).[22] It is itself a kind of moving target, something never wholly captured by its models and instantiations

but that nonetheless leaves excessive traces and palpable reve
in its passage through various interactions-in-the-making. For
qualities that are also signs, mobility can do little on its own
materialized through people, objects, words, and other embodie
Yet once actualized through a particular thing, it also inevitably ̲ ̲ ̲ ̲ ̲ ̲ ̲ ̲ ̲
entangled with the other features of whatever material form it inhabits.
When embodied by a passenger on a plane, for instance, mobility cannot help being bundled with other qualities like speed, lightness, or cosmopolitan privilege, just as it cannot avoid insinuations of inefficiency,
danger, or deprivation when embodied by a stowaway traveling across the
ocean in a shipping container. It is this very materiality of the sign, as
Webb Keane (1997, 2003) has noted, that helps shape the conditions of
its recognition and in turn underscores the everyday hazards of its translation in social encounters. My aim is to shed light on the inherent contingencies and unexpected effects that occur in the transactional moment
when the various properties of persons and things converge to produce
mobility as a qualisign. As aspiring migrants in Fuzhou well understood
(see chapters 3–4), there were reciprocal effects in store when certain bodies, modes of transport, and paperwork (or lack thereof) came together in
the act of travel. Meanings could drift or be displaced. New subjects and
objects could be produced. Certain ontologies and relationalities could be
reconfigured. In such moments of translation, things themselves were
never just simple instruments or prostheses of the aspiring migrant.
Rather, as I will show, by commingling their own semiotic and material
properties with those of the person, such things as shipping containers,
passports, luggage, and dollars all actively worked as agents to consolidate
mobility as a discernible sign and ready index in the valuation of various
people, their relations, and their worlds.

The Inappropriate/d Other

Not quite the Same, not quite the Other, she stands in that undetermined threshold
place where she constantly drifts in and out.
—Trinh T. Minh-ha, "No Master Territories"

Funny how we all want to go there and *you* from over there—somehow you want to
come *here*?!
—Longyan resident

Aspiring migrants from the rural outskirts of coastal Fuzhou inhabited a particular volatile sense of difference. At once peripheral and well connected, peasant and cosmopolitan, they embodied distinctions that often seemed at cross-purposes within the dominant scheme of differentiation. Unlike recognized minority populations or agrarian peasant "subcultures" in the interior hinterlands of China, these Fuzhounese were not easily contained as an internal Other. Nor like cosmopolitan Beijing or Shanghai urbanites did they fit the clear profile of a privileged Same (see chapter 2). Instead, they often fell between all boundaries as what Trinh Minh-ha (1995) termed "the Inappropriate/d Other," their alterity replete with grating excesses, deficiencies, and unaccounted for miscellany, their differentiation a fraught site and dense jumble of margins-within-centers and centers-within-margins (cf. Haraway 1992). As I came to appreciate, certain Fuzhounese articulations of difference did not easily fit into a pre-existing grid of the Same and the Other but rather "drift[ed] in and out," tainted, and ultimately reworked the grid itself.

This attentiveness to what Trinh has called "the undetermined threshold" of difference emerged largely out of the liminal space I wound up forging with the people of Longyan, with whom I shared a mutual recognition as an Inappropriate/d Other: in this case, as both foreigner yet not foreign.[24] This was not just due to our overlapping yet distinctive positionings as Chinese Han co-ethnics. We also possessed divergent yet intersecting transnational trajectories, with them edging from rural Fuzhou toward the United States and me traversing from their cross-Straits neighbor Taiwan as a child to the United States and then around to Fuzhou for fieldwork with a promised final return back to the United States. As a first-generation Chinese American, I was probably not so different from what aspiring Longyan migrants imagined they might become once they crossed the South China Sea. There was in fact quite a bit of reverse anthropology during my time in Longyan, where I felt the returned gaze and scrutiny of those around me trying to discern the subtle or not-so-subtle differences of gait, dress, habit, and logic between us. My left-handedness, coffee drinking, and bad chopstick form were especially active catalysts for headnotes (if not field notes) collected by villagers bound for where I had come from. Some of these instances of reverse anthropology are interwoven into this book in order to highlight the reciprocal recognition of difference *within* sameness (and vice versa) that developed empirically as well as theoretically out of my relations in Longyan.

Clearly, no one mistook me for a "native" anthropologist in their midst. In addition to the fact that I grew up with English as my primary language in the United States, my original Chinese dialect—*minnan hua* or Taiwanese—was virtually unintelligible and useless to a Fuzhounese speaker. Nine months of intensive Fuzhounese lessons got me only so far in listening comprehension of the local chitchat in Longyan. Once I opened my mouth and needed to communicate predominantly in the national dialect of Mandarin (with a smattering of simple Fuzhounese), phenotype be damned—my foreignness was marked.

Yet I was also never an essential or oppositional Other to the residents of Longyan. In fact, my ability to do the kind of field research I did largely hinged on my capacity to occupy more subtle and pliable grounds of differentiation, again as what I have designated an Inappropriate/d Other. Being able to trace roots to the southeast coast of China as well as a pathway overseas to the United States made me more of a kindred spirit, if not kin, to Longyan villagers with similar coordinates and desired trajectories. Though never a perfect fit, I could be located among these U.S.-connected villagers in vernacular terms of distinction already developed for their own kind. I was a Miwo Nëüng (American), someone would say with familiarity in Fuzhounese, a bona fide *sidising* (U.S. citizen, transliterated) who was not unlike Longyan's most fortunate members abroad. Whatever differences I embodied were often perceived to be more of gradation and privilege than exclusion and essence.

Over the course of my fieldwork, which comprised a three-month stint around Fuzhou (May–August 2000) followed by an eleven-month residence specifically in Longyan (September 2001–July 2002), a return visit in May 2005, and ongoing follow-up work with those arriving in the United States (2002–present), I benefited from being positioned as a not-quite-foreign foreigner. Although I had never set foot in mainland China before I started this project and initially spoke pretty rusty Mandarin, I was quickly embraced by people I met in Fuzhou as a *huaqiao* (Fz. *huagiu*, overseas Chinese) and a *taibao* (Fz. *taibau*, Taiwanese compatriot). Admittedly, some of this had to do with the social savvy and generosity of my mother, who traveled with me during the early days of my first stint in China and helped situate me in terms most familiar and nonthreatening to the strangers we met—as somebody's daughter secured in a web of kin relations. Such a standing enabled people to locate me on vernacular cultural terrain and overlook some of the initially jarring and otherwise awkward aspects of my foreignness as a first-time single female researcher unattached to and unfamiliar with any locals or their institutions. Kin positionality as somebody's daughter also gave me smooth entrée to becoming somebody's student. This happened mostly via the initial rapport between my mother and my local teacher/adviser, who discussed the transfer of my supervision from one elder to another, while, in proper hierarchical place, I sat mostly in silence and listened. Similarly, being positioned as somebody's student enabled me to later become somebody's guest in Longyan—once more through the helpful exchange of my teacher and my Longyan hosts, while again I mostly sat on the sidelines.

Ultimately with the help of all these relations, kin and non-kin, I was able to make a smooth transition to being somebody's teacher myself by serving as a volunteer English instructor at Longyan's middle school. There one day a week, I taught beginning English conversation to all the seventh graders and tutored the best of the eighth graders, as well as the worst of the ninth. In total, I got to know some two hundred students and, largely through them, a wide range of families in Longyan. Most villagers, whether young or old, student or not, close friend or distant acquaintance, came to call me by the singular name "Sinnang"—meaning literally "mister" in Fuzhounese but mainly denoting "teacher." The distinct group of middle-school teachers I got to know also offered important insights into the opportunity structure facing villagers, as well as the often fraught cross-class resentments among urbanites and rural dwellers, village elites and commoners (see chapter 2).

While the school gave me an institutional home in Longyan, my actual village residence was provided by a prominent family of cadre members who opened their home and hospitality to me during the year of my village residence. The household I joined was a small one, consisting of the elderly widow of a former Longyan village head (cunzhang) and her teenage granddaughter, whose parents had been in the United States since she was a small child but were currently in the process of finally sending for her from abroad. Though this household itself was small, it was part of a larger gated family compound consisting of other prominent kin in the village elite. Our living quarters sat on one side of a courtyard across from a middle-aged cousin whose two adult children were both in the United States and adjacent to the fifty-year-old younger brother of the former mayor who was himself a recognized leading cadre member as well as an unofficial historian for the village. Like his surrounding kin, this cadre also had adult children overseas.

Living among village cadres turned out to provide a distinct set of benefits as well as drawbacks. On one hand, the brother of the former mayor, whom I called Shusha, or Uncle, became for me an important guide to village history as well as to other leading members of Longyan, including the village's two party secretaries and a prominent elderly village historian and retired cadre. On the other, the elite household in which I lived was singularly isolated from its commoner neighbors, most of whom seemed to not care for and even resent the privileged cadres of Longyan. Although I had hoped that my residence would provide an organic site for mingling with all sorts of villagers, what it actually offered was rich insight into the class tensions that existed between the peasants and non-peasant elites of Longyan (see chapter 2). Few people visited the family I lived with, and the ones who might have visited me personally ultimately preferred that I meet them elsewhere rather than set foot in this cadre residence. So I learned to do all my mingling with other folks outside of my living quarters.

Although most villagers with peasant status had little social intercourse with either the cadres or the teachers in Longyan, again I found that my positioning as an Inappropriate/d Other enabled me to move among these distinct groups without rousing the suspicion or rancor of any of them. In this case, it was not my shared affinities but rather my foreign distinction from all local constituencies that made people much more forgiving of my associations with those they disliked. My status as someone in but not of Longyan enabled commoners to separate me from the cadres with whom I lived as well as the teachers with whom I taught and in turn not associate their traditional class resentment toward these elites with me personally. Additionally, my gender and age (female in late twenties) also seemed to work to my benefit by undercutting the more potentially alienating and threatening aspects of my profile: my privileged education, ambitious local research agenda, and foreign status as a U.S. citizen.

While I circulated broadly through all corners of Longyan, even acquiring fictive kin (a godfather and sister) along the way, I also decided to concentrate my main efforts in one particular district of the village where I could get to know the dynamics among family, neighbors, and friends at a much more intimate level. With a population of five thousand and thirteen hundred households, Longyan was no simple village that I could easily survey and map out all by myself. Luckily another organic unit divided Longyan residents into communities of a more manageable size: districts organized around local territorial god cults and temples. As I will show, Longyan happened to be divided into two temple districts—one north and one south of the Min River (see chapter 1). Each district had one defining territorial god (*ditou shen*) and an ad hoc committee of elderly and mostly male leaders from the district who oversaw community ritual events and the collection of donations for those activities, as well as for temple maintenance and renovation. Beyond these loosely structured committees, there was no institutionalized temple authority in these districts—no spiritual leader in residence who took charge. Instead, people largely organized their own religious practices and temple exchanges with the gods and with one another. What the temples did provide were particular communal spaces for people to mingle and forge collective identities along district lines.

By happenstance around the time of Lunar New Year festivities in 2002, I found myself spending an immense amount of time among families who lived along the north bank of the Min River leading to a cluster of three temples at the foot of Longyan's signature marble bridge, the Flying Dragon (Feilong Qiao). The oldest and most prominent of the three temples happened to belong to this district's territorial god—the famous divine trickster, the Monkey King (see chapters 1 and 5). Eventually, I put a good deal of my time and energy into this district—attending all the ritual events, mingling with the various households surrounding the three temples, and collecting oral histories among some of its elder members and their kin. I got to know a dozen multigenerational and extended families particularly well in this district and through them came to understand the texture and nuances of their everyday dynamics with other relatives, neighbors, and friends—including those currently abroad—whom I encountered by spending time in these households. A number of these families dotted the road on the northern bank of the Min, where I eventually became most integrated as a Longyan resident, a familiar face among others on the street. There were other key folks who shared insights and became good friends with me—other temple members, store owners, plucky housewives, U.S.-bound youths, a videographer—who happened to live across the river in the other temple district, not to mention the two dozen teachers and slew of cadre elites with whom I had daily interaction.

Many of these people also appear in this book, although they do not play as central a role in the district-level and neighborhood dynamics that I am able to sketch in my analysis.

Organization of the Book

The following chapters are divided into three parts and organized around the paths and diversions of various things-in-motion: a shifting built landscape (chapter 1), the contested trajectories of peasant subjects (chapter 2), the charting of paper and paperless routes overseas (chapters 3–4), the multicentric flows of spirit and market currencies (chapter 5), and the alienability of various sentimental substances and gendered bodies in transnational circulation (chapter 6). In following these different things-in-motion, my aim is to illuminate the centrality of mobility as a qualisign in contemporary projects for capitalist modernity in China, as well as to situate Fuzhounese migration amid other flows that shape the context for mobile, cosmopolitan desires. Part I focuses primarily on the tensions of emplacement resulting from recent Fuzhounese efforts to remake their social landscape and themselves through claims of overseas status and success. Part II examines the pragmatics of emigration out of China and particularly the different calculative agencies and technical competencies involved in charting successful departures vis-à-vis successful arrivals in the United States. Part III grapples with village aspirations for and anxieties over the flow of new money into Longyan from abroad. Specifically, it examines the ways money's circulation was regulated through various religious, gendered, and kin incitements of debt amid strong temptations for money's diversion into other things and relations. The conclusion attempts to draw together the central themes of this book by inviting the reader to ponder the various stakes and skills involved in one of the most common pastimes and models of fortune writ small in Longyan—the unpredictable and fast-paced game of mahjong.

PART I

Edgy Dispositions

MOST OBSERVERS OF CONTEMPORARY FUZHOU point to its long maritime tradition and legacy of overseas dispersal through the South China Sea (Chin 1999; Guest 2003; Hood 1997; Kwong 1997; Pieke et al. 2004). Fuzhou's rich history as an intercultural contact zone of an "Indian Ocean trading ecumene" (Clark 1990) or a prior China-centered "world system" (Abu-Lughod 1989; Frank 1998) has been well documented by many scholars, as well as by such famous mercantile traders as Marco Polo, who noted in his celebrated late-thirteenth-century travelogue of passing through this "splendid city" and "important commercial center," which, as he boasted, was "so well provided with every amenity that it is a veritable marvel" (Polo and Latham 1958, 233–35). A century after Marco Polo's travels through Yuan dynasty China, the revered Ming admiral Zheng He—the "Chinese Columbus" (Snow 1988)—would launch his legendary naval expeditions through the Middle East and Africa from the port of Fuzhou in 1405. Another famed hero named Zheng—the late-Ming-era general Zheng Chenggong (or Koxinga)—made Fuzhou into a central military site and geopolitical battleground against the new Qing government, with the city's subsequent loss to the ruling Manchus providing much of the impetus for the general's successful cross–Strait venture to wrangle Taiwan from colonial Dutch control in 1661. Later in the Qing dynasty, following China's defeat by the British in the First Opium War (1839–1842), Fuzhou became one of the five treaty ports forcibly opened to Western trade and, by extension, to Western missionaries. Centuries of maritime trade and foreign contact also enabled the Fuzhounese to establish some overseas communities throughout Southeast Asia and, more recently, in North America and Europe. In fact, since the mid-1990s, Fujian—of which Fuzhou is the administrative capital—has even surpassed Guangdong to rank first in emigration flows among China's provinces, largely due to the phenomenon of massive and steady outmigration from the Fuzhou countryside (Liang 2001; Liang and Ye 2001).[1]

Alongside this tradition of global exchange and connectedness, however, Fuzhou has an equally significant, if seemingly contradictory, history as an isolated and outer edge of China, a dangerous frontier of rebels, bandits, pirates, smugglers, and other illicit elements (Andrade 2005; Kwong 1997; MacNair 1924; Madancy 2001). Most famously, the Triad—the most notorious Chinese criminal syndicate—traces its mythic origins to Fujian Province (Hood 1997; Ownby 1996; Pan 1990). Across the Strait from the unruly island of Taiwan and cut off from much of inland China by foreboding mountain ranges to the north and west,[2] Fujian's distinctive topography has long made it a feared breeding ground of domestic revolt and foreign collusion from early imperial times to Mao's Communist regime (1949–1978).[3] In particular, as the first area to be possibly invaded and taken over by Taiwan after the Communist Revolution (1949), Fujian suffered from wholesale isolation and marginalization under state socialism, receiving a mere 1.5 percent of China's total capital investment between 1949 and 1978, the fourth lowest amount among all the provinces. During this period, Fujian Province failed to get a single key investment project from the central government, while its major and strategic industrial plants were all relocated inland (Shieh 2000, 85; Lau and Lee 2000, 45). The province's vast and long-standing ties to overseas Chinese also did not contribute to its standing in a government increasingly suspicious and antagonistic toward subjects with foreign connections (C-y. Chang 2000; Fitzgerald 1972; Wu 1967). On the cusp of post-Mao economic reforms, Fujian was the poorest province along the coast, its per capita income ranking last among all coastal provinces in 1979 and constituting just one-tenth of Shanghai's (Yeung and Chu 2000, 8). Ironically, with the push for China's "opening up" (*kaifang*) to global trade in the 1980s and '90s, the same factors that once hampered and isolated Fujian—its proximity to Taiwan and its overseas connections—quickly turned into its major selling points for leading the way in state experiments with economic liberalization.

As the next two chapters will show, there has long been a fine and easily blurred line between Fujian's positioning as a lagging or leading edge of China. These two aspects were in fact integrally linked in the central government's choice of the province, along with Guangdong, as the initial region for instituting "special policies and flexible measures" for intensive market liberalization in 1979 (Lyons 1998; Pieke et al. 2004). As Shawn Shieh aptly observed, "Ironically, Fujian's relative isolation and backwardness strengthened its case for getting the 'special policies.' Central leaders were more inclined to allow experiments in these provinces because they were far away from Beijing and did not constitute important centres of industry or sources of revenue. Any political or economic fallout that resulted from opening up to the outside world would, therefore, be limited" (2000, 94). Following Xiamen's rechristening as one of China's first "special economic zones" in 1980, Fuzhou was designated an "open coastal city" in 1984 (Pieke et. al. 2004, 42). By 1996, 122 economic development zones had been created along the coastal area of Fujian (X. Hu and Hu 2000; Pieke et al. 2004). In only five years, between 1990 and 1995, foreign capital investment in Fujian rose more than ten times—from $379 million to $4.1 billion (Liang 2001, 696). During this same period, emigration from Fujian more than doubled—from 32,000 in 1990 to 66,200 in 1995 (696), bolstering the province's shifting position once more from socialist backwater to cosmopolitan vanguard in the post-Mao era.

This section examines the problems of emplacement for subjects historically situated in China's geopolitical terrain on a tricky double edge—both cutting and peripheral. I have borrowed this notion of the edge and edginess from Robert Weller's description of Taiwan (2000), with which Fujian shares more than a passing affinity.[4] Like its cross-Strait neighbor Taiwan, Fujian also has a legacy as both "a backwater frontier" and a critical link and interface positioned "at the boundaries of the world" (Weller 2000, 477). This duality of edginess—as both a backward and outward edge of the nation—also compels the Fujianese to "wonder whether they are part of China or perhaps someplace else altogether" (477), though admittedly without the same intensity and single-mindedness as the Taiwanese debate over national identity. More significant, what my subjects in rural Fuzhou share with the residents of this anomalous non-state and non-nation of Taiwan is the implied insecurity of living on an edge, teetering uncertainly between being left behind, breaking away and ahead, or "fall[ing] between all boundaries" (479).

As the following two chapters will demonstrate, this sense of insecurity has been particularly palpable among the inhabitants of Longyan—the site of my research in the Fuzhou countryside, with a current population of around five thousand and another three thousand plus dispersed overseas. A former regional commercial center, military outpost since the

Ming, and a "hundred-surname village" (*baixingcun*), Longyan
served as a contact zone and point of dispersal for all sorts of t
and transnational flows. Situated along a key stretch of the Min R
major tributary in Fujian, flowing from the South China Sea to
walled entry into Fuzhou City, Longyan has been the kind of edgy si
often "falls between all boundaries" and exhibits confusions of "place."
As chapter 1 will show, people living in Longyan today cannot even agree
on whether it is properly a "village" or a "town," part of rural or urban
Fuzhou, or part of some other transnational social field altogether. Currently, 85 percent of all households in Longyan have at least one member
overseas, and this trend of outmigration shows no signs of abatement.[5]

For simplicity's sake, I refer to Longyan as a village and its residents as
villagers throughout this book, partly because as far as I can tell, "village"
remains the official classification of this community and partly because I
believe "village" also best evokes the tensions and taint of peasant identification that, as chapter 2 will demonstrate, shadows and propels these
subjects' cosmopolitan desires. Ultimately, I hope my contextualization of
these people's lives is enough to conjure the invisible quotes around the
terms "village" and "villager" that I deploy throughout this work.

One other nuance of insecurity and edginess is worth highlighting
about Longyan and its residents: their sense of inferiority as perpetual
second fiddles or also-rans to the actual cutting edge, always stumbling
and falling just short of taking a lead in China. In particular, Longyan suf-
fers from what could be described as a nested set of inferiority complexes.
Nationally, it is part of the uncouth and mongrel south compared to a
more civilized and purified north. Regionally as part of the coastal provinces, Fujian has largely been outpaced and overshadowed by the spectacular expansion and reach of its southern neighbor, Guangdong, including
during the last two decades of economic reforms. As part of a group of
port cities, Fuzhou paled in comparison first to its provincial neighbor
Quanzhou for much of its early history, then to the cosmopolitan port of
Shanghai following the Opium Wars in the nineteenth century, and most
recently to Guangzhou, Shenzhen, and Xiamen (another Fujian port to
its south) under China's policies for "opening up." Reportedly, the British
were so disappointed with Fuzhou's performance as a commercial port
after the Treaty of Nanjing in 1842 that there was even discussion of swap-
ping it for another city with better prospects at the time (Fairbank 1969,

375, 379; Spence 1999, 164). Similarly, for most of the two decades since the initiation of economic reform, Fuzhou has been the mediocre disappointment among the initial target areas of a modernizing China, lagging behind not only the special economic zones in Guangdong Province but also Xiamen in its own province as well. In fact, despite Fuzhou's status as the administrative capital of Fujian, it has trailed Xiamen not only in recent economic development but also for much of its history, lagging way behind it in the one area that most pertains to this discussion: emigration flows from China.

Probably the most egregious elision made by contemporary observers of Chinese emigration is that between Fuzhou's recent phenomenon of human smuggling and a more long-standing "Fujianese" tradition of overseas dispersal. Folding contemporary Fuzhounese migrants into this provincial legacy, most analysts refer to the recent massive constituency of Chinese smuggled abroad as "Fujianese," a designation that I would argue is too broad and misleading given the distinctive regional histories of the populations divided by the Min River. Along with the Min River, mountainous ranges cutting across the province managed not only to isolate Fujian from the rest of China over its long history but also to divide its internal population into distinctive and incommensurable regional groups. Fujian's linguistic diversity—it has the most heterogeneous dialects of any province in China—particularly attests to the historical separation and cultural divergence of its parts. As it has turned out, the "Fujianese" tradition of emigrant flows has been largely a phenomenon of the populations speaking in the Minnan dialect, groups situated south of the Min River (the *nan* or "south" in Minnan), including Quanzhou and Xiamen. Fuzhou, which lies north of this region in an area usually termed Mindong, meaning east of the Min River, has played only a minor role in dispersing "Fujianese" overseas for most of the province's starry history as the common "home" of diasporic Chinese.[6] Notwithstanding the odd pocket of Fuzhounese in Borneo or amid the mines of Mexico (Guest 2003, 56), most of the Fujianese comprising the diasporic Nanyang (Southern Ocean) or Southeast Asian Chinese population have hailed from the distinctive Minnan region and have had very little to do with the Fuzhou area. Of the 3 million or so Fujianese dispersed overseas, little more than 10 percent claimed Fuzhou as their origin (Guest 2003, 55; Pieke et. al. 2004, 40). From the latter part of the Qing until the Communist Revolution (1871–1949), only 4 percent of overseas remittances flowing into Fujian Province were directed to Fuzhou (Guozhi Lin and Lin 1982).

I do not mean to suggest that there was no legacy of Fuzhounese traveling overseas before the recent trend of mass migration via human smuggling, only that it was, at best, a minor current overshadowed by the phenomenal flows out of a very different Minnan region (cf. Pieke et. al. 2004, 39–40). While the notion of a "Fujianese" emigration tradition has certainly colored Fuzhounese people's own reinterpretation of their recent flows abroad, I argue that this provincial legacy has contributed more to Fuzhou's long-standing inferiority complex as the lesser "home" of overseas Chinese next to the dominant Minnan region.

In fact, Longyan itself did not have a significant tradition of steady overseas emigration before the post-Mao era. Though always a site of intercultural contact and dispersal, Longyan's mobile channels via occupations in fishing, construction, the military, and transportation tended to disperse people translocally and regionally along internal river and coastal routes rather than transnationally across foreign waters to settlement overseas. Before 1985, less than a dozen households could claim relatives overseas.[7] There were certainly other villages and townships in Longyan's vicinity that had greater ties to diasporic Chinese and contributed more to the small seed population in New York City that eventually blossomed into the massive human smuggling phenomenon along Fuzhou's rural outskirts. In fact, by villagers' own accounts, Longyan was rather a late-comer to the emigration trend in its immediate region, sending its first significant batch of residents overseas well after other nearby villages and towns had already garnered significant reputations as emergent *qiaoxiang*, or emigrant villages. As with its trailing position at other levels of differentiation, this slow start only added to Longyan's sense of inferiority within its immediate vicinity.

One last strand of inferiority is noteworthy: Longyan's local positioning as part of the rural outskirts of Fuzhou vis-à-vis the more "advanced" urban center. Situated in the countryside of the greater Fuzhou area or *jiaoqu*, Longyan stands in both close physical proximity and significant social distance from Fujian's provincial capital (see chapter 1). As a long-standing hub of translocal circulation just outside of the city, Longyan has often distinguished itself from its rural neighbors and insisted that it was not just any "peasant village." Yet Fuzhou City has also persistently distanced itself from sites like Longyan by walling itself off—literally in imperial times and later bureaucratically under state socialism—from a surrounding and peripheralized countryside (see chapter 2). Again, this was another edgy instance of Longyan's "falling between all boundaries" as neither a proper, idyllic "peasant village" nor a welcomed extension of urban life. Ultimately, as this section will suggest, such tensions of emplacement compelled Longyan residents to embrace the post-Mao call for "opening up" in ways that both exceeded and remade state expectations of their lives as "peasant" subjects on the move in China.

CHAPTER ONE

To Be Emplaced

Fuzhounese Migration and the Geography of Desire

An old convention of ethnographic presentation is to open with a map as a way for framing the field site as a locatable and knowable "place." Though a great flood of scholarship in recent years has challenged the assumptions of "place" as simply the staging grounds or container of social life, the territorial map has remained a powerful conceptual shorthand for situating anthropologists and the "areas" we study. Nonetheless, I also begin this chapter with a map in order to provide a general orientation to my field site, which I call Longyan. But in lieu of an image situating Longyan within the territorial and administrative borders of China (the nation-state), I offer an alternative geography of the five boroughs of New York City rendered in Chinese and English (figure 1). The map itself appears on the back cover of a book titled *Practical English for People Working in Chinese Restaurants*, which is published in New York. It has circulated broadly within Longyan; first through the efforts of overseas relatives who purchased and shipped copies of it from the United States to China and later through the technological wonder of copy machines, which made this map ubiquitous among all those who aspired to go abroad, mainly with the ideal of finding restaurant work in one of New York's three Chinatowns. As both a material link to overseas connections and a mediator of social imaginaries, this map has become much more integral than a regional map of China ever could to people's understandings of what it means to be a *dangdiren* or "local person" in Longyan today.

What I especially love about this image of the map here are the greasy fingerprint smudges on it pointing to the materiality of its circulation from restaurant workers abroad to their relatives in the village. This particular copy of *Practical English* belonged to Zou Shu, the wife of a short-order cook working just outside of New York City; he had sent her the book

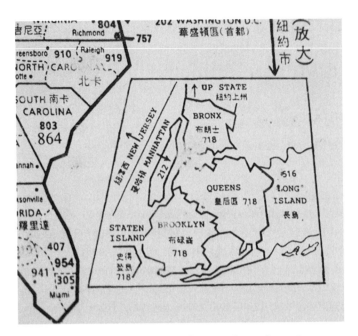

FIGURE 1 Map of the five boroughs of New York City from a Longyan villager's worn copy of a "Restaurant English" book.

along with its accompanying audio tapes and a Walkman cassette player to help her prepare for her impending venture and anticipated life overseas as a restaurant worker by his side. This book was already tattered by the time it reached her in Longyan, she told me. Inside its well-worn covers, scrawled notes in Chinese scattered along the margins enabled this villager to imagine her husband's studiousness, as well as his struggles overseas during their many years of physical separation. Inspired by these leftover traces of her absent husband's linguistic labors, she also scribbled in the margins as she studied from this book herself, adding her own distinctive marks as part of their continuity of efforts and momentum for connecting overseas and for remaking the scale of their everyday life as transnational subjects on the move.

• • •

This chapter offers an exploration of what it means to be emplaced amid the various spatial and temporal streams currently flowing through my field site in the Fuzhou countryside along the southeast coast of China. These flows include both transnational currents resulting from two and a half decades of mass emigration to the United States and other foreign destinations and national and translocal currents driven in part by post-Mao reforms for market liberalization and China's "opening up." Like other scholars working in the vein of transnationalism (Appadurai 1991; Basch et al. 1994; Clifford 1997; Kearney 2000; Levitt 2001; Ong and Nonini 1997; Rouse 1991), my aim is to highlight the complications of locality—its unsettled boundaries and experiences—among subjects differentially connected and on the move in contemporary Longyan.

The notion of a cultural and economic gap between one's "home" and "settlement" country has long informed much of the analysis concerning both motivations for migration and the possibilities for assimilation in receiving nations. Typically, scholars of international migration have assumed that the movement from "home" to "settlement" is naturally strange and alienating, while "to go home is to be where one belongs" (Malkki 1995, 509). This assumption that one's identity and experiences are only whole and well when rooted in a territorial homeland has been critiqued by anthropologist Liisa Malkki, among others, as the "sedentarist analytic bias" of research on migration (508).

"Diaspora" as a key unit of analysis beyond the territorially bounded nation has provided important challenges to the dominant assumptions of migration studies by foregrounding the multiplicity and hybridity of cultural identities among immigrants and refugees. Responding to an era of decolonization in the "Third" World and deindustrialization in the "First" World, works on diaspora, particularly in postcolonial and British cultural studies, have been among the first to analyze the important historical transformations of the global political-economic order in relation to the formation of cultural identities and political communities among displaced and mobile people. For instance, in observing the mass movement of former colonial subjects into the former metropoles of European empires, Stuart Hall (1991; Hall et al. 1996) challenges the conceptual distancing of "home" and "settlement," peripheries and centers, and other spatial metaphors emphasizing the boundedness and purity of people, places, and cultures. As Hall notes, far from being alienating and strange, these postcolonial migrations are the logical culmination of long-standing political and social ties, an experience less about social rupture than about historical continuity. Moreover, this kind of analysis has contributed to a blurring of distinction between economic migrants and refugees by historicizing the inextricable links between political and economic oppression.

Paul Gilroy's conceptualization of a "Black Atlantic" and the "double consciousness" of its diasporic African subjects has also provided important critiques of the essentialized conflations of cultural identity with discrete nation-states (1991; cf. Gilroy 1993). Specifically, Gilroy notes how the ongoing experience of displacement is the grounds, not a barrier, for forging an alternative cultural identity anchored in a diasporic network (that is, "the Black Atlantic") outside the territorial confines of any particular nation-state (cf. Hall et al. 1996: 235). Displacement, in this sense, refers to the shared experience of feeling out of "place" within and across the boundaries of the nation-state.

Unfortunately, in much of the scholarship concerned with diaspora, critiques of assimilationist ideologies and primordial ties to territorial nations often privilege the idea of displacement to such an extent that "home" countries become devalued as proper sites for research. This is because displacement is usually construed as the *result* of the physical departure of people from a prior literal or imagined "home," an analytic move that logically excludes these "home" sites as significant domains for examining diasporic conditions. At best, such sites simply get reinterpreted as immigrant nostalgia for a shared mythical homeland and desire for impossible returns (cf. Safran 1991).

My research in Longyan, which currently has 49 percent of its population overseas, aims to provide a corrective to this overemphasis (and sometimes celebration) of displacement as an experience outside of "home" and, moreover, to the mystification of "home" sites as simply imaginary places of longing and belonging. Approaching issues of migrant identities and social formations from the location of dispersion rather than arrival enabled me to critically examine and situate these analytic assumptions of displacement alongside local theorizations of *emplacement* made by those who stayed put (or rather "stuck") in my field site as others moved around them. As I will show for my Fuzhounese subjects, the ultimate form of displacement was seen and experienced as the result of *immobility* rather than physical departure from a "home."

This examination of emplacement presupposes the imbrication of "home" sites in diasporic formations while at the same time it contributes to the continual intellectual project on "diaspora" for relativizing (though not discounting) bounded and autochthonous assumptions of belonging to the nation-state, the primordial homeland, or the pristine "local" (against a penetrating globalization "from above") (cf. Brecher et al. 2000). I do not wish to suggest that territorial boundaries no longer matter in an era of transnational and global flows. Rather, my goal is to show how villagers' quest for emigration shifted the very grounds of both mobility and enclosure (Cunningham and Heyman 2004). It reshaped the geography of desire, expanding the possibilities of emplacement for some while contracting the terms of belonging for others. As I will show, not everyone was localized (or globalized) in the same way in Longyan. There were, in fact, multiple scale-making projects that shaped villagers' sense of belonging in the world. Scale, as Anna Tsing has noted, "is not just a neutral frame for viewing the world; scale must be brought into being: proposed, practiced, and evaded, as well as taken for granted" (Tsing 2005, 58).[1]

In the remainder of this chapter, I focus on these processes of scale-making and particularly on the resonances, tensions, and confusions of "place" such processes have generated among Longyan residents. Following a general overview of village experiences of locality, I offer three ethnographic sketches of how architecture and landscape could enable concurrent as well as conflicting senses of scale and emplacement among villagers. These three sketches will spotlight transformations first in housing, then in temples, and finally in roads. As a means for understanding Fuzhounese migration, the built environment is a particularly good starting point since scholars and journalists often seemed so puzzled by Fuzhounese desires to spend overseas remittances on the building of lavish temples and houses rather than on what most critics consider more "rational" economic activities like investments in local enterprises or public works. Overseas remittances currently comprise approximately 70 percent of all income in Longyan, and according to the local party secretary's office, an estimated two-thirds of these remittances go to the renovation and construction of houses and temples.[2] While these construction projects are commonly dismissed by local officials and elites as the unproductive result of newly wealthy but "low cultured" residents (di wenhua), my aim here is to move this discussion of value and value production beyond the economic terms of rational utility. Instead, I ask: How do these transformations of the built environment contribute to the production of locality as a structure of feeling? Specifically, how do they complicate the possibilities and terms of place and emplacement among the various members of this community? I conclude this chapter with some final thoughts on scale-making by returning to the spatial imaginaries conjured by "Restaurant English" and its practitioners in Longyan.

Placing on Locality

In many ways, Longyan appeared to be an idyllic rural village, surrounded as it was by verdant mountains on three sides and the flowing waters of the Min River as it splinters off and winds into the South China Sea. The small, flat valley bounded by the mountains, river, and sea contained most of the houses for village residents, as well as more than thirty Buddhist-Daoist temples, one Protestant church, an elementary and a middle school, a local government office, a few patches of farmland, and a green market at the end of two short and intersecting commercial streets of small shops. One of these two streets, River Head Road (Jiang Tou Lu), has long served as the vibrant hub for Longyan residents, though its luster as the commercial center for neighboring and even far-flung places up until the Communist Revolution no longer exists except in the youthful recollections of its oldest members. Though not much has changed about River Head Road's practical functions over the past century and a half, the street's spatial significance—like that of Longyan itself—has undergone several challenges and revisions since the Republican Era in China (1912–1949).

In regard to Longyan as a whole, as noted, there is some debate about whether this community is (or should be) properly called a "village" (*cun*) or a "town" (*zhen*). Though Longyan's physical boundaries remain intact, its emplacement within regional, national, and (more recently) transnational spatial hierarchies has been anything but stable through the years. The shifts are evident in Longyan's official "place" markers over the last century: from a regional township and military command center in the late Qing to a small district within a larger rural commune (*gongshe*) under Mao to a discrete "peasant village" (*nongcun*) under decollectivization and, finally, to its recent and ongoing transformation as a cosmopolitan home village of overseas Chinese (*qiaoxiang*). These various designations of place evoke quite different structures of feeling for being "local" in Longyan.[3] Moreover, they have not succeeded one another as linearly and neatly as the official changes made to Longyan's "place" designation would suggest. Rather, as I discovered through my research, all of these distinct senses of locality still resonated in Longyan, though not necessarily at the same frequency or force.

Town, commune, peasant village, and overseas village channeled different spatial and temporal imaginings of what it meant to be a "local person" in Longyan. Some figurations of the "local," like "town," conjured up nostalgia for the pre-Communist days of regional prestige and influence, while others, like "peasant village," evoked ever-present anxieties of the stagnation and narrowing limits of one's social world since the Communist Revolution. Yet another term, like "commune," carried entangled associations of political obsolescence, moral idealism, and personal bitterness over utopic aspirations and material deprivations in the recent and still reverberating past. All these senses of locality have persisted in memory and embodied experience beyond their functional purposes for political administration by different state regimes in China. In fact, they have not only coexisted with but also centrally shaped Longyan residents' current efforts and collective claims for being an "overseas village."

Anthropologist Arjun Appadurai has observed how contingent and fragile imaginations and experiences of the "local" can be, especially in the contemporary context of increasingly transnational and globalizing forces. As he notes, "Locality is ephemeral unless hard and regular work is undertaken to produce and maintain its materiality" (1997, 181). In trying to understand the unrelenting desires of the Fuzhounese to migrate through human smuggling networks, I found that I was also tracking this process for the production, transformation, and maintenance of locality in Longyan. As Appadurai argued, locality is not merely the given, stable grounds for identity formation and collective action but also in itself "a relational achievement" (186) and "property of social life" (182). Not only were there different and contested ways for being "local" in Longyan, but some people also became more local-ized than others in the process.

Not everyone who resided in Longyan was considered a "local person" (*dangdiren*). Many in the population who had migrated from Sichuan and other interior provinces of China were commonly referred to as "outsiders" (*waidiren*), as were the small corps of teachers and school administrators who mainly hailed from Fuzhou City and held urban residence status in the Chinese state's household registration system (*hukou*). It goes without saying that as a resident of Longyan, I also occupied this position of "outsider." Though all these "outsiders" shared spaces of habitation and sociality in Longyan, they did not all share the same material and embodied sense of locality. These distinctions were based not only on where people were from, but also, and perhaps more importantly, on where they were potentially *going* in the increasingly fluid context of a globalizing post-Mao China. Some people were better positioned amid regional, national, and transnational flows to imagine themselves as mobile and forward-looking (or "modern") subjects in a cosmopolitan context. Others less connected to such currents easily became "stuck" in the most narrow and confining sense of locality—as unchanging peasants in an equally stagnant and backward peasant village.

Over the past two decades, traveling through human smuggling networks has been one crucial technique for people's spatial-temporal extension beyond the imagined and material limitations of peasant life in China. Despite people's knowledge of the great physical dangers and staggering economic costs of human smuggling, aspirations for leaving China persisted in Longyan because in many ways, such migrant yearnings enabled residents to embody a more privileged sense of locality among other existing and competing notions of the local. But what I want to show in this chapter is how one did not need to physically *leave* China to feel emplaced within a larger global and transnational social field. Likewise, one could experience displacement while remaining at "home" simply because the boundaries of one's social world had shifted or come under contestation (cf. Mahler 1992; Verdery 1998). All these discontinuities and dissonances of locality were already present in Longyan and could be felt in very material and embodied ways through the built environment itself.

House: Up, Up, Away

In less than a decade, a new crop of brightly tiled enormous houses has rapidly emerged at the center of Longyan, replacing plots of farmland along both sides of the Min River. Commonly referred to as the homes of "American guests" (*Meiguoke*), these distinctive buildings marked the newfound prosperity of households with members in the United States and with abundant remittances flowing into Longyan (figure 2). Typically rectangular in form and rising four or five stories high in flashy shades of bubble gum pink or peach, these buildings not only dwarfed other houses around them in size and aesthetic dazzle, but they also exhibited the competitive spirit of their owners, who tried to outdo one another with each new and successive construction and renovation project. Although most residents in Longyan viewed the completion of each new house with a combination of collective pride and personal envy, they also tended to gripe about the general—and *literal*—escalation of competitive house-

FIGURE 2 "American guest" mansions in Longyan.

building among those with overseas connections. As Old Man Liu (Lao Liu), my self-proclaimed godfather in Longyan, observed one day while walking around with me, "They keep getting taller and taller." Shaking his head and pointing to specific houses, he noted, "First, this one had a three-story house, then over there—four stories, then five. . . . It's really getting excessive!" Incidentally, it may be worth noting that Old Man Liu had a four-story home himself, and as one could guess, he was less than pleased about being outdone by the newest houses.

Shortly after I settled into Longyan in the fall of 2001, the debut of yet another new house, nestled between the mountains and the southern bank of the Min River, would spark even greater debates and gossip about distinction and prosperity among village residents. This house (figure 3) not only upped the ante in height—rising six stories instead of the usual five—but it also offered a novel facade of elegant white tiles, jade green windows, and warm terracotta roofing that contrasted sharply with the

FIGURE 3 New house in Longyan, Lunar New Year 2002.

pink and peach uniformity of previous "American guest" mansions. Like most of the other new houses, this one was built with overseas remittances by Longyan villagers who had emigrated to the United States in the late 1980s through transnational human smuggling networks. The owners had since achieved a level of prosperity by starting their own family-run Chinese restaurant abroad. Because of ongoing chain migration, this family had no members left in Longyan to actually reside in the new mansion on a permanent, full-time basis.

Like so many other enormous houses in the vicinity with dwindling or no members remaining because of continual emigration, this new mansion was expected to be mostly unoccupied, aside from the occasional return visit or future retirement plans of its various overseas members. But the fact that this house had been built without definite residents in mind did not deter other Longyan inhabitants from imagining what it would be like to occupy that space. Even though most people had seen this mansion only from a distance—partly because the owners were rarely there to have visitors—gossip still abounded about what the interiors might look like and especially about its relative luxury among other new houses. My favorite uncorroborated rumor concerned the existence of an elevator located dead center in the house for easy and speedy access to all six floors. Though this house turned out to have only a staircase like all the other new mansions, this imaginary elevator made sense to people as the kind of distinctive, innovative feature of the interior that would complement the novel, modern look of the building's exterior.

Ultimately, the fact that the mansion's family had not actually built an elevator mattered less than the sense of lack others felt from imagining this new and superior mode of habitation and mobility among them. Through the elevator, people extended and concretized their imagination of the kind of superior, modern *habitus* this family must have acquired as successful overseas Chinese, with an ease of coming and going beyond the narrow terms of Longyan as a simple peasant village.[4] Figuratively if not literally, the elevator offered a new means for judging the relative mobility of Longyan residents, both in dwelling and in traveling.

When it came to understanding the various possibilities for emplacement, the two aspects of dwelling and traveling were inextricably linked in Longyan, as they were in other locations (and as previously noted by Clifford 1997). Houses of all sizes and styles, including these "American guest" mansions, were structured not only by different imaginations and conditions of dwelling, but also through distinctive trajectories of various residents moving in and about Longyan in space and time. I learned to appreciate the different temporal and spatial contours of the built environment early on in my research, when Longyan's party secretary guided me to the panoramic view from his office window and proceeded to narrate a history of village transformation through the various housing styles visible in the landscape. Pointing at different buildings in our view, Party Secretary Chen traced three distinct styles and eras : (1) red exterior, (2) white exterior, and (3) tiled exterior (*hongzhuang, baizhuang,* and *cizhuang* respectively). These three kinds of housing (which can be seen especially clearly in figure 4) concretized for Secretary Chen a spatial-temporal order of prosperity among Longyan residents.

Specifically, each successively larger and more grandiose style of housing marked a distinct point of departure in people's imagination and embodied experiences of modern and prosperous living in Longyan. First, the red-exterior houses evoked the initial era of prosperity before mass emigration, when, following China's economic reforms, Longyan residents first branched out from compulsory farming into several lucrative enterprises mainly involving building materials, construction, and renovation work in and around Fuzhou City. Between 1978 and 1985, these red-brick structures dramatically transformed the social landscape of Longyan by rapidly replacing the majority of old-style wooden housing and offering

FIGURE 4 Various housing styles in the changing village landscape.

a new and superior mode of habitation linked to success in the booming construction industry.

In the mid-1980s, the emergence of the white-exterior dwellings became associated with a diversifying profile of wealth involving not only those in construction but also an increasing number of families with members in the United States. As Party Secretary Chen noted, "From 1985 to 1990, every year at least ten people went abroad. First year, there were ten or so. In '86, twenty or so. In '87, forty to fifty. By 1990, massive numbers were going abroad." Like those who had achieved success through construction, the first residents with overseas connections also celebrated their newfound wealth by upgrading their houses to reflect the reigning imaginations of modern living at the time.

By the early 1990s, those who had achieved their success from construction increasingly lost momentum and faced mounting difficulties keeping up with the standards of prosperity set by residents with overseas connections. These difficulties came about partly because as people left for abroad in growing numbers and sent increasing remittances home, a new flow of migrants from China's interior provinces, like Sichuan, also began to move into Longyan and replace longtime residents in all sorts of village occupations from agriculture to the crucial industry of construction. Many residents, who were either displaced or simply disillusioned by the growing presence of internal migrants in local industries, ultimately joined a second, more massive exodus out of China to the United States beginning in the 1990s. During this period, the first houses associated solely with overseas wealth emerged in the social landscape. This new style of architecture was distinguished by its tiled exterior. Known locally as "American guest" houses, they immediately dominated and overwhelmed all other dwellings in their surroundings through their sheer height and sense of spaciousness.

This sense of spaciousness did not simply concern the actual square footage so much as it reflected people's new attentiveness to the nature of occupancy in different housing situations. For what most distinguished the "American guest" mansions from previous styles of habitation was the small and dwindling number of occupants in these spaces. While residents who had made their wealth locally tended to fully occupy and furnish all the rooms of their new houses, those with overseas connections commonly left their mansions nearly or completely empty, with very few occupants and with only the barest of amenities on one or two of the bottom floors. In fact, despite the fancy tiled exteriors, most floors, if not all, were left totally unfinished, with neither electrical connections nor plumbing installed, not to mention an utter lack of interior design. Some of these houses, like the new six-story mansion discussed above, had no occupants at all because of ongoing chain migration, and they sat absolutely vacant. Though the overseas families could have rented their empty houses to others, especially given the flow of internal migrants into Longyan, most preferred to keep them totally unoccupied and bare in their absence. Villagers often showed me how to identify the emptiness of these houses from the outside by the lack of curtains adorning their windows. Unlike occupied and furnished dwellings, these houses had no use for curtains, people told me, since there was nothing, including nobody, to shield from prying eyes.

The emptiness of the "American guest" houses was in fact central to the distinct sense of overseas prosperity and luxury surrounding them, marking both their overseas connections and the immense wealth of their absent owners. As villagers saw it, only those earning plenty of money abroad could afford to build a gigantic house in Longyan and then leave it completely vacant and therefore nonproductive (that is, neither in use nor generating income). Through the emptiness of these mansions, villagers could also evaluate just how constraining and crammed their own quarters and ways of habitation were without access to overseas connections. On the streets, the vacant interiors of these mansions served as embodied reminders of the superior mobility of absent owners with dual residences abroad and in Longyan, while others remained stuck within the confining boundaries of the village.

People also imagined that those living abroad must reside in housing as spacious and luxurious as the mansions they built for themselves in Longyan. Often while accompanying me on the streets, villagers would point out some of these houses and ask me questions like, "American houses all look like this high-rise mansion (*gaolou dasha*), right?" Initially, it seemed perplexing to me that people could imagine American dwellings through houses that I took to be distinctly non-American in aesthetics and architectural structure. But though I tried to describe my sense of American housing styles—the sprawling suburban home, East Coast brownstones, high-rise apartment complexes—as something quite distinct from these rectangular tiled buildings, villagers were rarely convinced by my explanations and refutations of their imaginative comparisons. People simply assumed that my knowledge of American housing styles was partial at best (which is true) and that somewhere in the vast geography of the United States—particularly where they imagined their own relatives—these same peach- and pink-tiled mansions were rising triumphantly from the modern American cityscape.

This imagined resemblance between Longyan mansions and American houses began to make sense to me only when I noticed similar high-rising tiled buildings in various states of construction, renovation, and grand opening all over Fuzhou City. Like the houses in rural Longyan, these new buildings in the city proper were being imagined in local advertisements and everyday conversations as a more cosmopolitan, modern, and Western-inflected style of habitation in an increasingly open and globalizing China. Just like Longyan villagers, Fuzhou urbanites were also caught up in an immense housing and construction craze as household incomes rose steadily over the past decade and new middle-class aspirations were nurtured through a growing consumer market and newspapers and television programs promoting the joys of shopping, interior decorating, and the ownership of new cars and houses. Similar to the "American guest" mansions in Longyan, the new five- and six-story tiled buildings in Fuzhou City were commonly referred to as "high-risers" and looked upon with pride by urban residents as a superior way of dwelling.

The affinities between Longyan and city imaginations of housing suggest how villagers' assumptions of Americanness in this case were refracted less through transnational ties than through Fuzhou's urban dreamscape of modern and cosmopolitan modes of living. The similarities, however, end here. While the buildings in Longyan remained mostly empty, a similar (though somewhat larger) structure in Fuzhou City would most likely be filled to capacity, with each floor divided into two residential units for a total of ten households under the same roof.

An even more pronounced difference between city and village high-risers became apparent upon entry into these domestic spaces. While the city residences usually opened into spacious living rooms—a fairly recent shift according to my urban sources—village mansions typically led people initially into a space of worship, where a large altar displaying ancestral tablets, household gods, incense holders, and food offerings would sit in the center. In contrast, most city high-risers positioned altars for worship in marginal spaces, such as a small corner of an office or an open kitchen shelf—if such religious shrines were displayed at all. Many urban dwellings I visited, in fact, had no place for worship at all, while in most village residences, regardless of housing style, a central altar room at or close to the entrance was the norm.[5]

I want to stress that this difference between having or not having an altar of worship bears little correspondence to a neat, normative assumption of "traditional" village and "modern" urban lifestyles. Although ritual life was certainly central to Longyan villagers, the next section will demonstrate how religious practices were actually integral to villagers' imaginations and aspirations for a modern, cosmopolitan lifestyle rather than barriers to such aspirations.

As I learned in Longyan, the grounds of "tradition" and "modernity" were constantly shifting and under contestation as people strategized, adapted, and adjusted life courses in response to material and symbolic transformations of the village landscape over the past two decades and beyond. What were once the shining symbols of new prosperity in the early 1980s—the red-exterior houses—were by the early 1990s the ramshackle signs of lowly living among newer imaginative structures of modern and cosmopolitan dwelling. While what was usually considered the most "traditional" kind of housing—the wooden compounds—was virtually all gone by the time I arrived in Longyan, both the red- and white-exterior houses had lost their novelty by the 1990s and increasingly became stand-ins for the "traditional" and the "backward" (*luohou*) among village dwellings and styles of habitation. This was especially true of red-exterior housing, which was commonly rented out to poorer internal migrants when local residents built new tiled-exterior mansions with overseas wealth. This meant that longtime village residents who were still living in red-exterior dwellings were now inhabiting the same kinds of spaces as the "outsiders" they considered more provincial and inferior to themselves.

Starting in the mid-1980s, without physically moving or transforming their ways of dwelling, the old residents of these red-exterior houses felt the privileged boundaries of locality shift beneath them, and by the 1990s, they found themselves newly displaced in the emerging social terrain of Longyan as an overseas village. Those like the Lin family, who lived in a red-exterior house along the Min River, could still recall with pride how they had the best home on the street in the early days of the local construction boom, when they were bona fide successes in Longyan. But such memories of superior dwelling now highlighted disjunctures with newer forms of habitation and made these former spaces of "modern" living seem hopelessly crammed, dilapidated, and backward in the present era. Dwelling in such comparatively confining quarters was now an embodied reminder of one's marginalization and failed capacities in the era of "American guest" mansions and mass emigration to the United States.

Temple: Spirits of the Time

Two temples sitting side by side at the end of a Tang-style stone bridge along the Min River offer contrasting narratives of the recent history of religious revivalism in Longyan (figure 5). On the left, the low-slung Qing-era temple with the elaborate curving eaves (built during the imperial reign of Jiaqing [1796–1820]) houses the Monkey King (Qitian Dasheng), the divine trickster made famous in the classic Chinese tale *Journey to the West*, about the quest to retrieve the Mahayana Buddhist scriptures from India in the early Tang period. On the right, the tall, burgundy-tiled temple provides the newest space for Guanyin, the Buddhist goddess of mercy and, among other things, the patient guardian of the mischievous Monkey King. Although it is hard to imagine from this picture, for most of these two temples' histories, the Monkey King temple dominated the visual landscape on its side of the Min River. In fact, less than half a year before this picture was taken, the temple on the right could not even be

FIGURE 5 Tang-era bridge leading to the Monkey King Temple (left) and the newly expanded Guanyin Temple (right).

seen from the bridge, tucked as it was in the sloping hill almost directly behind the ornate roof of the Monkey King temple.

Although technically Guanyin is considered a more powerful deity than the Monkey King, the temple of this goddess was always meant to play a supporting role to the Monkey King temple in Longyan. Legend has it that in the Republican Era villagers first built the Guanyin temple after a tragic but awe-inspiring opera performance of *Journey to the West* took place on the bridge in front of the Monkey King's temple. At the height of a chase scene, when the trickster Monkey loses his pursuers by destroying a bridge and flying over the rushing waters, Longyan's own bridge supposedly collapsed with scores of audience members on it. But in the midst of this disaster, something miraculous also happened: the opera performer playing the Monkey King was seen soaring over the gaping waters and the heads of shaken audience members and landing on the other side of the river, as the real trickster god had done in the original tale.[6]

Witnesses of this event took it as a sign to build the Guanyin temple as a tribute to the Monkey King's divine efficacy. The Buddhist goddess was brought to this site behind the Monkey King to serve as the trickster god's guardian and anchor, as she does in the original *Journey to the West*. With this smaller temple, villagers believed that the compassionate Guanyin would watch the Monkey King's back and, moreover, keep the mischievous trickster in his place. As the old caretaker of the Monkey King temple noted, "So he won't fly off again and cause trouble."

Village residents on this side of the Min River had every reason to want to keep the Monkey King in his place. The trickster, after all, was the titular district god for this part of the village, responsible for overseeing the well-being of all who lived on the south side of the river since this temple was built. Before the Communist Revolution, when popular religion thrived in China, Longyan was reportedly divided into four separate temple districts, each with its own territorial god to watch over a discrete quadrant of village residents. But after decades of vigilant Communist denouncement and destruction of ritual life and temples, only two of these four temple districts were able to effectively revive and blossom in the 1980s and '90s. The two others eventually got incorporated into the already flourishing temple districts, so the entire village was divided roughly into two cosmological zones—north and south of the Min River. As long as villagers could remember, the Monkey King had served as the designated district god for the half of the village south of the Min River.

Because of the Monkey King's singular importance south of the Min River, residents in his temple district were increasingly frustrated with the unchanging facade of his temple as all others, including the Guanyin temple next door, underwent drastic renovation and construction under loosening state policies on religion and growing overseas prosperity. In particular, as villagers began to succeed in their risky journeys abroad, overseas remittances began to flow back into Longyan with the designated purpose of thanking the gods through new temple construction and other lavish ritual activities. In the 1990s, at least 4 million renminbi (RMB) (approximately $500,000)—the majority from overseas remittances—was invested on the renovation, expansion, and new construction of temples in Longyan. The Guanyin temple alone underwent two expensive makeovers—a renovation for 70,000 RMB in 1989, followed by a more elaborate expansion and construction of a new high-rising building in 2002 (pictured in figure 5), currently towering over the old Monkey King temple at a cost of over 300,000 RMB. In fact, aside from the Monkey King temple, every major temple in Longyan, including the temple of the other territorial god, Hua Guang Dadi, had drastically expanded in size and height over the decade of the 1990s.

In the meantime, the Monkey King temple had weathered all the ups and downs of ritual life in Longyan since it had first opened nearly two hundred years ago and had maintained practically the same aesthetic and architectural form. It was in fact the temple's historical value that both saved it during the worst years of the Cultural Revolution and (as villagers saw it) doomed it in the present era of increasingly competitive temple renovation and construction. While more than forty temples in Longyan were either demolished or collapsed from disrepair between the bombing and looting of the Japanese invasion and civil war (1937–1949) and the equally destructive acts of the Cultural Revolution, the Monkey King temple managed to stave off disaster and preserve its integrity, first by chance and later through the sheer gumption of one of its worshippers. Specifically, during the height of the Cultural Revolution, as clashing Red Guard factions tried to outdo each other by tearing down all signs of "backward superstition" in Longyan, one persistent villager succeeded after twelve tries in persuading the Fujian provincial administration to decree the historical preservation of the Monkey King temple and the interlocking stone bridge leading to its entrance. Although the temple itself was converted into cadre offices during this period, the provincial recognition of its historical value guaranteed that the integrity of the structure itself would be unharmed and unchanged through the years.

In the present era, this administrative order for historical preservation had become the key obstacle for villagers to demonstrate their gratitude to the Monkey King for protecting them on dangerous smuggling ventures and helping them secure overseas prosperity. Although during the heyday of Mao the temple's preserved architecture was a sign of the superior power of the Monkey King to defy Communist plans for obliterating ritual life, its unchanged form now evoked its relative austerity and obsolescence among the newly built or expanded temples. Twice, in 1990 and 1999, villagers on the south side of the river gathered funds to renovate the interior of the Monkey King temple as a celebration of their collective overseas prosperity and as gratitude to the god for successfully overseeing their temple district. But with the prohibition against the transformation and expansion of the structure, worshippers of the Monkey King simply could not keep up with the pace of temple reconstruction among other newly successful and grateful worshippers—especially the followers of Hua Guang Dadi, who could completely raze and rebuild their temple to fit a more modern and grand sensibility with no spending limits or administrative obstacles.

These temple construction projects reflected more than a competitive dynamic between village districts trying to outdo each other in the display of newfound overseas prosperity. They also highlighted the complexities of religious revitalization as a kind of collective, forward-looking project among villagers. In particular, through their unremorseful enthusiasm for the tearing down and complete rebuilding of ritual spaces—regardless of "historical value"—villagers promoted their temples and their gods *not* as nostalgic bearers of "traditional" morals and lifestyles but rather as the crucial *vanguards* of modern, cosmopolitan ways. As villagers understood them, gods were fundamentally coeval subjects who both inhabited and exceeded the same spatial and temporal spheres as their worshippers. In other words, the gods were not timeless but *timely*. Or more accurately, as prescient beings with divine power over the progress and fate of their worshippers, gods were the ultimate trendsetters, always steps ahead of the temporal curve of humanity. Not surprisingly, as villagers transformed their habitats to reflect newer imaginations of modern, cosmopolitan lifestyles, they also worked on updating their spaces of worship. In fact, in general they prioritized the renovation of temples over that of their own houses, funneling the first batch of overseas wealth to their gods rather than to themselves as recognition of the gods' superior positioning as modern subjects in the temporal-spatial order.

In this sense, the historical preservation of the Monkey King temple was never a nostalgic, ideological project about "traditional" values but rather a strategy of last resort for survival in desperate times. Now that the climate for ritual life had considerably improved, residents south of the river could only express frustration that the district god responsible for forwarding their newly improved lifestyles was not dwelling in an even more modern and cosmopolitan space than their own "American guest" mansions. After all, the trickster god, like all other divine beings with the power to leap over rivers, mountains, and distant lands in a single step, already embodied and in fact surpassed the kind of worldly transnational mobility to which most villagers aspired in the contemporary era. For villagers, it only made sense that the Monkey King should inhabit a space representative of his superior mobility and worldliness, particularly as these aspects had trickled down and positively affected the residents in his district. The god's continual residence in a small and relatively humble space was seen by his worshippers as unjust and dissonant—a frustrating displacement and marginalization of the Monkey King's obvious divine efficacy on behalf of his prosperous and grateful followers.

In contrast to the Monkey King temple, the new Guanyin site articulated village imaginations of proper dwellings for their modern and cosmopolitan gods. In fact, these new temples bore an uncanny resemblance to the villagers' "American guest" mansions in their height, tiled exteriors, and utilitarian lines. Only, as villagers often pointed out, their houses did not have the lavish decorative eaves or the complete and carefully remodeled interiors as the Guanyin temple had; thus, this divine space could be seen as just a bit more advanced than people's own dwellings, as it should be according to village understandings.

Road: High-Speed Horizons

In this final sketch of the built environment, I want to direct our attention to travel as an aspect of social relations and a condition of dwelling in Longyan. As I have argued above (with reference to James Clifford), traveling and dwelling are inextricably linked to the production of locality and people's experiences of relative emplacement among others in their social world. Dwellings themselves—whether "American guest" houses or new-style temples—were not just immobile sites of residence. They were also emanations of travel relations and what Doreen Massey (1993) calls "differentiated mobility" among the people of Longyan.[7]

In a very concrete and literal fashion, figure 6 highlights yet another aspect of how people's sense of place and locality is currently being transformed. Cutting across the valley landscape of the village, the pristine strip of a new highway curving into the infinite distance promises in the very near future to connect Longyan in an even more high-speed and direct fashion to the mobile flows of China's cosmopolitan centers, from Beijing and Shanghai in the north to Guangzhou in the south. The road required significant encroachments on fertile village land for its construction, not to mention massive demolition and drilling for a cavernous tunnel through the solid center of one of Longyan's imposing sacred mountains. Despite the loss of productive agricultural land and the major alteration of one of their mountains, villagers all seemed to eye this long

FIGURE 6 The newly constructed highway stretching across village farmland to connect Longyan to Shanghai in the north. It was still closed to traffic as of August 2002.

stretch of highway with considerable pride and optimism. As I was taking this picture, the villager who had hiked up with me to see the highway from above nudged me approvingly and noted, "Look how pretty it is." She added, "In the future, when you want to come and go between the countryside and the city, it will be even more convenient, even speedier. Then it won't seem so far between here and there."

Less than a decade ago, villagers still recalled the necessities of traveling for more than two hours along dirt and pockmarked roads to reach Fuzhou City from rural Longyan. Those who could remember further back, to the Republican Era, also reminded younger villagers (and me) of how better-connected Longyan had been to the city and other places before the Japanese invasion and the Communist Revolution had reduced it to an isolated peasant village in the countryside. On the eve of the Japanese invasion in 1937, some could still point to the completion of a new road stretching from Longyan to the South China Sea, meant to function as a major thoroughfare for troops and goods in the high era of Longyan's prestige as an administrative town and military command center in the region.

Less than a year later, this road would be obliterated in the first stages of war with Japan, when military commanders under the Chinese Nationalist Party (Guomingdang or KMT) ordered the same local servicemen who had built the road to dig it up in a defensive effort to stymie the advancing Japanese military. The Japanese managed to reach the village nonetheless, older residents recalled bitterly, while the KMT forces, who were supposed to defend the village, fled for their own self-protection and left Longyan at the mercy of the Japanese. In the ensuing devastation, the Japanese not only killed, looted, and raped in the village but also left many dead along this road until survivors came by to identify and bury them in shallow graves by the roadside. Until the era of mass emigration, this road remained in the same devastated and haunted state as a constant reminder of Longyan's past regional influence and superior connectedness and its reduction by war and revolution to an out-of-the-way, marginal place—an isolated peasant village.

Since the era of mass emigration and overseas remittances in Longyan, significant reconstruction of roads has helped reduce the travel time to Fuzhou City from a couple hours to about forty-five minutes. Still, villagers held even higher hopes for the new highway running through the middle of their landscape, which was in the last stages of completion at the end of the summer of 2002. Where I saw air pollution, traffic congestion, and other environmental hazards, people glimpsed the promise of greater embodied mobility and social connectedness and, moreover, the hope for recentering their social world as a locality of extended reach and import. Whatever nostalgia I felt for the soon-to-be outmoded village landscape and pace of life seemed quite unwarranted to these no-nonsense, modern(izing) villagers. As I learned whenever romanticized sentiments about the "peasant village" threatened to creep into my engagements with Longyan residents, these were subjects with no desire to remain where they presently were or, worse, return to a glorified version of their past, despite Longyan's prestigious and rich history as a military and commercial center in the region.

Although much scholarship on migration and diaspora has led us to consider "home" sites as places of nostalgic longing and view the articulation of displacement as a migrant's "politics of return" (cf. M. Smith 1994), what Longyan residents showed me through their aspirations, imaginations, and everyday practices of dwelling was the *necessity* of mobility and travel to the experience of emplacement in their contemporary context. How one came to embody a superior mode of living had less to do with a "politics of return" than a politics of *destination*. To be the ideal modern, cosmopolitan subject in Longyan, one needed to find ways to be always better connected and more fluidly on the move, even as one remained in the same "home" site. To revisit and revise a well-known insight of Paul Gilroy's (1991) about diasporic conditions—that is, the notion "It ain't where you're from, it's where you're at"—I would argue that for these Longyan residents, ultimately "It ain't where you're at, it's where you're going" that matters (cf. Ang 1994, 10). Nowhere was this more evident than in the various classes of Restaurant English scattered around Longyan, where for a few hours every weekday a slew of villagers gathered to actively stage scenes of anticipated encounter at destinations overseas. To conclude this chapter, let me offer some final insights into the shifting contours of the Fuzhounese world as imagined through various editions and renditions of Restaurant English lessons in Longyan.

What's in General Tso's Chicken?

Zhong-Tang Tso was a famous Chinese General. The Chinese dish he liked the best was named after him. This is one of the favorite dishes of Americans. The chicken is battered and deep-fried to crispy brown and then sautéed in a sweet, sour, and hot sauce. It tastes delicious.
—Yuan Dai, *Practical English for People Working in Chinese Restaurants*

1) My food is ____	tasteless
	flavorless
2) This dish tastes ____	strange
	awful
	very bad
3) This sauce is too ____	light
	salty

—Andy Yang and Ann Lincoln, *Practical English for Chinese Restaurants*

China man: "Refers to Chinese male, carries humiliating, insulting characterization."
—Yuan Dai, *Practical English for People Working in Chinese Restaurants*

For 100 RMB each per month, anywhere from a dozen to over thirty villagers gathered in the converted sitting room of Chen Tao's house every

Monday through Friday to practice English passages like the ones above. With Chen's direction, these villagers would collectively bark out lines like "For here or to go?" or "What's in General Tso's Chicken?" in a speedy, discordant jumble against the repeated playback of a terribly warped, third-generation cassette of a seemingly proper American female voice elocuting the same lines with ease. Chen Tao's Restaurant English course was only one of many being taught in dispersed corners of Longyan, as well as in other similar villages in the Fuzhou countryside, where a critical mass of U.S.-bound residents could be found.

Like the worn copy of *Practical English for People Working in Chinese Restaurants* (Yuan Dai 1995), discussed at the beginning of this chapter, the text and tape used in Chen Tao's classes also made their way from New York to Longyan via relatives overseas. All the students in Chen's class worked from photocopied versions of another book, *The Most Practical (Eat-In, Take-Out) Restaurant English* (A. Yang and Lincoln n.d.), also published in the New York area. Both of these books had gone through multiple printings in the United States, with different editions circulating among the villagers in various forms—original and photocopied, tattered and new. In Longyan I encountered two editions of each of these books— 1995 and 1996 editions of the former and two undated versions of the latter, which had been renamed *Practical English for Chinese Restaurants* in its later revised and updated edition.[8] As the "practical" in their various titles suggested, all of these books promised to offer lessons not just of English but also of restaurant work overseas. Chock full of maps and sample restaurant menus, as well as detailed recipes for common stir-fry sauces and cocktail mixes, these texts were in fact more like survival guides for those navigating the Chinese restaurant industry overseas, be they clueless new immigrants encountering English and restaurant work for the first time in New York City or savvy restaurant owners negotiating tricky business leases, health inspections, and public relations in suburban or small-town America. Studying these books from cover to cover, one would not only proceed from the basic English alphabet to complex English dialogues involving restaurant customers, landlords, and lawyers; along the way, one would also encounter whole texts in Chinese providing detailed descriptions and tips about everything from the different working environments of take-out, buffet-style, and more upscale, sit-down restaurants to the proper etiquette, responsibilities, and skills required of various restaurant workers—from delivery person, cashier, and host to waiter, manager, and boss. The following passage from the 1995 edition of *Practical English for People Working in Chinese Restaurants* illustrates some of the extralinguistic knowledge available in these books:

> Within Chinese restaurants in the United States, there is a kind of store specializing in take-out. Their scale is usually smaller, usually with three to five workers and with the most having about ten. This kind of take-out restaurant in the United States is extremely common. In many areas, they can be found in every town and district, and even within a small range of neighboring streets, there is commonly one restaurant on every block. Because these take-out restaurants have fewer employees, every worker's workload is bigger. . . . Because every take-out restaurant is similar in major aspects, though different in minor points, customer service becomes a main point for attracting business. Here are key points for good interaction:
> 1. You have to be friendly. First impression is crucial.
> 2. You can briefly exchange greetings and be on friendly terms with the customer, but don't talk about sensitive topics such as politics, marriage, race, yearly income, etc. (Reader can consult section on conversations with guests).
> 3. You must keep clothes and appearance clean and tidy. Fingernails must be kept short and rinsed clean. Also make sure that the work area is clean.
> 4. When serving a customer, you will commonly face all sorts of questions or problems. In order to respect the customer's argument, you should use appropriate words and behavior to solve the problem.
> 5. When the customer leaves, you must remember to say thanks to him/her. (Yuan Dai 1995, 54–55)

Restaurant English lessons like the one above incited villagers to engage in what Douglas Holmes and George Marcus (2006) have termed "para-ethnography." In particular, through such texts, aspiring migrants from Longyan were developing a specialized knowledge of cultural practices and life overseas in ways both familiar and entangled with the very project of ethnography, including and especially my own. Like me, the students in Chen Tao's class studied the maps and passages in Restaurant English books in hopes of gaining a better insight and foothold into a social world in which they were not yet conversant or fully situated. Every single one of the seventeen students I met during my visits to Chen Tao's morning sessions already had plans in motion for leaving China. In fact, attending Restaurant English classes was itself a declaration of imminent departure for overseas, something recognizable in Longyan as a scale-making practice for pushing the terms of emplacement beyond the provincial boundaries of village life. Five days a week, Chen Tao's makeshift classroom provided a staging ground for these students to make claims of belonging to the world conjured up through Restaurant English.

Yet as I learned in Longyan, Restaurant English was merely the starting point, not the end, for enacting spatial imaginaries. In fact, the text Chen Tao's students recited in class offered not just one but several divergent possibilities for emplacement, its various lessons leading the reader through an ambiguous and shifting social landscape from the backroom kitchens of Chinese take-outs in New York City to business dealings and everyday life in the suburban and rural outskirts of the United States. Perhaps most striking about these classes was that claims to scale oscillated from lesson to lesson and student to student. While dialogues set in New York's Chinese restaurants occupied the bulk of these books, aspiring migrants also had the opportunity to imagine alternative geographies through scattered English lessons for catching long-distance buses to Philadelphia and Washington, D.C., for checking into a motel while scouting restaurant locations in the Midwest, and for getting a driver's license and a car in small-town America. Even more illuminating were sections orienting students to the possibilities of emplacement in what villagers termed zaqu ("mixed" or multiracial neighborhoods overseas). These included a chapter on Spanish translations of typical Chinese foods and restaurant dialogue (Yuan Dai 1995, 1996; Yang and Lincoln n.d.) and a dictionary of common racial slurs and profanities (Yuan Dai 1995, 1996) that began with the following list:

1. Chinaman
2. Chink
3. Chinky
4. Nip
5. Jap
6. Slant-eye
7. Slope-face
8. Flat-head
9. Gook. (Yuan Dai 1995, 307)

Chen Tao's students did not all embrace the various scenarios and settings evoked by the lessons of Restaurant English in the same way. Some, like the shy but earnest Zou Shu, were drawn to the tensions that occasionally rippled through these texts and looked for opportunities in class to map out the hazards of racism and marginalization overseas. Others, like the outgoing and ambitious young bachelor Wang He, who had already failed once to emigrate, preferred to hone in on the entrepreneurial side of things, perking up in class only when reading the English dialogues and Chinese texts that pointed the way to climbing the restaurant industry ladder from humble busboy to successful boss in the United States. Then there were two teenage boys, Zhao Yongjun and Lin Zhu, who sat in the back corner of the room and spent most of their time conspicuously playing checkers with each other while the rest of the class recited English words and dialogues together. While Zhou Shu pondered a hostile terrain of enclosure and exile and Wang He strove to inhabit an expansive one of upward mobility, these two youths merely registered their grudging presence and obvious reluctance for belonging to a world mediated by Restaurant English. Though all these students shared a general orientation to destinations overseas, clearly there were tensions and divergences in the ways they claimed their "place" within and beyond Chen Tao's classroom. As the next chapter will show, such tensions of scale only intensified when village aspirations for emplacement were juxtaposed against state expectations of their lives as "peasant" subjects.

CHAPTER TWO

Stepping Out

Contesting the Moral Career from
Peasant to Overseas Chinese

Before, we loved the two characters *geming* [revolution] the most. People all said,
"No revolution, no way [forward]. . . ." Now it's all about the *kaifang* [opening up]
model. No opening up, no way [forward].
—Party Secretary Liu, Longyan Non-Peasant Resident Committee

On the third day of the new lunar year in 2002, an unprecedented crowd
of more than fifteen hundred people packed into the last plot of farmland
along the south side of the river in Longyan. On this occasion, the only
barren dirt plot remaining amid cemented roads and colorfully tiled five-
and six-story mansions had been transformed into an enormous outdoor
banquet in order to celebrate the grand opening of an adjacent high-rise
senior center and a new kindergarten nearby. Along the wide paved road
leading into the banquet area, a line of heavily rouged school girls in sailor
outfits waved silk flowers above their heads in time to a blaring marching
band, greeting pedestrians with a synchronized flutter of hands as they
approached the celebration.

This was just the beginning of the visual dazzle the festivities had to offer. Inside the banquet area, guests seated at one of the 150 round dining tables were treated to a smorgasbord of musical and dance performances on
a large stage constructed at the front and center of the plot. Beyond ballad
singers, drumming troupes, and folk dancers, the entertainment show-
cased a daring acrobatic troupe who electrified the audience by alternately
jumping through hoops of fire and bursting into back-spinning break-
dancing moves including an occasional moonwalk. But perhaps the most
dazzling sight of all hovered above the heads of the guests in the form

FIGURE 7 Grand opening celebration for Longyan's new senior center and kindergarten. Balloons overhead list contributing organizations, including several overseas Chinese groups.

of twenty-seven gigantic multicolored balloons swaying gently in the sky (figure 7).

Large, flowing banners attached to each balloon named the major sponsors for the banquet and the new buildings, which the festival was celebrating. Seven of these banners displayed the names of overseas Chinese organizations, including the U.S.-Longyan United Association (Meiguo Longyan Lianhehui). To foreground the presence of overseas Chinese even more, another large banner, stretching across the face of the senior center, gave specific thanks to "village relatives abroad" (haiwai xiangqin).

In a succession of speeches on stage, officials, local luminaries, and representatives from overseas Chinese organizations singled out the growing overseas population as a sign of Longyan's arrival at the doorstep of modernity. "Today, we at last can say right here that we've succeeded! Longyan's succeeded!" declared Party Secretary Chen, the village cadre leader responsible for peasant administration. Boasting of the more than three thousand village relatives abroad and their large financial contribution to these construction projects, Secretary Chen spoke optimistically of continual overseas support for state-sponsored projects, noting that with more collaboration between officials and overseas Chinese, "Our ancient exuberant Longyan can go from today's springboard to tomorrow's glorious prosperity with real and rapid speed!"

Following Secretary Chen's lead, the next three speakers—all representatives of the overseas population—touted the commitment and contributions of the overseas Chinese toward the progress and modernization of their community. On stage with the same ceremonial red sash and bow, the overseas representatives and officials from provincial, city, district, and village administrations all linked arms in front of the banquet guests at one point, prompting Secretary Chen to announce through the loudspeaker, "Reporters, please come take your photos now."

This orchestrated show of united leadership and cooperation had nearly run its course when one of the last speakers, a representative of the Fujian-U.S. government office, punctured the celebratory mood by casting doubt on the priorities and collaborative spirit of overseas villagers. Following some initial upbeat remarks, the official paused tentatively before declaring that he was there "to remind our overseas Chinese residing abroad [luwai huaqiao] to give a portion of supportive funding to their native homes." Striking a less confident tone than other speakers, the official soberly urged the audience to "carry on the village-loving, nation-loving spirit from this event to more building of schools, less building of temples." He continued: "Let's use funds from abroad on education, on useful things. We encourage you to follow this direction. Look at how things are here today; it's probably very difficult to successfully get us provincial, city, district leaders—major leaders at different levels—to participate in this banquet. This just goes to show how concerned all of us at different levels of government are for overseas Chinese, how we hope that they care more about their native homes, about construction, education, the building up of these aspects."

The official's comments sent a ripple through the audience, some of whom laughed and shook their heads while others whispered into each other's ears. He had clearly touched a nerve by highlighting the social distinctions between officials and village residents, a point that previous speakers had carefully papered over with more congratulatory and unifying remarks. Not only did he suggest that Longyan residents were lucky to be eating at the same banquet as "major leaders," but he also suggested that all these leaders were at the celebration only because they were not quite convinced that villagers and their overseas kin had successfully transformed themselves into the kind of dynamic, productive subjects that the label *huaqiao* suggested.[1]

Without so many words, the official had managed to raise the specter of the "peasant" (*nongmin*)—the official state identification most people in the audience still held, despite their links to a large overseas population. Although most people I knew identified themselves as members of *huaqiao* families, as long as they themselves were still stuck in Longyan, they remained self-conscious of their political classification as peasants under village administration.

• • •

This chapter examines some of the tensions and contradictions in villagers' transition from peasant identification to overseas Chinese status. Specifically, I offer a cross-class analysis of the divergent and often clashing narratives of peasant mobility among village cadres, urbanites, and Longyan's state-classified peasants themselves. In order to understand villagers' current aspirations and strategies for going abroad, I argue that we need to look first at the political classifications established under the household registration system (*hukou*) in the late 1950s, which effectively reordered and immobilized the majority of Longyan residents under the category of "peasant." The bureaucratic paper trail that circumscribed people's lives under the household registration system made villagers highly conscious not only of their "file selves" (Chatterji 1998; Goffman 1962) but also of the divergent futures enabled by different political classifications.

As I will show, state identifications not only legalized claims to personhood, but they also entitled their possessors to enact particular "moral careers"—that is, what Erving Goffman described as the possible sequence of changes and transitions over a life course that constituted both one's "image of self and felt identity" and one's "framework for judging [the self] and others" (1962, 127–28). At once public and personal, moral careers produced social "selves," as Goffman noted, by conflating "common character" and "common fate" (129). As such, moral careers worked to naturalize social differences by tracing certain pasts to certain futures for distinct categories of persons. They did this dialectically through the internalization of "felt identity," on the one hand, and through the externalization of official, juridical, and socially legible forms of identification on the other. This chapter focuses on the latter aspect of moral careers and particularly on the ways state identification has mediated social horizons and destinies in China over the Mao and post-Mao years. The people of Longyan, as I will show, were precisely *not* the kind of state subjects expected to chart trajectories abroad as Chinese cosmopolitans. In turn, to fully understand their desires and struggles for becoming overseas Chinese, it is necessary to examine what moral careers Longyan residents could imagine in the first place and specifically what it meant for villagers to inhabit the state classification of "peasant" in China. As this chapter argues, the kinds of strategies Longyan residents developed for going overseas have roots in the socialist registration system, where people long sought unauthorized means for transcending state expectations of peasant subjects. Ultimately, villagers' views of state identification as a sign of potentiality rather than ontology or unchanging essence provide the key for understanding their current approach to questions of legality and morality as would-be migrants and aspiring overseas Chinese.

The Moral Career of the Peasant

Nongmin, commonly translated as "peasant" in English, was the kind of state identification that reeked of social and economic limitations, both in Longyan and in other places across China. To be identified as such was to be cast into the static backwaters of Chinese society as part of the "backward," "superstitious," and unproductive rural masses. The figure of the *nongmin*, as Myron Cohen has argued, was a modern cultural invention of early-twentieth-century Chinese elites—both Communist and non-Communist—constructed precisely as "an image of the old society that had to be rejected" in order to create a "new liberated society" (1993, 152–53; Guldin 2001; Kipnis 1995b; Ruf 1998). Cohen notes that in the elite urban imagination *nongmin* described a rural population that was "intellectually and culturally crippled by 'superstition' . . . a major obstacle to national development and salvation" (1993, 154).

Although the term *nongmin* was already in circulation before the Communist Revolution, it was not until the Maoist regime that the label was formally adopted and solidified as part of the Chinese state's official system of political classification and registration (Cohen 1993; Potter and Potter 1990a). While in rhetoric Mao himself often sang the praises of poor peasants as the backbone of the Communist Revolution, in practice the Maoist regime instituted distinctions between the rural and the urban populations that were far from favorable to state-classified peasants.[2]

By the late 1950s under the policy of household registration, the central government established a residential system that essentially fixed people "permanently on the basis of their birth place or their husband's residence" (Solinger 1999, 35). The main distinction was between agricultural and nonagricultural status, which roughly corresponded to rural and urban residence respectively (T. Cheng and Selden 1997; MacKenzie 2002; Potter and Potter 1990a; Torpey 1997). Although the registration system was initially intended to establish people's residence mainly for monitoring population distributions and movement, following the economic catastrophe and famines of the Great Leap Forward (1958–1960), it quickly ossified into what anthropologists Sulamith Potter and Jack Potter (1990a) described as "a caste-like system of social stratification," isolating rural inhabitants from the more privileged urban dwellers.

From the late 1950s forward, a veritable paper barrier was established between rural and urban areas. Under the household registration system, a peasant could not gain physical entrance into cities or access to rationed food, employment, housing, or any other state resources without first presenting all sorts of registration-related paperwork—a certificate of urban employment, proof of school admission, "moving-in" and "moving-out" certificates issued by the police in one's destination and current residence respectively (T. Cheng and Selden 1997; Torpey 1997).[3] In effect, household registration became an internal passport system, fixing the entire population within a "spatial hierarchy" of unequal and bounded rural and urban entities (T. Cheng and Selden 1997). Between cities and rural areas, there were great disparities in the quality of life and opportunities for advancement.[4] As Dorothy Solinger noted, "The *hukou*—very much as a badge of citizenship in a Western society would do—determined a person's entire life chances, including social rank, wage, welfare, food rations (when these were in use), and housing" (1999, 4). "In every sphere," Tiejun Cheng and Mark Selden argued, "city was privileged over the countryside, state-sector workers over collective farmers" (1997, 46).

In a place like Longyan, which had mainly relied on nonagricultural and translocal kinds of labor (such as from the military, fishing, construction, and transportation) before the Second World War, the reclassification of most people as peasants was experienced as an extremely artificial imposition from above and their confinement to compulsory agricultural

work in the countryside as a dramatic narrowing of their social worl
life chances under Mao. Though some villagers classified as pea:
were occasionally dispatched as temporary workers on particular no
ricultural projects in Fuzhou City, people tended to paper over such complications when describing the generally immobilizing effects of peasant
status under state socialism. For instance, when recalling life under the
rural commune system (1958–1979), villagers routinely launched into a
long litany of laborious tasks—hoeing the fields, drawing water, planting
sweet potatoes in the mountains, collecting timber and edible wild herbs
and weeds—to illustrate just how all-consuming and "very bitter" (*hen ku*)
it was to embody a peasant identity during the Mao years. Typically, this
outline of dawn-to-dusk hard labor would be followed by memories of
meager meals and hunger. I was always particularly struck by the consistency of people's narratives of eating wild herbs (*yecai*) scrounged from
the mountains surrounding Longyan. As one elderly man noted, "For us
there were many hungry stomachs, a lot of people with their feet swollen
this big [as a result of hunger] and who had to go gather wild herbs to eat.
All you get is this bit of vegetables to eat, never really feeling full."

Maoist policies promoting provincial self-sufficiency in grain production were particularly disastrous for a region like Fujian, which, with only
10 percent arable land, had traditionally depended on translocal trade, remittances, and food inflows to feed its population (Lyons 1999; Yeung
and Chu 2000). Villages like Longyan along Fujian's coast, which had
never relied on farming for survival, were especially hampered by Maoist
development strategies tying the "peasants'" well-being to their success in
producing grain for both the urban industrial workforce and themselves.
Moreover, because only urban residents were entitled to state allocations
of food and other basic resources, "peasants" like those in Longyan were
expected to distribute the bulk of their agricultural output to first feed
their urban neighbors before fending for themselves with whatever happened to be left over. Given the limited agricultural land and work experience of the many state-classified peasants who farmed under the rural
commune system in coastal Fujian, it was not surprising that urban centers like Fuzhou were sustained largely through the impoverishment and,
at times, starvation of those farming on its rural outskirts. As economist
Thomas Lyons has shown through a comparison of county-level data in
Fujian during the Mao era, huge disparities in income between Fuzhou
City and its adjacent rural counties pointed to how "cities became islands

of wealth, with very little in the way of spillovers affecting welfare outside its borders" (1999, 964).

Beyond inadequate access to food and other basic staples, many, like Zhu Huarong, a married mother of two in her forties, also resented that such backbreaking work in the fields and mountains kept villagers from attaining the same educational levels as city residents. Zhu Huarong specifically told me that she was forced to drop out of the second grade when her mother fell ill and needed someone else in the family to assume her burden of agricultural labor and household chores during the Mao era. Her mother, she told me with pride, had had the leisure to learn how to write before the Communist Revolution, a skill Zhu Huarong had never had the chance to master as a "peasant." While older residents like Zhu Huarong's mother fondly recalled the early Mao years (1949–1956) as a period of much optimism and prosperity for peasants, almost everyone who had lived through rural collectivization and the disastrous Great Leap Forward pointed to "peasant" identification as a source of sufferings and persistent disadvantages under the CCP.

Inequalities experienced by the peasant population in Longyan were sharpened by the existence of a small minority of villagers with nonagricultural status, most significantly party cadres but also teachers, workers, and a few others, all of whom were assigned to work units. Since I happened to be living with a family of cadre members and worked among teachers as a volunteer at the middle school, I often witnessed the lived tensions and divisions among people of different household registration status. Most people in fact pointed explicitly to *hukou* identifications as the root of social inequalities among Longyan residents. Non-peasants, however, were much more likely to naturalize *hukou* status as ontology and explain peasant disadvantages as a result of the peasants' entire way of being, an expected outcome of their inherent "peasantness," so to speak. Middle-school teachers I knew—most of whom had grown up in Fuzhou City—often criticized the poor performance and undisciplined behavior of their students by noting that "peasants are just this way" (*nongmin jiushi zheiyang*). In contrast, Zhang Wen, a young mother in her early thirties, told me that it was because of the unfair stigma of peasant status itself that her older sister had failed to gain admission to high school, even though she had consistently gotten higher marks than a classmate from a cadre household who went on to become a college professor. Although her sister was at the top of her class, Zhang Wen believed that this other student's superior status as a non-peasant had entitled her to prefere treatment for high school admissions. In this case, Zhang Wen saw ring natural about peasant identification, only unjust structural disad tages, which she blamed for her sister's dashed prospects.

While reform-era policies in the past two decades have eased the physical restriction of peasants to the countryside, they have done little to close the social and economic gaps between those with urban and rural *hukou* identifications. By the early 1980s, following the end of the rural commune system and the decollectivization of agricultural land, Longyan residents classified as peasants were no longer bound to agricultural labor in the village. However, although the economic reform policies gave new incentives for people to branch out into village enterprises and a variety of other productive labor, most villagers remained "administrative peasants" under the household registration system (Cohen 1993, 166).

Those from Longyan who ventured into Fuzhou City in the early-to-mid-1980s mainly discovered how closed off the urban world of state privileges and opportunities remained for people like them, who were still officially registered as rural peasants. The Lin clan of five brothers, for instance, all ended up as day laborers in Fuzhou City, mainly scraping together unofficial temporary jobs in construction while remaining cut off from the city safety net of housing, health, and other welfare resources. Although the Lin brothers fared relatively well compared to the growing mass of unemployed in Longyan, they understood that "there wasn't any kind of future" in the city for them as long as they remained state-classified peasants. The legitimate trajectory to urban status and success—via the high school and college entrance exam system to official placement in an urban work unit—continued to be an impossibility for most villagers given the inferior educational infrastructure and resources in Longyan. But becoming part of the "floating population" of unregistered rural migrants in the city was hardly a step up, particularly when villagers began to face growing competition from other peasants coming from the interior and more distant regions of China who were often willing to settle for lower wages for the same kinds of itinerant labor.[5] Beyond economic competition, most Longyan residents simply refused to work alongside migrants from China's interior, whom they dismissed as even more "peasant," and hence socially inferior, than people like themselves, who identified as coastal subjects first and as "peasants" only by administrative default. Amid the influx of internal migrants in the mid-1980s, people from Longyan quickly grew disillusioned with the opportunities available for "peasants" in China's cities and continued to view Fuzhou as an uninhabitable and exclusionary place.

Ultimately, whether they were running small food stands, doing day labor in Fuzhou City, or simply were unemployed (as most became under economic reform), the majority of Longyan residents I knew still retained their peasant status, tethered to a state identification that now represented less a shared form of labor (farming) than a "distinct and backward cultural category" of persons (Cohen 1993, 166). Even under reform, the expected moral career of the peasant continued to be one of social stasis and limitation in the countryside; the peasant was "one held by definition to be incapable of creative and autonomous participation in China's reconstruction" (Cohen 1993, 154). In fact, whatever signs of creativity and autonomy were displayed by Longyan residents tended to be viewed by elites as the antisocial and destabilizing effects of peasant ignorance and low culture (di wenhua). While the revival of temples and popular rituals in Longyan confirmed the "superstitious" nature of the peasant, the persistence of "unplanned" births highlighted the unruly and unproductive excess of peasant bodies despite state agendas for population control. These were traces of peasant autonomy that officials sought to stamp out through a series of political campaigns and often violent crackdowns on Longyan residents; for religious worshippers, such crackdowns persisted from the heyday of Mao through the mid-1990s, and for families with unauthorized pregnancies, from the early 1980s to the present. Along with the policing of unregistered rural migrants in the city, such crackdowns in the countryside not only reiterated the inferiority of the peasant but, moreover, imparted a new criminality to peasant aspirations and movements under economic reform.

Not surprisingly, Longyan's celebration of its transformation from peasant village to a modern home of overseas Chinese would appear suspect to someone like the official from the Fujian-U.S. government office. While local cadre like Party Secretary Chen often tried to downplay the peasantness of villagers in favor of their upwardly mobile overseas connections, higher-level officials and urban elites seemed less convinced of the population's legitimate transformation into the kind of modern(izing), cosmopolitan subjects that the identification of "overseas Chinese" implied. The government official's plea for "less temple-building" highlighted these suspicions of villagers' persistent backwardness and their odd fit into the category of "overseas Chinese."

Those who sat next to me at the banquet, like Zou Jin, the wife of an undocumented Chinese take-out cook in New York, clearly did not resemble the kind of "nation-loving," entrepreneurial professionals imagined by the ccp in its promotion of overseas-Chinese-friendly policies since economic reform (see Barabantseva 2005; Nyíri 2002; Thunø 2001). For one thing, Zou Jin's husband had knowingly violated Chinese law by leaving the country without proper papers through a boat-smuggling venture. For another, he was currently applying for political asylum in the United States by specifically claiming persecution by the Chinese government under the "one-child" policy—a claim that surely contradicted both the patriotic and the collaborative spirit of the overseas Chinese that were being promoted by the succession of banquet speeches. If Zou Jin thanked anyone for her overseas status, it would certainly be the gods to whom she routinely prayed for supporting her husband's efforts abroad—and not the Chinese state. Such considerations did not fit neatly into the moral career of the model overseas Chinese, a figure imagined as an urban-dwelling elite venturing abroad—with formal approval of the Chinese state—to pursue higher education or some highly skilled or entrepreneurial professional venture. Aside from the questionable legality of travel, the typical Longyan emigrant like Zou Jin's husband was lucky to possess a middle-school education and find a minimum-wage job abroad washing dishes in a Chinese restaurant. Ultimately, despite a public show of unity among village cadre, outside elites, and Longyan's overseas representatives, these three groups had quite divergent and often conflicting understandings of villagers' claims to the overseas Chinese success story.

Village Cadre: The Disappearing Peasant

Although human smuggling, asylum claims, and divine worship were openly discussed in everyday conversations as part of villagers' strategies for becoming overseas Chinese, these were not aspects of the *huaqiao* success story that local officials wanted to highlight. The top two cadre leaders in Longyan—Party Secretary Chen of the peasant administration and Party Secretary Liu of the non-peasant (*jumin*) administration—both told me in separate interviews that the village did not have a human smuggling problem.[6] Both insisted that since the 1980s economic reform policies have supported, rather than worked against, the outmigration of Longyan residents. In fact, as both saw it, no legal or political obstacles have stood in the way of people's quests for overseas success since the launching of China's economic reforms. Instead, they suggested that the greatest barrier for going abroad had been cultural—a problem of "ideological outlook" (*sixiang guannian*).

Specifically, Secretary Liu described the problem as a result of being "closed off from worldly ways" (*biguan shigu*). "Over hundreds of years of being closed off has led people to become narrow-minded," he explained to me. "This has been a part of our Chinese people's tradition, one of the most totalizing kinds of backwardness." Secretary Liu went on to explain that because people were penned in by Longyan's natural topography with "three sides of winding mountains, one side a surging river" and its scarcity of fertile land, over time villagers became complacent, content simply to survive under such unfavorable conditions. "There was a kind of very easy satisfaction that 'If I can survive, that's good enough'" Secretary Liu noted. "This was a kind of psychological solution," he added.

Not wanting to suggest that complacency was a natural characteristic of the villagers, Secretary Liu also pointed out that the same geographic environment had encouraged people to "go outside of the village to attract development" before the Communist Revolution. As a result of these prior translocal connections, Secretary Liu also argued that Longyan residents were never quite like other rural inhabitants in the area. "We Longyan folks were stepping out [of the village] long before [people in] other places, and because of business contacts with outsiders, we were not at all like a rural village," he insisted. In education, hygiene, and other aspects of life, Longyan residents were in fact much closer to urbanites, Secretary Liu argued. In fact, despite the classification of Longyan as a "rural village" under Mao, Secretary Liu noted that work teams from Fuzhou City who came to evaluate Longyan's productivity all instantly recognized the villagers' social superiority to other peasants. As he recalled, "One brief look and 'Huh!' they would exclaim. Longyan's hundred-surname workforce may have few resources compared to other village folks, but they thought the quality of our [people] was better."[7]

Party Secretary Liu acknowledged that during the Mao years, "The registration system and other circumstances greatly clamped down on mobility"; he even noted that in terms of "mobility and hardship, it was a bit more favorable before than after liberation." While cadre leaders refrained from harshly criticizing the Mao years in discussions with me, both Secretary Liu and Secretary Chen described the period before economic reform as one of social stasis in Longyan. Secretary Liu remembered the state mantra, "No revolution, no way [forward]" (*bugeming buxing*) as a kind of empty slogan, leading to little positive transformation during the Mao years: "People all said, 'No revolution, no way [forward].' Yet as we stood here over time, other people in the world developed while we didn't even develop." While cadre leaders insisted that Longyan residents were never like other rural folks, the Mao years seemed to have nurtured their "closed off" complacent tendencies rather than their dynamic translocal ones.

According to village cadre, it was only after the initiation of reform in the late 1970s that Longyan residents were finally able to expunge the remaining signs of peasantness. In particular, village leaders offered a utopian narrative of their population as model subjects under economic reform, responding to "Deng Xiaoping's great vision" for China to open up. "After reform," Secretary Liu continued, "the biggest change that we Chinese people brought forward, that came to be the change that we Longyan folks brought forward, was precisely what is called 'stepping out' (*zou chuqu*)." As Secretary Liu and Secretary Chen understood it, Longyan folks were part of the vanguard of those "stepping out"—literally in this case—from the social stasis of "closed off" and "backward" villagers to modern cosmopolitan subjects with the singular drive "to walk forward from the front and break through from the back." Secretary Liu continued: "The best aspect of change since reform has been the transformation of ideological outlook, people boldly stepping out (*renmen dadande zou chuqu*). The country's policy permits this. And the people? They also meet the qualifications and also want to go abroad. Moreover, once abroad, they truly and honestly (*shishizaizaide*) succeed in launching overseas careers. When we also bring contributions back to our home village, the transformation domestically is great."

By emphasizing supportive state policies, people's "qualifications," and their honesty in pursuits abroad, village leaders deliberately tried to counter assumptions of human smuggling and to steer clear of other criminalizing or "uncivilized" (*bu wenming*) aspects associated with peasant migrants, such as the lack of education, meager resources, and general disregard for law and order. When prodded, village cadres did concede that earlier emigrants from Longyan—those termed "old overseas Chinese" (*lao huaqiao*), who had emigrated before reform—did not have the highest qualifications and were often illiterate travelers seeking menial labor abroad. But they also insisted that the current generation abroad was qualitatively different; they were beneficiaries of the sacrifices the old overseas Chinese had made to ensure the superior education of their children and their access to legal status abroad. In effect, the past became a receptacle for all the problematic aspects of Longyan emigration, including the necessity for human smuggling. As Secretary Liu told me, "It's not like people think, 'If you don't let me leave, I'll just get smuggled out somewhere.' The ones who wanted to leave [this way] have all left. There's no need to stow away now."

Though the cadres admitted that some aspects of "backwardness" had hampered Longyan residents in the past, they tried to limit such associations of "peasantness" to "ideological outlook." This problem of outlook, moreover, was never all-encompassing but, at best, a partial effect of the same geographic constraints that had historically fostered villagers' translocal inclinations for "stepping out." In this narrative, the figure of the peasant was lodged so far in the past that by the time Communist work units were dispatched to Longyan in the 1950s, it was already clear that "peasantness" was on its way out. So, as the cadres argued, it only took the slight nudge of reform policies for villagers to expunge the final traces and transition with ease into the kind of modern, cosmopolitan subjects toward which they were developing all along. The model overseas Chinese, in other words, was a natural fit for Longyan residents.

For village cadres, the transition from peasant to overseas Chinese meant more than economic or juridical changes in status; rather it highlighted the wholesale transformation of embodied subjectivity among Longyan residents. Villagers not only assumed the legal status of overseas Chinese but also an entire way of being—outlook, appearance, health, propriety—that visibly marked their social superiority to their peasant neighbors. Secretary Liu told me that much like the Communist work teams in the 1950s, leaders coming from outside to observe Longyan's development under reform could tell "just from appearances that the changes were dramatic." When I asked for clarification, he continued:

> Since people's spirits have become more optimistic [*leguan*] after reform, they pay more attention to their bodies, outside appearances, and inner pro-

priety [*zishen, waibiao, neidaide xiuyang*]. By outside appearances, I'm not talking about just making oneself up but also about the exterior's polish—when a person goes out, to dress very neatly is to give others a kind of respect. Before people all left the house looking disheveled [*qiqibaba*]; now this is unacceptable. On the street, you have to suggest your quality as a person, your education as a person, so you have to pay attention to the impression of your outside appearance.

Beyond a newfound respect for the sociality of appearance, villagers' embodiment of overseas Chinese status extended to significant improvements in eating habits, hygiene, and other aspects of life, including a more cosmopolitan drive to "keep up with the developments of the times," which was a direct result of "closer contact with foreigners." Village cadres admitted that despite overseas connections, most Longyan residents retained peasant registration status. But they also insisted that "the household registration system hasn't had an influence on us here that counts as significant," noting not only the disappearing signs of "peasantness" among villagers but also the growing similarity and even superiority of Longyan to the "quality" of urban life. Although Secretary Liu noted that to legitimately move to Fuzhou City one still needed to change registration status, he added, "But even if you told me to move, I still wouldn't want to move. . . . Why? Because it's even better here." Secretary Liu then boasted of how his house in Longyan was just as big if not larger than those of urban residents and how his son, a graduate of Xiamen University, was just as educated and professionally skilled as urbanites. In fact, not only did Longyan provide the same kinds of opportunities for doing business as "going to the city," but according to village cadres, it also offered a more breezy (*qingsong*) lifestyle. Though people's official registration may have been the same, the qualisigns of Longyan's superior mobility were legible everywhere, local officials suggested—materialized in well-dressed villagers, the food they ate, their spacious mansions, and other visible markers of cosmopolitan embodiment. In fact, whatever remaining gaps still existed between Longyan and Fuzhou City, they were shrinking so quickly that Secretary Liu told me, "When you come back to Longyan, it's possible that Longyan will be part of the city's interior, so there won't be any kind of a peasant village left." Secretary Liu's prediction was more than just a reflection of scholarly observations of the "townization" of rural areas in post-Mao China (Guldin 2001). More important, it was meant to naturalize

Longyan's urbanization as an expected outcome for villagers who, as local cadres argued, had always been less like their rural neighbors than like the cosmopolitan urbanites in nearby Fuzhou City.

Urban Outsiders: Quantity, Not Quality

Outsiders like the official from the Fujian-U.S. government office and other urbanites also offered an ontologizing narrative of Longyan villagers' transformation from peasant to overseas Chinese. However, unlike the village cadres' utopian tale of smooth transitions and model subjects, urbanites pointed to a dystopic vision of lingering and intractable "peasantness," encroaching on city spaces and destabilizing China's development in general. While village cadres suggested that Longyan inhabitants were becoming more like city folks every day, most urban residents I knew tended to distance themselves and their own aspirations for going overseas by lumping together and delegitimizing peasant migrations in general, whether originating from China's interior to coastal cities or from places like Longyan to destinations abroad. Just as the flow of internal migrants into cities was often blamed for rising urban crime, the flow of rural migrants abroad was viewed with suspicion by Fuzhou's urban residents. In direct contrast to village cadres, many urbanites conflated rural emigration with human smuggling. They particularly often pointed to shady and violent associations with smugglers as the definitive aspect of peasant strategies for going abroad.

Longyan teachers, all of whom held non-peasant registration and lived in or close to the city, were especially vociferous in their critiques of the emigration aspirations and strategies of peasants in the village. Although they taught and interacted with Longyan peasants on a daily basis, the majority were not local residents but urban outsiders placed in Longyan schools after finishing their vocational training in the city. As such, most did not see themselves as part of the local population and often took pains to distinguish their urban identity from the village residents around them. In fact, I found that their views of emigration resonated much more with other city residents than with local villagers.[8] As I discovered, many of these teachers also had designs for becoming overseas Chinese, though they always stressed that unlike the local peasants, they would never resort to such desperate and illegal means as human smuggling. Since Deng Xiaoping had first promoted the Chinese overseas as a key component of China's reconstruction in the late '70s, aspirations for overseas Chinese status had become fairly common, not only in rural places like Longyan but also in cities like Fuzhou.[9] Ads scattered across city buses and streets attested to the widespread interest of Fuzhou urbanites in becoming foreign students abroad, improving their English, obtaining travel visas, and finding work opportunities overseas. Popular media also promoted the overseas Chinese as successful and dynamic subjects, particularly in soap operas on national television, where they had become fairly common as central protagonists (see Sun 2002; M. Yang 1997).

While village cadre tried to avoid the term *toudu* (human smuggling or to stow away) when discussing the outmigration of villagers, urbanites often referred to peasant migrants explicitly as *touduke* (stowaways) to distinguish them from the more legitimizing and celebrated figure of the *huaqiao*.[10] Like others around her, Wang Lizhi, a thirty-one-year-old Longyan teacher who commuted from the city, also harbored overseas Chinese aspirations. On and off for the past few years, Wang Lizhi had considered and tried to find different legal routes to study or work abroad. But she also believed that her chances for obtaining a foreign visa had been compromised by the international notoriety of Fuzhou as China's human smuggling capital. That was why her husband had recently been rejected when he had applied for a travel visa overseas, she told me. Like other urbanites, Wang Lizhi resented the success of peasant migrants from Fuzhou's countryside and blamed their continual and mostly illegal flow overseas for undermining what she believed was her legal and more legitimate claim to overseas Chinese status. In particular, Wang Lizhi suggested that Longyan villagers simply did not have the moral disposition and cultural capital to thrive overseas and transform themselves into successful cosmopolitan subjects. "Their culture [*wenhua*] is not high enough, their quality [*suzhi*] too low," she complained about Longyan peasants. While educated urbanites like Wang Lizhi aspired to attain additional schooling and entrepreneurial success abroad, aspiring migrants from Longyan "only think of going overseas to wash dishes in restaurants." Moreover, their "low quality" explained why they were willing to violate laws in the first place and risk life and limb in dangerous smuggling ventures overseas.

Beyond issues of legality and legitimacy, the terms *huaqiao* and *toudu* suggested very different experiences of travel and mobility. *Huaqiao* invoked imaginations of a privileged class of cosmopolitan professionals jet-setting across borders with the greatest ease.[11] In sharp contrast, *toudu* (the characters for which represent "to steal" and "to cross a river or sea"), conjured up harrowing images of illicit and lowly travel on crammed and suffocating boats. Unlike the celebrated *huaqiao*, the *touduke* offered cautionary tales of peasant ignorance and desperation, tracing the dangerous and tragic pitfalls of illegal migration in concrete and embodied ways. Typically *toudu* evoked descriptions of inefficient and slow journeys, full of squalor, risk, and suffering through rough seas and rugged terrain. Such experiences warranted significant media attention only when gruesome deaths were involved.

In October 2002, Wang Lizhi brought my attention to the media frenzy around a particularly tragic case of boat smuggling in which twenty-five people died and the remaining stowaways were captured off the shores of South Korea. This case provoked horror and indignation not only because a group of stowaways had slowly suffocated to death in a sealed ship container but also because the smuggler and his crew had dumped their corpses into the ocean to hide evidence of the tragedy from the approaching coast guard. For urbanites like Wang Lizhi, this case confirmed all the degrading and unruly aspects of peasant mobility—the peasants' lack of resources and alternatives, their blind willingness to break laws and risk death, their general disregard for the quality and value of their own lives. The dumping of the bodies provided a particularly sad illustration of the cheapness and expendability of peasant lives as part of the unemployed surplus of China's population. "It's like they used their own lives for gambling," Wang Lizhi noted with disapproval. She added, "It's really too terrifying. Who would dare do it?" Definitely not city folks like her, she implied.

With a mixture of admiration and disdain, Wang Lizhi pointed to the *danzi*, or courage, of peasants as the key distinction between rural and urban aspirations for overseas prosperity. While many urbanites also had overseas aspirations, most admitted they lacked the boldness of rural migrants to "gamble their lives" on risky human smuggling ventures. "People like me read the paper, hear about smuggling, and become too scared," Wang Lizhi admitted. In this case, Wang Lizhi believed that "peasants had more nerve" (*bijiao you danzi*) simply because they did not know better. As many urban observers of human smuggling told me, the lower the *wenhua* (education/culture), the greater the *danzi* (courage/nerve). This correlation between cultural capital and courage was affirmed by the common Chinese saying, "One who lacks knowledge lacks fear" (*wuzhizhe wuwei*). The boldness of aspiring rural migrants was mentioned not only by urban critics, but also by village cadres, who uniformly cited this characteristic among Longyan residents. But while local officials celebrated this trait as part of the modernizing disposition of villagers to venture into the broader world and step out of the comfortable complacency of rural life, urban observers dismissed it as a symptom of various peasant deficiencies—a lack of wisdom and moral propriety, "low culture," and low social expectations.

The peasants in Longyan, Yang Xiumei told me, were willing to gamble their lives on smuggling ventures overseas only because they did not have much else to lose. "Human smuggling to America is their one road out (*chulu weiyi*)," she told me. Yang Xiumei, the thirty-three-year-old daughter of the cadre household with whom I lived, had been a city resident for at least a decade and considered herself, much like Wang Lizhi, as an urban outsider with special ties and insights into Longyan peasant life. Though Yang Xiumei had little love for her childhood village, which she described as terribly boring and backward, my presence in her mother's house had something to do with her frequent extended trips back to Longyan from Fuzhou City. As I found out, like Wang Lizhi, she had also had emigrant aspirations since being laid off from her bookkeeping job in a city work unit. Currently awaiting approval for a visa to Canada, Yang Xiumei was eager to spend some time with me in hopes of learning more about life overseas and perhaps even practicing her English. As one of the few former villagers who claimed urban status, she served as a unique and especially compelling interlocutor on peasant mobility. Even more than teachers like Wang Lizhi, Yang Xiumei made great efforts to distance herself from local peasants and their aspirations for going abroad.

In particular, Yang Xiumei liked to stress that unlike Longyan peasants with overseas aspirations, she had other opportunities for prosperity in China. Though she was currently unemployed, she told me she had had the chance to take the placement exam for another city job. She also pointed to a friend in Kunming who had offered her an open invitation to join his private company as a saleswoman. In turning both of these options down for the chance to emigrate, Yang Xiumei emphasized that she had a choice in the matter, in contrast to the desperate situation of other would-be migrants from Longyan. "There are no jobs, no industries in Longyan," she pointed out. The one paper factory she remembered as a teenager had long since gone bankrupt, while the remaining menial jobs, from plowing the few plots of village farmland to construction and domestic work, had mostly been taken over by even poorer rural migrants from Sichuan and other interior provinces over the years. Moreover, since most peasants did not thrive in school, few could successfully pursue the entrance exam route via high school and college into placement in state jobs. Because, as Yang Xiumei argued, "the people here do not have any kind of future if they do not leave," they were therefore more willing to embark on risky and illicit journeys to go overseas. Peasant courage, in this case, was seen as the product not only of ignorance but also of the desperation of unskilled and uneducated rural masses who were out of work and out of options for survival in China.

Like the unruly flows of rural migrants from the interior provinces to the developing coast, the massive outmigration from the Fuzhou countryside to overseas destinations was largely viewed by urbanites as part of the same "population problem" (renkou wenti) facing post-Mao China as it moved toward market liberalization and opening up to globalization. As various China scholars have observed, questions over the quantity and quality of China's population had become central to the project of economic development and modernization in the reform era (Anagnost 1995, 2004; Fong 2004, 2007; Greenhalgh 1994, 2003; Kipnis 2006; Pun 2003; H. Yan 2003, 2008). From the initiation of the one-child policy in 1978 to recurring party rhetoric for "raising the quality of the people," the population—its excessive size and lack of education and other resources—has emerged as a pervasive source of blame for China's persistent failures of achieving modernity in the past. Ann Anagnost (1995) has noted that the notion of a population problem played especially well among intellectuals and urbanites when the rural masses served as the referents for the "low quality" and unproductive surplus of the Chinese nation-state.

As I found out, the "low quality" of migrants from Fuzhou's countryside was also one of the most common critiques made by urbanites eager to distinguish their own overseas aspirations from those of their rural neighbors. Much like the "floating population" of internal migrants, the stowaways smuggled out of rural Fuzhou were imagined as a kind of undisciplined swarming mass on China's economic and political periphery who were more of a destabilizing drain than a productive resource. Unskilled and underemployed, wandering rural bodies—whether bound for the cities or overseas—constituted the part of China's population that was considered quantity rather than quality. As urbanites imagined, these were not the kind of overseas migrants who would be sorely missed as part of the elite "brain drain" from China's population. Rather, as Yang Xiumei argued, would-be migrants from Fuzhou's countryside were akin to other rural migrants from the interior—low-quality surplus bodies pushed into motion out of necessity, not choice, as a result of the competitive Malthussian pressures of overpopulation in the midst of market liberalization. Widespread media depictions of smuggled Fuzhounese as faceless masses desperately crammed into illegal and suffocating shipping containers, produce trucks, and other tight quarters only bolstered urban imaginations of the triumph of quantity over quality in these rural flows overseas.

Whether internally or transnationally, peasants on the move were largely viewed by city residents as problematic and undisciplined subjects tending toward criminality. By virtue of leaving their rural homes without authorization, both the "floating population" and the stowaways were already marked as illegal migrants in violation of state policies for travel and residency. Additionally, while urbanites blamed internal migrants for rising crime rates in Fuzhou City, they lambasted their U.S.-bound rural neighbors for abetting transnational criminal networks and, in turn, tainting Fuzhou's regional reputation—and that of its upstanding city residents—with the notoriety of human smuggling. This sense of the transgressive movement of peasants extended to images of overpopulation in the countryside, where pregnant women in violation of the one-child policy were known to flee and hide from authorities in large numbers. It is interesting that the terms for both unauthorized births and unauthorized travel abroad shared the character *tou*, which means "to steal." While the common term for surplus births outside the one-child policy was *toushen*, meaning "to steal a birth," human smuggling, or *toudu*, referred to "the stealing of passages." Both pregnant women in hiding and roaming rural migrants conveyed the illicit nature of mobile peasant bodies in contradiction to state plans and disciplinary aims for managing the quantity and quality of the population.

In fact, it was common to hear urbanites describe human smuggling as the logical culmination of rural overpopulation itself. One reason peasants wanted so many children, some people told me, was so that they could increase the odds of future success overseas. According to this theory, the more children peasants had, the more expendable were the lives to be gambled on smuggling ventures. In this case, surplus children born outside of the state's birth planning agenda became exemplary signs of the triumph of quantity over quality in the countryside. In contrast to state discourses for having the "quality" single child—a notion largely embraced by urbanites (Fong 2004, 2007; Kipnis 2006)—Longyan teachers often described how hordes of peasant children roamed village streets without adequate care or discipline from parents. "As soon as they can walk, their parents don't mind them," one teacher complained about peasant reproductive strategies. Deficient in care and excessive in numbers, this surplus of unruly peasant children would inevitably become the kind of "low-quality" subjects bound for desperate and illicit smuggling ventures overseas. By linking unregistered births to undocumented travel, urbanites generally denounced peasant mobility as deviant and subaltern in nature. Far from the natural progression described by village cadres, the trajectory of peasants overseas was largely critiqued by urbanites as part of a series of aberrations, the digressive moves of unproductive subjects off the grid of state networks for controlling population flows and quality.

The "low quality" of rural flows overseas had to do not only with the illegal means of travel but also with what many urban observers critiqued as the general problem of peasant culture. Whether describing the blind courage, criminal disposition, or problematic reproductive and productive capacities of rural populations, urbanites almost always punctuated their comments with broad statements that "their *wenhua* is just too low." While the term *wenhua* can be translated narrowly as "education," these complaints typically conveyed peasant deficiencies not only in schooling but also in an entire way of being that better reflected the broader definition of *wenhua* as "culture." Urban observers often pointed to the blossoming of "superstition" (*mixin*) or popular religious practices in the village as clear evidence of the intractable backwardness of peasant culture. Villagers' reliance on prayer and divination as part of the calculus for emigration particularly drew scorn from urbanites as "unscientific" (*bu kexue*) and superstitious folly. In addition, the massive sums overseas villagers donated to build temples and other ritual activities were often ruefully described as a "very wasteful" (*hen langfei*) and "meaningless" (*meiyisi*) use of remittances. The plea for "more building of schools, less building of temples" by the Fujian-U.S. government official also indicated the widespread frustration of higher-level officials—above village cadres—over the channeling of overseas capital toward popular religion rather than toward state-sanctioned economic development and modernization. While Long-yan officials always avoided talking about villagers' interest in popular religion and drew a blank when I would bring the topic up, urbanites of all stripes commonly pointed to the resurgence of peasant religiosity as proof of their hopelessly retrograde ontological makeup. As many urban observers decried, the successes of Longyan villagers overseas contributed very little to state desires for China's modernity but rather only managed to resuscitate "feudal superstitions" and other social ills long stamped out under Mao.

Beyond popular religion, the rise of a peasant *nouveau riche* with remittances to squander generated widespread distaste and resentment among urbanites. Specifically, as the previous caste-like system of registration distinctions shifted to a more flexible hierarchy of class and capital in the era of reform, many urbanites found themselves increasingly sharing the same banquet tables and social milieus as their upwardly mobile peasant neighbors. Longyan teachers and others, like Yang Xiumei, who prided themselves on their non-peasant privileges, felt especially threatened by the new class mobility of peasants with overseas wealth. Just as Fuzhou's urbanites criticized their rural neighbors for tainting their more legitimate overseas aspirations, so they also resented newly wealthy and overseas-connected villagers for crowding in on and spoiling what they perceived as their exclusive and entitled social spaces.

Among all the non-peasants I knew, Yang Xiumei and her two sisters drew my attention the most to distinctions between their urban lifestyles and the class pretensions of Longyan's rich peasants. Perhaps because the three Yang sisters were among the elite few from Longyan who had managed to become city residents, they guarded their privileged status from the perceived encroachment of their peasant neighbors with particularly visceral tenacity. The daughters of a former village head who was deceased, over the past decade and a half the sisters had all managed to finesse their cadre family connections into finding entrances into Fuzhou City. The oldest and most successful sister had navigated the difficult state exam system to become a city professor and was married to a provincial official to boot. The youngest sister, who did not fare as well in school, happened to marry a wealthy entrepreneur in the city. While Yang Xiumei neither excelled in school nor found an urban spouse, she had managed with the help of her sisters and their well-connected husbands to land a low-level job in a city work unit until her recent layoff. Few other families in Longyan were as elite as this cadre household, and even fewer could boast of so many members who legitimately resided in the city. Though the sisters also had a brother who had gone overseas via human smuggling in the early '90s, they were catty about his success and disassociated themselves by blaming his "low culture" and general peasantness on the bad influence of his wife.

While Yang Xiumei made the most visits back to see her widowed mother in Longyan, the other two sisters also occasionally gathered in their village house, especially for holidays like Lunar New Year and the Dragon Boat Festival. Although it is hard to say what kind of influence my presence in the house had on their interactions, it seemed that when the three sisters gathered around the kitchen table in their village home, the conversation almost always turned into an extended rant against the vulgarity of their newly wealthy peasant neighbors. Of the new mansions around Longyan, Yang Xiumei and her younger sister disdainfully noted that they were merely poor copies of urban residences. "If you look very carefully," the youngest Yang sister instructed me, "you'll see that the materials they use are all the cheapest, the insides are hollow, and the outside—not even a few flowers or plants." In contrast, she noted that city folks cared about interior decorating and outside landscaping because such small details added to the quality of life for urbanites. For peasants, the grandiosity of housing was just all for show, yet another example of the peasant interest in quantity over quality.

This sense of overseas-connected peasants as subjects flush with cash but not class was further reinforced by the eldest Yang sister one afternoon shortly after Lunar New Year when she returned to her village home after attending her Longyan middle school reunion up the street. Sitting down with her sisters and me over some tea around the dining table, the she described the unexpected peasant wives who showed up at the reunion. Usually, she told me, only those who had achieved some level of respect and success would dare show their faces at these banquets, partly because they were expected to contribute some funds to the school by the end of the event. She then proceeded to list some of her classmates— a savvy entrepreneur, a doctor, another college graduate, and so forth— who she felt qualified to be at the same banquet table with her. With equal parts humor and aversion, she then went on to describe other surprising guests—female classmates who had never amounted to much—whose main claim to success was the boast, "My old man is in America." As she parroted this line to her sisters in a wry tone, Yang Xiumei rolled her eyes and exclaimed with disgust, "What nerve (*zhen shi*)!" Though she herself had plans to emigrate, Yang Xiumei was the most vocal of the three sisters in denouncing these women for thinking that their overseas connections and new wealth could compensate for deficiencies in status and culture. Unlike her older sister, who took the fundraising part of the banquet seriously, Yang Xiumei suggested that these women were there only to be seen in the company of their more elite classmates and—even worse—for the vulgar fanfare of banquet food and entertainment. This uncouth aspect of village banquets, with peasants crowding elites for food and visibility, was one reason that no one from the Yang household wanted to attend the grand opening celebration of the senior center I described at the beginning of this chapter. Even the Yang widow wrinkled her nose disdainfully when I asked her about her invitation to this highly anticipated banquet. "She doesn't see the point," Yang Xiumei explained for her mother. Yang Xiumei went on to describe her mother's and her own distaste for the sight of their peasant neighbors hoarding party favors and leftovers at the end of these kinds of banquets.

By highlighting intractable distinctions between peasants and non-peasants in such minute and embodied ways as etiquette and dining habits, Yang Xiumei refuted the local cadres' insistence on the natural forward momentum of the villagers, who, as Party Secretary Liu argued, were not only closing in on urbanites as modernizing subjects but even exceeding their urban neighbors in achieving prosperity and comfort at home. In contrast, urban critics of peasant mobility argued that new wealth gained through such lowly illicit means as human smuggling was incommensurable with the more elusive class privileges of taste and breeding—what Bourdieu famously referred to as cultural capital (1977, 1986). Overseas connections and new money may have enabled peasants to buy their way into the same banquets as non-peasant elites. But as Yang Xiumei suggested, their social bearing and consumer habits at these kinds of events continued to betray the incontrovertible peasantness of their embodied subjectivity. In this case, hoarding food and party favors offered yet another example of the persistent peasant disposition to quantity over quality and, in turn, villagers' ill fit into the overseas success story as more elevated and cosmopolitan subjects.

Longyan Residents: The Networked Body

Despite their clashing interpretations of rural migration overseas, both village cadres and urbanites seemed to agree that "peasant" encompassed an entire way of being characterized unfavorably by social stasis and backwardness. Just as cadres naturalized villagers' transition to overseas identity by describing the wholesale transformation of people's habits and dispositions, urbanites fixated on these same embodied details to essentialize Longyan residents as unchanging peasants. From housing to food, they simply inverted many of the qualisigns embraced by village cadres as the markers of Longyan's legitimate upward mobility and newfound cosmopolitanism into indexes of its perennial "low quality" and "low culture."

In contrast to this interest in the ontological signs and material traces of peasantness (or lack thereof), villagers classified as peasants tended to emphasize the more narrow legal and political aspects of their identification. Far from essence and ontology, those who described themselves as peasants typically evoked the state inequalities and structural disadvantages associated with this juridical status. One of the most striking things about peasant self-descriptions was that they seemed to resonate—at least on the surface—with outside critiques of their deficiencies. In particular, not unlike their urban critics, villagers commonly told me about how they lacked *wenhua* because they were "only peasants." But in contrast to urban references to "low *wenhua*" as a wholesale deficiency in peasant culture, Longyan residents typically used the notion of *wenhua* more narrowly to describe the dearth of educational resources and opportunities available to those who occupied the state category of peasant. Villagers who were self-conscious about their poor literacy or Mandarin speaking skills frequently apologized for their lack of schooling by describing the political and economic disadvantages of being labeled peasants. Like Zhu Huarong, mentioned above, many peasant residents of Longyan suggested that state demands for agricultural labor in the past had detracted from their ability to excel in school or even to attend school in the first place. Many who had little more than an elementary education told me that they were forced to drop out of school to help their parents labor in the fields or take responsibility for domestic duties. Most also believed that non-peasants in the village, particularly among the cadres, had unfair privileges and connections for putting themselves and their children through the tough exam system into high school, college, and ultimately state placement in a secure job. While the few elites, like the Yang family, could mobilize superior resources and social networks to ensure the smooth passage of their children into urban employment and residence, most villagers argued that by virtue of their peasant classification this same trajectory from Longyan to Fuzhou City was closed off to them. As Zhang Wen's story about the dashed prospects of her gifted sister suggested, many Longyan peasants suggested that the divergent destinies of non-peasants and themselves had less to do with the innate talents and "quality" of different populations than with the pragmatic institutional and social inequalities linked to state-imposed identifications.

This sense of the peasants' institutional disadvantage was typically manifested in villagers' descriptions of themselves as people "without a work unit" (*meiyou danwei*). Along with complaints about the lack of educational resources, people commonly pointed to their exclusion from the state system of work unit placement as a key component of peasant identification. In tandem with the household registration system, the socialist work unit system emerged in the 1950s as part of the state's agenda for harnessing labor power and resources for rapid industrialization and modernization through a centralized planned economy. Just as the household registration system divided the population along rural and urban lines, the work unit system became an organizational tool for privileging an urban industrial workforce at the expense of a rural majority (Perry 1997; Solinger 1999). *Danwei* mainly referred to the basic organizing unit of welfare benefits and bureaucratic administration through which urban and nonagricultural populations were placed. Peasants tethered to rural communes under Mao were not considered part of this system and in turn were excluded from the supportive and secure network of permanent state employment and comprehensive benefits provided by the work unit to its members. While the socialist state initially idealized rural communes as "iron rice bowls" (*tie fan wan*), with comparable guarantees of job and welfare security as work units, the famine during the Great Leap Forward and its aftermath highlighted pronounced inequalities between those who starved in communes and those who survived on state-allocated grain in work units. As He Xinghuan noted, far from the ideal "iron rice bowl" of lifetime state provisions, rural communes instead offered "an 'iron walled enclosure' (*tie weiqiang*)," excluding peasants from the privileges of city work units (cited in Dutton 1998, 48).

Beyond the allocation of state resources from food and clothing to housing and health care, the work unit, as Michael Dutton has argued, emerged "as the ethically privileged space of contemporary Chinese Marxism" (1992, 190). Many scholars have also noted how fundamental the work unit system was as an organizing principle and basic unit of social life, particularly in urban China, where people commonly introduced themselves by naming their particular work unit (Dutton 1998; Lü and Perry 1997; M. Yang 1989). More than just a workplace, the work unit functioned as an encompassing social community and total institution with far-reaching jurisdiction over not only labor and welfare but also, more centrally, the moral discipline of its subjects. From surveillance and indoctrination to the regulation of marriage, childbirth, and divorce, the work unit served as the hub of state discipline and subjectification, tracking and sorting people through the careful administration of the personal dossier file (*dangan*) and producing collective identities for its members. This totalizing nature of the work unit was nicely captured by He Xinghuan. As He argued, "The work unit doesn't just constitute a kind of identity certificate. It also relates to subsistence and to other issues from birth through to death and also to the value attributed to the individual. If one is in a good work unit, one is set for life and one's status can even be inherited by one's children." He added that even if one belonged to a less than perfect work unit, "it [was] preferable to being lonely and roaming around in society without one" (cited in Dutton 1998, 45, 47).

In contemporary Fuzhou City and its surrounding countryside, I found that the work unit continued to dominate people's vision of social organization and emplacement through the early 2000s. In fact, it was still such a basic category for understanding social difference while I was conducting fieldwork in 2001–2 that people often tried to place me in the United States by inquiring about my own "work unit" overseas. Urbanites and rural residents alike frequently commented on what a good unit I must belong to as an advanced graduate student in the United States at the time. They also typically assumed that my current unit (that is, my university) would automatically secure a good job for me in a comparable or superior unit after I completed my PhD. People in both Fuzhou City and Longyan were often quite surprised when I explained that I did not belong to a work unit, like graduate students did in China, and that there was no state-guaranteed track to employment for me after I finished school.

While the general benefits and prestige of the work unit system have waned over the past decade, what the *danwei* long provided its members—

and what Longyan peasants resented not having—was a sense of security and social insulation from the vicissitudes of state agendas for development since the high tide of the Maoist regime in the 1950s. The famine during the Great Leap was perhaps the most striking example of how peasants felt cut off from the state's protection of its urban industrializing forces in the face of the disastrous effects of its own modernizing drive. But there were also more subtle and long-term instabilities that Longyan residents attributed to the disadvantages of peasant identification. Land reform, for instance, raised the uniform ire of older villagers, especially those who could remember as far back as the transition to communism in 1949—the historical turning point commonly referred to as *jiefang*, or "liberation." Specifically, while most Longyan seniors with peasant status spoke positively of the initial years after liberation, when many received their first piece of farmland under initial state policies for redistribution, they also resented that their property was confiscated only a few years later in the transition to rural collectivization in the mid-1950s. Most also viewed the last wave of land redistribution following the dismantling of the commune system in the late 1970s with a great deal of cynicism, as part of a continual seesaw of land reform policies toward peasant subjects. Many villagers complained particularly about how the majority of the plots allocated to peasants in 1980 were again confiscated by local officials by the end of the decade. While cadres justified these land seizures by pointing to their lack of productive use by residents increasingly bound for emigration, most Longyan peasants denounced these seizures as evidence of the continual instability and capriciousness of the state in regard to the rural masses.

Villagers' sense of the mercurial nature of state policies toward peasants was also manifested in discussions about the local policing of popular religious practices since the 1950s and the one-child policy since the early '80s. In both cases, the state's reliance on intense but short-lived political campaigns for periodically cracking down on rural populations contributed to villagers' sense of a perpetually unstable and unpredictable social field for pursuing their religious and reproductive interests. A hallmark of Maoist politics, the strategy of launching the occasional campaign to target a particular social problem or crime was exemplified by villagers' memories of the seemingly arbitrary rhythm of anti-"superstition" raids on homes that extended from the 1950s through the mid-'90s.[12] As Longyan residents remembered, in every decade since the Communist Revolution such campaigns against popular religion would periodically emerge as short bursts of official political fervor, followed by long, indefinite stretches of informal apathy and non-enforcement. By all accounts, enforcement of the one-child policy since the early 1980s had also been subject to similar sporadic but zealous and draconian campaigns—with the last one in 1991 resulting in at least one late-term abortion, the partial destruction of two houses, and the incarceration of several elderly parents and in-laws, who were held mainly as ransom to lure their pregnant daughters or daughters-in-law out of hiding for mandatory abortion and sterilization. Not only did the inconsistency of these campaigns render them ineffectual over the long run, but also the intense and brutal nature of their execution only made those caught up in them feel unjustly and arbitrarily singled out for punishment.

Peasant complaints of injustice typically took highly personalized forms as indictments against Longyan officials, who were largely suspected of doling out scarce resources and draconian punishments on the basis of nepotism and social connections. For instance, many saw the Yang family, with its cadre members and urban ties, as a prime example of entrenched privilege built upon an insular personal network of state connections and favoritism. Desired resources like prime agricultural land and the sole factory in Longyan—not to mention a legitimate ticket to urban residency—all seemed to wind up in the hands of the Yangs and their social web of cadres, kin, and friends. Those inside this charmed circle also seemed less susceptible to the punitive whims of local law enforcement. Rumor had it that the most prominent elderly villager in Longyan was even able to get his son cleared of murder charges because of his superior personal connections, or *guanxi*, with state authorities. Despite the fact that the son had been caught and convicted for killing a man who had tried to seduce his wife, people told me that he did not spend more than a few years in prison before his well-connected father found a way to secure his release and passage out of China to the United States.

In contrast, those less attached to the centers of state authority—mainly villagers classified as peasants—often complained that they were subject to disproportionate fines and punishments for relatively minor infractions. For example, people told me that only those without state connections were ever fined for such widespread practices as the ritual burning of spirit money (offered on behalf of the dead)—an official fire-hazard public health violation. Such discriminatory fines were often cynically described as a kind of extortion by local officials hoping to fill their personal coffers with the resources of the marginalized peasant masses. One woman even told me that it was not unusual for peasants to pay multiple fines for the same one-time infraction. She complained that several years after she was first fined for evading the one-child policy, local officials came by her house to demand yet another payment for the same violation. Even after paying two fines, she told me that she would not be surprised if officials used this past infraction yet again to extract more money from her down the road. Like others in Longyan, she attributed this unpredictable climate for local persecution and extortion to her lowly status as a peasant cut off from state favoritism and protection.

Being outside of the elite circle of village cadres as well as the privileged safety net of urban work units meant greater vulnerability to the whims of state agendas and the traumatic reversals of fortune that accompanied them over the years. While most villagers acknowledged that the political fervor of the Cultural Revolution upended Longyan elites more than the common peasant, this kind of elite dislocation was seen as an isolated and exceptional case within a longer and more steady history of peasant marginalization and displacement under state socialism, beginning with the seizure of land for rural collectivization. As Friedman et al. noted for peasants in northern China, collectivization along with the standardization of the household registration system entrenched divisions between "the favored few and the excluded many" and highlighted the informal networks that "channeled scarce resources—jobs, travel, medicine, investment, technicians, and so on—to favored communities, regions and families" (1991, xvii). Longyan critiques of policing and punishment suggested that the law itself was one of the resources that could be harnessed by the centrally networked and well-connected against the more socially peripheral and isolated others.

Rather than an emanation of a correct moral order, the law could be better described by villagers as a flexible and dynamic field for the production of personal connections (guanxi)—a social testament at any one time to the relative depth and breadth of one's network of loyalty and reciprocity.[13] For Longyan peasants, the household registration system was probably the most enduring and salient example of how legality could become a privileged currency for some over others. Particularly for a population accustomed to translocal mobility and ties before the Communist Revolution, registration classifications—with their segregation of urbanites from rural residents, non-peasants from peasants—ultimately pointed less to ontological difference than to the state's "monopolization of the legitimate means of movement" (Torpey 2000, 5). At the most basic level, peasant identification itself became a badge of lawful if unjust immobilization, its imposition a legal curtailment of people's social and physical mobility outside the sedentary, agrarian assumptions of peasant ontology. This did not mean that most Longyan residents were resigned to their fates as state-classified peasants tethered to the land. If anything, the solidification of the household registration system as an internal passport system only highlighted how those who could finesse superior state connections also legalized better destinies and futures.

As people noted, it was usually the few well-positioned cadres like the Yangs who accessed the state channels from rural registration to city work unit. But while this legal trajectory was not available to most, Longyan residents sought out other pathways for legitimizing destinies beyond state limitations on peasant subjects. In particular, people's sense of legality as more of a flexible resource than a moral valuation was exemplified by their pride in successful maneuvers around the state's one-child policy. Initially, I was quite surprised when villagers would casually point to a child and openly declare, "This one is *toushen*" (that is, born outside of the one-child policy). But as I later found out, violations of the one-child policy were not only widespread but also quite normalized as part of a routine process for transforming illegal births into legalized children. Although children born outside of the state's birth-planning agenda were officially excluded from registration and state eligibility for benefits, villagers seemed to negotiate with local cadres on a regular basis for obtaining legal status for unregistered offspring. Except when there were spikes in law enforcement during campaign drives against unplanned births, it seemed commonplace for villagers to simply pay a fee for registering illegal births after the fact of violation. On several different occasions, people described how the cost and expediency of this process—from state evasion to legalization—depended largely on one's interpersonal skills and connections with local bureaucrats and leaders. For instance, Deng Feiyan, a mother of three in her mid-thirties, not only recounted how she had outsmarted and escaped from local police when they tried to arrest her while pregnant with her second child, but she also capped her triumphant narrative by boasting of how skillful bargaining with officials later enabled her to get a huge reduction off the payment for registering her unauthorized child. When it came to such payments, another woman noted how informal things were and how contingent on local officials: "It's all according to whatever they say." Specifically, when I asked her about the standard costs of penalties for one-child policy violations, she shrugged and said, "However much they want to fine, they'll just fine." So much depended on "seeing who you are," she added.

For villagers, ascertaining "who someone was" required a relational appreciation for persons as networked bodies—a collective, rather than individualized, sense of subjects as particular nodal points and extensions of various affective and material ties.[14] While certain identities like "non-peasant" provided evidence of an expansive web of relations and superior alignment with state forces, villagers also believed that state identification was ultimately less totalizing as ontology and more partial as a contingent aspect of one's positioning within a larger, dynamic social network in which state ties comprised only one relational strand. This weblike and pliable sense of identification was highlighted by Lin Mengya's dramatic tale of reproductive defiance and triumph during the especially volatile 1991 campaign against unauthorized births in Longyan. Lin Mengya, a thirty-three-year-old mother of three, and I had reached a hilltop temple for Guanyin, the Buddhist goddess of mercy, near her mother's home just outside of Longyan, when she first recounted her troubles with the one-child policy. The sight of this temple under renovation had jogged Lin Mengya's memories of how she had hidden with her husband and oldest daughter at this place when she was pregnant for the third time about a decade ago. In particular, she described how when she was more than eight months pregnant, she slept on the bare, hard floor of the courtyard in front of the temple for days while more than twenty local officers and cadres raided her mother's home not more than forty steps away at the bottom of the hill from this site. Had the authorities climbed these forty steps, she told me she would probably have faced abortion, fines, and incarceration. This was, after all, the fate that had befallen her cousin, who was also almost due to give birth when she was captured at a friend's house not far from the hilltop temple where Lin Mengya was hiding around the same time.

Lin Mengya attributed the divergent outcomes of her cousin's pregnancy and her own to the relative strength of their social networks. In particular, at the time of this intensified campaign, Lin Mengya recounted that local officials everywhere had been offering monetary rewards to people who revealed the hideouts of pregnant women in violation of the one-child policy. This incentive became a true test of interpersonal savvy and social bonds, pitting group loyalties against personal financial benefit and revealing the instabilities of certain people's webs of relations. Lin Mengya suggested that her cousin was a victim of a shaky and untrustworthy social network at that time. For one thing, hiding at a friend's house pointed to the lack of closer relations (that is, kin) for the cousin to count on. Ultimately, her capture also highlighted the disloyalty and greed of the friend, who Lin Mengya suspected had turned her cousin in for the reward money. In contrast, Lin Mengya noted that she benefited from the widespread respect and loyalty commanded by her parents while she was hiding in her natal home. As a result of her parents' tight-knit web of relations, Lin Mengya described how knowing and watchful neighbors not only shielded her whereabouts from Longyan authorities but also warned her as the police were finally approaching to raid her mother's home. Even the local party secretary of her natal village had protected her informally out of respect and loyalty to her parents. Though this cadre knew Lin Mengya was hiding in his jurisdiction, he never turned her in to Longyan officials but instead warned her to be careful and on the lookout for signs of approaching authorities.

Susan Greenhalgh has observed that in the countryside, "local cadres often colluded with peasant resisters because of unwillingness or simply [their] inability to enforce the state's strict limits on fertility" (2003, 206). In part, such lack of enforcement could be attributed to the more dispersed and disorganized nature of rural cadre power, particularly after the dismantling of communes, a step that decentralized control over rural subsistence (Greenhalgh 1995, 2003). In contrast, city work units, with their highly centralized administration of welfare and punishment, tended to assert more uniform and strict discipline over their subjects' fertility, which became tightly bound with the allocation of urban resources, from jobs and housing to health and retirement benefits. Ironically, being outside the work unit's encompassing network of benefits enabled Longyan peasants to evade the state's firm grasp over the reproductive capacity of its urban subjects. More important, exclusion from the tight-knit, paternalistic web of state support and discipline allowed villagers to envision and plot moral careers beyond what was considered legally correct for peasant subjects.

Though Lin Mengya did not initially have the law on her side, she could point to an alternative anchor of moral support—her informal network of kin, neighbors, and even officials—who not only collectively protected her against state intervention in her multiple pregnancies but also helped legitimize her actions later on by enabling her to obtain legal status for her children from the same disapproving state. Although she was finally arrested and incarcerated by Longyan officials after she returned to the village with her third newborn, her husband was able to finesse cadre connections, along with a 1,500 RMB payment, to secure her prompt release. These connections came in handy once more when her husband was unexpectedly arrested much later for this same one-child policy violation and held for more than ten days in jail. In the end, with the help of a relative who worked in the local administration, Lin Mengya not only got her husband free but in the process also secured household registration for her three children—all of whom had been unregistered until that point—with another 6,000 RMB payment. Although it was common to pay a fine for legalizing unregistered children, she told me that less connected villagers had paid over 10,000 RMB for the same registration. Moreover, during the last intensive campaign in 1991, those who lacked the protection of loyal and expansive networks encountered harsher threats and punitive measures, including wide-sweeping arrests of their family members and the tearing down of their houses in Longyan.

In contrast to urban critics, who dismissed surplus births as ontological signs of peasant criminality and low culture, villagers like Lin Mengya emphasized the processual and tactical nuances in rural reproductive practices for moving from state evasion to incorporation. In this case, legality and illegality could not be seen as exclusive positions of being, marking intractable differences between civilized urbanites and unruly peasants, but rather as distinct phases in a trajectory of becoming. Just as one could move from unregistered birth to registration, one could also legitimize illegal emigration with later acquisition of legal status and prosperity overseas. While the strategies for becoming overseas Chinese will be discussed in greater detail in part II, here I mainly want to point out that there were precedents for villagers who wanted to circumvent state channels and constraints in the pursuit of destinies and moral careers beyond normative expectations of "peasantness." It is important to note that villagers' approaches to the one-child policy revealed that the legality of being could not be conflated with the morality of becoming.

While much has been written about one-child policy violations as strategies of "peasant resistance," it is interesting to me here that village maneuverings for extra children, as well as for going overseas, ultimately have less to do with outright opposition to state impositions of difference and ontology than with desires for reincorporation into privileged subject positions. Specifically, it seems important to note that those with illegal trajectories mostly had legal destinations in mind—whether from unregistered birth to registered child or from undocumented stowaway to passport-toting cosmopolitan Chinese. In this sense, maneuverings for moral careers beyond the teleological assumptions of peasant backwardness and stasis might be better described as counter-hegemonic moves always retrievable and circumscribed by a larger hegemonic order or, in Michel de Certeau's terms, as more of a tactic than a strategy that "insinuates itself into the other's place, fragmentarily, without taking it over in its entirety, without being able to keep it at a distance" (1984, xix). By "insinuating themselves into the other's place"—in this case, the privileged position of overseas Chinese—the villagers took a classificatory system that they could not fully escape and made it serve alternative practices and meanings foreign to it. It was neither simple resistance nor submission. As de Certeau argues, "They metaphorized the dominant order: they made it function in another register" (1984, 32).

For Lin Mengya, this alternative register was crystallized on the fateful day when she hid at the hilltop temple not more than forty steps above the swarm of local officials raiding her mother's house. Until this point, she told me she had been skeptical about the divine powers and compassion of gods, putting her faith in more certain human resources like the informal web of helpers who had protected her thus far in her unauthorized pregnancy. But when she found herself alone beyond the security of her social network and only forty steps away from capture, she realized she had exhausted her protective circle and for the first time pleaded with the gods to keep her safe. Her vigilant prayers, she told me, were answered that day when the local police somehow managed to overlook the steps leading up to the temple and pursued another path leading away from her. Rather than simple chance, she saw the police's stray trajectory as clear evidence of the superiority of divine efficacy and, in turn, as moral affirmation of her reproductive efforts against state regulation. From that point forward, she told me she had been a loyal follower of local gods and a generous contributor to the revitalization of temples and ritual life in Longyan.

I have much more to say in subsequent chapters about the repositioning of state power within a more encompassing order of divine authority (see especially chapter 5). For now, I just want to point out that this alignment of villagers with gods was not necessarily anti-state or anti-modern simply because it supported local practices that villagers (as well as their urban critics) commonly described as a continuity of "customs" (*xisu*). As mentioned in chapter 1, gods themselves were not imagined as unchanging and stolid forces in contemporary Longyan but rather as forward-looking, cosmopolitan subjects. In turn, alignment with the gods over the state was a means for villagers to better access, not oppose, the dream of modernity. They did so by trying to shed the categorical constraints of household registration status, particularly the backward associations of peasant identification, which they denaturalized as a sign of institutional disadvantage and state expropriation rather than as an index of their inherent quality as persons. From the famine during the Great Leap Forward to recurring campaigns against religious and reproductive practices, villagers linked an uncertain and turbulent terrain for livelihood and prosperity to their institutional marginalization as state-classified peasants. Having children outside the state plan was itself not simply a matter of incorrigible peasant "tradition" but a response to the socioeconomic insecurities of life outside the state's embrace. In particular, villagers often argued that urbanites could afford to have one child only because they had the work unit to support them in poor health and retirement. However, multiple children were viewed not only as necessary insurance for old age among rural residents, but they were also fundamental extensions of one's social possibilities and moral legacy as a networked body.

While critics focused on surplus children as expendable by-products of peasant criminality, villagers themselves pointed to these same children as part of their success in solidifying and expanding their reach as moral persons positioned in a reciprocal and loyal web of relations. In an important way this desire for what Nancy Munn (1986) termed the "spatial-temporal extension" of subjects went beyond the material vicissitudes of life to the sustainability of one's social influence and reputation well after death as a beloved ancestor with far-reaching and thriving intergenerational ties. In contrast to dystopic images of rural children as the unruly excesses of China, villagers openly pointed to unauthorized children as networked achievements in circumventing state constraints to legalization. Moreover, they singled out another kind of child beyond the Chinese state's grasp as evidence of their superior spatial-temporal extension—the "American child," or in Fuzhounese, the *Miwo giang*. This term mainly referred to children born overseas who were sent back as infants and toddlers to be raised by village kin, especially grandparents. More than any other figure, the returned "American child" offered proof of the overseas success story villagers were crafting against state expectations. Not only were these children the culmination of transnational journeys from state evasion to privileged legalization, but also, armed with U.S. citizenship, the "American child" promised to be a superior networked body, full of generative potential as a resourceful link and legal channel to future overseas status for those still immobilized as village peasants. Even without emigrating, Longyan residents, particularly those too old to imagine ventures overseas, could point to the transfer of these children to their care as evidence of their own elevated positioning within an expanded transnational circuit of exchange. Nurturing the "American child" not only opened flows of remittances from abroad to villagers but for elderly grandparents, it also extended and strengthened the intergenerational ties essential for their imagined futures as formidable ancestors, still transnationally networked and connected in the afterlife.

The Ins and Outs of Moral Careers

Erving Goffman described moral careers as "any social strand of any person's course through life" in which "unique outcomes are neglected in favor of such changes over time as are basic and common to members of a social category, although occurring independently to each of them" (1962, 127). This concept of career, he suggested, was dialectical in nature: "one side is linked to internal matters held dearly and closely, such as image of self and felt identity; the other side concerns official position, jural relations, and style of life, and is part of a publicly accessible institutional complex" (127). Central to every moral career was the reconstruction of a fateful past leading to one's present arrival and future destination. Retracing and contesting such trajectories are part of what I call a "politics of destination" among my subjects in rural Fuzhou.

Specifically this chapter has examined three divergent narratives of "fateful pasts" leading up to the village-wide banquet celebration of Longyan's new senior center and kindergarten in early 2002, when officials and villagers linked arms in front of a crowd of thousands and declared that Longyan had finally "arrived" as a modern, cosmopolitan home to overseas Chinese. As I have suggested, this triumphant tale of villagers' smooth transition to overseas Chinese status was best represented by Longyan's cadres, who tried hard to efface all teleological signs of peasant backwardness from their accounts of village transformation. They argued that it was natural and inevitable for villagers to move from a position of ideologically clouded but translocally mobile subjects before the Communist Revolution to enlightened, cosmopolitan vanguards for China's modernization and opening up in the post-Mao era of economic reform. Even during their confinement to the stasis of the rural commune system, cadres emphasized the positive impressions of visiting party elites who observed that Longyan residents were clearly not like "other peasants." By downplaying peasant status and illicit links to human smuggling, cadres argued that it was villagers' moral destiny to step out and become successful overseas Chinese. They even suggested that state policies directly served as supports and catalysts—not legal obstacles—for villagers' overseas aspirations, enabling them not only to catch up to their urban neighbors but even to surpass them in terms of the pace of modernization. They pointed to all sorts of embodied forms of newfound prosperity as the indexical signs of villagers' superior quality and growing cosmopolitanism as an overseas-connected population.

Urbanites refuted this account of a fateful past to a cosmopolitan future by interpreting many of the same qualisigns celebrated by village cadres—from housing to food to social etiquette—as the inverse markers of intractable peasantness among Longyan's newly mobile residents. Far from a natural evolution of the peasants with state support and legitimacy, non-peasant critics emphasized all the transgressive and unruly aspects of rural emigration from Fuzhou's countryside to distinguish these transnational flows from the more elevated assumptions of the overseas Chinese as jet-setting cosmopolitan professionals. Not only did they reference overseas villagers as stowaways rather than overseas Chinese to highlight their criminal dispositions for "stealing a passage," but they also linked illegal migration to the larger population problem of unproductive rural surplus—itself a result of illicit peasant tendencies for having excessive and expendable children in violation of the one-child policy. Along with the peasants' continual backward and superstitious practices, these evasions of state regulations suggested how far Longyan villagers were from the model subjects of economic reform promoted by local cadres. Despite their urban and worldly pretensions, villagers with overseas connections continued to embody the quantity rather than quality part of the population, as exemplified by their disregard for civic order and their squandering of remittances on vulgar consumerism. As their critics argued, villagers remained incorrigible peasants, displaying all the ontological signs of backwardness that disqualified them from moral careers as China's cosmopolitan vanguards.

Despite their obvious clashes, these two retracings of village trajectories from peasant to overseas Chinese shared some fundamental assumptions of ontology and entitlement anchored to the state classificatory grid of distinct and unequal state identifications. Cadres did not dispute urbanites' claims that peasant culture was fundamentally incompatible with overseas Chinese identity, disagreeing only over the degree that villagers ever embodied the qualisigns of peasantness in the first place. In both cases, the state's taxonomy of difference and identity was taken as the natural order of things, its bureaucratically regulated channels understood as the encompassing road map to divergent moral careers. While non-peasant status put one on the track from school to work unit, peasant status usually meant either a future of categorical stasis and immobilization or aimless wandering and dislocation off of state trajectories. Villagers did not disagree with this assessment of the available pathways for state subjects. But they also emphasized the institutional inequalities leading to such divergent destinies and in the process denaturalized state distinctions like household registration as the ontological grounds for charting moral careers.

Since Deng Xiaoping called on people to "step out" in the late 1970s, new trajectories overseas also opened to Chinese subjects for serving as productive "bridges" (the "*qiao*" in the term *huaqiao*) to global ties and resources. While the legal channels abroad largely remained the province of university graduates and elite professionals, state desires for an inflow of overseas capital inspired officials—high and low—to court a wider circle of mobile Chinese currently overseas—from third-generation foreign nationals to recent emigrants like Longyan villagers—under the same celebratory rubric as "overseas Chinese."[15] The slippage of this designation between urban elites authorized for travel and mobile others questionably bound to state regulations has made it possible for people to imagine moral careers from state evasion to privileged reincorporation. More important, I have argued here that precedents for such moral careers could be found in people's approaches to the household registration system, particularly around the status for unauthorized children, where legality was understood more as a resource than a moral valuation, more a phase than a state of being. In the delinking of legality and morality under the registration system, villagers could look to state identification more for potentiality than ontology, more as networked achievements than as natural entitlements in a given order of things.

PART II   *Exits and Entrances*

My wallet was already crammed full with my passport, visa, plane ticket, and a wad of related documents—the fruits of one year and eleven months of difficult struggle. This wallet was firmly attached to my belt; unless somebody ripped off my trousers, it would be quite impossible to lose it. May the designer of this wallet be richly rewarded in this life and the next—that's what I was thinking at the time.

—Tie-sheng Shi, "Fate"

IN SHI TIE-SHENG'S SHORT STORY "FATE," the paraplegic protagonist Mo Fei retraces the last moments before his disabling accident by recalling his magnanimous thoughts toward the maker of his tightly secured wallet, whose contents held not only the fruits of almost two years of "difficult struggle" but also the key to his dreams for studying and traveling abroad. Going over the inventory of documents in his wallet, Mo Fei contemplates his good luck while riding his bicycle and imagines all the places "on the other side of the world" he will soon get to see (Shi 2001, 24). Starting with vacation plans for the Grand Canyon and Niagara Falls, his travel fantasies grow increasingly elaborate and exuberant: from the great pyramids in Egypt to St. Mark's Cathedral in Venice "to the Louvre in Paris, the Tower of London, Mt. Fuji in Japan, and the wild game reserve in Tanzania." (24). "I will see them all," Mo Fei remembers thinking optimistically, just moments before his bike turns into a narrow street, runs over a slippery eggplant, and swerves violently into a screeching car. Sometime later in the story, Mo Fei would return to the memory of his fat wallet, this time as a lament for his immobility as a paraplegic stuck in China. From his sickbed in the hospital, Mo Fei would recall that "The documents in my wallet were still there, silent as an ancient tomb preserving the records of innumerable heart-rending legends" (30–31).

Such a poetic contemplation of documents would not be out of place in Longyan, where going abroad has also occupied most people's minds. Like Mo Fei, many villagers have imagined their futures through the accumulation of travel documents and blamed their dashed hopes on incomplete and aborted paper trails. They would also agree that it was a "difficult struggle" to obtain all the documents that allowed Mo Fei to legitimately leave the country, though the "one year and eleven months" that Mo Fei needed to acquire all his paperwork would surely qualify as speedy and lucky for a would-be migrant in Longyan. For unlike the fictional Mo Fei, a bona fide urban elite, almost no one in Longyan could imagine entering the United States as a prospective doctoral student. For state-classified peasants, the trajectory to becoming an "American guest" would usually be much more circuitous and convoluted than the fairly straightforward path of Shi's privileged urban protagonist.

To acquire *shenfen* (literally, "identity" or legal status) abroad was a widely acknowledged achievement among residents in Longyan. It distinguished the able and successful migrant from the average smuggled stowaway, who toiled away abroad without clear prospects of reuniting with his family. Yet for the most part, when one thinks of the current wave of Fuzhounese migration, it is of illicit smuggling ventures by sea and land—routes that bypass state-authorized points of entry and exit and circumvent the ritualized exchanges of paperwork and narrative with state gatekeepers so integral to the production of legality in travel. Illegal migrants, one assumes, are *undocumented* subjects—those that embark on paperless routes or, at the very least, lack legible and complete file selves that can be emplaced and traced within and across the territorial grid of nation-states.

Ethnographers working with undocumented U.S. migrants, particularly among Spanish-speaking populations from Mexico and Central America (see, for example, Chavez 1992; Coutin 2000; Mahler 1992), have described the move from state-authorized identity to illegal migrant subjectivity as a distinct rite of passage in which one is stripped bare of all identifying markers of personhood in the course of travel. The narratives of undocumented migrants often recount a litany of personal material dispossessions—money swindled, mementoes lost, food disappearing, even clothes and shoes stripped off, as well as (of course) passports, visas, and other identifying documents tossed, destroyed, or confiscated—in the process of one's emerging paperless, illicit, and often physically bare and vulnerable on the U.S. side of the border. As Coutin observes of this process of state dispossession, "As unauthorized immigrants are materially constituted as illicit, they simultaneously experience themselves as lacking a right to papers" (2000, 58). This equation of statelessness and paperlessness, I argue, also resonates strongly with popular understandings of the "illegal alien," a status that most Fuzhounese in the United States are assumed to occupy.

Fuzhounese narratives of journeys overseas do sometimes recall these accounts of Mexican and Central American migrants. But what struck me during my fieldwork among the Fuzhounese was the preponderance of paperwork—rather than a lack thereof—in people's strategies for charting routes overseas. While many who emigrated through the 1980s and early '90s left without papers through boat smuggling ventures, changes in immigration policies abroad—particularly the U.S. alien amnesty program in 1986 and new refugee and asylum priorities since the Tiananmen Square incident in 1989—opened new possibilities of legal status for those already overseas, as well as for new prospective migrants.[1] By the time I settled into Longyan, most people aspired to find paper trails out of China rather than resorting to long and cumbersome undocumented journeys (also see Chin 1999). After more than a decade and a half of mass emigration out of Longyan, most villagers had acquired enough knowledge and even personal experience of harrowing smuggling ventures to be fearful of undocumented routes out of China. To obtain legal status was widely acknowledged as the highest aspiration (and, more important, an increasingly *plausible* aspiration) by residents in Longyan. This did not mean that people just stopped traveling clandestinely via cargo ships across the South China Sea or on foot across the rugged mountain border between Yunnan and Vietnam. It did, however, mark those who still chose these more strenuous routes as both less able and less privileged than their documented counterparts. As I will show, the possible strategies for going abroad were not only diverse in Longyan but also served as key markers of social differentiation among villagers. Though being paperless certainly made aspiring migrants feel stateless, the variety of documents one could acquire also highlighted what a broad and relative range there was for feeling state-*ful* (cf. Painter 2006).

This section extends the themes of the last chapter concerning villagers' quests to rewrite their moral careers as state-classified peasants in China. While chapter 2 mainly concerned state subjectification and discourses of peasant and overseas Chinese morality, the two chapters in this part focus on the mundane and material practices for transforming state identification in villagers' attempts to chart trajectories abroad. Specifically, I consider how villagers' quests for emigration complicate some of the basic associations of state identification with ontology and particularly, in the case of immigration and travel documents, with the isomorphism of people, place, and culture.

In chapters 3–4, I offer a detailed examination of the interlocking relationship of paper and flesh, inscription and performance, in the constitution of state identification among Longyan villagers in search of transnational mobility. In delineating villagers' interests and strategies for achieving legal status abroad, I highlight what Bruno Latour has referred to as "the simple craftsmanship" of inscription—that is, the acts of writing and imaging deployed by both state agents and Longyan residents that enable these "groups of people [to] argue with one another using paper, signs, prints and diagrams" (1986, 3) over the facticity of identity and its relation to state inclusion and national belonging.[2] Such encounters over identification required not only the exchange of documents but also the enactment of narratives of emplacement—that is, the entitlement of particular persons to particular locations. Though it is important to acknowledge the structuring power of states to set the grounds for identification and mobility (particularly in terms of "the nation"), I focus here on the indeterminacies and disjunctures in the encounters between different state agents and would-be migrants over "proof" of identification and claims for legitimate movement. As I will show, these indeterminacies enabled villagers to revalue passports, visas, and other state documents as achievements of personal skill and social networks rather than as the natural entitlements of certain state subjects.

While research focusing on already "settled" immigrants rarely looks at border crossing as more than an abstract transition from "home" to "settlement," the following chapters will also show that there are qualitative differences in the ways exits and entrances are forged by would-be migrants aspiring for destinations and legal status overseas (cf. Cunningham and Heyman 2004; Cunningham 2004). In particular, I elaborate here on the materiality and pragmatics of transnational movement by distinguishing in my ethnographic account between the processes for making exits (chapter 3) and those for making entrances (chapter 4) across state boundaries. Not only are exits from nation-states generally easier to achieve than entrances into them, but as I will show, such border-crossing distinctions can also point to the incommensurability of state inclusion and national belonging, particularly when exits lead to such non-entrances as immigration detention centers, where one may be folded into a state's carceral grip while simultaneously being excluded from its national embrace. Ultimately, by focusing on the staging of exits and entrances, this section looks at how il/legality comes to be recognized as a legible marker of various mobile subjects—that is, as a qualisign for stratifying people along a hierarchy of travel.

Snakeheads and Paper Trails

The Making of Exits

Shortly after I became known on village streets as the *sinnang* (teacher) from America, Longyan residents started showing up at my doorstep with a dizzying array of official correspondence and bureaucratic forms from the U.S. Immigration and Naturalization Service (INS) and other comparable institutions in Canada and the United Kingdom. Mostly they wanted to know what the documents said. But sometimes they also asked for help in filling out the forms with passive appeals to my privileged capacities and positions. "Wow," someone would say with a smile, an approving nod, or a bouncing thumbs-up, "we hear your English is really super, *Sinnang*, that you're an authentic American. A *sidising* (U.S. citizen)."

This was always a fascinating but tricky territory for me to negotiate as an anthropologist. While for reciprocity's sake, I tried to offer some assistance, I always feared that people would ask me for legal advice or perhaps even proposition me for legal sponsorship abroad in exchange for money.[1] Over the course of fieldwork, I did have to refuse a handful of "fake-marriage" (*jia jiehun*) proposals, but thankfully no one ever thought I was qualified to give immigration advice. In fact, most people thought that they were more knowledgeable on migration strategies than I was (which was true) and often took much pride in dispensing this knowledge for my benefit. It turned out that for villagers, my privileges also implied a kind of naiveté and lack of strategic finesse for negotiating the various bureaucratic and informal hurdles necessary for travel and emigration from rural Fuzhou.

Indeed, the various bureaucratic instructions and long checklists that I sometimes translated for villagers seeking legal emigration seemed much more unfamiliar and daunting to me than to them. Almost everyone in Longyan could point to some relative or friend who had successfully maneuvered through various channels for emigration and who therefore could serve as coach and model for their own attempts for leaving China. Many people also had insights and experiences of their own from having failed in previous efforts. In fact, initial failures often pointed less to defeat than to incremental gains in the kinds of skills and knowledge necessary for future attempts at emigration. Too many failed attempts, however, could become an embarrassment and raise questions of the would-be migrant's competence and potential for success overseas.

This chapter explores the production and mobilization of village knowledge, skills, and other resources for making exits out of China. In particular, it examines how emigration as a project is translated and actualized as various strategies—both legal and illegal—for exit. As I will show, there were diverse options for would-be migrants. Most villagers, in fact, could tick off a long list of possibilities off the top of their heads and, moreover, rank these options in terms of cost and desirability. As I learned, an aspiring migrant's success was never just about one's capacity to leave China, but, more important, it was about the *kind* of route one was able to chart overseas.

The aims of this chapter are twofold. One aim is to track the various modes of calculation and expertise that shape village expectations and efforts for departing China. The other is to show how the very pragmatics and materialities of departure worked to qualify emigration as a differentially valued achievement and, by extension, to stratify villagers as differentially mobile subjects along a hierarchy of travel. Ultimately, I am interested here in the zone of indeterminacy between migrant aspirations and their actualization as different embodied experiences of mobility. In particular, I hope to highlight the ways villagers cope with the uncertainties of departure by honing skills for identifying, evaluating, and anticipating the risks of emigration while still "stuck" in Longyan. The risks I discuss here mainly concern what can be described as the hazards of translation, by which, by way of Keane (1997) and Latour (1999), I mean the chain of mediation through which different persons and things—from money-lenders, smugglers, and state bureaucrats to shipping containers, travel documents, and immigration checkpoints—come to exchange various properties and goals and together enable aspiring migrants to assemble a program of action. Specifically, my aim is to shed light on the necessary displacements and unexpected effects that occur when the semiotic and material properties of traveling cultures and traveling bodies collide and in the process consolidate mobility as a qualisign.[2]

Translating Transport

It is by mistake, or unfairness, that our headlines read "Man flies," "Woman goes into space." Flying is a property of the whole association of entities that includes airports and planes, launch pads and ticket counters. B-52s do not fly, the U.S. Air Force flies.

—Bruno Latour, *Pandora's Hope*

Hong Jianyi was one of the many Longyan residents who had already tried multiple times to leave for the United States. Although he could claim significant knowledge of migration strategies from two failed experiences, he was also beginning to lose credibility as a twenty-six-year-old unemployed husband and father still stuck in Longyan. This situation made him quite self-conscious and cautious about publicly discussing his current attempt to find a route abroad, particularly on village streets and in other impersonal social situations such as banquets and temple gatherings, where he often seemed reticent and aloof.[3] Everyone may have suspected that he was searching for another viable route overseas, but he knew that if he kept quiet, people would not dare ask about his current plans. In the intimate setting of his own home, though, Hong Jianyi spoke openly and confidently to me about migration strategies, including his own continual aspirations for leaving China. Beyond his own experiences, Hong Jianyi derived much of his knowledge and hope for emigration from the successes of two older sisters who were already residing in the United States with legal status, as well as a brother-in-law with U.S. citizenship who was currently processing an immigration application for his wife (Hong Jianyi's other sister) and infant child in Longyan.

In his two previous attempts, Hong Jianyi had tried to get smuggled out by boat and both times had been caught and sent back to Fuzhou before reaching his destination. Each time he and his family had suffered a significant financial setback from losing the down payment for the smuggling services (usually a nonrefundable fee of a few thousand dollars) and from the punitive fines for illegal migration and arrest by state authorities. Hong Jianyi also noted that until quite recently, boat smuggling had been the most viable option of emigration for Longyan residents like himself. Though there was a high risk of failure and much danger involved in these ventures, human smuggling had been widely accepted as part of the moral career of Longyan migrants. It had certainly not been anything to be ashamed about in the past.

Over the past decade, however, people had begun to imagine other possibilities as a growing number of overseas relatives established legal status abroad. In addition, increasingly sophisticated smugglers responded to heightened international policing of boat smuggling by diversifying their services to include counterfeit travel documents, fake-marriage arrangements, and other alternative paper routes out of China. By the time Hong Jianyi was considering his third attempt abroad, boat smuggling had lost its respectability and was considered a lowly last resort. Pragmatically, Hong Jianyi noted that boat smuggling was still appealing because it was significantly cheaper than other smuggling services—a difference of roughly $20,000, equal to a year of earnings overseas. The downside, he admitted, was the hardships and dangers of the journey itself, which he did not relish from his own past experiences and described matter-of-factly as "going gambling with your own life" (*na zijide shengming qu dubo*). Though Hong Jianyi did not rule out the possibility of future attempts via boat smuggling, for the time being he was placing his hopes on obtaining a travel visa for visiting one of his legalized relatives abroad.

As it turned out, the crucial factor for Hong Jianyi, as for other would-be migrants, concerned the embodied experience of travel itself. When considering their migration options, most people distinguished between paper and paperless routes by describing embodied differences in plane and boat transport respectively. These descriptions were less about issues of legality or financial costs per se than about people's sense of control over their experience of mobility. Such concerns nicely recall what Doreen Massey termed "differentiated mobility." As Massey noted, "The point concerns not merely the issue of who moves and who doesn't, although that is an important element of it; it is also about power in relation *to* flows and the movement. Different social groups have distinct relationships to this. . . . Some are more in charge of [mobility] than others; some indicate flows and movement, others don't; some are more on the receiving end of it than others; some are effectively imprisoned by it" (Massey 1993, 61).

The stories people shared about their own attempts to emigrate as well as other tales heard through gossip constituted a distinct body of knowledge in village life. Offered as preambles to declarations of plans in motion or as illustrations of lessons learned and expertise gained, these were narratives of valuation meant to calibrate migrant aspirations to the textures and rhythms of bodies in transit. Translating the goals for going overseas into various tales of junky freighters and shipping containers, airports and airplanes, long-distance trucks and back-road hikes, villagers pointed to the ways emigration could transform persons, for better and for worse, through the very routes they traveled and the conveyances they took.

For instance, one cannot easily forget the stifling darkness and pervasive disorientation of being crammed into the hull of a ship or into a steel shipping container for anywhere from fourteen to ninety days. Most people in Longyan who have been smuggled this way describe the experience of travel as a kind of entombment at sea where one is led under the deck or into a container and shut in a tight space with others with the barest of provisions. Like Hong Jianyi, Zhang Yin, the thirty-three-year-old wife of a villager overseas, recalled her one attempt to get smuggled by boat into the United States as a "very terrifying" (hen kongbu) experience akin to "gambling with your life." Over lunch with Chen Mingming, another villager with a husband overseas, Zhang Yin described her journey by fixating on the physicality of travel by sea. She recounted her sense of confinement and near suffocation from the density of people, the dank heat, and the foul smells trapped in the locked hull. She described experiences of hunger punctuated only by the periodic frenzy among stowaways when the door to the hull would suddenly swing open so that a few buckets of sustenance could be lowered down for the masses. Last but not least, there was the unremitting darkness and the general disorientation of space and time from being submerged at sea, of being nowhere and out of touch between China and a destination yet to be reached.

One of the most common complaints about boat smuggling ventures concerned the lack of control over one's embodied mobility, including the time frame for one's departure and arrival abroad. Snakeheads arranging boat smuggling routes often subjected their clients to long delays for departure while expecting them to pack up and leave at a day's notice. Moreover, once journeys began, there was no control over the duration, route, or forms of transport. All these aspects could vary depending on the smuggler's transnational connections and the unpredictability of obstacles such as police raids or travel accidents encountered along the way. A smuggling venture via a single ship could easily expand into unanticipated and complicated transport by truck or train and even by foot. Villagers who were promised smooth journeys lasting a couple of weeks often found themselves on long circuitous routes with multiple stopovers in other countries like Thailand, Russia, and Guatemala that could last more than a year. In addition, they were subjected to the unpredictable whims of snakeheads who often demanded more money for complications in travel arrangements and who were capable of using violence and abandoning clients in the midst of journeys. Most residents had enough accumulated knowledge and experience of such complications to understand that once someone embarked on a boat smuggling venture, there was no telling when or if they would arrive at their desired destination. These were excruciating experiences of limbo not only for the smuggled passengers but also for relatives left behind, who often lost complete contact with their loved ones during the journeys and could only pray (often at temples) for their safe emergence at their destination in the indefinite future.

Chen Mingming, who had been listening to Zhang Yin's account of her smuggling venture with a knowing smile and occasional nod of commiseration, explained that this was why she herself had been trying for the past five years to secure travel documents through a snakehead so that she could leave China by air instead of by sea. It may cost more to get smuggled via a convoluted itinerary of connecting flights and fake documents through several international airports around the world. But as far as Chen Mingming was concerned, it was well worth avoiding the kind of abject experience her husband had suffered in transit when he was adrift at sea with a boatload of stowaways for three whole months before finally reaching the United States. It was so dehumanizing, she said. The snakeheads, so cunning and unreliable, always offered comforting words and promising scenarios to hook their clients for these boat smuggling ventures. Yet, as Chen Mingming and Zhang Yin agreed, they rarely ever cared about the people they transported as much as they did about the money to be made off them. A case in point, Chen Mingming noted, was that snakeheads always prepared just enough food for the minimum number of days of expected travel; if and when they had to extend the journey, people were just expected to starve the rest of the way, as her husband did during the final stretch of his smuggling venture. It did not matter to the smugglers that her husband went hungry and had to struggle to survive. It only mattered that in the end he made it through the journey, if barely, so that they could claim their fees.

Traveling under such conditions made one feel "not like a human being" (*buxiangren*), Chen Mingming noted. Instead, one became merely human cargo, a thing to be delivered intact overseas, not catered to while in transit, as more privileged international travelers would be. To further illustrate the dangers and depravities of boat smuggling, Chen Mingming pointed to the soap opera *Broken Dream, Heavenly Country* (*Meng duan tian guo*), which had just concluded its run on television at the time. A melodrama about Chinese migrants in Seattle who were entangled in a human smuggling ring, this serial featured lurid scenes of suffering, violence, and death among stowaways crammed into shipping containers. Though not very popular in Longyan because of its grim depictions of illicit migration, the show had captured Chen Mingming's imagination because of her husband's experience at sea and the lessons she said she had learned from his struggles, as well as from others who had traveled through these channels. In fact, Chen Mingming said that the soap opera resonated so much with her own accumulated knowledge of boat smuggling that she made her two daughters watch it with her as a reality check on their migrant aspirations. By exposing them to the horrors of smuggling as depicted on TV, Chen Mingming hoped that her daughters would learn, as she had, to avoid such ventures in the future.

As villagers like Chen Mingming came to appreciate through a combination of embodied experience, others' personal stories, and public culture, one needed a certain kind of constitution to endure the physical and psychic hardships associated with this kind of travel. In fact, because of such hardships boat smuggling was largely seen as a particularly masculine form of transit, an option more suited to the gendered capacities of aspiring male migrants than to those of women like Chen Mingming and her daughters.[4] Though in reality many female villagers, including Zhang Yin, had tried to leave China through these channels, it was working-age men who were assumed to be the ideal candidates and who made up the majority of the passengers for these smuggling ventures over the years.[5] In the mid-1980s and early '90s, when boat smuggling was virtually the only viable option for those with overseas ambitions, most women like Chen Mingming simply learned to bide their time at home, sending their husbands and brothers ahead of them while searching for alternative paper trails and air routes for themselves. Even women like Zhang Yin, who had dared to venture abroad by sea, agreed that boat smuggling was more appropriate for men while air travel was better for women.[6]

Local valuations of emigration strategies not only gendered traveling bodies and their modes of transport but at the same time imparted certain class distinctions. It was, after all, not only women who preferred to leave China with travel documents and plane tickets in tow. These days, Chen Mingming noted, all who had the means were arranging papers for *tanqin* (travel visas to visit overseas relatives) or fake marriage to a U.S. citizen so that they could leave China by air. Only the lowly and the desperate who could not muster the skills and resources for other options still resorted to boat smuggling. While everyone agreed that plane travel was superior to undocumented travel by sea, villagers also made fine distinctions among the kinds of paper routes people established to depart through airports. In fact, most people could list an astonishing array of strategies for establishing paper routes abroad. The range of possibilities included counterfeit documents (that is, passports, visas); official but temporary visas (for example, for travel or business, work authorizations, and visas for fiancé[e]s); and processes for permanent immigration (that is, legal sponsorship by a foreign citizen, permanent resident, or political refugee).

In the hierarchy of travel options, obtaining false travel documents through a snakehead ranked only slightly above paperless routes. Often villagers referred to this kind of paper arrangement, along with boat smuggling, as a strategy of human smuggling—not only because of the centrality of snakeheads in making such arrangements but also because of the perceived illegitimacy and unreliability of counterfeit papers. While the possibility of plane transport made traveling with false documents more appealing than undocumented boat ventures, people complained about the unpredictable complications and high risks of failure in trying to pass through airports with false documents. In fact, people who relied on smugglers for counterfeit documents typically had just as little control over their itineraries as those who traveled by boat. In order to avoid suspicion at the airport of destination, smugglers often arranged convoluted flights for their clients through secondary and tertiary foreign countries, where they would use and then discard different sets of false papers. Like boat smuggling ventures, these roundabout travel arrangements were subject to complications that could prolong the journey, force changes in itinerary or transportation along the way, leave the traveler stranded in some intermediate foreign site or, worst of all, abruptly end in arrest and deportation. Ultimately, the term *toudu* (human smuggling) best described not a particular form of transport or access to certain travel papers but a circuitous and messy route some travelers were forced to take without official state approval. In contrast, obtaining proper legal papers for travel meant that one could exit airports with greater ease and most likely succeed in getting on a direct flight to one's chosen destination.

Villagers assessing travel options often described how the qualities of passengers and their mode of transport became intimately entangled through the very practice of traveling. Air transport elevated passengers literally and figuratively, distinguishing a privileged class of mobile subjects from that of smuggled passengers, whose lesser capacities and lowly status were indexed by the very inefficiencies and abject conditions of their journeys through smuggling channels. At the phenomenological level, perhaps nothing captured the differences between air and sea transport better than the problem of waste management in transit. Those who had experienced smuggling often noted how difficult it could be to simply breathe amid the stale air and olfactory oppressiveness of bodies crammed together. Boat smuggling, especially via shipping containers, was notorious for trapping its passengers with the collective odors, trash, and human waste they generated over the days and weeks of their journey. While people in planes could count on an infrastructure of regulated air circulation, private restrooms, and flight attendants to alleviate some of the physical burdens and polluting effects of long-distance travel in tight quarters, smuggled passengers could rarely escape the taint of garbage and human waste, which at best could be relegated only to a discrete corner of the space people inhabited for the duration of their trip.

This kind of contamination was not only experienced by those being smuggled but also materially and discursively reinforced by border police and customs officials, who routinely relied on techniques and technologies for detecting the olfactory and visual signs of human waste as a means of identifying stowaways in and around ports of entry. "Stowaway detectors," including carbon dioxide monitors, looked for traces of human waste as part of the distinctive chemical profile and olfactory signature of migrants smuggled through shipping containers. An article reviewing a new profiling technology, "the zNose 4200," noted the following:

In recent years, smugglers have put humans inside cargo containers to slip them into the country. The presence of human cargo might be signaled by the odor of human waste, which contains a high percentage of E. coli bacteria. E. coli produce a very recognizable olfactory image, which is dominated by the chemical indole. The presence of molds and fungus in cargo containers can contaminate and even damage sensitive cargo. These life-forms produce distinctive olfactory images and unique, detectable chemicals called microbial volatile organic compounds (Staples 2004, 25–26).

Images of garbage-strewn shipping containers and descriptions of reeking waste also commonly appeared in stories about Chinese human smuggling circulated by the U.S. Immigration and Customs Enforcement (ICE), as well as by the U.S. news media.[7] For instance, in a report about the discovery of twenty-nine Chinese migrants at the Port of Los Angeles in April 2006, ICE officials noted, "The circumstances of this latest incident are similar to those of past human smuggling scenarios. Officers at the scene say the stench coming from the containers was overwhelming. Inside, agents found piles of discarded food packages, blankets, and containers overflowing with human waste" ("ICE Fighting Chinese Human Smugglers" 2005). Such stench and garbage became so indexical of the Chinese stowaway in border enforcement that one reporter concluded, "even if they make it here alive, they are easy to spot . . . because of the smell of waste they create" (cited in Grossberg 2006).[8]

What both aspiring migrants and state authorities recognized were the reciprocal effects that occurred when bodies and transport came together in the act of traveling. Mode of transport was more than a simple instrument or prosthesis of the traveling person. Rather, something like a shipping container actively shaped the traveler both materially and symbolically, just as passengers gathered in the container transformed its various properties from its air quality and chemical composition to its uses and meanings. The merger of container with human passengers even produced new life-forms, like the E. coli in human waste, and new technologies, like stowaway detectors, that together could then act as new mediators of il/legality in global shipping and border control. While flying— with its own chain of mediators from air circulation and in-flight services to plane tickets and passports—endowed traveling bodies with superior directionality, speed, and comfort, smuggling by sea stripped passengers down to their corporeal burdens and "bare life" (Agamben 1998) as human cargo struggling to survive the mutual production and dehumanizing taint of waste and illegality in their travels.

Enframing Lawfulness

Plane passengers were certainly not immune from suspicions of illicit travel. Yet what villagers appreciated was how differently mobility could be embodied because of the mediating effects of transportation, paperwork, snakeheads, and state authorities, which together helped constitute the pragmatics of international travel. Though villagers used the term *toudu* to encompass unauthorized journeys by both air and sea, they also recognized how differently illegality (as well as lawfulness) could be experienced by travelers moving through airports and planes versus those being smuggled in a cargo ship. For one thing, it was only in boat smuggling that something like the waste generated in transit could become such an indexical sign of illegality among Chinese migrants. In contrast, air transport heightened villagers' attention to the various effects that travel documents could have as mediators of legal status.

It is interesting that in distinguishing between smuggling and legitimate travel by plane, most villagers cared little about how a passport and visas were attained, whether with the help of smugglers or with less than accurate claims for travel. Fake-marriage arrangements, for instance, were rarely described as "smuggling" because the travel documents one acquired through this strategy were considered "real" (*zhende*). As many people saw it, fake marriage was perfectly "legal" (*hefa*) because what mattered most was not the truth value of one's claims but the authenticity of one's travel documents as direct products of state institutions. In this sense, what determined the lawfulness of paper routes was the degree of engagement with state agencies in the making of exits. Aside from traveling with only counterfeit documents, all paper trails abroad required travelers to pass through some state institutions—both domestic and foreign—in order to secure official clearance for leaving China. At the very least, one needed to be physically present for an interview at a foreign consulate in order to obtain final authorization for a visa, whether for temporary travel or for permanent immigration overseas.

Aspiring migrants hoping to become lawful in transit commonly described this process as a rite of passage through a series of state checkpoints; to succeed, one had to master the art of "going through formalities" (*ban shouxu*). Particularly for those trying to leave China legally, no reason for failure seemed more embarrassing and demoralizing than the notion of "incomplete formalities" (*shouxu buwanzheng*), a shorthand for one's inability to both assemble all the proper papers and convince state agents of one's entitlement to travel. Bungling formalities always exposed the procedural hurdles involved in the production of lawfulness in travel. It highlighted how various technicalities could get one in trouble, from missed appointments and incomplete forms to nervous twitches and inconsistent responses in exit interviews with airport security.[9] In turn, these formalities pointed to certain disciplinary hoops and competencies necessary for making oneself legible to state gatekeepers as a subject deserving legal exit and entry across national borders.

In fact, legality itself can be seen as an artifact produced through the orchestration of formalities, something made intelligible among traveling bodies only through the everyday practices and relations sustained by such state procedures and rituals.[10] Specifically, here I want to draw on Timothy Mitchell's (1991) notion of enframing, which he described as the techniques of coordination and arrangement that create the appearance of an ontological divide between an outside and inside, material form and meaning, physical reality and its representations. In immigration and travel procedures, such enframing practices can be seen through the staging of inside and outside, inspector and inspected, through the various bureaucratic hoops and checkpoints set up for those seeking legal passage. As Veena Das and Deborah Poole observed, "Inherent in this imagination of the figure of the law was the creation of boundaries between those practices and spaces that were seen to form part of the state and those that were excluded from it. Legitimacy, in turn, emerged as a function of this boundary-making effect of state practices" (2004, 7). It was not just the would-be migrant but also various state agents—from health examiners to consulate officers to airport security personnel—who were enlisted through the immigration process to routinely enact the "reality effect" of lawfulness in travel.

In their quest for legal status, would-be migrants had to establish what Benedict Anderson described as "traffic habits"—a pattern of flows through a mesh of state institutions that ultimately gave form and "real social life to earlier state fantasies" of the "nation" (Anderson 1991, 169). While for most people, such "traffic habits" were gradual experiences dispersed throughout a lifetime, they became a much more explicit and intensified part of everyday life for those seeking to cross national borders legally and, in the process, transform state identifications. Consider, for instance, the following list, required for obtaining a U.S. visa like the K-1, issued for the foreign fiancé(e) of an American citizen. By the time applicants arrived at the U.S. consulate to interview for this visa—a process that took a minimum of ten months (and could last indefinitely)—they were expected to have all the following original documents in their hands:

Chinese passport

Application forms from the appointment packet completed in English

Application fee receipt from making a payment of 830 RMB (about $100) at an approved bank

Four visa photos attached to application form

Notarized birth certificate

Notarized marital status certificate, including divorce certificates for each previous marriage

Notarized police certificates issued by local municipal notary offices for each place in which the applicant had resided for at least six months since the age of sixteen

Medical report, including medical history and physical exam worksheet, vaccination documentation, chest X-ray, and classification worksheet completed by the staff of a hospital approved by the U.S. consulate

Affidavit of support and copy of the most recent tax returns from the U.S. sponsor of the applicant

Documentary evidence of the relationship between the foreign fiancé(e) and U.S. sponsor, such as mail and telephone correspondence and photographs of the applicant and sponsor together

Translations of police certificates from other countries not in English or in the official language of the country. These translations must be certified by a competent translator and sworn to before a notary public.[11]

This intimidating list does not even take into account the additional resources needed for travel and lodging in Guangzhou, where the U.S. consulate is located, not to mention the interpersonal skills necessary for securing and coordinating with a U.S. sponsor in the first place or winning the final approval from a consulate official during the face-to-face interview for the visa.

By moving through various state institutions to obtain and complete paperwork, would-be migrants were demonstrating more than their skills at mobilizing various resources and allies. They were also mapping out the entire network of relationships in which they could be located—literally and figuratively—as the particular subjects of a nation-state. To accumulate all the required documents on the K-1 visa checklist was to gather all the instances of one's engagements with various state agencies, to sum up one's proper emplacement within the national order of things. Specifically, it is important to note here that the immigration process compelled people to do the work of coordination among scattered state institutions. The very demands of paperwork required the visa applicant to bring together what would otherwise be dispersed and uncoordinated experiences of "the nation-state" into "an optically consistent space" (Latour 1986, 29). As Latour notes, it is only through the "power of paper shuffling" that "domains which are far apart become literally inches apart; domains which are convoluted and hidden, become flat; thousands of occurrences can be looked at synoptically" (28). In turn, by gathering up the dispersed traces of their institutional appearances through paperwork, applicants not only solidified their "file selves" before the U.S. consulate but also consolidated the very idea of the nation-state as a centralized, coordinated, and bounded "imagined community" (Anderson 1991). While Benedict Anderson most famously highlighted the importance of print capitalism, particularly the spread of newspapers, in enabling these national imaginings of difference, one could argue that identification and travel documents, as a kind of print media, also contributed significantly to the forging of such "imagined communities."[12] In fact, even more than newspapers, identification papers highlight how the national "style of imagining" could operate not only in ideational terms but also in deeply material and embodied ones.

Despite the multiplicity and divergence of particular claims to legal travel and immigration, one cannot help but note the astonishing uniformity of passport and visa applications among contemporary nation-states.[13] The standardized demands for certain kinds of paperwork—birth certificates, photographs, health records, and so forth—specifically recall what Anderson has described as the "grammar" of nation-states:

> The "warp" of this thinking was a totalizing classificatory grid, which could be applied with endless flexibility to anything under the state's real or contemplated control: peoples, regions, religions, languages, products, monuments, and so forth. The effect of the grid was always to be able to say of anything that it was this, not that; it belonged here, not there. It

was bounded, determinate, and therefore—in principle—countable. . . . The "weft" was what one could call serialization: the assumption that the world was made up of replicable plurals. The particular always stood as a provisional representative of a series, and was to be handled in this light (1991, 184).

Like pieces on a checkerboard, aspiring migrants needed to first affirm their place within the "classificatory grid" of nation-states, to show that they "belonged here, not there," before they could legitimize their move into another country.

Distinguishing "here" from "there" was not simply a matter of crossing "the border" at an immigration checkpoint. Rather, as the K-1 visa checklist makes clear, one first needed state clearance through several other institutional checkpoints, like the state hospital for a health exam, the public security bureau for the passport, and the U.S. consulate for the visa. In this sense, there was an extended zone of crossings, a procedural trajectory of hurdles through which one could gain passage and in turn achieve legality only by engaging in a series of ritualized exchanges of paperwork and narratives with various state bureaucrats and inspectors.[14] "Going through formalities" enlisted aspiring migrants in what James Scott (1998) has described as the state project of legibility (cf. Das and Poole 2004; Gordillo 2006; Kim n.d.; Trouillot 2001). To become lawful, one had to be legible to state agents in the form of paperwork and embodied passage through designated checkpoints.

Yet as Das and Poole have argued, the checkpoint is also "a tension-filled space" where "assumptions about the security of identities and rights can become suddenly and sometimes violently unsettled" and where ultimately "the state is continually both experienced and undone through the *illegibility* of its own practices, documents and words" (2004, 10; emphasis in original). Villagers hoping to refashion themselves as legal travelers both took advantage of and contributed to such illegibilities in state practice and law. For instance, even as they sought legibility as lawful subjects, most villagers also tried to find shortcuts through the formal bureaucratic process for departure by capitalizing on personal connections with state agents, a strategy commonly referred to as "walking in through the back door" (*zou houmen*). Those who could bypass bureaucratic hoops through "back doors" were often admired for their interpersonal skills and superior network of social connections (*guanxi*). The most successful smugglers, for instance, were seen as masters at "walking in through the back door," with deep and expansive ties to officials and other agents of migration across several countries. In fact, migration via boat smuggling or fake documents relied solely on smugglers' command of "back doors." But it was not just smuggling that produced illegibilities. "Front door" strategies like fake-marriage arrangements also pointed to the ways legal inscriptions and effects could depend on the obfuscation and bracketing of certain crucial practices, including the employment of smugglers, personal favors from officials, and commodified relations with legal sponsors like foreign spouses. In particular, the fact that aspiring migrants often paid smugglers and other middlemen to secure passages they considered "legal" indicates the extent to which illegibilities could be imbricated in the very production of legible and lawful travel.

Money and Creditability

Ideally one would already have the appropriate overseas connections and bureaucratic know-how for successfully accumulating all the required travel papers on one's own for departing through airports. Many Longyan residents, however, still needed to hire smugglers and other middlemen to help them find viable legal sponsors abroad and navigate the circuit of state agencies necessary for obtaining travel permits. Even though most people had relatives and friends overseas, they often did not know anyone with legal status who was in a position to sponsor them and was, moreover, *willing* to do so with or without some kind of payment.[15] In lieu of adequate personal connections and bureaucratic knowledge, one needed first and foremost to amass the requisite funds for eliciting the services of mediators. The large sums of money needed to underwrite most village efforts for legal status stood in sharp contrast with the small administrative fees made legible as part of the application process. Like snakeheads, personal connections, and "back doors," such funds could be seen as part of the necessary illegibilities produced alongside the legibilities of legal travel.

For most villagers, it was already a monumental feat to summon the funds required for the cheapest undocumented smuggling venture, let alone for gathering up the papers and state allies necessary for legalized travel. Contrary to popular assumptions, most would-be migrants did not finance their travels as indentured servants under human smugglers.

Rather, they were typically expected to deposit an initial down payment in China (usually $2,000–3,000) and then pay the balance upon completion of their journeys. Such a financial arrangement required travelers to have ready access to a large sum of cash—anywhere between $35,000 and $100,000. To obtain such funds, most villagers needed to borrow from many friends and relatives, mainly from those already abroad and earning dollars. The higher the costs of travel, the more one's reputation and personal connections mattered in securing a patchwork of loans. In turn, those who could finance paper routes out of China were assumed to have superior creditability (*xinyong*) among a broader, wealthier network of supporters than those opting for cheaper smuggling ventures.

When it came to mobilizing financial resources, "the most crucial thing," Lin Mengya told me, "was that you as a person have creditability." Lin Mengya, who had defied the one-child policy (as discussed in chapter 2), was the wife of an overseas villager; she had just cleared off her husband's smuggling debt when I first met her in the winter of 2001. While she was happy to finally be debt-free after nine years of frugal living and lonely separation from her husband, who had left in 1992, she seemed to be most proud of the maintenance and expansion of her reputation as a trustworthy person capable of assuming and paying off debt. Over the course of my fieldwork I learned that Lin Mengya indeed had an impeccable reputation among village residents as an honest, responsible, and generally moral person—in other words, someone of creditability. This reputation preceded her husband's attempts in the late 1980s and early '90s to go abroad and came in handy when she needed to inspire possible creditors to lend her money for his travels. When Lin Mengya's husband left in 1992, it was such a peak period of mass emigration in Longyan that she often had to compete with other villagers to secure loans from a small and overlapping pool of relatives and friends. Many of the same people already working abroad and amassing some savings in U.S. dollars were being besieged by multiple requests for loans from Longyan. In such a competitive environment, one's reputation often became the key for mobilizing funds. Lin Mengya viewed it as an honor for others to lend her money, even those outside of her close network, who charged her sky-high interest on loans.[16]

To be able to mobilize funds, whether from a close relative or a stranger, was a hard-earned achievement and a social confirmation of one's trustworthiness. In fact, smugglers themselves were reluctant to accept clients who did not have good creditability and often demanded evidence of ready cash from those whom they did not trust. Still one's reputation, however honorable, was usually not enough to sway upwards of thirty people to each loan anywhere from a few hundred to several thousand dollars. When Lin Mengya had exhausted her circle of relatives and friends, like other villagers, she expanded her network by "borrowing other people's face" (*jie bierende mianzi*)—that is, getting others to vouch for her creditability among more distant and unknown lenders. Lin Mengya had such good relations with some distant relatives living near Fuzhou City that when she ran out of options, they gladly took her to see their own circle of friends and staked their own reputations, or "faces," on her ability to pay back her lenders. This was an even more impressive feat of mobilization because it demonstrated her ability to inspire not only financial creditors but also other equally important and necessary allies.

Villagers discussing smuggling debts often pointed to the sociality of lending as an important sign of a person's creditability. It mattered to them how smuggling ventures were financed, not only how much money they cost. This emphasis on the social pragmatics of credit is embedded in the term *xinyong*, which literally means the use or applicability (*yong*) of trustworthiness (*xin*). Though securing loans was the most obvious application of one's claim to social trust, Lin Mengya's story of creditability was less about the specific economics of debt than how one can move others to act on one's behalf, both financially and otherwise, through the cultivation of a good reputation and personal ties.

Personal ties were typically evoked by villagers through the notion of *guanxi*, which has been translated alternately as relationship, as informal personal ties, and as the social web or network of such ties. Besides improving one's capacity to borrow money, superior *guanxi* was highly valued because it enabled people to better navigate through the various bureaucratic channels necessary for obtaining travel documents. As mentioned above, having the right social connections could enable one to "walk in through the back door" and bypass hurdles in the application process for passports and visas. This was particularly true for encounters with local Chinese officials and other bureaucrats in the Fuzhou area where the possibilities for asserting personal connections, even those of kinship, were greater and often critical in economizing the energy and time spent on paperwork. For instance, having a brother-in-law in a provincial-level government office enabled Yang Xiumei (the adult daughter of the cadre members with whom I lived) to secure health clearance for the sponsor of her "fake marriage" arrangement, despite the fact that this sponsor was in questionable health and had twice failed his medical exam.

Though few villagers outside of cadre members like Yang Xiumei or powerful snakeheads had the kind of clout to easily open "back doors," even a distant connection or casual acquaintance could sometimes help speed up the bureaucratic process for achieving travel authorization. Most people believed that their ability to control the tempo of state encounters had everything to do with their relative social distance from key state agents. For example, when I described my own frustrating attempts to secure my temporary residence card in Fuzhou, people were not surprised that as a foreigner with no connections, I needed to make repeated trips to the same office in search of a perpetually absent stamp holder. Some thought it was common for state agents to deliberately not see someone on a first, second, or even third visit, just to point to that person's social distance and status as a stranger. As one friend eloquently put it, without adequate *guanxi* in state encounters, "it's not like what you say in English—'a straight line from A to B'—but more like making a 'W.'" Knowing someone behind the counter at the passport agency or at the Fujian provincial hospital could minimize delays and avoid the futility of making repeated, fruitless visits. With the right connections one could assert more control over one's movements through state encounters, rather than being controlled by a frustrating and unpredictable bureaucracy.

While *guanxi* relations were clearly used instrumentally, most people stressed the importance of sentiment and trust in cementing personal ties and mobilizing supporters.[17] For instance, villagers often complained about fake marriages with total strangers by pointing to the strictly material and amoral foundations of such arrangements. Although forging an instrumental relationship was better than having no connections at all, people often doubted the "quality" and creditability of strangers willing to help them solely out of material interests. Moreover, the indifference of these kinds of allies did not reflect well on the reputation of villagers and their ability to inspire respect and loyalty from others.

Creditability, in its fullest sense, was about cultivating one's standing in personal relationships of owing and being owed rather than just connecting the means and ends of debt. Though money and creditability were certainly related, the latter was considered a more crucial resource and better measure of village achievements in emigration. In fact, creditability could be said to encompass money. As Lin Mengya's success suggested, superior creditability highlighted not only one's skills for mobilizing economic resources, but more importantly, one's morality as a trustworthy person. Even without adequate money to finance plane travel, having better creditability could still lead to qualitative differences in the experience of mobility and travel among the lowliest stowaways. Lin Mengya told me that because the snakehead's nephew had vouched for her husband's good character, he was treated with more decency and respect than other clients over the course of his smuggling venture. Once he arrived in the United States, good creditability enabled her husband to preserve some dignity and avoid the threats of daily beatings that less trustworthy, and less connected, clients faced when they were all confined to a safe house while the smuggler awaited full payment for his services.

The "Work" in Paperwork

Although villagers could sometimes take advantage of their local connections or reputations in interactions with smugglers and Chinese bureaucrats, they usually had to resort to other strategies for garnering the support of foreign agents at the INS, the U.S. consulate, and other immigration agencies for countries such as Canada and the United Kingdom.[18] It is in encounters with foreign state institutions that the "work" in paperwork comes into the sharpest focus. Unlike encounters with the Chinese bureaucracy, where people often looked for personal ties and other informal means of persuasion, dealing with foreign agencies foregrounded the necessity of documents themselves in mediating relations.

In a typical INS application, for example, aspiring migrants had two kinds of interaction with U.S. officials before their actual departure from China. The first and more frequent involved long-distance correspondence, through which they received and responded to various official documents—notices of case status, instructions for completing applications, standardized forms to be filled out and returned by mail. This paper correspondence spanned the entire period of the application process and, if successfully negotiated, usually culminated in the applicant's second kind of interaction: a discreet face-to-face interview at the U.S. consulate in Guangzhou City, some five hundred miles away in neighboring Guangdong Province. In this final hoop, applicants needed to not only present their embodied selves before a foreign state agent but also, and more important, hand over the accumulated evidence of their "file selves" in the form of completed application materials. The exchange of paperwork was just as critical to an applicant's consulate interview as the long-distance correspondence had been.

For aspiring migrants, one of the most unfamiliar and challenging aspects of establishing a paper route was the material practice of inscription itself—specifically, the filling out of complicated English forms and the coordination of on-the-record narratives (usually in paper form) between applicant and sponsor. For starters, almost everyone lacked the most basic and essential skill for initiating and maintaining contact with a foreign immigration agency—namely, the capacity to community in the agency's national language. Aside from some documents from the U.S. consulate in Guangzhou that included Chinese translations, almost all paper correspondence with the INS required the applicant to read and respond through written English. On their own, most people were in the dark about the content of INS documents that arrived in the mail and paralyzed about what to do with them without outside assistance. Though I never felt that I did very much, I was always surprised at how much gratitude and relief people expressed when I could tell them that an INS letter simply stated that their application had been received and their case was pending or if I could print their names, birth dates, and other basic information in English on the simplest bureaucratic forms. I was even more stunned to find out that these simple practices of inscription and translation were, in fact, saving people serious money and time (not to mention, anxiety), including long trips to Fuzhou City, where they could elicit services from English scribes at travel service agencies. As it turned out, these were such valuable and needed services that a whole industry of translators and scribes had emerged in Fuzhou over the past decade and was charging a few hundred RMB for each discrete service of reading and writing. While aspiring migrants who were eliciting the services of snakeheads could sometimes rely on their smugglers to take care of all the paperwork, more often than not, applicants were left to their own devices when it came to deciphering and responding to documents from foreign immigration agencies. While most people made the trip to travel service agencies to pay for the translation and filling out of forms, those who had adequate connections preferred to send their forms abroad and elicit favors from someone trustworthy and competent in English or, in very rare cases, appeal to someone at home with superior English skills (like me). Although taking a day trip to Fuzhou City was probably more efficient than sending forms abroad to be completed, people did not always have as much confidence in paid services as in assistance based on personal ties. This became evident to me when those who had already paid for English services sought me out to translate and double-check the data filled in by these agencies.

To be described as someone whose "English is really super" (*yingyu hen bang*) was more than a compliment about language competence. I often heard villagers boast about someone's overseas success by referring specifically to superb English ability. Though language competence was certainly not equivalent to bureaucratic savvy or legal knowledge, English proficiency was in many ways a marker of one's vernacular expertise on migration matters, a sign of one's worldly command over transnational flows and relations, particularly one's facility of movement through foreign checkpoints and bureaucracies. At the most immediate level, having English ability meant that an aspiring migrant could seize direct and immediate control over the practices of inscription in correspondence and not be subjected to the long delays and risky inaccuracies involved in exchanging information through paid translators or overseas relatives.

Of all the practices in English—reading, writing, and correspondence—the one thing no mediator could do for an applicant was to achieve mastery over a distinct and replicable signature on bureaucratic forms. I realized what a confusing challenge this small task of inscription could be when I watched people hesitate and agonize over the one blank space on forms that they needed to fill in for themselves. For starters, Chinese bureaucracy has been predominantly a stamp culture, which privileged the inked marks of individual seals and fingerprints as signs of identification and official authorization over handwritten names. To encounter the need for producing a signature was simply not the kind of rote experience for Longyan villagers as it was for Americans. People were not always certain whether they needed to sign for themselves or could elicit the help of some relative with better penmanship. Moreover, they were often confused about whether their signature needed to be in English or whether it could be written in Chinese. This was an especially important concern for older applicants, who were often barely literate in Chinese, let alone familiar with the English letters for romanizing Mandarin under the pinyin system. The most poignant and frustrating case over a signature I encountered concerned a frail, elderly applicant in her eighties who could neither see nor write well enough to sign a name on an INS form for her green card application. When I pointed out the blank line for signature on the form her family asked me to help read and fill in, the old woman and her two adult daughters collectively panicked over the necessity for her to reproduce a signature. "I can't sign for her?" one daughter asked me almost pleadingly. "Can't she write it in Chinese?" the other daughter piped in. Having failed to provide answers and help them sort out the issue of the signature, I left them with the one blank space on the form still looming before them like an insurmountable hurdle. Later, when I ran into one of the daughters, she informed me that in the end, over a course of three weeks her sister had helped her mother practice writing her name over and over again until there was some consistency to the old woman's control over pen and paper.

Examples such as the one above illustrated that the signature, like learning to write between margins or check off boxes on a form, was a distinct disciplinary practice that required inculcation and training on the part of the would-be migrant. It was part of the *habitus*, so to speak, of state identification and legibility. In particular, beyond English competence itself, the demand for a signature nicely captured the performative aspect of inscription in the production and exchange of immigration papers. Filling out bureaucratic forms required not only English ability but also the capacity to put the kind of coherent and convincing narrative of oneself on paper that could be repeatedly performed in other state encounters, whether in person or through further paper correspondence. The signature as a reiterative and self-authorizing act of identification was only the most blatant and clear-cut example of this inextricable link between inscription and performance in immigration procedures. In fact, most people in Longyan were quite self-conscious about all the personal information they recorded on standardized forms in general and particularly the necessity for all these inscriptions to add up to a consistent and replicable narrative of one's legitimate claim to mobility.

Most INS forms demanded more than a disclosure of verifiable personal information; they also required the demonstration of transnational connection and coordination between aspiring migrants and their legal sponsors abroad. Typically, applicants needed to repeatedly gather both their own personal data and those of their sponsors into the same standardized forms (for example, see figure 8). This meant that forms often

B. Information about you. | **C. Information about your relative.**

B. Information about you.	C. Information about your relative.
1. Name (Family name in CAPS) (First) (Middle)	1. Name (Family name in CAPS) (First) (Middle)
2. Address (Number and Street) (Apt.No.)	2. Address (Number and Street) (Apt. No.)
(Town or City) (State/Country) (Zip/Postal Code)	(Town or City) (State/Country) (Zip/Postal Code)
3. Place of Birth (Town or City) (State/Country)	3. Place of Birth (Town or City) (State/Country)
4. Date of Birth (mm/dd/yyyy) 5. Gender ☐ Male ☐ Female 6. Marital Status ☐ Married ☐ Single ☐ Widowed ☐ Divorced	4. Date of Birth (mm/dd/yyyy) 5. Gender ☐ Male ☐ Female 6. Marital Status ☐ Married ☐ Single ☐ Widowed ☐ Divorced
7. Other Names Used (including maiden name)	7. Other Names Used (including maiden name)
8. Date and Place of Present Marriage (if married)	8. Date and Place of Present Marriage (if married)
9. U.S. Social Security Number (if any) 10. Alien Registration Number	9. U. S. Social Security Number (if any) 10. Alien Registration Number
11. Name(s) of Prior Husband(s)/Wive(s) 12. Date(s) Marriage(s) Ended	11. Name(s) of Prior Husband(s)/Wive(s) 12. Date(s) Marriage(s) Ended

FIGURE 8 Form I-130, Petition for Alien Relative, to be submitted by the sponsor of a migrant's green card.

could not be completed without the continual cooperation and relay of information from the sponsor abroad, usually through long-distance phone calls or international mail. In this sense, the practice of filling out forms itself tested the applicant's claim to a transnational relationship of trust and support with someone overseas. Moreover, beyond the sponsor's name, birth date, and social security number, applicants commonly needed to obtain many other personal documents from the sponsor, such as the sponsor's most recent income tax returns, an affidavit of support with the sponsor's signature, a copy of his or her naturalization papers, and a notarized letter of current employment in the United States.

Transnational coordination also extended to the more basic need for applicants and sponsors to reproduce the same narrative in their separate and joint interactions with INS agents, from the first petition for application filed overseas to the final face-to-face interview for approval of travel or emigration. There were enough stories of failure that centered on poorly filled-out forms, incomplete documentation, and unsatisfactory interviews for most people to know that once a narrative was inscribed in state records, all divergences undermined the legitimacy of one's case.

Much of the concern with procedure manifested through villagers' fixations on documents themselves, especially as applicants drew closer to their scheduled interviews at the U.S. consulate in Guangzhou. In particular, as aspiring migrants moved further from encounters based on more informal, personal relations with mediators, they often shifted their concerns to paperwork in anticipation of more formal and unfamiliar exchanges with foreign state agents. Aside from procedures involving counterfeit documents, all paper routes eventually led aspiring migrants to a consulate or embassy of the country of destination, where they were expected to make their final appeal for departure through a convincing interweaving of paper evidence and embodied performance. Even when smugglers and other mediators could shorten some of the application process for would-be migrants through "back door" tactics—particularly, as noted, on the Chinese end of state encounters—the foreign consulate always stood out as the one necessary "front door" through which villagers had to pass in order to secure a legitimate paper route out of China. Having mobilized the necessary funds and allies to reach the consular interview, the villagers' task was now to translate these socioeconomic resources into intelligible signs of "legal creditability"—a standard based on performative ideals such as narrative rationality; the external consistency of personal story, paperwork, and "known" facts; and the appropriate display of embodied affect, such as confidence and ease among legal travelers or fear and sorrow among asylum seekers (McKinnon 2009; Melloy 2007; Sweeney 2009).

In Longyan, "going to Guangzhou" had become a common rite of passage among those seeking to establish a paper route to the United States. In fact, it was both the culmination of one's efforts in mobilization and the first litmus test of one's capacity for consolidating paperwork and performance into a convincing case before a foreign gatekeeper. While most villagers expressed anxiety over the unpredictability of the interviews, from the mood of the consular official to the nature and degree of interrogation, they also tried to prepare for the encounter as much as possible. On the streets, at mahjong games, and in everyday interactions, villagers often traded information about past successes or failures at the U.S. consulate. Though stories of failure often pointed to uncontrollable factors, such as changes in immigration policy or the random draw of a hostile interviewer, the one aspect that always reflected poorly on applicants was a general lack of command over their "file selves" in the interview situation. Of all the facets of the consular interview, the paper component was the one thing that most villagers believed they could best control.

More importantly, paperwork was a key site through which one's claim to creditability—in both the socioeconomic and legal sense—could be teased out and consolidated. To show up at the U.S. consulate with complete and orderly documents in hand and, moreover, with intimate knowledge of their content were the basic criteria for success in the interview. For villagers, these criteria also indexed an applicant's general diligence as a person, distinguishing the promising and deserving from the incompetent. Even though most aspiring migrants worked through smugglers, translators, and a host of other mediators in order to assemble their "file selves," villagers often made moral judgments about applicants themselves when their cases failed on the basis of botched paperwork. People who could not recall the basic facts of their cases, such as the sponsor's date of birth or overseas address, or who did not bother to make sure their paperwork was complete had only themselves to blame when they were rejected at their consular interviews. A lack of mastery over one's file self was already an index of one's lack of credible commitment to the project of emigration. Despite the centrality of mediators and the unpredictability of the application process itself, most villagers shared Lin Mengya's view: "No matter what, you yourself have to put the materials in order and take care of procedures [ban shouxu]. It's your responsibility." Someone who pored over application materials and proved themselves to be "conscientious" (renzhen) about paperwork inspired confidence for going overseas. In fact, even when such "conscientious" people encountered rejection at their consulate interviews, they often could still retain, and in some instances even extend, their claims to creditability as worthy candidates for future emigration (see chapter 4).

A high level of preparedness over paperwork was not always possible, however, especially for applicants relying on smugglers and other socially distant allies such as unfamiliar sponsors in fake-marriage arrangements. Unlike villagers applying through close relatives, those depending on smugglers and strangers often had neither much control over the quality and kind of materials assembled for their cases nor the time to become familiar enough with the documents to get their stories straight for the consular interviews. But even in these more uncontrollable situations, prior experience with the "work" performed by paperwork could help applicants minimize and even prevent a disastrous encounter at the consulate. For instance, even when faced with certain failure during her last trip to Guangzhou, Deng Feiyan still had the opportunity to display her superior savvy over paperwork and in turn distinguish herself from the other, less competent, applicants in her party. In this case, a smuggler had lead Deng Feiyan and four middle-aged men to the U.S. consulate to try to get them a business visa as a group. The trip was an utter disaster, marred by the poor organization of the applicants, who were given only one day to prepare for their interviews and get their stories straight. Moreover, the applications were hampered by shoddy supporting documents, which Deng Feiyan promptly pulled out for my benefit when she got back to Fuzhou. The papers consisted of a fake company resume for Deng Feiyan, a letter from an advertising company in Fuzhou attesting to her present employment there and authorization for business travel, an invitation from a Florida media company filled with grammatically incorrect English and lacking a signature and proper letterhead, and the Chinese translation of the invitation without any official stamp of notarization. "Can you believe this?" Deng Feiyan complained, "They gave me this when I got on the plane [to Guangzhou] and told me, 'You have one day to memorize it all.'" Deng Feiyan said it was 10 p.m. by the time her group arrived at a hotel in Guangzhou, and she ended up staying up all night trying to read and memorize her application for an early morning interview the next day. At the consulate, when she saw the men in her party rejected for a visa one after another while she was waiting for her own turn, Deng Feiyan said she refused to go to her interview. Given the poor preparation and paperwork, she knew she would be rejected as well and did not want to risk having her passport marred by a stamp of rejection from the consulate. Those who did not know better thought of their interview "like it was gambling," she told me with disdain. But she knew that every time a rejection was stamped on a passport, it left a record behind, and she was determined to keep her passport and personal file pristine. While ignorance made the men in her group reckless in their approach, Deng Feiyan believed that her superior understanding and management of paperwork—in this case her passport—helped her assess the situation better and preserve the possibility of a more successful encounter at the consulate in the future. Like embodied knowledge of travel or English proficiency, mastery over the "work" in paperwork enabled aspiring migrants like Deng Feiyan to claim some vernacular expertise over the hazards involved in the pursuit of exits from China. By displaying conscientiousness through paperwork, Deng Feiyan was also making a more general moral claim as a creditworthy person capable of redeeming the continual good faith of villagers—that is, the social and financial credits extended—through future attempts at emigration and in the performance of "legal creditability."

Calculating Luck

Ultimately, no matter how prepared one was or how much money, connections, or expertise one could mobilize, there was still an element of randomness or luck (*yunqi*) involved in every effort for making an exit. For this reason people often evoked gambling as a metaphor not only for the experience of boat smuggling but for consulate encounters as well. Though the stakes were certainly not as high as in boat smuggling (where life itself was often the "gamble"), even the most prepared applicants for legal emigration faced unfavorable odds in an interview situation. Residents from Longyan tended to fail consular interviews not only because of poorly prepared paperwork (as in the case of Deng Feiyan) but also because of foreign consulates' increasing suspicion of applicants from the Fuzhou area, with its notoriety as China's human smuggling capital. When Li Guang, a twenty-one-year-old aspiring migrant, was preparing his INS application via a fake-marriage arrangement, he described to me how bad his odds were by recounting the recent consular experience of a group of aspiring migrants that included a few of his close friends. Though this group of nine all had the same supporting documents for student visas, only one of them managed to obtain approval for travel after they emerged from their individual interviews at the U.S. consulate. "It's really terrifying," Li Guang concluded while contemplating this failed example and his own expectations for an upcoming interview. "Seems to be just like gambling," he noted with a shudder. When his time at the consulate arrived half a year later, Li Guang believed his success had more to do with random luck than preparation or skill. Of all the interviews that day, Li Guang believed he was the only young male applicant to gain approval at the U.S. consulate. The luck of his draw was made even more explicit when he noted with gratitude that his interviewer had approved his application even though she pointedly told him that she did not quite believe his case. In the end, this consular official also told Li Guang that she hoped he would prove her suspicions wrong through his future conduct as an upstanding American resident.

While boat smuggling still contained more unpredictable variables than applications for travel papers, both processes shared similar uncontrollable rhythms, including long, anxious periods of waiting and limbo and short, stressful bursts of activity for gathering up money, documents, and even oneself (along with luggage) in time for departure. Whether they were traveling by boat or plane, aspiring migrants always seemed to be either waiting in a state of uncertainty or rushing madly to meet specific deadlines for leaving China. These fits and starts made the experience of going abroad seem even more chaotic and uncontrollable, even for those already familiar with the cycle from prior attempts at emigration. In fact, many failures not only heightened all the uncontrollable elements involved in the process but also made people question their luck and karmic fate (*mingyun*) in general.

For most villagers, the moral lesson to be learned from both smuggling disasters and failed legal travel was about the calculus of luck. Thus regardless of the means of departure, most villagers felt the need to mobilize local gods—the agents of luck and karma—to help manage all the factors that they themselves could not anticipate or control. Strategies for managing luck included daily prayer at home and at local temples, the seeking of divination through spirit mediums, the interpretation of religious almanacs, and the tossing of fortune sticks or divination blocks at the shrine of a particular god. At local temples and at their own home altars, villagers constantly appealed to gods for advice and answers concerning the reliability of certain snakeheads or routes, the status of their cases, and the possible obstacles or outcomes of their attempts. Through daily offerings and more elaborate donations, aspiring migrants and their relatives also mobilized gods to intervene proactively in their cases, from ensuring safety at sea to arranging favorable state encounters with more lenient and sympathetic officials.

After multiple failures through boat transport, Hong Jianyi was hoping to change his luck not only by choosing a different route of departure but also by making greater investments in ritual activities, from more intensive participation in temple worship to larger monetary donations as appeals to gods for ensuring the success of his next attempt. Some said Hong Jianyi was so convinced his past failures stemmed from cosmological sources that he had even married on the advice of a local god as part of a scheme to change his luck. When he finally made arrangements with a cousin in the United States to sponsor him for a travel visa, Hong Jianyi consulted both his network of overseas relatives and friends and a circuit of gods at popular local temples in order to determine the feasibility of his plan. Though he managed to gather all the necessary papers from his cousin abroad, in the end Hong Jianyi decided to scratch this arrangement. But this time Hong Jianyi's problem did not involve a dearth of paperwork, money, or even preparation. He simply believed that luck was not yet on his side. When I ran into him outside of his house a few weeks after he had shown me a packet of application documents from his cousin overseas, Hong Jianyi informed me about his change of plans in the typical self-conscious and defeated demeanor he displayed in public. "Right now it's impossible to pass through [the consulate]," he told me with quiet chagrin. Not only had he heard that the approval rate for a travel visa had plummeted to "about 1 percent" since the 9/11 attacks on the World Trade Center in New York the previous fall, but Hong Jianyi had also been told by a god in a recent temple visit that his luck was on the wane and would not improve until after the next lunar new year in 2003, which was more than nine months away. This cosmic accounting killed whatever remaining optimism Hong Jianyi had had about trying his luck (against the "1 percent" odds) at the U.S. consulate and convinced him that he needed to continue his search for another paper route out of China. Like other aspiring migrants from Longyan, Hong Jianyi tried to anticipate the risks of departure by calculating his odds in terms of not only human probability but also cosmic efficacy. Luck and karma did not replace human agency in Hong Jianyi's account. They were simply recognized as central variables among others in his assessment of potential success. Perhaps even more important, such cosmic factors were seen as calculable by the gods, if not directly by people, and therefore open to divine as well as human intervention.[19] When I left Longyan, Hong Jianyi was still biding his time for a viable departure while working to improve his luck on the advice of the gods.

Zones of Departure

Even if Hong Jianyi had gone through with his application and obtained approval from the U.S. consulate, his paper route would have lead him to a paperless end once his travel visa expired. Like many villagers who had managed to make their exits abroad, Hong Jianyi would also have found himself exiled in the United States without legal status and, in the worse-case scenario, even facing INS detention or deportation to China.

As these possible outcomes suggest, successful exits from China often did not equate with successful entrances abroad.

Even though there were many options for exiting China, almost none lead directly to a proper entrance and legal status overseas. In fact, aside from legal sponsorship for permanent immigration by a spouse, parent, or adult child (including successful fake-marriage arrangements), all who exited China usually ended up without legal status in the country of destination because they had either circumvented ports of entry altogether (as in the case of boat smuggling) or passed through checkpoints with fake papers or visas that became invalid after a short stay abroad. Although many aspiring migrants were able to forge exits through "back door" strategies, most of these routes dead-ended in what Erving Goffman (1986, 81) has aptly called "back places"—the marginalized sites where the socially stigmatized found themselves isolated among their own kind. Even when undocumented migrants worked for citizens as cooks, deliverymen, gardeners, housecleaners, and so forth, many still remained in what Susan Coutin (2000) described as "spaces of nonexistence," their presence rendered invisible in the daily lives of the privileged. Such spaces included not only the small ethnic circuit of Chinatowns and their take-out restaurants, warehouses, and Fuzhounese boarding houses and apartments, where many undocumented migrants found themselves confined, but also extended to immigrant detention facilities, where the most unfortunate were even more effectively immobilized as "illegal aliens."

Less than a year after Li Guang had successfully arrived in the United States with a K-1 visa through his fake-marriage arrangement, he told me his legal sponsor had decided to withdraw her support for his green card application and give up the remaining $42,000 he would have paid her (out of $62,000) for successfully completing their legal marriage and the three years of INS scrutiny necessary for final approval of his permanent residency. Having left China with the privilege of plane tickets and legitimate papers, he now found himself with his visa expired and no other possibilities for legal status in sight. When I caught up with him on the phone, Li Guang was in Miami, working in a Fuzhounese-run kitchen supply warehouse and trying to lay low for a while as he sorted out his finances and options. At some point before his fake-marriage arrangement had fallen apart, he had managed to get a legitimate driver's license and a cell phone. But he had not managed to get a bank account or a proper place to live. Instead, he slept on a cot in the warehouse and hoped his boss, who promised to keep the wages he was earning in a safe place for him, turned out to be an honorable man. When I asked him if all the English lessons he had diligently taken in Fuzhou before his departure were being put to good use, he told me that things here were nothing like he had imagined before he left China. "English?" he scoffed. "No way! Day in and day out, all I hear is Fuzhounese. In fact, this is the first time I've spoken Mandarin since I've been here in Miami."

Over time, celebrations of successful exits from Longyan commonly turned into despair over the exile of a loved one abroad who, without proper papers and legal entrance into the United States, could neither reenter China without penalty or easily reunite with those left behind by sponsoring their legal emigration. In fact, many women I knew in Longyan had been separated from their husbands for over a decade, with no end in sight and with infant children growing into teenagers in the interim without the least memory or sentiment for their fathers (see chapter 6). As all of these women discovered when they found themselves and their husbands equally stuck in their respective places, a successful exit did not necessarily entail better command over mobility and transnational flows.

Despite the daunting tasks for mobilizing resources and managing the cycle of waiting and rushing necessary for leaving China, most people understood that it would be even more difficult to make a proper entrance abroad. At the most basic level, the difference between exits and entrances can be gleaned from the management of flows at international airports, where as a rule arrivals always involve more arduous security checks and elaborate bureaucratic hoops than departures. Post-9/11 efforts to make entrances into the United States more secure have worked explicitly to extend the zones of departure while pushing back the legal points of arrival. In particular, initiatives since 2001, like the US VISIT program, have taken steps to widen the liminal space between exits and entrance in international travel by imposing additional domestic and foreign checkpoints and employing new policing technologies (for example, "dataveillance" and "smart" passports)—all in the hopes of filtering out undesirable subjects *before* they reach the ports of entry (Amoore 2006).

Hong Jianyi's diagnosis of 9/11 as one cause of his plummeting odds for departure was, in fact, empirically supported in Longyan by the extended hoops and long lines reported by other villagers trying to leave China legally since 2001. In the aftermath of the World Trade Center attacks, it seemed like much of the embodied knowledge and vernacular expertise that villagers had developed about the spatial-temporal rhythms and procedures of legal travel had imploded overnight. Those who had expected a two-year wait to get refugee visas already approved by the United States ended up lingering in Longyan for four to five years. Others, like Hong Jianyi, saw common pathways to legal exits (like visas to visit relatives overseas) disappear from their realm of possibilities. Still others found themselves facing unexpected callbacks from foreign consulates while watching long-established, if undocumented, relatives overseas suddenly rounded up and deported back to Fuzhou. Even for those who managed to secure a departure from China, the difficulties of arrival often persisted. As the next chapter will show, the problems of entrance were not only heightened by new border-policing protocols in the post-9/11 era; they also extended to the general rigors necessary for achieving and maintaining legal status once a migrant was overseas, which, even more than in the making of exits, required the migrant to interact with state agents through a convincing continual display of paperwork and performance.

Bad Subjects

Human Smuggling, Legality, and the Problem of Entrance

The passport that you hold in your hand as you approach the immigration officer has a purpose and coherence that is governed by its own rules. The passport chooses to tell its story about you. Is that story one of your own making? Can it ever be?

—Amitava Kumar, *Passport Photos*

At the end of the summer of 2000, fifty-eight would-be Fuzhounese migrants turned up dead in a sealed container truck in Dover, England, and made international headlines. Shortly after, I returned to the United States from Fuzhou for the first time. In the fast lane for U.S. citizens at Los Angeles International Airport (LAX), I was waved forward by the immigration officer to his booth. He took my passport and casually flipped through the pages of visa attachments. "So where were you in China?" he asked. "Fuzhou in Fujian Province," I replied. "Fuzhou, huh?" he perked up and scanned my face against my documents with considerably more interest. "What were you doing *there*?" he inquired with a raised eyebrow. All of a sudden I became very aware of my resemblance to my research subjects and the importance of the words that were about to come out of my mouth. As I tried to explain my status as a student doing research in Fuzhou, I found myself inadvertently monitoring the pronunciation of words and their flow. I threw in some friendly small talk for good measure. "Pretty humid there, so it's good to be home," I let it be known. Seemingly satisfied with my display of citizenship, the officer chuckled and stamped my passport. "Yeah, Fuzhou," he told me with a resigned smile and shake of the head. "You know, that's a bad, *bad* place."

Fuzhou's notoriety as China's human smuggling capital was already widespread in the international media and among immigration gatekeepers by the time I had this encounter at the airport. As I later learned in Longyan, most villagers expected this story of Fuzhou as "a bad, *bad* place" to frame their own exchanges with immigration officials at airports and other entrance checkpoints. "When they hear 'Fuzhou, Fujian' they immediately think human smuggling," Zheng Hui complained to me. "It's as if the Fuzhounese are all bad." Zheng Hui, a jaded villager in her early twenties, was speaking from her own experience as a victim of two deportations from failed entries into the United States. I had been telling Zheng Hui and two of her friends about my encounter at LAX when she revealed her own familiarity with arrival procedures at this particular airport. "Los Angeles seems really comfortable," she interjected wistfully in the middle of our conversation. "At least the bits I saw gave me a good impression," she added. These "bits" turned out to be no more than the interior of the airport, from where Zheng Hui was immediately deported the first time she tried to enter the country, and the view from a car ride from LAX to a nearby INS detention center, where she spent more than ten months after her second failed effort to gain entry.

Like most aspiring migrants who had been thwarted in recent years, Zheng Hui believed that in both of her attempts at entry, her difficulties with immigration officials began the moment her place of residence—Fuzhou, Fujian—was revealed. Fuzhou residence indexed a narrative of illicit mobility, smugglers, and frauds that by now most aspiring migrants like Zheng Hui found inescapable in their encounters with foreign gatekeepers of travel. The regional association with Fuzhou often meant heightened suspicion and scrutiny by immigration officials.

After more than twenty years of mass emigration from the region, alongside a steady stream of well-publicized human smuggling disasters, most villagers, including Zheng Hui, believed it was now more difficult than ever to make a successful entrance abroad because of Fuzhou's outsized reputation as the launching pad of snakeheads and stowaways. Whether they actually relied on smugglers or not, most villagers worried about the impression their status as Fuzhou residents would make on immigration officials. As Zheng Hui concluded from her own failures, "Xiamen, Sichuan . . . any place is better than Fuzhou." Some people were even changing their legal residence in China's household registration system as a means of minimizing the taint of Fuzhou in their personal records and "file selves." Many more thought they could undermine the bad impression of Fuzhounese migrants abroad through convincing embodied performances as a more legitimate and entitled kind of Chinese subject—the sort of cosmopolitan, jet-setting overseas Chinese who, in the popular imagination, always moved with ease and familiarity through foreign airports and other points of entry.

This emphasis on performance made me, an outsider most villagers identified as an overseas Chinese, something of a curiosity, especially for women like Zheng Hui and her friends, who often took much interest in the distinctions of clothes, gait, and general bearing that they believed separated me from the local population. Such scrutiny sometimes put me in the uncomfortable position of having to refute the generalizations people made about "overseas Chineseness" and "Americanness" based on my appearance and behavior. For instance, my limited wardrobe, consisting largely of T-shirts and jeans, gave some the impression that "You Americans seem to dress more casually [suibian]" and in one case even prompted Deng Feiyan to ask me, "Would I look more modern [modeng] in a T-shirt?" as she imagined her future passage through the immigration line of some U.S. airport. Though people knew that I too was not immune from the taint of Fuzhou, as my LAX encounter had illustrated, some, like Deng Feiyan and Zheng Hui, still sought me out as a sounding board (if not model) for their theories and trial runs for persuasive performances and smooth entrances in their destinations overseas.

"Bad subjects," the title of this chapter, refers, on the one hand, to all the unseemly aspects of Fuzhounese migration—human smuggling, fake-marriage arrangements, religious divination, and other unauthorized strategies for mobility—that have troubled (and have been troubling for) China's celebratory narratives of its "opening up" and its legitimate emplacement among other modern nation-states in the global order. "Bad subjects" also refers to Longyan residents themselves, who in their quest for emigration have problematized the whole apparatus of state subjectification and its firm grip on disciplined, legible bodies. The title itself was inspired by reformers in the nascent First French Republic who lobbied for fixing state identification to individual bodily markers (for example, color of hair and eyes) by sounding alarms over "the complete liberty given to bad subjects" to elude state capture under the old passport system (Torpey 2000, 39).[1] "Bad subjecthood" is less an exemplar of resistance among the Fuzhounese than an acknowledgment of the compromises

ke in order to maintain some semblance of control over their
oth physical and social) and the terms of "self-making" (Ong
e face of ongoing state disenfranchisement—in this case, by
and the United States. These strategies for mobility have involved more than the pragmatics for exiting China; as this chapter will
show, they have extended to goals and practices for achieving legal entrances overseas. As aspiring migrants shifted their focus from exits to
entrances, their concerns no longer revolved around the accumulation of
supporting documents but around one's capacity for bringing these documents and their claims of entitlement to life in direct, embodied encounters with foreign gatekeepers of immigration. In the remainder of this
chapter, I focus on the two most common checkpoints villagers discussed
when it came to the problems of entrance: (1) the most immediate and
highly anticipated hoop of airport arrivals, and (2) at the other end of the
spectrum, the last chance for legality through pleas for asylum in court
hearings. Here I want to suggest, following anthropologists like Aihwa
Ong, that "It is perhaps much more useful to talk about the 'concrete
assemblages' produced by converging rationalities that function in connection with other assemblages, and about what effects such divergent
mixes have on the citizenship forms [and migrant identifications] in different social milieus" (2003, 10; cf. Ong and Collier 2005). In particular,
by examining the entangled practices of inscription and performance that
go into the production of legal entrances, my aim is to shift the analytic
frame from "the state" as a coherent and monolithic regulator of national
borders to the circuits of state agents and allies that villagers routinely
tried to marshal in support of their various claims to legality and, in turn,
to possible moral careers overseas.

Travel English

Any day now, Liu Ming told me, he would be getting on a plane armed
with his real passport and some additional fake documents a snakehead
was currently procuring for him at the cost of $60,000. When I met this
twenty-three-year-old aspiring migrant in Longyan, he already had a bag
packed and was simply waiting for the final word from the smuggler
about his date of departure. This would be Liu Ming's first attempt at
emigration, and he was hoping for a short and painless experience on a
direct international flight to the United States. "Of course I am nervous,"

he told me. "Many people, after ten or more times [*shijici*], still haven't succeeded," he added. Liu Ming's father, a devout worshipper at local temples, had recently stepped up his participation in religious activities in an effort to ensure his son's smooth passage. It was at one of these temple events—a birthday banquet for Guanyin—that the old man first told me about his son's impending travels and confessed his anxieties about Liu Ming's passage through airport inspections in the United States.

Liu Ming had never been on a plane and knew almost no English. Moreover, though his smuggler had given him a sheet of the kinds of English sentences commonly exchanged at airport inspections in the United States, Liu Ming had not yet studied it, let alone mastered the English alphabet. While his lack of plane experience could not be helped, Liu Ming's failure to improve his English reflected poorly on both his travel prospects and his character. "He's not very conscientious [*renzhen*]," some villagers gossiped to me while predicting his chances for success.

Liu Ming's father was well aware of the village gossip surrounding his son's impending trip overseas. Over lunch at his home, he confided to me that he too was worried about Liu Ming's capacity to get through airport security in the United States. Liu Ming had never shown much motivation or aptitude for learning, let alone having to master specialized English phrases about travel plans and legal status in a hurry. He barely made it through fifth grade before dropping out of school, his father told me. Unlike his older sister, who had studiously practiced her "Travel English" (*Liyou Yingyu*) before sailing through airport inspection overseas, Liu Ming was making his father very nervous because he had yet to glance at the sheet of English dialogue his smuggler had given him even though he could be leaving tomorrow.

As with Restaurant English (see chapter 1), most Longyan residents believed it was vital to practice Travel English well before departure. Even the local middle school had acknowledged the importance of Travel English by providing training in it for its worst ninth-grade students, who, without any hopes for further education, were expected to be the first youths to leave Longyan. While the students I observed in these courses often seemed bewildered or bored by the specialized dialogues and vocabulary they recited about "flight attendants," "carry-on baggage," and visits with "my sister/uncle/cousin in Los Angeles/Chicago/Honolulu," their presence in class at least assured relatives of their potential for entering the United States successfully. In contrast, someone like Liu Ming, who seemed either too indifferent or incompetent to grasp the basic English alphabet, was considered to be at a serious disadvantage in encounters with immigration officials. The better their command of Travel English, the more villagers believed they could distance themselves from the typical impression of Fuzhounese migrants as illiterate greenhorns disoriented by the procedures for airport arrival. While Travel English dialogues did not offer scenarios involving hostile immigration inspectors or extended interrogations, they did provide aspiring migrants a chance to practice simple exchanges of questions and responses (for example, "How long do you plan to visit? Two weeks."), which in turn could serve as general, if idealized, scripts for imagining and preparing for their encounters with immigration officers at ports of entry.[2] Along with a mastery of one's paperwork, studiousness in Travel English was one way of displaying a credible commitment to the project of emigration.

Deportable Knowledge

Even though Zheng Hui had already failed to enter the United States twice, she had managed to make dramatic improvements in English during the interim, particularly while in INS detention, where she was forced to use English in most interactions with guards and fellow inmates. Unlike Liu Ming, Zheng Hui's gumption and capacity for making the best out of her failures gave those around her much confidence in her ability to eventually make a successful entrance into the United States. In fact, far from feeling defeated by her failures, Zheng Hui often used what she had learned from these experiences to position herself as more of an expert among her circle of friends in Longyan. When I would meet up with Zheng Hui and her two best friends, all of whom currently had immigration applications in progress, Zheng Hui always seemed to dominate the conversation with fascinating theories and tips for moving successfully through airport entry. Not only had deportation failed to keep her from trying to leave China again, but its trials and tribulations also provided her practical training and knowledge, which Zheng Hui touted as advantages for her next venture overseas.

When she had first attempted to enter the United States, Zheng Hui said she did not yet understand why the immigration official at LAX seemed to be suspicious of her after just a few simple questions about where she was from and how long she planned to stay. While other travelers passed through immigration after similar questioning, Zheng Hui's interviewer held her back and began to closely inspect her travel documents by typing their ID numbers into the computer system and swiping one of them through some magnetic stripe-reading machine. This was not at all what she had expected from all her Travel English lessons in Longyan. Unfortunately for Zheng Hui, the documents in her possession that time—a doctored passport and U.S. green card provided by a snakehead— did not hold up under scrutiny, and she was sent on the next international flight back to China. Only when she was held up by immigration officials at LAX during her second attempt to enter the United States did Zheng Hui realize that her troubles in the first encounter stemmed from her Fuzhou association. This time Zheng Hui noticed that when she told the official that she was from Fujian, he immediately asked her, "Fujian . . . *Fuzhou?*" When she affirmed his hunch about her origins, Zheng Hui said he began shaking his head in knowing disapproval, as if he already knew what her story was all about.

Zheng Hui's tough interrogations and deportations gave her some valuable insights into the general profiling techniques and embodied signs that state gatekeepers relied on to interpellate and capture travelers like herself as "bad subjects" deserving apprehension and removal. More important, by analyzing her own practices and assumptions in these encounters, Zheng Hui had learned to recognize her complicity in producing the signs of illegality. Not unlike stories of successful entrances abroad, stories of deportation also generated knowledge about the making of il/ legality in international travel. In reflecting on her own failures, Zheng Hui had the chance to hone her skills for identifying the pitfalls in trying to pass as a legalized subject. Far from its being simply negative, the state power to illegalize and remove travelers proved to be productive, in the Foucauldian sense of creating new knowledge and relations. Deportation did not just return people unchanged to pick up life in Longyan where they had left it (Peutz 2006). It qualified people, for better or worse, in terms of the trials they encountered and the resources they gained as mobile subjects. Perhaps because initial failures in emigration were so common among aspiring migrants in Longyan, many first- and second-time deportees like Zheng Hui returned to China not so much diminished by their forced removals as better positioned with new claims to knowledge and skills for their next journey.[3] While there was a limit to how many failures one could chalk up to lessons learned and experiences gained,

Zheng Hui still had enough good faith among villagers (unlike someone like Liu Ming) to claim her two deportations as valuable training for her next attempt at emigration. Moreover, by converting her experiences of illegalization into useful lessons for others, Zheng Hui not only bolstered her own privileged positioning on migration matters in Longyan, but also helped to shape the very social landscape of legal knowledge and practice among villagers aspiring toward successful entrances abroad.

Airport Habitus

As Zheng Hui saw it, many Fuzhounese simply did not understand the general protocols for passing through airport inspections and gave themselves away at the basic level of bodily conduct. "A lot of people get caught because when they arrive at the airport, they just stand there stupidly [*sha-shade*]," Zheng Hui told her friends one evening as we discussed their various plans for legal entry overseas. As the only one in her social circle with relevant experience, Zheng Hui relished the opportunity to describe all the embodied qualities and mundane practices that could trigger suspicions about Fuzhounese travelers. Looking disoriented, confused, or nervous upon arrival immediately roused the unwanted attention of airport personnel, she told her friends. Similarly, Zheng Hui warned that many Chinese travelers made a bad impression by impatiently crowding and jostling while waiting for their turn with immigration officers. The worst and most visible offense, Zheng Hui noted, came from the failure to respect the yellow boundary markers on the floor separating those waiting for an interview with immigration officials from those already being interviewed. Even though there were signs in English and Chinese that instructed people how to line up behind these boundary markers, "many Chinese still don't know how to stand in line," Zheng Hui complained. This kind of clueless, unruly behavior did not help travelers blend in or make a persuasive case for themselves as cosmopolitan overseas Chinese at ease in the world of international travel. It did not show their practical mastery over what we might call airport *habitus*, following Mauss's (1992) and Bourdieu's (1977) insights into the embodied aspects of tacit cultural belonging.

Zheng Hui believed that many newcomers incriminated themselves as "bad subjects" ill-suited to international travel by showing a lack of procedural familiarity and sense of direction in moving smoothly through airport arrivals. Such physical disorientation extended through baggage claim, where people sometimes lost their way among the vast sea of rotating carousels while searching for their luggage. Zheng Hui said she knew of cases where people were so overwhelmed and confused by the baggage claim system that they simply gave up and tried to leave without their bags. She added that the lack the luggage ultimately made these travelers seem even more suspect to airport inspectors and sabotaged their chances for success.

As it turned out, people's self-consciousness about the impression they made in airport arrivals extended beyond dress and demeanor to concerns over the quantity and content of their luggage. While Zheng Hui thought a dearth of bags aroused suspicions among airport gatekeepers, Yang Xiumei railed against the tendency of Fuzhounese migrants to cram all their possessions—even pots and pans—into a bloated, excessive assortment of luggage. No privileged, self-respecting overseas Chinese, she reasoned, would have the need or desire to pack up and transport the entire contents of their house, especially cheap and expendable goods like housewares, which were easily replaceable in the United States. "It's only peasants who would do this," Yang Xiumei noted with disdain. For her own impending trip overseas, Yang Xiumei planned to bring one simple suitcase with casual clothes and basic personal items in order to distinguish herself from the typical peasant markers of illicit Fuzhounese travelers. In the meantime, Lin Mengya, who was busy assembling the kind of luggage collection that Yang Xiumei shunned, began to worry about the strange impression some of her packed items might make on American airport inspectors. She was particularly nervous about the kind of scrutiny she might invite if she transported the smoke-stained wooden statue of the god she had worshipped at home for over a decade, along with the sacred vessel that held the incense and ashes on the god's shrine. To show proper respect for the god as a divine being (as opposed to a common object), Lin Mengya knew she needed to hand-carry the statue and incense holder onto the plane and through all the steps of airport arrival. But she also dreaded the way she would probably stand out with these peculiar items in hand and wondered how much suspicion and explanation she would have to juggle to make it through.

In the end, what Lin Mengya and other would-be migrants feared the most was triggering the kind of extended interrogation that could derail their chances for a successful entry. Because enactments of "legal credibility" were always contingent on the reception of state agents, who often did not share the same readings of the law and its enforcement, one could never be sure whether encounters with officials would lead to easy passage or extended interrogation. And as most villagers knew, to be subjected to additional questioning only increased the chances of apprehension and removal by already suspicious inspectors. Even villagers like Lin Mengya, who were assembling the most complete and legitimate travel papers, could not be certain that their every word and gesture would ultimately support their claims to legality rather than betray them under the stress of heightened scrutiny. Because of such uncertainties, people often tried to imagine ways for passing more smoothly and inconspicuously through airport entry and specifically why they fixated on the very physical and performative aspects of self-presentation that might help them minimize questions and undo the taint of Fuzhou, which inevitably marked them as bad subjects in the eyes of foreign state agents.[4] These efforts included attention to the material culture of travel and particularly to the necessary props supporting their performances of lawfulness, from the class markers of luggage to the aesthetics of paperwork.

No doubt the most dreaded moment of airport arrival involved the exchange of paperwork and narratives with immigration officers, when most villagers' links to Fuzhou could be easily gleaned from Chinese passports (which include a line for place of residence). Aside from the consular interview in Guangzhou, the encounter with airport inspectors at entry was probably the most anticipated and feared rite of passage for would-be migrants in Longyan. While having legitimate, state-issued travel documents boosted people's confidence for success, most aspiring migrants in Longyan knew that the ultimate test came during face-to-face encounters with foreign gatekeepers when the correspondence between one's personal claim to entrance and the state-authorized signs of entitlement (passports, visas, and the like) needed to be proven.

In particular, the challenge was to persuade immigration officials of one's rightful emplacement abroad by providing not only convincing paperwork but also a credible display of local knowledge about one's place of arrival and final destination. The latter could be as simple as projecting confidence and a sense of direction and belonging through body language—anything that might help one blend in during arrival procedures, as discussed above. It extended to the first impression made on immigration officers, from the way one stood in line to the look on one's face and the first words out of one's mouth. For nearly three months, when Deng Feiyan was gearing up for an anticipated trip abroad, she often tried to imagine this moment of first contact and prepare for it by asking me to evaluate her trial performances for approaching airport immigration inspectors. "Little Sister, look," she would motion to me as she put on a smile and practiced walking toward an imagined official at a U.S. airport. "How am I this way? Good or no good?" She would continue, "Should I say 'Hello,' or is 'Hi' better? What about 'How are you?' Am I saying it correctly?" She would then try these different combinations of English greetings, with and without a smile or a small wave of the hand, at a casual or determined walking pace, and so forth, refining her performance until she had gained some level of confidence about her chance for success. "Don't I look like an American?" she would ask me at the end of these practice encounters. "No problem, right?"

The tougher and even more intimidating test of local knowledge involved answering questions posed by immigration officers about the traveler's purpose in the United States, place of origin, final destination, and whatever else they deemed necessary for judging the legitimacy of claims for entrance. While most villagers lacked a solid grasp of English, many hoped that beyond a simple "Hello" or "Hi," a decent command of a few Travel English sentences might help them appear more like an overseas Chinese or Chinese American—that is, someone who already had a legitimate place in the United States. But whether they knew any English or not, most aspiring migrants worried more generally about the content of their interrogation and specifically their capacity to answer questions in a way that reinforced rather than detracted from the narrative of entitlement already inscribed in their travel papers. Much like rejections at consular interviews, one of the most disgraceful kinds of failure at airport arrivals was to be deported because of one's self-sabotage through confused, incomplete, or simply wrong answers to questions posed by immigration officers either directly or through a Chinese interpreter. Above all, there was no excuse for one's neglect or sheer ignorance of the weight of words exchanged in these encounters. In fact, it was often better to be silent than to give ill-informed and rash responses because, as Lin Mengya noted, "Whatever you say, there will be a record." Since one's words were bound for immediate inscription in these situations, there was nothing worse than saying the wrong things and thereby putting a story on record that contradicted official, existing narratives of oneself and one's entitlement to mobility.[5] This was especially true for aspiring migrants with temporary or counterfeit travel papers or, moreover, without any documents at all, who sometimes came up against the clashing narratives they put in place between initial airport encounters and later applications for political asylum.

While most villagers understood that poor and inconsistent answers could jeopardize the legitimacy of their claims on paper, they also believed that a great performance could compensate for the bad quality of (fake) travel documents. For all the countless examples of muddled responses and failed paperwork, villagers could also cite a few successful tales of quick thinking and savvy performance in the face of almost certain rejection. Deng Feiyan, for instance, drew comfort from the miraculous story of her nineteen-year-old niece, who managed to find a way into the United States despite all odds. After the smuggler had ditched this niece and her larger group of U.S.-bound travelers in Australia, the girl decided to head for the United States on a direct international flight by herself with little more than some shoddy counterfeit travel papers she had scraped together during her short stint working and improving her English in Australia. Deng Feiyan said her niece knew she was in trouble when the immigration officer at the U.S. airport had her escorted to a private room, away from the lines of arriving travelers, where she was subjected to further questioning by a Chinese-speaking inspector (who Deng Feiyan assumed was also ethnically Chinese). Despite three grueling hours of interrogation, the niece ultimately managed to make it through this hurdle by sheer poise and willpower. "No matter what they asked her, she wouldn't say one word," Deng Feiyan noted admiringly. "She would be like this," Deng Feiyan told me while demonstrating the imagined guise of her niece, her body slumped in silence, eyes downcast, and lips pursed into a tight, immobile frown. Deng Feiyan believed that this silent protest moved the interrogator because when he finally let her go, instead of sending her to INS detention or on the next flight back to China, he surprisingly gave her some words of friendly advice. "Next time, you better make sure you prepare your documents better," he purportedly told her while stamping her obviously fake passport. This comment by the officer helped Deng Feiyan humanize the process of airport entry and imagine the possibilities for overcoming the greatest (paper) barriers through sympathetic, convincing performances in direct encounters. The making of lawful entrances was not just a rational juridical process; it also overflowed with embodied affect. While not all immigration officers could be expected to be so easily swayed by such performances, the moral lesson Deng Feiyan drew from her niece's success story was that "no matter what, [the inspector] is a person. You are also a person." As such, there was always room for appeals to compassion and commonality despite the formality and privileging of paperwork in legalizing claims for entrance.

Going to Court

For the many who had failed to gain legal status upon arrival in the United States and found themselves undocumented and/or facing deportation, one of the last possibilities for obtaining legal status involved appeals for political asylum. Like airport arrival procedures, the process for claiming political asylum generated a great deal of conversation and general strategizing among aspiring migrants and their village kin in Longyan. "Going to court" (*shang ting*), as asylum applications were commonly termed, often evoked even more anxiety than airport entry because it was usually seen as the last hope for those who had exhausted all other options.

As the shorthand "going to court" indicates, most Longyan residents tended to think of political asylum as a judicial event rather than as a series of bureaucratic procedures like other applications for immigration and travel abroad. Even more than other encounters with state agents, villagers often emphasized the performative aspects of asylum applications in INS hearings and particularly their urgency. Unlike other procedures for legal status, political asylum applications could not be initiated until the aspiring migrants had set foot in the country of destination.[6] While those filing for permanent immigration or legal travel abroad often had to deal with significant paperwork and state agents before actual departures from China in order to prove their legitimacy and desirability as state subjects, those claiming government persecution and life endangerment were expected to evade those same disciplinary processes in fleeing from their country of oppression. For those with no papers, political asylum was the one claim that could open the legal doors to U.S. entry. It was also the only kind of application through which one's status as a "bad subject," who had knowingly violated immigration (and other) laws in defiance of the state, could be legitimized on the politically charged grounds of wrongful government persecution. While all other INS applications required migrants to present themselves as model subjects of state discipline, financial abundance, and bodily health, asylum cases demanded the exact opposite from applicants, whose success hinged on biographies of violation, deprivation, and bodily vulnerability. Instead of outlining a network of supporters and creditors from their country of origin, asylum claimants needed to sketch the dangerous webs of state persecutors and potential executioners that made fleeing China without papers seem reasonable and returning there impossible. The desperation and high stakes of such claims were not only narrated through paperwork and live testimonies in immigration court but also often deeply felt by both applicants and their village kin in Longyan, most of whom understood the zero-sum nature of these cases, which either lead to legal status or set deportation procedures in motion. Though some migrants managed to evade deportation even after losing their cases, most people believed that there were no further possibilities for achieving legal status after final denials of political asylum were handed down. At best, asylum rejections meant that one would be permanently undocumented abroad and therefore truly stuck in exile.

Even successful adjudications of political asylum presented a double bind to aspiring migrants from Longyan. As Hong Jianyi explained to me, "By going to court, you can get legal status, but because [in] this kind of political refugee [case], you say 'My life is in danger, the government will beat me,' et cetera, you still can't come back whenever [you want to] to see family." Because ideally most aspiring migrants hoped that legal status would give them freedom to move back and forth between China and their U.S. outposts, the granting of political asylum was often seen as a more partial achievement than other kinds of legal status. Although those who were granted political asylum could eventually trade up for permanent residence and although they could immediately sponsor their spouses and minor children for immigration to the United States, they themselves could not readily return to China because of the nature of their claims. Hong Jianyi shook his head vigorously when he contemplated the possibility of reentering China with asylum status abroad. "There's no way," he told me. "If you come back with this kind of legal status, you have to give up everything since you wouldn't be able to leave again." In this sense, asylum legalized only the unidirectional flow of migrants and their immediate families but did not provide a license for the kind of transnational coming and going most villagers desired.

Still, people in Longyan had great cause for celebrating when their overseas kin achieved political asylum since the alternative in most cases would have been immediate deportation. Because a great number of migrants from Longyan claimed political asylum when detained by the INS at ports of entry or at some later point (for example, immigration raids on workplaces), most filed their cases against the urgency of deportation orders already in process. These "defensive" asylum applications, as they are generally known, were commonly adjudicated by INS judges in court hearings, which is why Longyan residents referred to these cases as "going to court." Though villagers, including previously deported migrants, had little knowledge of most aspects of the asylum application process, almost everyone could imagine and discuss in great detail the actual event of "going to court."

The lack of knowledge about other aspects of the asylum application process was probably due to the fact that almost all aspiring migrants from Longyan put their wholesale trust in lawyers and other mediators, like snakeheads, to take care of the paperwork and other bureaucratic requirements for their applications. While those gathering materials for other immigration applications often did quite a bit of the work themselves, especially on the Chinese end of paperwork, asylum claimants seemed to count on lawyers completely to do everything leading up to the anticipated court hearings. When I asked villagers about the various aspects of asylum applications prior to court appointments, people typically told me, "I don't know. The lawyer takes care of it all." In fact, people seem to have detailed knowledge only about the various narratives their overseas relatives had told INS agents between the time they were first detained and the point at which they made their bid for political asylum.

More often than not, people recalled the initial testimonies of their overseas kin with regret and frustration because so many initial INS interrogations resulted in shaky performances and contradictory or inadequate responses to support asylum claims. Although many aspiring migrants tried to rectify the flaws in their narratives by the time they reached court, they often worried about the damage done to their cases by the initial stories they put on record during prior INS interrogations and detentions.[7] Some problems resulted from the poor coaching of snakeheads, who sometimes advised their clients to claim asylum upon arrival, usually through some rote narrative involving either persecution under China's stringent one-child policy or, increasingly, on religious grounds. Although a number of Longyan residents probably had strong cases for claiming asylum on these grounds, those who were coached often suffered in presenting their claims in rehearsed and nondescript terms, which were both not of their own making and were most likely already suspicious and familiar to INS agents who had had prior encounters with other Fuzhounese migrants relying on similar coaching.[8] In other cases, some who later claimed asylum simply failed to provide the biography of suffering and persecution expected of asylum applicants because they were initially trying to project themselves as the *other* kind of legal immigrant—resplendent of good fortune and resources and blessed with state legitimacy in the country of origin. Taking this position did not mean that these migrants lacked support for meeting the legal standards of political asylum under U.S. immigration law. Rather, people's preference for trying other means first had more to do with their chances for success and the implications of the various outcomes for transnational mobility. Because asylum decisions seemed so unpredictable and the consequences of rejection so disastrous, even those with perfectly legitimate claims tended to view asylum as a strategy of last resort.[9]

Once asylum applications were initiated, people often invested incredible resources and hope in the lawyers they hired. As mentioned above, aspiring migrants tended to rely completely on their lawyers to take care of all aspects of their applications leading to their hearings. While aspiring migrants imagined their own role as a series of performative moments culminating in their testimony in court, they also saw their lawyers as the directors of their most dramatic and critical scene before the immigration judge. People often went to great lengths to comply with their lawyer's advice for giving convincing performances in court. For instance, Lin Mengya's sister went to the trouble of finding and paying a courier $1,000 to transport her toddler from Longyan to the United States on the advice of her lawyer, who thought she would appear more sympathetic with the baby in her arms. When I expressed my surprise to Lin Mengya at such an expensive and elaborate orchestration, she shrugged and responded, "Anyway, the lawyer said we need to do it this way, so we'll just do it this way." Because people invested their lawyers with so much faith and authority (not to mention money) during the application process, it was not surprising that villagers often evaluated the outcomes in equally strong and extreme terms. In everyday conversations about asylum cases, I often noticed the bipolar descriptions people offered about their past and present lawyers—either saintly heroes who could do no wrong or immoral predators draining their clients of money while leading them to catastrophe.[10] Because villagers mostly accepted the power relation between commanding lawyers and compliant clients, the good lawyer/bad lawyer morality tales mainly impressed upon them the importance for assembling the right mediators for their cases.

While personal references (sometimes via smugglers) and word of mouth about a lawyer's record of successes were often seen as important components in the search for reliable representation, many people also believed that the overall placement of specific lawyers, judges, and asylum seekers in immigration court had as much, if not more, to do with the luck or fate (*yuanfen*) of the applicants. As in consular interviews and other situations where luck seemed an important factor, aspiring migrants often sought the intervention of particular gods in Longyan to positively orchestrate this triangulation of lawyer, judge, and petitioner. This is where villagers in Longyan often played their most direct and central role in the entire asylum application process. While most asylum cases unfolded overseas only after aspiring migrants had set foot in the United States, religious interventions in the process remained the primary responsibility of villagers still in Longyan. Beyond routine prayers and offerings made to gods to ensure the general success of their kin, villagers in Longyan also performed specific ritual activities tailored for the asylum hearings of their loved ones. For instance, when Lin Mengya's sister was approaching her date in immigration court, she dispatched her mother in Longyan to visit a couple of local temples with specific information, including the court date and time, street address, judge's name, and court circuit code—all written in English on pieces of thin red paper. Along with the burning of incense, food offerings, and prayers, these little red notes were left on the altars of gods so they would have the exact coordinates to intervene and make their presence felt at the hearing. Such red pieces of paper could also commonly be found on people's home altars as their relatives approached asylum hearings. In the case of Lin Mengya's sister, the family in Longyan hoped to mobilize gods to help "soften the heart of the judge" presiding over the hearing. Although nothing could ensure that the sister would deliver a stellar performance during her testimony, Lin Mengya and her family believed that through their transnational coordination of court information and ritual offerings, they could at least motivate gods to watch over the court proceedings and make sure that factors of luck, such as a judge's mood swings or political inclinations, were shaped in the sister's favor.

The fact that Lin Mengya's sister requested this divine intervention illustrates how much aspiring migrants believed their success ultimately hinged on contingencies beyond human control—that is, beyond both their own personal agency and the collective but disjunctive efforts of various immigration gatekeepers. At the same time, the little red notes on altars in Longyan show just how rich and extensive was the transnational coordination between villagers and their overseas kin in their collective effort to establish legality abroad. For these notes to arrive on village shrines and take their full divine effect abroad, court information had to be relayed from overseas to someone who could transcribe it onto ritual paper in English and then incorporate it into the proper sequence of ritual offerings and prayers necessary to move gods to action. These activities also point out that aspiring migrants' views of necessary allies extended beyond narrow legal and bureaucratic state parameters to include more informal and locally recognized (but transnational) networks involving gods as well as personal creditors and human smugglers. While gods and snakeheads were not the kinds of supporters one made legible before state agents, their practical importance to the making of exits and entrances highlights the kinds of unauthorized and even oppositional strategies that aspiring migrants deployed to meet specific state disciplinary demands for travel and immigration.

Lines of Flight

In one way or the other, the animal is more a fleer than a fighter, but its flights are also conquests, creations. Territorialities, then, are shot through with lines of flight testifying to the presence within them of movements of deterritorialization and reterritorialization.

—Gilles Deleuze and Felix Guattari, *A Thousand Plateaus*

Villagers' quest for legal status overseas did more than articulate the "traffic habits" and "grammar" of nation-states (Anderson 1991). It also produced what Deleuze and Guattari (1987) have aptly described as "lines of flight" toward destinations and linkages beyond state capture.[11] In particular, by seeking alliances with both state agents and gods, Longyan residents showed that the pursuit of legal entrances could simultaneously reiterate both the "reality effect" of territorial borders and the cosmic efficacy of divine support. In fact, the "effect" of state boundaries was most deeply felt in the loss, not achievement, of legal status, when one became undocumented and therefore stateless abroad. While people tended to attribute their success equally to gods and personal agency—the importance of which I will elaborate on in the next two chapters—failures often led villagers to focus on the nation-state, particularly in the form of critiques of its structural inequalities and persecution of those on its margins. When Zhang Yuan, a thirty-five-year-old mother of two and wife of an undocumented day laborer working in New Jersey, found out her husband's asylum claim had been rejected by the INS shortly after his lawyer was arrested and indicted for filing fraudulent claims for clients, she did not blame the lawyer but rather the U.S. government for her husband's exile and possible deportation. "It's all because of you Americans, that [President] Bush—that's the problem," she huffed when she thought about her husband's dead-end position as an undocumented migrant in the United States. "If we go to court and lose, then we won't be able to come back. But if you Americans only gave that legal status to us, then it wouldn't be this difficult," Zhang Yuan grieved. (Zhang Yuan's story is discussed in more detail in chapter 5.)

Perhaps the most revealing story of failed entrance and government persecution was told in the aftermath of 9/11 by my next-door neighbor, Yang Libin, a middle-aged cousin of the widow with whom I lived. Not long after the United States launched its military offensive against the Taliban in Afghanistan for the Al Qaeda attacks on 9/11, I was sitting with the widow and two of her visiting daughters when Yang Libin came bursting in from across the courtyard waving her knitting needles and the unraveling sweater attached to them. Though it was already old news that her son had been rejected for asylum in the United States, she announced in a frenzied panic that in a call with her cousin overseas she had learned that her son had recently received an official letter from the U.S. government demanding *not* his deportation but rather his mandatory conscription as a soldier in the current war against Afghanistan. Alarmed by this "draft notice," the son quickly abandoned his residence in the New York area and began making his way north to the Canadian border. At the time Yang Libin told us this story, she had yet to hear confirmation of her son's safe crossing into Canada, out of the reach of the American armed forces.

This incredible piece of news did not seem to surprise anyone except me. Instead, it was simply seen as yet another example of all the known cruelty and persecution perpetrated by the U.S. government toward marginalized immigrants, especially those who were undocumented. Though certainly I sympathized with the truth of these sentiments, I also felt compelled to play devil's advocate. Gently I asked whether it was possible that Yang Libin's son had simply misread this "official" letter? Perhaps this was just a form letter from a mass-mailing campaign for army recruitment, I surmised, because it did not seem plausible that the U.S. government would reinstate any kind of a draft in the current political climate, particularly not for subjects like undocumented migrants, whose loyalty and trust were inherently suspect. Despite my insistent questions, and arguments, people merely waved me aside as terribly naïve and fundamentally biased. I could defend the U.S. government, they implied, only because I was too shielded as part of the nation-state's privileged center to understand its capacity for persecution on the margins. "You don't understand," Yang Libin shook her head forcefully. "What you say all concerns what a government *should* do. But what you don't know is that there isn't *anything* that they wouldn't do." In speaking of the nation-state in the plural as "they," Yang Libin extended her critique to include both the United States and China as persecutors of the marginalized and stateless.

In the end, it did not matter what precisely was in that letter that set Yang Libin's son on the run. The fact that he fled was itself an enactment of the conditions of marginality and exception that he already inhabited as a subject suspended between exits and entrances in "the national order of things." Yang Libin's insistence that "there isn't *anything* that [governments] wouldn't do" strongly echoed arguments that scholars like Carl Schmitt (2005) and Giorgio Agamben (1998, 2005) have made about the constitutive sovereign power of states to exempt themselves from the norms of law and to relegate certain subjects like "illegal aliens" and "enemy combatants" to "zones of abandonment" (Biehl 2001) outside the juridical order. Having already been stripped of his claims to state protection, perhaps Yang Libin's son did not need much to be convinced that his struggle for "bare life"—for salvaging a life forfeited by the state and thus rendered "killable by anyone" (Agamben 1998)—could take such an explicit form as forced military combat and exposure to violence and death in Afghanistan. His line of flight only made clear to his mother and others in Longyan that one could not count on nation-states to secure the basic conditions of life, let alone the possibilities of "the good life." Yang Libin responded to news of her son's flight by praying for the protection of the gods at local temples and especially at her own domestic altar, where she added a little red paper with the address of her son's destination—Toronto, Canada—to the list of coordinates for Linshui Furen, a goddess of fertility, to keep a watch over. As the ultimate guarantors of lives not only in their present incarnations but also in their transformative karmic cycles through past lives, afterlives, and rebirths, gods like Linshui Furen promised to be powerful allies. They were the only ones, in fact, who could trump state claims over the management of life and death and redeem the "gambles" many villagers already made as mobile lives outside the security of the state's embrace. For as Yang Libin and others in Longyan knew, it was only through the gods that one could discern not just the this-worldly contours of lines of flight but also the other-worldly sources that helped set them in motion.

Toward the Good (After)Life

This chapter has attempted to sketch a more dispersed and on-the-ground account of how legal status can be consolidated while allowing for the persistence of illegible and unruly subjects outside the firm grip of "the state." As chapters 2–4 have shown, achieving legal status at home or abroad, whether in the form of a superior household registration or U.S. citizenship, was not just about state subjectification and the disciplining of bodies, though such forces certainly shaped people's aspirations and practices. Many "back door" efforts and illegible alliances were activated in the process—some leading to shortcuts along bureaucratic trails toward a privileged state positioning, others diverging off the path of state valorization to support dissonant aspirations for spatial-temporal extension, for a discrepant cosmopolitanism, for surplus children, and for expanded divine relations and credit.

As I first argued in chapter 2, the networked body—a nodal rather than individualized notion of the subject—offered a better way to understand how villagers approached state identification as achievement rather than as ontology or entitlement. Through this notion, I have tried not only to show the relevance of longstanding Chinese concepts like *guanxi* in dealing with "the state" but also to extend the notion of "networking" to include all sorts of mediating, if illegible, agents and allies—smugglers, personal creditors, local gods—well beyond the limited institutional boundaries of bureaucratic state encounters. Religious practices, as I have shown, have been a central part of the "work" in paperwork, even though such strategies are rarely evident when one strictly limits the field for negotiating and achieving state identification to bounded and reified institutions.

In describing the fetishization of passports and particularly the emergence of the multiple passport-toting transnational Chinese, Aihwa Ong has noted that such state identifications have become "less and less attestations of citizenship, let alone of loyalty to a protective nation-state, than of claims to participate in labor markets. The truth claims of the state that are enshrined in the passport are gradually being replaced by its counterfeit use in response to the claims of global capitalism" (1999, 2). Certainly my subjects' disheartening and cynical views of both the U.S. and Chinese states support Ong's argument for the declining significance of passports, citizenship, and other state identifications as markers of "loyalty to a protective nation-state."

I would also argue that migrants aspire to state identifications for other reasons beyond ambition to participate in labor markets.[12] For instance, the push and pull of labor markets cannot account for INS applicants like the frail eighty-two-year-old woman who had spent a good month trying to achieve mastery over her signature on bureaucratic forms (discussed in chapter 3). Nearly blind and having difficulty walking, this woman could hardly be seen as a respondent to the "claims of global capitalism." Nor was she subject to the pull of some American dream of prosperity as the outward-bound Fuzhounese are often said to be. In fact, she confessed that she had no intention of either moving to the United States or visiting there since on her one and only trip to see her son she had had a thoroughly isolating and terrible time. Instead, achieving U.S. status was part of her preparation for another personal journey altogether—to secure burial rights (and *rites*) for a smooth and prosperous afterlife rather than submit to the new local mandatory cremation policy.[13] As I discovered when other elderly villagers starting showing up at my doorstep with green card applications in hand, this woman was not alone in her quest for what Barbara Myerhoff (1978) once noted as "the good death" or, perhaps even more accurately, the good afterlife. Old Man Liu, my own self-proclaimed godfather, was himself an avid proponent and covert supporter of those in his cohort seeking to circumvent mandatory cremation—a practice that most of the elderly vaguely described as sacrilegious and fearful for disrupting the proper passage from this world to the next.[14] "To us old people, this is a very terrifying situation," Old Man Liu told me. Since the local administration began vigilantly enforcing a policy of mandatory cremation among villagers in the late 1990s, Old Man Liu, a skilled woodworker, had often been called upon to secretly build a coffin whenever someone passed away in Longyan and its neighboring villages. In fact, this state policy was seen as so unacceptable that when it was first announced in Longyan, people claimed that some ailing elderly persons had committed suicide or, in the most miraculous cases, had willed their own timely deaths to beat the deadline for the launch of mandatory cremation. For those who missed the small window between the policy's announcement and its enforcement, the one alternative to wholesale defiance and violation of the policy was to claim exemption as a subject under the rule and protection of a foreign state. "If you have legal status elsewhere, then the government can't drag you to be burned," Old Man Liu explained. This is why desires for a U.S. green card had become a local epiphenomenon among Longyan's elderly population.

Here we can glimpse how the social life of IDs can extend well beyond the boundaries of nation-states to a larger cosmology of heavens and hells, where one looked for smooth passage beyond the territories of this-worldly life. In particular, by reframing the very terms for thinking about personhood beyond life itself, elderly applicants suggested that what was at stake in IDs was not just the biopolitical subject of reproductive and economic value but also the *cosmo*-political subject of karmic credit and rebirth. As I discovered, differentiated mobility—the submission to or mastery of flows and movements—was not just a condition of the living in Longyan. It also extended to the spirits of the deceased, distinguishing the dangerous, wandering limbo of those without proper deaths and burials—the hungry ghosts—from the confident, directional movements of well-cared-for ancestors, some of whom were making their way toward a favorable rebirth with the help of green cards and U.S. dollars. These insinuations of transnational ties into the good afterlife were evident all around in Longyan and will be elaborated on in the next chapter. For now, I close this chapter with one last trace of the divergent paths that state identifications could take.

In a small, hilly cemetery above the Min River in Longyan, I encountered a personal memorial to the achievement of paperwork and its reverberations into the afterlife. Amid a uniform row of marbled tombstones

FIGURE 9 Tombstone duplicating image of the U.S. green card.

etched with full-frontal portraits of bland and somber faces, there stood a three-quarter profile of a young man surrounded by an ornate American seal and a personal alien registration number. For those familiar with INS documents, this image was instantly recognizable as the U.S. green card (figure 9). What was it about a dead man's identification with a nation-state elsewhere that could inspire these etchings of mourning and remembrance? Was it a marker of a lost overseas status or its extension beyond the grave? Though I can offer only questions since I never knew the deceased or his relations, the last section of this book aims to provide some resolution by pursuing a slightly different line of inquiry into another cosmic thing-in-motion: the U.S. dollar.

PART III   *Debts and Diversions*

"FORGET ABOUT ALL THE 'ISMS' [ZHUYI]," Yang Shuhsu told me with a dismissive wave of his hand. This retired cadre went on to explain about his neighbors in Longyan: "Whatever is called 'communism' [gongchan-zhuyi], whatever is called 'capitalism' [zibenzhuyi], they really don't have the slightest clue. There's really only one thing they all understand," he concluded, "and that one thing is money."

Yang Shushu was not the first person to suggest that money was the key to understanding the logics of contemporary transformations in Longyan. He was, however, the most explicit in pointing to money as distinct from and irreducible to the "isms" conventionally used to evaluate social change in post-Mao China. Capitalism? Communism? Such designations had little purchase for those managing complexity amid the flux of everyday life in Longyan. Money, on the other hand, could be grasped. In fact, it was exceptionally knowable, Yang Shushu argued—the "one thing" comprehensible to all villagers.

Exactly what kind of "one thing" was money? What made it legible and diagnosable to someone like Yang Shushu as the one thing—a shared singularity among villagers—rather than as a divergence and overflow of many things, potentialities, and effects? To be sure, there was some condescension in this former cadre's assessment of money as a simple knowable object among his common "peasant" neighbors. Yet there was no denying that money often topped the list of reasons people gave for their ongoing projects of emigration. When I asked villagers why they would risk life and limb to travel clandestinely through hazardous human smuggling networks to reach the United States, no response was repeated more often than the Chinese-U.S. exchange rate at the time: *ba bi yi* (8 to 1). U.S. dollars, many openly proclaimed, were simply "bigger" (*bijiao da*) and "better" (*bijiao hao*) than Chinese RMB.

Yet as I learned much later in my fieldwork, money also turned out to be more ambiguous in other common sayings people quietly shared with each other in their intimate circles (see chapter 5). Despite the seeming certainty of public pronouncements and the elegance of numerical equations (for example, the ratio of 8:1), money's simplicity as the "one thing" held in common in village life turned out to be a more tenuous proposition. After all, as another villager, Zhang Yuan, was apt to remind me, sometimes in a register of longing and optimism and other times out of caution and despondence, "with money, one can do *anything*."

Part III of this book examines the tensions and resonances in money's circulation through Longyan as both singularity and multiplicity, both a thing and no-thing. In particular, I am interested in the various claims and practices that enable money to cohere as one thing knowable, however contingently, above and beyond its divergent possibilities as the agent of anything. In this case, I look at how money comes to be recognizable in Longyan, though not without contests and doubts, as the touchstone of generalized debt.

Since Marcel Mauss (1967) pointed to debt and its obligatory claim to repayment as the *modus operandi* of gift economies, there has been no shortage of research on the divergence of transactional orders shaped by the entangling effects of social credit-debt, on the one hand, and the disentangling effects of money capital on the other.[1] Mauss's own intervention was meant to disrupt the economist's origin story of the market's emergence from a world of natural self-interests and utilitarian dispositions to "truck, barter, and exchange" (A. Smith 1999).[2] With its incitement of debts and obligations, the gift as a form of exchange offered a productive counterpoint to the usual seamless tale of the modern economy's development from the commensurability of objects in barter into the equivalence of money in commodity exchange.[3] To point out the persistence and prevalence of the gift (and its debts) in contemporary systems of exchange, as Mauss did, was to interrupt the *homo economicus* narrative of value production, in which money dominated as a social force for extracting personal profit from impersonal transactions.

While debt and money may often conjure distinct modalities of exchange, ethnographic research has also attested to the enmeshments and complicities between these modes in social practice. Claims to social debt can be commodifiable in the form of money, just as money can be circulated as a gift to sustain relations of social indebtedness. Such could be the case even when the ideological opposition between "giving" and "selling" is embraced and articulated by local populations (Akin and Robbins 1999;

Thomas 1991).[4] In fact, far from simply being money's foil, debt can also be seen as an enabler of monetization, especially in the development of money's functions as a currency of trust and a mode of accounting.[5] In arguing for a labor theory of value, Karl Marx himself pointed to the importance of debt and its manipulation in capitalist transactions, through which asymmetries between the labor power advanced as credit by workers and the payment later made in money by capitalists could lead to surplus value.[6] For Marx, the problem of labor's alienation and exploitation was not about money's mediation of equivalence per se but rather its erasure of the remainder owed to workers through the misrecognition and reappropriation of such debt as private surplus at the capitalist's disposal. Disavowing debt disentangled relations of exchange from the promise of ongoing, mutual returns; it enabled the remainder to appear as an alienable thing-in-itself subject to zero-sum claims of individual profit with no strings attached.

Ultimately, whether one sees debt as the foil or handmaiden to money's development as capital, we can draw one conclusion from these discussions: debt has a tendency to entangle its various subjects and objects by demanding recognition for remainders across transactions. That such recognition could be denied, as in Marx's analysis of the surplus in wage labor, only emphasizes the very contingencies of debt's hold as a normative figure for ordering the sociality of exchange. To claim debt is to conjure a world of binding, asymmetrical ties in which deferred gains and promised returns have not yet, if ever, evened out. It requires a commitment to the remainder as an agent of ongoing relationality rather than as an object for appropriation and alienation through exchange. This is not to suggest that recognition of debt always reinforces the social in the nostalgic terms of collective solidarity. If anything, debt's extension of asymmetries in exchange has proven to be a common source of friction in social life, whether it is articulated in the nonmarket form of gift transactions or the capitalized form of financial lending. With respect to the latter, for instance, anthropologists have shown how debt can entangle people in "the market" in profoundly disabling ways even as it claims to extricate them from other disempowering modes of sociality through the promise of money's liberating capacities (Elyachar 2005; Roitman 2003, 2005).

In the case of Longyan, the most obvious starting point for thinking about money and debt is the huge sums people borrowed to support human smuggling ventures. There is no denying that most villagers and their overseas relations have become deeply enmeshed in financial debt over the past two decades of mass migration. By the time I was doing research in Longyan, debt had become such a pervasive mediator of social relations that one could hardly find someone in the village (particularly at the household level) who was not either in the process of securing financing for emigration, paying off loans for past smuggling ventures, or lending funds to others. In fact, it was not at all unusual to find villagers or their overseas relatives simultaneously playing both debtor and creditor, lending money to someone while still paying off a long-standing smuggling debt to someone else. As mentioned in chapter 3, such debt was even embraced as a marker of expansive sociability, a hard-earned achievement that villagers like Lin Mengya touted as confirmation of others' respect and confidence in their credit-ability.

Here liability ceases to be merely incidental, aberrant, and external to the person but instead emerges as a generalized, even ontological, condition (Roitman 2003). It is at this juncture that I focus my query on money's translatability and efficacies as debt in Longyan. Chapters 5–6 explore money's capacity to incite indebtedness as a modality of exchange and sociality amid its more touted dispositions for enabling relations of equivalence, alienation, and commodification. While chapter 5 focuses on the repertoire of ritual and mundane monetary transactions that have worked to stabilize debt as the grounds for value production, chapter 6 examines the everyday frictions and gendered asymmetries that have unsettled the hegemonies of this kind of distributional order. Together, these two chapters look at the ways money's circulation through Longyan could be regulated through claims to debt's entanglements amid strong temptations for its diversion into other things and relations.

CHAPTER FIVE

For Use in Heaven or Hell

The Circulation of the U.S. Dollar among Gods,

Ghosts, and Ancestors

It was the allure of firecrackers—their snap, crackle, and pop somewhere in our midst—that sent Teacher Wang and me headlong into the middle of a long and boisterous funeral procession. I had been in my field site not more than two months when I got my first full sensorial experience of ritual life with the ear-tingling explosion of firecrackers, the canned wails of stone-faced mourners, and the tapping and twirling of the drumming female troupe shuffling past us. Teacher Wang, a city scholar with a nose for ritual, had come in from Fuzhou on this occasion to help me get more settled in the village. But I had barely greeted him off the city bus when I found myself half-jogging to keep up with him as he zipped along the narrow cobblestoned streets in hot pursuit of a funeral in progress.

Following the wafting firecracker smoke, we trailed the parade of mourners as they carried the deceased through every major walkway of the village. Sometimes, with a quick sprint in anticipation of the ritual route ahead, we would intersect with the crowd of onlookers dotting both sides of the road and watch the approaching procession, announced first by the exploding red confetti of firecrackers and a brightly painted quartet of unsmiling young women. Decked in pink satin, the women carried color-coordinated giant paper lanterns and red lacquered signs announcing the identity of the deceased and bearing messages of farewell and good luck, including the prosaic "Have a safe journey" (*Yilu pingan*). A brass marching band of army-clad performers, all somber, weary, and middle-aged, followed with a mid-tempo militaristic elegy as if summoning the old spirit of Mao to rally a small, lethargic throng of stoic mourners behind them. More young women in pink flashed by with multicolored sequined and paper wreaths the size of patio umbrellas before we got our first glimpse of the deceased in the form of a black and white picture. The photo of a frowning old man gazing blankly into the camera had all the personality of a passport photo. Yet mounted on a polished wooden shrine and carried along the shoulders of four men like an imperial sedan, this image floated by with a certain foreboding and depersonalized authority. From behind the photo, the soft lilts and whines of traditional Chinese music emanated from a ragtag troupe of erhu, gong, and cymbal players and set the tone for the passing of the coffin. This was followed by a group of the deceased's closest kin, who had wrapped white cloth around their waists and heads. While few actually shed tears, a couple of dry-eyed mourners held portable boom boxes that emitted heart-wrenching cries and moans on cassette. After a second marching band and more mourners passed by, a troupe of female performers in red Tang-style costumes shimmied down the road to the beat of drums tied around their hips. At the tail end of the procession, two men balanced baskets of incense and food offerings while another trio of men accompanied a cartload of firecrackers. With wads of tissue paper stuffed in their ears, the latter group lit and flung large red coils of firecrackers with abandon and with a certain swaggering nonchalance about the proximity of exploding gunpowder to onlookers and to themselves.

As I stood mesmerized at the end of the procession and more than a bit shell-shocked as the firecrackers went off all around me, Teacher Wang remained strangely indifferent, his attention fully consumed by a single flimsy piece of yellow paper he had picked up off the ground. "It's *mailuqian!*" he exclaimed as he nudged it into my view. Amid the hoopla of the parade, I had not noticed the paper bills scattered along the ritual route until Teacher Wang pointed to the ground in front of us. Literally translated as "money to buy the road," this was ritual money used to secure the road from the threat of ghosts and demons as the spirit of the deceased made the journey to the afterlife. Here was an artifact in familiar form—a plain yellow bill with rough slits down the middle—long written about by observers and scholars of Chinese ritual life and alternately called mock-money or spirit money.[1] As I glanced down at the paper-strewn street before us, though, another oddly familiar currency came into view. "Is that a U.S. dollar?" I asked Teacher Wang. "Oh, yes," he snickered. "It's the *modern* kind."

Teacher Wang's bemused response provided a segue into a personal anecdote with a punch line. Apparently, he told me, his own mother had scattered this kind of modern spirit money along the funeral route in his home village when his father passed away. Shortly after the burial, his mother arranged a conversation with the deceased father through a spirit medium to find out about how he was settling into the afterworld. "All those U.S. dollars you sent me," the father griped. "They're no good. The bank here won't exchange them!"

Like most Fuzhounese urbanites observing the spectacular revitalization of popular religion in the nearby countryside, Teacher Wang told me this story with a good deal of perplexed humor and shrugging embarrassment over the pesky remnants of peasant backwardness that have stubbornly shadowed the signs of China's modernity. "Religious beliefs have to do with every aspect of Chinese history and culture," he told me with equal parts fascination and chagrin. "Look at all the great Chinese inventions," he continued with some amusement. "With gunpowder, what did we do? We made firecrackers to celebrate the Lunar New Year and so forth. With the compass, we practiced *feng shui*.[2] And with paper money? We burned it for gods, for ancestors. Meanwhile, Westerners were using these inventions to conquer the rest of the world."

Reminiscent of what Michael Herzfeld (2005) has described as the embarrassment of cultural intimacy (also see Shryock 2004), Teacher Wang's humorous remarks simultaneously recognized and disavowed popular religion's importance to China's cultural and historical development. As Teacher Wang saw it, spirit money in U.S. dollars was simply the newest sign of a long-standing Chinese disposition to squander the potential resources and tools of modernity on the irrationalities of ritual life. While the critique of spirit money as inherently worthless in form (as "fake" money) and practice (as a destructive act of scattering and burning) was familiar, Teacher Wang's anecdote was uniquely funny because the spirit world itself rejected the value of this "modern" form of currency. Even the Bank of Hell, an invention of people with "low culture," had its rational limits. The ultimate butt of the joke, though, remained the well-meaning country folks, who kept spinning the futile wheel of superstition (*mixin*) despite their good intentions and desires for modern prosperity.

Of course, this punch line works only if we assume a series of binary oppositions between modernity and superstition, real money and spirit money, elite rationality and peasant irrationality that make the circulation of U.S. dollars fundamentally incompatible with the logics of the Bank of Hell. Without denying the structuring power of binary logic, this chapter highlights the instability of such oppositional categories in the very task of people trying to stabilize the terms of value production through various totalizing incitements of the order of things. Such a task includes not only those interested in promoting a world of expanding market rationality but also the village worshippers involved in the revitalization of an encompassing ritual economy. While these interests may appear distinct, their differentiation actually depends on the resonance and reproduction of similar boundary-making projects, which draw from overlapping and finite pools of material and symbolic resources. As I will show, through the circulation of the U.S. dollar, villagers themselves tried to firm up certain boundaries between non-peasant elites and themselves, productivity and waste, progress and backwardness, in order to anchor newfound wealth in a meaningful and legitimizing world order. However, my interests here concern not only how such boundaries were drawn but also how they were maintained through and *in spite of* everyday encounters and practices that, in their diversity and idiosyncrasies, had a way of exceeding what Pierre Bourdieu has called the "generative schemas" of *habitus* (1977). My opening description of the funeral procession should already hint at some of the excesses of praxis that defied easy recuperation in conventional schemas like "tradition" versus "modernity."

This chapter examines not only how people made sense of the specific money form of wealth but also how the distinctions of cash—as U.S. dollars (USD) and Chinese RMB and as spiritual and market currencies—became meaningful markers of modernity, productivity, and morality through everyday practices of exchange. As anthropologist Alaina Lemon has observed, "Not all cash is alike" (1998, 22), so money, despite its much-touted capacities for abstraction and equivalence, can also crystallize certain social differences and asymmetries through its concrete manifestations and distinctive flows as various kinds of currencies.[3] Drawing from insights about the boundary-making (and breaking) effects of money and other objects in exchange (Gilbert 2005; F. Myers 2004; Spyer 1998; Thomas 1991; Zelizer 1994), my task here is ultimately to understand how Longyan residents made distinctions among forms of monetary wealth and why, specifically, it seemed appropriate to scatter the ritual version of U.S. dollars alongside the coarse yellow bills that have long fascinated foreign (and native) observers of China as markers of tradition and superstition. I approach this discussion from the very materiality of monetary notes as they were perceived, felt, handled, and exchanged in the making of distinctions in Longyan (Foster 1998; Keane 2002). This is an aspect often effaced in the analysis of money as a mere abstraction of value but that, as I argue, needs to be restored in order to make full sense of local differentiations between cash and its circulation in spiritual and market cosmologies.

In God(s) We Trust

Foreign observers of Chinese popular religion have long been fascinated with the materialism and monetization of the afterlife, where, unlike in Judeo-Christian cosmologies, spirits still needed food, shelter, and especially money after leaving their mortal bodies behind. Some Chinese even imagined a central bank in hell through which living relatives could remit money to their ancestors to pay off cosmic debts incurred during previous lives and to help buy their way into a more favorable rebirth in this world.[4] Notwithstanding some nuanced differences in the analyses of Chinese popular religion, there has been a general consensus among scholars that such other-worldly currencies roughly fall into three hierarchically ranked forms and distinct spheres of exchange: the most valuable—gold—form of money was typically reserved for the gods (occasionally for ancestors), middling silver for middling ancestors (occasionally for ghosts), and small change for the poor and hungry ghosts (never for the gods).[5] Yet while scholars have highlighted a rich array of spirit monies—gold, silver, copper, and material goods—and their various flows from this world to the next, few have ever mentioned the circulation of state-backed paper currencies, let alone the U.S. dollar, in the Chinese ritual economy. Though we know from some missionary accounts that spirit money in the form of "foreign cash" has been present in Fuzhou at least since the mid-nineteenth century,[6] very little attention has been devoted to this kind of currency in the academic literature.[7]

It is useful, then, to begin with a closer look at the dollar form of spirit money. The bill itself replicates not only the precise dimensions of a U.S. $100 note but also all of that note's key aesthetic features, from its greenish-gray ink and the filigreed weave around the border to its bureaucratic indices of authenticity—the official seals, serial number, and series date.[8] Like the actual $100 note, the spirit form also provides a central iconic figure of authority and announces its sphere of legitimacy in the form of a three-dimensional banner floating above the figure. But in lieu of Benjamin Franklin and "The United States of America," the spirit money has substituted the image of the Jade Emperor (Yuhuang Dadi), the highest

FIGURE 10 Spirit money in U.S. $100 denomination.

FIGURE 11 Actual $100 bill.

deity in the Daoist pantheon, and the phrase "For Use in Heaven or Hell" (*Tiangtang Difu Tongyong*). Above the banner, the words "Federal Reserve Bank Note" have been replaced by "the Bank of Hell" (Mingtong Ying-hang). In fact, if we compare the spirit dollar and the actual note (figures 10 and 11), we will notice how carefully the producers of the spirit money have substituted all the institutional signs structuring the U.S. currency with logical counterparts for the afterlife. Not only has the Federal Reserve been replaced by the spirit world's own currency-issuing institution, the Bank of Hell, but the Reserve's bureaucratic leaders, the secretary of the treasury and the treasurer of the United States, have also been supplanted by authorities from popular Chinese religion. In the bottom right of the U.S. note, where the signature of the secretary of the treasury is imprinted, we now find the red seal of the Jade Emperor (Yu Huang) under the title "Bank President" (Hang Zhang), while on the bottom left, the signature of the U.S. treasurer has been replaced by the authorizing seal of Yama (Yan Luo), the King of Hell, under the title "Bank Vice President" (Fu Hang Zhang).

This series of substitutions supports a bureaucratic logic of the afterlife that is consistent with other anthropological and missionary accounts of Chinese popular religion, particularly along China's southern coast and in Taiwan.[9] Longyan residents saw the Jade Emperor as the head of a highly elaborated bureaucracy of gods with specific jurisdictions and functions for overseeing the realm of the living as well as the dead. These deities ranged from territorial gods, who oversaw all activity within a specific village district, to specialized ones, who controlled particular aspects of well-being like female fertility or safety at sea. Under the Jade Emperor's supervision, all these gods were expected to operate according to certain regulations and were held accountable by their superiors, to whom they periodically reported. Within this structure, Yama, the King of Hell, functioned as the administrative head over the entire world of the dead, which consisted of courts for judging the lives of the newly deceased and a hierarchy of ten hells (and sub-hells within them) for meting out various punishments in preparing the dead for eventual rebirth (see Eberhard 1967; Orzech 1994; Teiser 1993 on the structuring of hell). Designating the Jade Emperor and Yama as president and vice president respectively of an underworld bank made sense in a bureaucratically imagined cosmology where they already occupied similar positions along the hierarchical chain of command.

The existence of U.S. spirit money also suggests the complexity of a deeply material understanding of the spirit world, where money is but one need among many for sustaining the well-being of deities and the dead. Alongside the U.S. dollar, there was in fact not only a variety of spirit money but also a range of material goods that villagers transmitted to the spirit world. The diversity of material needs among spirits was evident on the shelves of the several ritual specialty stores in Longyan, where paper models of prestige items like gold jewelry, American sports cars, and cell phones could be found alongside simulacra of clothing, umbrellas, and mahjong sets. One could even purchase a paper mansion the size of a large dollhouse, fully equipped with furniture, phones, TVs, and even female servants for the enjoyment of ancestors awaiting rebirth. As for spirit money, whole shelves in these stores displayed sheets of gold and silver in various sizes, while others contained stacks of state-issued bank notes including USD, RMB, Japanese yen, and Hong Kong currency. Like the spirit form of the USD, these other bank notes also relied on a logic of substitution to index their ritual purposes. In particular, all of these different bank notes were united by the image of the Jade Emperor, which uniformly replaced the state-specific icons of authority as if reordering these various currencies under a common spiritual sphere of exchange (figure 12).

Clearly, the producers of dollar spirit notes worked painstakingly from actual U.S. currency. Through a series of subtle substitutions, the spirit money retained all the formal aesthetic properties of the dollar bill while effacing all content that specifically referenced the United States. In this way, someone who had never encountered U.S. dollars would have no textual clues to identify the spirit money as U.S. currency, while others, like me, could recognize the formal resemblance to the dollar even as the bills lay partially obscured and trampled along the road. Longyan residents were no strangers to actual dollars given the massive and steady influx of overseas remittances from the United States, which in 1999 were estimated at $2,000 per capita (Ji 1999). In fact, dollars had become so prevalent in the local economy that the measure word used for banknotes, *zhang*, commonly referred to a $100 bill. For instance, when people said, "He just wired two bills to my account" or "I still have three bills in my purse," they were referring to $200 and $300 respectively. It should be no surprise then that the artifact we have been discussing is modeled specifically on the $100 note—both the front *and* the back, which duplicates the central image of Independence Hall in Philadelphia (figures 13 and 14).

Familiarity with U.S. dollars and their spiritual counterparts was not widespread outside of places like Longyan, with its huge overseas-connected population. The conditions for recognition became clear to me during one of my weekend trips to Fuzhou City when I excitedly waved my newfound artifact in front of a couple of friends who had never encountered genuine U.S. dollars. Though these city friends could identify these notes as spirit money, they were in fact quite shocked when I pointed out that these bills were in U.S. denominations. In contrast, the dollar form of this spirit money was evident to Longyan residents across distinctions of age, gender, class, and religious affiliation. It also seemed rather obvious to them that only the living who possessed actual dollars should remit spirit dollars to the dead in the first place.

FIGURE 12 Various spirit currencies with unifying images of the Jade Emperor. From top: Chinese RMB, Japanese yen, and Hong Kong dollar.

FIGURE 13 Back of U.S. dollar spirit money with image of Independence Hall in Philadelphia.

FIGURE 14 Back of actual $100 bill.

Whenever I asked why USD were sent to the spirit world, people typically conveyed the obviousness of such transactions in one of two ways. The first and more knee-jerk response to my question involved a quizzical look, followed by matter-of-fact statements like, "Well, because they have relatives in the United States," or "Well, because they happen to be 'American guests.'" The "well" (*la* in Mandarin) that punctuated these statements always indirectly emphasized the obviousness of the answer to what must have appeared like a very odd and stupid question. In the second and more self-effacing response, a small chuckle or shrug would usually preface the casual observation, "Oh, they're just making *mixin* (superstition)" or "It's just doing *mixin* (superstition)." These statements also were offered as if they were self-evident. But in this case, the use of a seemingly pejorative and opaque term like *mixin* had the double effect of obfuscating the ritual practices at hand. It was as if these practices were simply too trivial for a more cogent description. But what in fact was being *done* in the name of "superstition"?

Making Money, Making Mixin

Here it may be helpful to trace a brief genealogy of the notion of *mixin*. By all accounts, *mixin*, meaning "false belief" or "superstition," is not a term native to China. It probably entered the Chinese vocabulary, along with the contemporary word for religion, *zongjiao*, through Japanese translations of Western terminology around the late nineteenth or early twentieth century. In fact, *mixin* and *zongjiao* seemed to emerge as mutually constitutive concepts. Together, they worked to define the boundary between more institutionalized and permissible forms of religiosity and their heterodox and illicit counterparts at the turn of the last century (Anagnost 1987, 1994; Bosco 2003; Feuchtwang 2001; Feuchtwang and Wang 1991; Gladney 1994).[10] Taken up by Chinese reformists between the end of the Qing dynasty and the beginning of the Republican Era, *mixin* became a core concept against which the project for Chinese modernity and nation building was first defined. In fact, campaigns to "eradicate *mixin*," involving the persecution of shamans and the destruction of local temples, were already being launched in the name of a modernizing China by various regional administrators in the 1910s and later by the ruling Nationalist Party in the 1920s (Duara 1991, 1995). While such early campaigns against "superstition" were not as widespread or as notorious as later CCP crackdowns on popular religion, it is noteworthy how much continuity there has been in the deployment of *mixin* since its emergence as a popular neologism in the early twentieth century. Even amid ample evidence of popular religion's resurgence in the reform era (Chao 1999; Chau 2006; Dean 1993; Feuchtwang and Wang 1991; Kipnis 2001; Siu 1990; Tan 2006; M. Yang 2000), the category of *mixin* has not disappeared from official discourse so much as it has been pragmatically redefined to target practices mainly involving direct economic fraud, physical harm, or perceived threats to political order (the last as presented, for example, by the Falun Gong) while allowing most other ritual activities to operate under the more permissible categories of "custom," "tradition," and "folk belief" (Feuchtwang and Wang 1991). Whether used narrowly to crack down on particular ritual practices or broadly to criminalize all religious life, *mixin* has proven to be a persistent, if floating, signifier of lack and illegitimacy shared by various state regimes across the conventional Republican, Mao, and post-Mao divides. However defined, its illicitness as unauthorized practice has remained intact.

This pejorative connotation of the term only makes villagers' matter-of-fact descriptions of spirit money as the "doing" or "making" of *mixin* all the more curious in contemporary Longyan. The villagers were far from unaware of the negative implications of the term. Longyan, after all, has had its share of outspoken critics since the Republican Era who have singled out *mixin* as an obstacle to village development. While reading the memoirs of Longyan officials who were active in the 1930s and '40s, for instance, I was always struck by how they felt compelled to undercut their vivid descriptions of the various temples and ritual activities in their hometown with knowing, reproachful reminders of the backward nature of *mixin* and its local practitioners (J. Chen 1984; Li 1987; Zheng 1983). In the contemporary era, Longyan worshippers also regularly reminded me of their trying times under state socialism through common complaints of how "the cadres wouldn't let us do *mixin*." This seemed especially evident during the Cultural Revolution, when by all village accounts, spirit money was one of the many things that disappeared from public life after local cadres arrested and persecuted the one ritual paper maker and proprietor in the village for abetting counterrevolutionary *mixin*. While, like other aspects of Chinese popular religion, spirit money's reappearance on village streets has been generally seen as a post-Mao phenomenon, people were also quick to note that official crackdowns on ritual life persisted well into the mid-1990s of the reform era, during which occasional fines, arrests, and even police violence continued to shape the conditions of public worship in Longyan.

It is interesting that while village worshippers often singled out cadres as the source of their past troubles, in present-day Longyan, the most vocal critics of *mixin*, or "superstition," as we will refer to it here, have not turned out to be local officials at all. Instead, criticism has come predominantly from Longyan's small corps of teachers, as well as from outside observers like Teacher Wang and some higher-level officials who saw popular religion as a terrible drain on village resources and a continual obstacle to Longyan's modernization (see chapter 2).[11] In contrast to these two vociferous groups, village officials have been strangely subdued about the recent revitalization of ritual life in Longyan, often preferring to change the subject when I broached it in conversation or, at the very most, offering some mild apology for it as a rather harmless, if retrograde, survival of old village traditions. Some contemporary China scholars have suggested that the softening of official attitudes toward religion in the post-Mao era can be linked to state initiatives for attracting overseas Chinese investment, which has often worked by appealing to the nostalgic desires of diasporic Chinese to visit and/or restore old temples, ancestral cults, and other community rites in their home villages (Dean 1993, 1998; Eng 2006; Feuchtwang 2001; Feuchtwang and Wang 1991; Lin 1993; Liu 1998; Tan 2006; Thunø 2001; Woon 1990). Considering that 85 percent of Longyan households have members abroad, it certainly seems plausible that local officials' current stance had something to do with nurturing overseas investments in the village.

While officials have openly embraced and promoted the flow of remittances into Longyan through public speeches and written reports about the village, no one, let alone cadres, has been particularly interested in linking the resurgence of "superstition" to money's motivating effects on the deregulation of ritual life. This is not to suggest that people were simply victims of misrecognition, unable to locate the "real" source of the village's current success in revitalizing local popular religious practices. Rather, willful silences and active disavowals were at the very heart of official complicity with worshippers. They made it possible for villagers to recognize and reclaim the productivity of ritual life, including its monetary entanglements, in the distinctly defiant terms of "doing *mixin.*" Describing spirit money transactions in these terms entailed two things at once. First, it highlighted the continual illicitness of these practices, which, despite local cadres' passive tolerance, remained outside official state validation. Second and perhaps more important, it resituated "superstition" as an object of practice rather than of belief, as something "made" and "done" by its practitioners against the persistent threat of its undoing by disapproving state agents. To describe spirit money transactions in this way was to both acknowledge and recast the illicit as a morally legitimate, if not officially sanctioned, site of village practice and sociality. From human smuggling to undocumented labor overseas, certainly no one could deny that illicitness saturated village strategies for achieving prosperity. What is worth teasing out in the remainder of this chapter is how another set of illicit practices—spirit money transactions—enabled the village project of value production to be claimed as both distinct from and superior to the project of money making at home in China. To do so, I begin by sketching the pragmatics of ritual exchange in Longyan.

Some Rules of Exchange (or How to Get Ahead in the Afterlife)

Chen Mingming, a gregarious mother of two in her mid-thirties, inadvertently became my guide to the world of spirit money after accompanying me to see another funeral procession. This funeral was the third in a row I had seen with spirit USD scattered along the ground. Like other Longyan residents I had questioned, Chen Mingming offered similar responses about overseas connections and "doing superstition" when I asked her about the significance of these USD notes. Perhaps sensing my continual puzzlement over these answers, she explained that people of her generation and younger simply did not delve too deeply into the intricacies of "doing superstition." There were, however, some older villagers to whom people always turned for such knowledge, and she offered to take me to see them. The next day, Chen Mingming introduced me to one of these elders over the dusty glass counter of a tiny general store at the far end of the main commercial street in Longyan.

"The Boss" (Laoban), as Chen Mingming called him, was a lean old man in a gray Mao shirt with a toothy grin and Coke-bottle glasses. He was somewhere in his mid-seventies and had run this little store for a couple of decades. When Chen Mingming explained that I wanted to understand spirit money, the Boss enthusiastically began to pull stacks of different bills off shelves and even disappeared into a back room to rummage for some more unusual options. Meanwhile, his middle-aged daughter, who worked the counter with him, began to explain the array of spirit money before us. She called the plain yellow bills we had seen at funerals "small change" (*lingqian*) and explained that they were the smallest denomination of spirit money. Because ghosts were "like beggars" (*xiang qigai*) in the spirit world, they were the common recipients of such small change, she said. In fact, these plain yellow bills were the only kind of money ghosts usually received from the living. Another kind of currency, which the Boss's daughter called "ghost money" (*guiqian*), turned out not to be money at all but coarse sheets of paper with inked images of material goods like clothing, eyeglasses, and shoes (figure 15). Along with "small change" notes, these representations of nonmonetary handouts were at

FIGURE 15 Spirit money for ghosts.

the bottom of the hierarchy of spirit currencies, where they circulated mainly as alms for begging ghosts.[12] In fact, funeral processions were one of the few exceptions when ghosts received something other than small change and basic goods. On these occasions, the scattering of USD for ghosts highlighted the special importance people placed on securing the journey of the newly deceased to the afterlife. It also pointed to the heightened danger of ghosts toward those in the liminal state between the worlds of the living and the dead for whom small change and basic handouts were not enough.

For the newly dead, the difference between becoming an ancestor and a ghost hinged on the outcome of this journey to the afterlife, which Longyan residents imagined as uncertain and dangerous. There was no guarantee that one would reach the first level of hell, where court judgments of lives were made, especially without the support of living relatives who were responsible for sending a steady stream of food, material goods, and money for the entire period of travel. One needed not only money to bribe ghosts and demons who stood in the way but also nourishment in order to sustain a journey that some say lasted seven days and others as much as forty-nine days.[13] Without money and other material resources, the newly dead were susceptible to starvation and to losing their way on the road to hell. Not surprisingly, those who failed in their journeys into the spirit world were themselves imagined as "wandering" or "hungry" ghosts—that is, lost and impoverished spirits who languished in a state of limbo between death and rebirth.

While the sphere of ghosts was marked by the meager circulation of small change and simple handouts, the sphere of ancestors was distinguished by an abundance of prestigious goods—silk dresses, jade bracelets, sports cars, and mansions—which signaled an afterlife of security and comfort while the ancestors' spirits awaited rebirth. Ancestors were also entitled to spirit currencies of superior value, and the Boss and his daughter kindly organized these for us into two separate piles. First, among various stacks of spirit currency representing precious metals, the Boss singled out the smallest sheets of gold and silver as common offerings to ancestors. The larger versions of these sheets were deemed "too big" for ancestors and appropriate as offerings only for gods. "This kind we've had a very long time," the Boss explained as he passed around a coarse yellow sheet pasted over with tinted gold foil. "Before liberation, they were already available."[14] When I asked about their availability after liberation, the Boss continued, "It was difficult because the local cadre opposed it; they wouldn't let us do superstition." But he also recalled that some people managed to buy the coarse yellow paper and tinted foil that were used to make this spirit money, and they would cut, paste, and assemble these materials into proper form in the privacy of their own homes. The Boss smiled and shook his head in wonderment at the resourcefulness of people determined to use spirit money in the Mao era. Some people, he noted, even made currency for ghosts by covertly drawing material goods by hand on sheets of paper about a quarter the size of those currently being sold in the open.

It was not until the 1980s that mass-produced versions of these spirit currencies began to appear at stores like his, the Boss informed me. Moreover, beyond these few forms of spirit money, a whole plethora of "newer ones" (bijiao xinde) grew popular among Longyan villagers through the '80s. These constituted the second pile on the Boss's counter and consisted of various state-issued bank notes, including the USD. Like the small sheets of gold and silver, these kinds of spirit money were mainly earmarked for the use of ancestors. However, unlike the transfer of precious metals, the circulation of different bank notes was subject to certain restrictions in the spirit world.

"Before, in the '8os," the Boss explained, "Hong Kong dollars were the most popular because everyone fled to Hong Kong. Japanese yen too, because a lot of people went there. Now people all want these," the Boss said, while poking at a stack of USD with his index finger. "Let me tell you," the Boss's daughter piped in. "In Fuzhou [City], Putian, and other places, they all sell these USD. But they're not like us over here—not *this* popular. We just have so many 'American guests' now."

The logic of circulation could be summed up as follows: people sent only the kinds of foreign currency to ancestors that they themselves were receiving from overseas relatives. In this sense, giving USD to ancestors could not be seen as an act of wish fulfillment for wealth so much as an extension of existing monetary resources from the living to the dead. Simply stated, spirit USD functioned as overseas remittances for ancestors. The Boss noted that there were even penalties imposed on those who sent foreign currencies to ancestors without appropriate overseas connections. "When the money arrives down there," the Boss explained, "they [the gods] know who has relatives abroad and who doesn't. So if you don't, they can lock you up [in jail]." Given these rules of exchange, it made sense that Teacher Wang's father would be denied access to USD since his family had no overseas connections. In fact, it would seem that the father was treated rather mercifully considering there were no complaints of jail time to Teacher Wang's mother.

As for the RMB notes, the Boss told me that anyone could send them to ancestors, no doubt because everyone had access to this kind of currency. However, he also confessed that the RMB, unlike the USD, was not a popular choice among Longyan residents. In my subsequent survey of all the ritual specialty stores in the area, most of the store owners also noted the unpopularity of spirit RMB notes, which tended to linger on shelves collecting dust, while USD and the other more traditional forms of spirit money sold briskly.[15] In fact, despite their wide availability in stores, I myself never saw RMB used in any ritual practices in Longyan. Even on the annual Tomb-Sweeping Day (Qingmingjie), when the specialty stores all reported peak sales, RMB could not be found among the grand displays of spirit money covering ancestral tombs in the hills above Longyan.

Spirit USD, in contrast, could not be more pervasive as money for Longyan's dead and as an index of the overseas connections extending into the afterlife.

Setting the Gold Standard

On the first and fifteenth days of each month on the lunar calendar, throngs of Longyan residents could be found as early as 4 a.m. setting stacks of gold spirit money ablaze at one of the many temples in the village. Unlike the coarse yellow sheets or spirit USD scattered at funerals or graves, the large gold and silver bills fed to the flames on these occasions were meant for the resident gods of the temples where the activities took place. Typically, worshippers—mainly middle-aged women and the elderly, each representing a different household—visited a set number of temples where they felt they received cosmic protection and blessings. At these various sites, they burned incense, prayed, and prostrated themselves before the shrines of gods and offered spirit money by burning it in large metal bins or ceramic and tiled kilns. Often worshippers also sought divination from the gods, finding answers by tossing bamboo sticks (*chouqian*), interpreting almanacs, employing spirit mediums, and turning to a number of other methods. On these days, the circuit of worship always included a visit to the district god who oversaw the part of the village where the worshipper lived. It might also include the temple of a deity designated as the protector of one's household or a god who oversaw a special interest. Generally, the criteria for visiting temples boiled down to the worshipper's notion of the divine efficacy, or *ling*, of the resident god. The more efficacy the god was thought to have, the more spirit money was burned at that god's temple.

No doubt these bimonthly visits with the gods constituted the largest transfers of funds to the spirit world on a regular basis. The spirit money burned on these occasions represented the most valuable of the gold and silver currencies, the largest of the tinted yellow sheets the Boss had declared too big for ancestors. While they resembled the coarse yellow notes given as "spare change" to ghosts and the tinted notes offered to ancestors, these bills usually consisted of superior materials—finer paper and more lustrous foil. These bills were at the top of the hierarchy of spirit currencies and were circulated exclusively among the gods. Longyan residents often called these tinted notes "gold money" (*jinqian*) and "silver money"

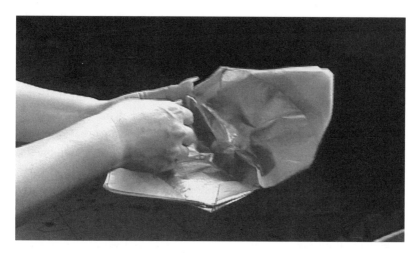

FIGURE 16 Gold spirit money for the gods.

(*yinqian*) in recognition of their status as precious metals in the spirit world. Between the two precious metals, the gold notes were considered more valuable than the silver of equal size. When the largest gold sheets were meticulously folded into the shapes of fans or boats, they became the most valuable currency among the spirit monies, literally serving as the gold standard for the spiritual economy (figure 16).

In this cosmology, currencies seemed to circulate within a set of nested hierarchies, with ghosts having access to the fewest and least valuable currencies while the sphere of ancestors and gods encompassed successively more diverse and valuable kinds of money.[16] The concept of nested hierarchies resonates quite strongly with other accounts of the structural ordering of spirit currencies in southern China and Taiwan (Feuchtwang 1974, 2001; McCreery 1990; Seaman 1982; A. Wolf 1978). What is notable here and is not mentioned elsewhere is that USD occupied a middle position along the hierarchy of value; they were highly prized for ancestors but not quite good enough for gods. People did tell me that theoretically one could give gods spirit USD, just as one could give ancestors "small change" notes and ghost money. However, while I have seen Longyan residents occasionally burn small change and basic goods for ancestors, I have never observed gods receiving any kind of spirit money besides the largest gold and silver currencies.

It is interesting that while residents usually did not offer spirit USD to gods, they did actively seek divine recognition for the terrestrial USD they gave for temple renovations and other ritual events for the gods. For instance, it was common to burn receipts of temple donations so that "the gods would know how much money you gave," as one woman informed me. Increasingly, such contributions were being made in USD and recorded on temple receipts and ledgers as USD amounts. Nowhere were these dollar amounts more prominently displayed than on giant stone steles or red donor posters at temples, which since the early 1990s have featured huge and growing lists of USD contributions alongside shrinking ones of RMB. In fact, though gods rarely received spirit USD from villagers, they seemed to be the most public and privileged recipients of the terrestrial USD remitted from overseas. According to local officials' estimate, in 1997 three-fifths of all incoming overseas remittances were going to ritual activities and the renovation of temples and houses in Longyan (and I would add that the renovation of temples was taking priority over houses).[17] In just three years, between 1994 and 1997, residents of one village district had donated an estimated $150,000 for the renovation of three joint temples in their neighborhood.[18] Outside this particular district, there were more than twenty other temples in Longyan that had either been newly built or significantly renovated with the support of dollar remittances over the last decade.

Whether the contributions to temples were given as USD or RMB notes, they were largely understood as the fruits of transnational migration, mainly generated in the United States. This transnational connection became especially clear to me when I visited one of the temples; the overseer guided me through the newly renovated space by pointing out the USD price of every new feature and religious object, as well as the transnational status of the contributor responsible for each improvement. Pointing to an intricately sculpted altar or an equally elaborate floral vase, he would ask me repeatedly, "Guess—how much is this?" The answer would inevitably begin with an amount in USD—"Five hundred U.S. dollars" or "Twelve hundred U.S. dollars"—and it would be followed by a short description of its source—"an old overseas Chinese living in New York" or "an 'American guest' who owns a restaurant there." At another temple, the overseer took out a large red poster listing the names of all contributors for a Lunar New Year ritual and proceeded to describe the transnational connections and emigration history of each person listed *and* that person's family members. Not surprisingly, the majority were described as "overseas Chinese" or, more specifically, "American guests."

Such public displays of ritual expenditures in China have commonly been analyzed by scholars as a means for worshippers to gain status or "face" (*mianzi*) in their social world (Basu 1991; Oxfeld 1992; M. Yang 2000). Local teachers and other critics have explained temple contributions to me in similar terms, albeit with a pejorative emphasis on *mianzi* as "a kind of vanity" rather than on its functionalist implications as social capital. Yet while few villagers would disagree that the social status of contributors mattered in the public display of U.S. dollars, my interactions with worshippers and temple caretakers also suggested something more complicated. Even in the most boastful accounts of dollar donations and transnational connections, temple caretakers never promoted the "face" of any specific contributor so much as they emphasized the cumulative divine efficacy of the temple's resident god. Similarly, while most worshippers were not without their suspicions of the vanity of some of the donors inscribed on temple steles, such critiques were always offered as contrasts to their own ritual expenditures, which few failed to attribute at least partly if not wholly to the efficacy of the gods.

Cosmic Debt and the Efficacy of Wealth

The importance of divine efficacy was supported by the way Longyan worshippers talked about temple contributions as repayments rather than as gifts. As in other Chinese communities engaged with popular religion, a concept of deep cosmic debt informed Longyan residents in their ritual uses of both spirit and actual money (Brokaw 1991; Cole 1998; Eberhard 1967; Hou 1975; Teiser 1988). This debt was understood both as a result of personal wrongdoing against other people accumulated in past and present lives and as indebtedness to gods for giving the dead new chances to settle their karmic accounts through reincarnation. While spirits also incurred debt to the parents, especially mothers, who had conceived them and suffered to give birth and raise them, they relied even more on gods, who provided them with new bodies and fates in rebirth.[19] In this sense, gods could be seen as the fundamental creditors of debt-ridden spirits, giving them literally a new lease on life and another chance to escape the mortal coil of death and rebirth perpetuated by deep cosmic debt (Hou 1975). This initial line of divine credit made all other accumulations of wealth—money, karmic merit, and otherwise—possible for the living and in this way anchored the entire mortal sphere of value production to the more basic and generative logic of an encompassing spiritual economy. Monetary wealth then could not be taken as mere surplus at the disposal of Longyan residents. Rather, it might be better understood as the material manifestation of one's spiritual solvency, as an extension of good credit, if you will, from gods who could never truly be paid back.

The primary importance of divine credit and the necessity for repaying gods was evident not only by the regularity and size of monetary transfers to deities but also by the way worshippers described these practices. When I asked Longyan villagers about their ritual expenditures, they commonly explained their offerings to gods in two distinct ways. First, worshippers often told me that they gave gods money—in both spirit and market forms—simply out of *xinyi*, a term that translates literally as "heartfelt meaning" and perhaps more accurately as sincerity or good faith. It mainly referred to routine provisions, including daily offerings of food and incense and the bimonthly transfers of spirit money to the gods.[20] These mundane ritual practices could be seen as everyday enactments of devotion and continual reciprocity driven by the initial generosity of the gods and the subsequent indebtedness of the worshippers. Second, beyond these regular offerings, worshippers also made more conspicuous one-time payments to certain gods for fulfilling specific requests. Typically, these offerings completed a kind of oral contract in which the worshipper promised to spend a large sum on behalf of a particular god in return for that god's specific intervention in matters ranging from safety in human smuggling ventures to success in political asylum applications and new businesses overseas.

To determine the compensation for a particular divine service, a worshipper usually made a verbal offer in front of the god's altar and then tossed divination blocks to see the god's response.[21] In this way, the god and worshipper agreed not only to specific amounts but also to the particular uses of the funds—most commonly for temple renovations or the entertainment of the god. In Lin Mengya's case, the god she enlisted for help even specified the kind of entertainment he preferred as compensation for ensuring her husband's successful asylum case in the United States. While it was most common to stage Fuzhounese opera for entertaining the gods,[22] Lin Mengya, in deference to her god's request, opted for showing movies on an outdoor screen instead. "I had already agreed with him [on this]," Lin Mengya said, "and if you say it, you should do it." In meeting her oral agreement with the god, Lin Mengya emphasized the moral authority of her ritual expenditures. Not only did the god meet her request—and in this sense extend her line of cosmic credit—but she also redeemed the divine trust by fulfilling her end of the bargain. Large dollar contributions for temple renovations and for entertaining gods simultaneously highlighted overseas success and, as contractual payments to gods, claimed a divine agency behind success. In this way, temple contributions enacted the moral credit-ability of the successful worshipper. While it was hard to deny the instrumentality of such transactions with the gods, worshippers like Lin Mengya also typically made a point of giving a little something extra—perhaps fifty or a hundred dollars more than stipulated—as an explicit gesture of heartfelt meaning on these occasions. As such, this extra expenditure aimed to neutralize the inherent economism of contractual payments by realigning such instrumental one-time offerings with the more humble and routine enactments of general devotion and indebtedness to the gods.

Ultimately, transfers of funds to the spirit world were imbued with varying degrees of instrumentality and affect that defied easy categorization as purely economic or, for that matter, as capitalistic in Longyan.[23] While offerings to ghosts appeared to be mainly instrumental as a means for preventing potential harm, payments to both ancestors and gods conveyed mixed messages of moral sentiment and rational utility.[24] As reasons for giving ancestral offerings, worshippers often cited the moral imperative of filiality and, to a lesser degree, fears of the wrath of neglected ancestors. Typically, people said they gave spirit USD to ancestors because they wanted to extend the fruits of overseas success as a gesture of continual support and devotion to dearly departed ones. However, they also sometimes noted that it was beneficial for them to make ancestral offerings not only in order to settle their individual cosmic debts to ancestors but also because the debt of the deceased could be inherited by living relatives. In this sense, worshippers made repayments on behalf of both ancestors and themselves to reduce their collective cosmic debt.[25]

Managing such debt was widely recognized in Longyan as part of the calculus for prosperity. This was true even among the professed skeptics and nonbelievers of "superstition," including local officials and teachers who, despite their personal doubts, rarely obstructed the efforts of loved ones to burn spirit money on their behalf. In fact, because it was common for just one family member, usually a wife or mother, to regularly pray and make offerings on behalf of the rest of the houschold, most villagers could be personally agnostic about spirit money transactions while still passively endorse such practices at the collective level as part of their project of value production. As many people like Chen Mingming acknowledged, even if they doubted the efficacy of giving money to the dead, it also could not hurt to have someone else look after their cosmic affairs just in case karmic debt did turn out to be the crucial factor for their well-being and success.

Far from being divisive, this kind of hedging had also been embraced by Longyan's active corps of worshippers as a rationale for the pragmatic upkeep and expansion of money's flow into ritual life. Largely feminized as the domestic duty of wives and mothers, repaying cosmic debt was easily folded into the calculative practices women already assumed as the daily managers of household budgets. But unlike food provisioning and other routine tasks of household management, cosmic debt's importance to family fortunes could rarely be accounted for with any positivist certainty so much as it could be conjured as a possibility that had yet to be disproved and therefore as something that families, especially the women in charge of their daily well-being, could not afford to neglect.

Ironically, after decades of concerted state efforts to erode villagers' faith in the existence of other-worldly agencies, it was precisely on the shared grounds of radical uncertainty that people, whether religious skeptics or practitioners, have come to regard the "doing of superstition" as something worth pursuing, regardless of the question of belief.[26] As part of a larger repertoire of calculative practices, such an "as if" approach to ritual transactions not only highlighted villagers' agnosticism about cosmic debt per se but, more important, it also revealed people's general uncertainty about the very ontology of human fortune—its generative sources, its stabilizing agencies. This uncertainty included widespread doubts about the state's claim to be the ultimate guarantor of this-worldly prosperity, especially given the common condition of insecurity people have struggled with as both state-identified "peasants" and disavowed "illegal aliens."

While the women who routinely sent money to the spirit world were generally less skeptical than others about the productivity of ritual transactions, they also acknowledged that uncertainty itself was integral to their engagements with cosmic debt. As many worshippers agreed, ritual transactions were inherently speculative because it was impossible to pinpoint the bottom line of one's cosmic account and, by extension, one's prospects in this world. Since every human action inherently produced karmic merit or demerit, the balance of cosmic debt was always in flux, its bottom line impossibly obscured through a process of accumulation spread across not only one lifetime of action but also across multiple lives, through which one had no recourse of memory. To scramble the equation of debt and repayment further, every cosmic account was also subject to unknown and unpredictable transfers of demerit from particularly wicked ancestors and/or living kin over the many cycles of one's life and rebirth. This is not to say that quantity and enumeration were unimportant in ritual calculations of cosmic fortunes. After all, the precise amounts of this-worldly money given to gods were always meticulously recorded in temple ledgers, publicly displayed in steles, and widely discussed among villagers as signs of one's spiritual solvency. However, it was also generally acknowledged that only the vague contour of one's cosmic account (for example, as either on the upswing or downswing) could ever be gleaned from this-worldly fortunes like money wealth. As villagers were apt to remind me, not all money made in this world was a reflection of karmic merit. Some money wealth, particularly when accumulated through ill-gotten means, might actually index mounting spiritual deficits, pointing to bad debt in an overdrawn cosmic account rather than good credit in the ritual economy.

If money itself could not be regarded as a good gauge of human fortunes, divine efficacy, in contrast, was always celebrated in ritual practices as a positive agent of value transformation, enabling overseas wealth to flow into Longyan and also reordering the villagers' social world in a way that was advantageous to committed worshippers. Unlike the powers of ancestors and ghosts, which mainly had negative and preventable effects, the notion of efficacy described a proactive cosmic force that not only counteracted supernatural harm but also brought about desired outcomes in this world. While ritual transactions with the dead, and particularly with ancestors, inspired villagers to see cosmic debt as immanent to all human actions and relations, offering to gods pointed to the promise of additional other-worldly redress in the form of extendable divine credit. To put it another way, debt and credit pointed to decidedly different orders of cosmic engagement. While cosmic debt, the domain of the living as well as the dead, was simply par for the course of karmic existence, cosmic credit, in contrast, was the distinctive prerogative of the gods, which only they had the capacity to extend to remake human fortunes. If cosmic debt could be regarded as intrinsic, even ontological, to village projects of value production, cosmic credit promised to be their transformative agent. In turn, only offerings to gods could appeal both to the highest moral imperative—that of human indebtedness—and to the greatest instrumental value—that of proactive divine efficacy in the world.

While some Longyan residents, as noted, continued to be very critical of the ritual uses of money, divine efficacy itself has been cited by worshippers for softening local policies against the doing of "superstition," including lavish ritual expenditures. Though the giving of USD in both actual and spirit form to gods, ghosts, and ancestors can be traced back as far as the late 1980s in Longyan, most people said it was only within the last decade that it became permissible to do so without fear of fines, incarceration, or violence from local cadres and police (*ganbu*). When villagers told me about this transformation in official policies toward ritual life, they always described it as a sudden about-face resulting from one particularly violent crackdown by local officials that provoked the wrath of the local gods. The defining moment took place in either 1994 or 1995 around the Lunar New Year during an annual week-long ritual called Youshen, or "Tour of the Gods," when the images of local deities are carried out of temples in imperial sedans and paraded through every village street. This event had been subject to some harassment by the local police ever since it had been unofficially revived in the early 1980s. But according to villagers, on this occasion, local party leaders crossed the line when they ordered the destruction of the divine images and wooden idols, which were thrown into a stream running through the village. People recalling this incident never failed to end their account with the same coda: shortly after this debacle, the head of the local cadre suffered a devastating stroke from which he never recovered; at the same time, both of his adult children, who had recently arrived in the United States, met disasters of their own that left them exiled without immigration status and deep in financial debt.

Villagers read these calamities as direct evidence of the gods' anger in being treated as nothing but empty vessels of superstition. As an instantiation of divine efficacy, the official's subsequent comeuppance not only provided vindication for embattled worshippers but also transformed many skeptics and opponents into ritual participants. People said that local cadres were simply too scared to crack down on religious activities after this series of events. In fact, some retired officials even became active temple members to the point of taking on leadership roles in ritual events and donation drives. By instantly striking down those who would oppose them and deny their existence, the gods, as villagers understood them, proved that they were irreducible to material objects and were in fact the ultimate dynamic agents of village life. Moreover, through this forceful show of their efficacy, the gods halted decades of official persecution of worshippers and opened the floodgates for public enactments of faith and indebtedness to them.

As common retellings of this story suggested, divine efficacy enabled villagers to reclaim the "doing of superstition"—that illicit category of ritual activity—as legitimate social practice. As mentioned above, it was striking how openly and matter-of-factly people in Longyan spoke of "doing/making superstition" to describe their various ritual practices. These utterances never seemed to tap into lingering fears of state persecution or conjure up nostalgia for the glory of "traditional" life before the Communist Revolution. In fact, it constantly amazed me that people tended to talk about "doing superstition" in terms of everything new and innovative in local ritual life. Contrary to critiques of its backwardness, "doing superstition" appeared in local discourse and practice as a firmly forward-looking project.

Seven years after the definitive Tour of the Gods, for instance, I listened to Old Zheng, the elderly overseer of the Temple of the Monkey King, describe the seven-day ritual as a blossoming parade of newness, with increasing numbers of participants and a dizzying array of previously unseen performers. This annual ritual, Old Zheng told me, had never been as festive (renao) and successful in the pre-Communist era as it was now. When I asked him why he thought this was the case, he explained that it had to do with the massive influx of overseas remittances since the 1980s. The more money people had, the more they wanted to participate in the ritual as a gesture of gratitude to the gods for their success. The more they participated, the more new and lavish elements they wanted to add to the procession. Watching my video footage of the Tour, Old Zheng poked his finger at successive elements of the ritual and proudly declared, "This is new; . . . this is also new," for three out of every four costumed troupes that paraded along the road. These novel elements included a lively troupe of little boys, costumed as the Monkey King, who intermittently shouted the following blessings:

The Monkey King is so efficacious!	(Fz: *Ieloma wei ling.*)
Peace to the whole village!	(Fz: *Zuong hüong taibing.*)
May you leave the country successfully!	(Fz: *Cuguo sunglei.*)
May your entire family emigrate!	(Fz: *Zuong ga ieming.*)

Through every major street of the village, the voices of these little boys proclaimed all the good fortunes that could flow from divine efficacy. Far from fettering modernity, "doing superstition" was being realigned with the forces of progress, mobility, and expanding wealth through ritual displays of divine efficacy.

It is important to note, though, that divine efficacy was not considered the only agent behind a worshipper's overseas success. Villagers like Old Zheng also recognized human agency as a necessary component, not simply a reflection, of divine efficacy. After all, people had to actively engage in both routine offerings and specific oral contracts with gods in order to secure divine intervention in the first place. Even then Lin Mengya suggested that "gods can only help you with a portion." As she explained further, "Gods make sure that when you're on the road, you won't run into any bad people who want to harm you. Or that when you are in court [for asylum in the United States], you get a judge who is more soft-hearted. But if you want to succeed, you still need ability. You still need to rely on yourself. Without ability, there's still no way." Manifestations of divine efficacy pointed to the cosmic regulation of social order, to a kind of divine "invisible hand" structuring the playing field for the accumulation of credit—both spiritual and otherwise—against the persistent backdrop of ontological karmic debt. Through worshippers' routine good-faith offerings, as well as specific contractual promises, gods could be motivated to structure this cosmological web of credit-debt relations to the advantage of worshippers and those for whom they prayed. But it was still up to people themselves to manage their own cosmic accounts and mobilize divine creditors for their projects, thus translating other-worldly advantages into this-worldly success. Divine support did not absolve people of the underlying cosmic debt they produced, and the debt continued to accrue over lifetimes of human interaction and entanglements. It only kept one from defaulting on such debts by extending credit for maintaining one's temporary hold over "the purchase on life" (Hou 1975). Illness and death, as villagers noted, were frequently signs of overdrawn cosmic accounts. Yet despite the demise of the former cadre leader after the Tour of the Gods incident, no one could deny that many other village officials and elites had achieved and retained significant prosperity through the years while actively working to suppress popular religion and debunk local claims to divine efficacy. In this sense the efficacy of the gods could never account for all the wealth made in this world so much as provide divine sanction for only certain means of achievement. The question then remains: Why did the display of usd become such a salient index of divine efficacy above all others?

Big Money, Small Money

At the temple of Beitang Gong—a local deity who was once a Ming-era general stationed in the area—a lovely courtyard was surrounded on two sides by giant black marbled walls, each etched in red and white characters with descriptions of specific donation drives, the names of donors, and the amounts of their contributions. One wall recounted the triumphant rebuilding of the temple in 1989 and the other the grand construction in 1991 of an adjacent theater for entertaining the god. In sheer size and sheen, these marbled steles were a spectacular sight to behold as a display of the collective wealth of worshippers and the divine efficacy of Beitang Gong, who was largely recognized as one of the most effective protectors of those journeying overseas. But of the many dollar contributions etched into these walls, the one that struck me the most was a humble donation of $20. Amid an impressive list of largesse in five currencies—rmb, usd, yen, and Taiwan and Hong Kong dollars—the $20 was by far the smallest amount listed in any denomination and stood out as an odd testament to the efficacy of the god. What was the point of declaring a measly $20 on a list with contributions in the tens of thousands? Why not convert that same $20 into the more impressive equivalent of 160 rmb? When I asked the temple overseer these questions, he shook his head at any suggestion of equivalence. "That's what that person gave—twenty usd," he explained. "You can't change that because dollars are just dollars; rmb are rmb."

The temple overseer's insistence on the incommensurability of usd and rmb suggested a distinction between these currencies beyond their much vaunted exchange rate of 1 usd to 8 rmb. Money in its particular material form was more than an abstraction of exchange value; it was also, as Lemon notes, "a sensual substance, both a thing in the Marxian sense and a visible surface that concentrates diffuse, mass-mediated associations as well as personalized memories" (1998, 29). In their narratives and practical handling of different currencies, Longyan residents constantly highlighted the irreducible materiality of money (cf. Foster 1998; Keane 2002).

In fact, dollars were merely the newest substance of value among a diverse array of cash that villagers have long tried to order into meaningful social difference. As in other parts of China, money has long circulated through Fuzhou as a diverse set of coexisting and even dueling currencies despite various state efforts since the Yuan dynasty (1279–1368) to prescribe a single medium of exchange (Von Glahn 1996; L-s. Yang 1952). Fuzhou's system of monetary exchange was so heterogeneous and complex by the Republican Era that it was even singled out in a U.S. Department of Commerce report as an exemplary case of China's "currency chaos" in the 1920s (F. Lee 1926; cf. Notar 2002).[27] That is, even before the current influx of dollar remittances, Longyan villagers were already quite attuned to money's multiplicity as an agent of exchange. Distinctions among hard currencies—their aesthetic and material properties, the way they circulated, and who possessed them—often mattered in the ways villagers imagined their past and future and in turn situated themselves in the spatial-temporal order. For instance, money was uniquely imbued with nostalgia in *My Hometown Longyan*, a widely circulated memoir of pre-Communist village life published in 1987 by a former Longyan mayor who had fled to Taiwan during the war of resistance against Japan in the 1940s (Zheng 1983). Writing from exile over forty years later, the author fondly recalled the privileged circulation of local currency while describing the former glory of Longyan as a political and cultural center of the region. All local cash issued by Longyan's private banks was "big money" (*daqian*), the author noted; in contrast to the "small money" (*xiaoqian*) of neighboring places, "big money" could be exchanged with the national currency at equal value rather than at a reduced rate. Moreover, Longyan's "big money" circulated widely outside the confines of the village, finding acceptance as legal tender in significant market towns to the north, south, and east. In the historical imagination of the author, "big money" became a salient marker of Longyan's superior sphere of influence before the war against Japan and the Communist Revolution reduced it to a poor peasant village like any other in the Fuzhou countryside. While Longyan residents "were not city folks" simply because they lived outside of Fuzhou's formal municipal borders, their possession of "big money" distinguished them from their rural neighbors in the pre-Communist era. Before the devastations of war and revolution in the 1940s, Longyan residents, as the author adamantly declared, "were also not country folks" with all the characteristics of backwardness and inferiority that those terms implied.

It is no secret that money became taboo as an object of desire in the Mao era and its possession or lack thereof, a means for separating the morally superior "red" class from the pariah "black" class of former capitalist oppressors. Yet despite the political denouncement of money in the abstract, people often reminded me that the RMB functioned as an important medium of exchange in everyday life, though the introduction of rations in the late 1950s also ensured that the RMB circulated less as a general currency than a specialized one under state socialism. Grain ration coupons (liang piao) in particular emerged as an even more important currency than RMB and weighed heavily in the memories of Longyan residents as an index of relative privilege in China's household registration system (see chapter 2). As a means for controlling population movement, such coupons specifically linked geographic mobility to social rank by making it impossible for peasants to purchase food in China's urban centers or, by extension, set up residence in the cities.[28] While Longyan's "big money" had signaled the wide circulation and regional influence of its residents in the Republican Era, grain ration coupons—or rather the lack thereof—became potent markers of villagers' new immobility and marginalization as state-classified "peasants" under Mao.

With the disappearance of rationing under economic reform, the RMB gained new salience as a general currency for market transactions and as a desired object of prosperity in the 1980s (Anagnost 1989; Croll 1994; Ikels 1996). But as Ann Anagnost notes, tension also emerged in "the practical redefinition of socialism around formerly condemned capitalist categories" like money wealth (1989, 215). Moreover, growing, rather than shrinking, economic disparities highlighted the contradictions in promoting the accumulation of money as part of the development of the PRC's so-called "socialism with Chinese characteristics." While state celebrations of "ten thousand yuan" households emphasized the contributions of the prosperous to the collective, people were often suspicious of the morality of wealth gained through RMB accumulation since the initiation of economic reform.

This suspicion was palpable in the practical handling of RMB notes in everyday market transactions in contemporary Longyan. In a typical exchange between buyer and seller, RMB notes were finely scrutinized for all signs of flaw or dishonesty. People were particularly suspicious about new prints and denominations, which, because of their unfamiliarity among consumers, were considered easier to counterfeit. But suspicion of the RMB extended beyond notes that seemed too crisp and new. People also refused to accept notes that were too tattered and old. At a cashier's counter, it was routine to witness both buyer and seller engrossed by the materiality of the RMB before them, to watch them holding bills to the light for official watermarks, rubbing their fingers against the grain of the ink, and folding them in thirds and halves to verify the proper alignment of the signs of authenticity. I myself was often prodded by friends to return old notes that cashiers had just handed me as change and to eye crisp new bills with comparable suspicion. In these transactions, one constantly fought against the sense of being duped as if unfair gain was inevitable in RMB exchanges.

This sense of unfair gain was often elaborated in villagers' critiques of local elites, who were largely viewed as the beneficiaries of RMB wealth. Many people complained that the wealth accumulated by these elites involved unfair advantages like better access to higher education and superior social connections. Moreover, there was widespread suspicion that RMB wealth involved dishonest means like embezzlement, bribery, favoritism, and other corrupt practices involving the abuse of political authority. If no secret corruption existed behind the accumulation of RMB, people reasoned, why did the honest and hard-working efforts of commoners not result in prosperity? In contrast to the unearned fortunes of local elites, the meager earnings of internal migrants from Sichuan were often cited as evidence of the futility of honest labor as a means to RMB wealth.

Dollars differed sharply from RMB in both local discourse and practical handling. Unlike RMB, USD notes were not used as a general currency for everyday market transactions but mainly given and received as loans, repayments, and remittances from overseas. While RMB notes were often individually scrutinized as commodities of suspicion in mundane consumer

exchanges, stacks of USD would usually change hands smoot[h]
the suspicion of both buyers and sellers in RMB exchanges, the
dollars in credit transactions was often quite one-sided. In my
of dollar exchanges, I was often impressed by the giver, wh[o]
purview of the recipient, would briskly shuffle through the stack of mun[ey],
to be handed over with the efficiency of a bank teller and the bravado of
a card player. In turn, the recipient would quickly stow away the stack of
bills without inspection, as if embarrassed by any suggestion of mistrust
or calculation on the receiving end. Regardless of whether it was a loan
from a neighbor or a contribution to gods at temples, the giver typically
did all the counting and handling while the receiver unquestioningly accepted the money. Unlike RMB exchanges, the giving and receiving of USD
enacted relations of confidence and trust.

This distinction between RMB and USD extended to the spirit forms of
these currencies, and it helps to explain why spirit RMB were so unpopular
among worshippers. As Lin Mengya explained, "People buy U.S. dollars
[for ancestors] because what they earn is U.S. dollars." She added that
"people may also buy [spirit] RMB because they regularly need RMB to buy
food, to buy things." Yet while worshippers like Lin Mengya claimed that
it was perfectly appropriate to use either RMB or USD in transactions with
the dead, it seemed that in ritual offerings all preferred to feature only the
USD they "earned" to the exclusion of the RMB they used to "buy things."
Though people could never explain why they made only USD offerings other
than to say that it was a personal choice, the widespread absence of RMB
in ritual transactions hints at that currency's suspect status as a pragmatic
and moral substance for binding the living to the dead.

Like the privileged currencies of previous eras, USD indexed social relations of superior pragmatic and moral value for Longyan residents. Dollars, as everyone told me, were "bigger" (*bijiao da*) than RMB, just as the
"big money" of pre-Communist Longyan trumped the "small money" of
neighboring villages. Not only did USD have a superior exchange value but
they also circulated more broadly, finding acceptance both domestically
and transnationally as a general currency and object of value. Moreover,
dollars tied what was considered an isolated and marginalized "peasant"
village in the Mao period to the desired cosmopolitanism and transnational capital flows of overseas Chinese in the new era of market liberalization. In the overseas Chinese both state and local discourses found a
common model of prosperity premised on a moral ethos of hard work and

sacrifice (see chapter 3).[29] While the suspicious wealth of the elites only reinscribed the status quo, the success of the overseas Chinese suggested that through the challenges of honest labor abroad, the most humble commoners could be transformed into the wealthy entrepreneurial vanguard of a new Chinese modernity. Dollars were powerful tokens of the rite of passage through which Longyan villagers transformed themselves from marginal "peasants" to overseas cosmopolitans. In displays of collective dollar wealth, Longyan residents indexed their transnational mobility and broader sphere of influence as a home to overseas Chinese amid isolated rural villages and other domestically confined places.

In Longyan, USD circulated as a currency of credit in the full sense of the word—both as an extension of capital for financing journeys abroad and as a token of social and divine merit. These two notions of credit were inextricably linked in local discourses of and transactions with dollar wealth, in contrast to understandings of RMB, where financial prosperity often contradicted, rather than reflected, moral value. Dollars provided Longyan residents with an alternative means for grounding the accumulation of money as "morally *earned* wealth" (Dorfman 1996, 275). As Diane Dorfman has observed for the peasants grappling with economic reform in northern China, Longyan villagers also turned to a "spiritual idiom" to find "a mandate for a moral market that involves offering moral wealth—wealth that is earned, not derived through corruption" (275). Through ritual exchange, "They give and receive what they condemn officials for appropriating, but render it discrete because it is the product of what the spirits define as a moral transaction" (275). Ritual expenditures reconstituted dollar wealth as the co-production of divine and human agencies, but, just as important, they broadened the latter category to recognize the work of not only wage laborers overseas but also the distinctly feminized and unpaid contributions of the worshippers in Longyan responsible for their households' spiritual solvency. In fact, such feminized work was arguably the most essential kind of human practice if one sourced money's staying power and productivity in this world to the extendability of cosmic credit in the next.

It may be useful here to remember that as a middling form of money not quite good enough for the gods, the USD was never imagined as the standard of value for structuring the various hierarchies of spiritual and market transactions. Rather, it was another kind of currency—a "gold standard" for divine credit—that underwrote one's spiritual (and worldly) solvency and in turn united the various economies of the living and the dead under the generative logic of karmic merit and retribution. As Alan Cole similarly observed for the Buddhist notion of cosmic credit, "All felicity and fertility would dry up should one's stock of merit collapse" (1998, 7). While the dollar's entrance into Longyan depended largely on wage labor overseas, it was ultimately through the feminized circuit of ritual exchange that its lasting value as a distinct project of money accumulation could be made legible and stabilized.

Ritual practices for transferring funds to the spirit world aimed to ensure that money made in this world was not ephemeral but anchored to a more permanent and generative source of prosperity. In this sense, spirit money transactions did not just reflect the existing fortunes of the living but rather enacted essential value transformations.[30] As villagers' emphasis on the "doing of superstition" suggested, ritual exchange might be best seen as productive action rather than as merely symbolic practice or ideological effect. This was not only an emic perspective but also an important analytic point that a number of anthropologists both in (Chau 2006; Sangren 2000) and outside of China (Graeber 2001; Munn 1986) have made with regard to various kinds of ritual exchange. Here action could be construed in the broadest Marxian sense as world- and self-making practice, as well as in the equally resonant terms of actor-network theory, as the stabilizing agencies of social ontologies and relationalities (Law 2002; Mol 1999). As a kind of world-ordering activity, spirit money transactions promised to secure the terms of value production amid radical uncertainty about the sources of human fortune. They did this by conjuring a particular cosmology of credit through which money's worth could be grasped not so much in terms of its circulation as market-versus-spiritual currency as its karmic implications as a form of merit-versus-demerit money.

By linking the market and spiritual forms of USD exchange, Longyan residents repositioned their money wealth in a different transactional order than what was imagined as "the market" in state agendas for economic reform. People did not deny the importance of market exchange and in fact recognized the RMB as the currency for everyday consumer transactions in this arena. However, by downplaying the market affinities of the RMB and the USD as state currencies in favor of their moral disparities as merit or demerit monies, they also destabilized certain normative claims on the money form as a universalizing and generic medium of exchange. Disavowing the RMB and USD as objects-in-kind enabled villagers to remake the boundaries for thinking about money's ontology and translatability as value. Rather than emphasizing money's generalizing capacities as a mediator of market relations, villagers highlighted its multiplicity as a set of discrete and specialized currencies, each moving according to its own pragmatic and moral trajectory within a "multicentric economy" (Bohannon 1959). While the RMB emerged here as a delimited and limiting currency good only for everyday consumption and suspect wealth accumulation, the USD was more broadly and generously constituted as a currency of credit for consolidating relations of trust and productivity across both human and spiritual domains of exchange. If the RMB and USD could not be any more different here, the market and spirit forms of the USD were, in contrast, easy to see as like objects in the service of like practices within the cosmic nexus of credit and debt.

Money to Burn

Local critics and foreign observers alike have long dismissed any affinities between spirit and market currencies by pointing to radical differences in the materiality and pragmatics of their exchange. The burning of spirit money, in particular, has often been cited as evidence of waste and destruction in ritual practice, as opposed to the productivity of money's circulation in market exchange. Paper incinerated into ashes could hardly be deemed "real" money, critics have noted, let alone share ontological grounds with market currencies as part of the same transactional order.[31] Yet a closer look at ritual burning would highlight not the reckless destruction of material objects but the diligence and care in the way worshippers fed their spiritual currencies to the flames. Typically, with a stack of spirit money in hand, a worshipper would deftly separate the bills and successively set each one on fire as if taking stock of every value transacted. Much like the handling of USD in credit transactions, there was a kind of banker's precision to the sorting and counting of the spirit currencies. The transfer of funds to the spirit world required not only the burning of currency but also enactments of trust and accountability through its proper handling. The burning of currency, in this sense, was never significant in itself but rather as a thing-in-motion (Zito n.d.) that needed to be expertly activated in ritual performances in order to connect the sphere of the living to that of gods, ghosts, and ancestors.[32]

Standing over a metal bin or ceramic kiln during an act of ritual burning, one would notice that spirit money was never just reduced to ashes but also transformed into the ephemeral but palpable form of smoke. Like the wafting fragrance of incense and the sweet aroma of daily fruit offerings, smoke resembled the kind of fluid sensual form that people imagined spirits assuming in human encounters. It resonated as a kind of liminal substance in between worlds that could be appropriated by spirits from the offerings of the living. Ashes were no more than the discarded shell of ritual paper in its actualization as the kind of money capable of connecting the visible world of humans to the invisible one of spirits. In particular, through the disappearing trail of smoke, worshippers burning spirit currencies were able to not only render the invisible visible but in the process also crystallize the very boundary of money's im/materiality as circulating value. Far from being destructive of the money form, acts of ritual burning simply shifted the locus of money's valuation from its object status (for example, paper or ashes) to its relational flow and movement as a mediator of exchange. Arguably, spirit currency was not so different from its market counterpart as "money" embodying exchange value, though admittedly the kind of exchange value produced here was being harnessed more to a cosmology of ontological debt and karmic repayment than to one of alienable surplus and capital accumulation.[33]

This is not to suggest that the logics of ritual transactions stood in some kind of direct opposition to those of capital in Longyan.[34] As Robert Weller has usefully observed, "Religion shows less a preadaptation [or, I would add, antagonism] to capitalism than an ability to reproportion itself to the new context" (1998, 93). The fact that Longyan villagers described "doing superstition" as a positive force of modernity and "morally earned wealth" is a testament to the complicated entanglement of socialist, capitalist, and religious imaginaries in the post-Mao era. One would be hard-pressed to peg these ritual practices to either a clear repudiation or embodiment of the spirit of capitalism (as we know it), though it is clear that through ritual activity people tried to concretize and shape the various invisible forces already in play in their lives to their advantage.

In the end, the encompassing spiritual economy I have sketched above also needs to be recognized as a normative project itself. For like the cosmology of capitalism (see Sahlins 1994; M. Yang 2000), village incitements of a cosmic web of karmic debt and divine credit reinscribed certain inequalities and hegemonies among Longyan residents even as they challenged other dominant ideologies. While ritual practices suggested a critical stance toward the accumulation of money within the domestic economy, they also valorized notions of overseas Chinese prosperity via global markets. Though not an embrace of capitalism per se, "doing superstition" clearly involved an awkward tango with different capitalist modalities. Similarly, village understandings of ritual exchanges as the household duty of women hinted at certain gendered disparities in the moral regulation of money wealth and moneyed persons, a topic that I will pursue further in the next chapter. In practice, not all Longyan residents had both the capacity and privilege necessary to display "morally *earned* wealth" or to marshal evidence of divine efficacy for their practices, especially when they were faced with disastrous human smuggling ventures, indefinite conjugal separations, restaurant bankruptcies, and other hazards in the rites of passage of overseas Chinese. A final anecdote illustrates both the perpetual vulnerability of Longyan's spiritual economy and its resilience as a normative construct despite the recurring disappointments and devastating failures of some worshippers.

"Tears for Dollars": Zhang Yuan's Wager

Many people in Longyan told me compelling stories of their uninterrupted devotion to the gods in the worst of times. They described how during the Cultural Revolution they saved precious relics from temples about to be destroyed and secretly worshipped at altars tucked away in hidden upstairs closets in their homes. And they told me how through the mid-1990s they faced down the violent cadre forces and withstood beatings, fines, and incarceration in order to revive the annual Tour of the Gods ritual and pry open the locked doors of their beloved old temples for a renewal of public and routine worship. In these dominant narratives of religious continuity against all odds, bright glimpses of divine efficacy were cited in the sudden death of a particularly cruel official or in the barrenness of corrupt families or in the simple fact that one survived and stayed afloat amid famine, political torment, and the allure of suicide. Ultimately, people noted that these dark decades of secret and subversive religious devotion led to their current payoff: overseas success and the flow of dollars into the community.

With one blunt sentence, Zhang Yuan managed to throw this entire narrative of village religiosity into question for me. "Praying has resulted in nothing," she declared when I first sat down with her on the eve of Lunar New Year. Like other villagers, Zhang Yuan had prayed to the gods for her husband's overseas success, but unlike other testimonies of divine efficacy, her tale was one of disillusionment and bitterness over prosperity deferred and mounting debt. Despite several contracts with gods, her requests for her husband's success have never been fulfilled, she complained. The first time her husband tried to go abroad, in 1996, he got only as far as Thailand before he was caught and sent back. The second time, he had barely boarded the boat before officials raided it and carted off the entire group of stowaways for fines and a month in prison. The third attempt was even worse because he was caught and sent back to China after he had already paid the full smuggling fee for what turned out to be a ten-day stint in Japan. Deep in debt from three unsuccessful ventures, Zhang Yuan nonetheless continued to pray for her husband's successful emigration. But though he finally found a route into the United States in 1999, the results did not suggest the blessing of the gods.

For this last effort, Zhang Yuan and her husband had paid extra money for the safer option of plane transport. But the snakehead led her husband's group only on a short flight to Hong Kong before he made them board a ship for the duration of their journey to the United States. Zhang Yuan was visibly bitter as she recounted her husband's ordeal under the untrustworthy and domineering smuggler who changed the terms of their original agreement. In Hong Kong, her husband was even ordered to pay an extra sum to continue the journey by boat. There was no choice involved, she recalled: "If you didn't pay, they would lock you up and not give you food until they got their money." Things did not get better after Zhang Yuan's husband arrived in the United States. His jobs as an undocumented laborer garnered meager wages and made the debt they had incurred seem insurmountable. When her husband lost all possibility for political asylum and it became clear that their separation would be interminable, Zhang Yuan angrily denounced her religious efforts and finally stopped going to temples. "I prayed day after day, but it was just useless," she complained. "My luck was just this bad."

Though technically Zhang Yuan now belonged to the family of an "American guest," she privately griped to me about the dominant assumptions of overseas prosperity and critiqued social pressures for ritual expenditure. She not only questioned the efficacy of her own prayers but also challenged stories of persistent and true devotion among her neighbors.

Against celebrations of divine efficacy and dollars, Zhang Yuan told me of a bitter saying that quietly circulated among wives left behind: "U.S. dollars are really easy to use, but you secretly shed tears."[35] Amid her disillusionment with religious devotion, Zhang Yuan also highlighted an underlying disenchantment with dollar wealth.

Less than a week after her initial rant against the efficacy of dollars, Zhang Yuan and her younger sister took me on a hike through the overgrown weedy trails of Dragonhead Mountain (Longtou Shan), a sacred village landmark. Despite their shared cynicism about religious life, the two sisters happily volunteered to take me through the rough and tricky terrain to get to a famed temple of the Minyue king Wuzhu that was perched on the mountain's peak. Part of their enthusiasm to serve as my temple guides no doubt stemmed from their local reputations for fearless athleticism as part of a family of five tomboy daughters. Though Zhang Yuan had recently sprained her back when she had fallen off a tree she had climbed to pick apricots, for my benefit she deftly scaled another tree at the foot of the mountain to deposit some of our extraneous jackets as we geared up to tackle the hilly trail on a hot afternoon. Decked in three-inch heels, both sisters maneuvered quickly and confidently around overgrown weeds and slippery boulders while I trampled awkwardly behind them in my surprisingly less surefooted hiking boots. Even a broken heel could not stop the steady pace Zhang Yuan and her sister set for moving onward and upward to the temple on top. Zhang Yuan simply snapped off her intact heel and cheerfully marched forward in her now evenly flat shoes.

All along the way, the disillusionment over religion and money deepened. I learned that Zhang Yuan's sense of bad luck extended to her sister, Zhang Wen, whose husband's overseas journey had also led to devastating results. Caught with a counterfeit passport upon entry at airport customs in Las Vegas, Zhang Wen's husband had been locked up in INS detention for almost three years, without recourse to the typical parole given to those petitioning for asylum in his situation.[36] Her husband's atypical detention had made Zhang Wen and her extended family (including Zhang Yuan) the laughingstock of their entire neighborhood. Since the detained relatives of other villagers could often wrangle parole from the INS in a month or two, people assumed that some physical or mental deficiency was preventing Zhang Wen's husband from doing so or that there was some deeper cosmic curse on the entire family that could explain such misfortunes.

It turned out that the idea of a family curse could be extended to Zhang Yuan's parents, who in their prime had been scorned by neighbors for giving birth to five daughters and no sons. The two sisters angrily recalled how their paternal uncle, who had two sons, once publicly humiliated their father by joking that their family was doomed to "look at the asses of sons" (kan erzi de pigu). Zhang Yuan's mother had been doubly cursed as a young woman under the new Mao regime when she was classified as a member of the black pariah class because her father, who passed away when she was a child, had been a notable village teacher. Despite the fact that her mother had grown up as a poor orphan, she was denied sympathy by the local party cadre and often cut out of food allocations made to the official "peasants" of Longyan. While Zhang Yuan's father continued to get his equal share of resources as a "peasant" under the newly formed village collective during the Mao years, the family as a whole had to rely on less than others because of the political marginalization of their mother.

In the contemporary context, the two sisters continued to rant against the political injustices inflicted on their family. During the period of decollectivization in the early 1980s, Zhang Yuan's mother was once again denied an allotment of land because of her political classification. Furthermore, both sisters recalled that on separate occasions the last village head had squandered large sums of money they had paid him for adjusting their household registration status without making the promised changes. Zhang Yuan recalled that she had stormed into the village-head's office and demanded her 2,000 RMB back, only to have him shamelessly tell her that a refund was impossible because he had already spent the money. Soon after this encounter, Zhang Yuan said, the village head himself paid a large sum to get smuggled into the United States, financed no doubt by swindled money like hers that had been diverted into his personal account. Commenting on the amorality of money accumulation, Zhang Yuan shook her head and noted with disgust, "Right now, for those with money, anything can be done" (Xianzai youqian, shenme dou bande dao). There was no moral comfort in the ideal of overseas Chinese prosperity if the former village head could also occupy that subject position.

Considering the bitter and cynical comments that accompanied our uphill trek, I was quite surprised, once we reached the temple, at how the two sisters recounted local stories of the divine Wuzhu with what seemed like genuine awe. Even more unexpectedly, they lead me to a donation plaque commemorating the recent reconstruction of the temple and proudly pointed out their husbands' names and contributions. While we were touring the temple, a couple of monks and a lay caretaker had been busy putting up decorations to ready the place for Lunar New Year celebrations. Though they paid scant attention to us beyond an initial greeting, Zhang Yuan and her sister approached them on our way out and engaged them in friendly patter about the upcoming festivities. The conversation ended with Zhang Yuan spontaneously emptying her pockets of all money—about 130 RMB—and handing it over to the temple caretaker as a donation. This off-the-cuff act of largesse took not only me by surprise but also the caretaker, who seemed quite disoriented as she scurried off to find a donation ledger in which to properly record Zhang Yuan's contribution.

On the way downhill, Zhang Yuan grew pensive about her desires for going abroad. Perhaps things would be better once her back healed, she said, when she would be able to find a way into the United States to join her husband so they could pay off their loans faster. Pretty soon, she told me, her thirteen-year-old daughter would also be mature enough to make the journey abroad, so together they could work off their debt and possibly finance the dreams of higher education for her only son. Maybe he could be the one to go abroad legally as a foreign student, a legitimate overseas Chinese in the eyes of the state and urban elites. Perhaps the ideal of overseas prosperity was still within reach with a little bit more sacrifice and sustained faith in one's choices. Perhaps Zhang Yuan just needed to bide her time for manifestations of divine efficacy in her own life.

After this temple tour, I often encountered Zhang Yuan in her old form, denouncing the effectiveness of ritual practice and the morality of dollar wealth. At the peak of her despondency, she railed against the value of her and her husband's sacrifices for overseas prosperity. "It's like tears exchanged for dollars, beloved village exchanged for dollars," she lamented. "People all say it's like this here," she added as if marshaling collective support for her family's continual suffering and its seeming incommensurability to any future returns of dollar wealth.

Despite these strong critiques, Zhang Yuan continued to make surprising gestures of faith at local ritual events. These enactments of religiosity culminated in her family's participation in a week-long event for "the returning of resources" (*huanyuan*), through which worshippers tried to pay off their ancestors' legacy of cosmic debt in order to change their own luck in the present and the future. More than a half year after I first encountered Zhang Yuan, I ran into her at the temple of the Monkey King while I was accompanying a family of devout worshippers who were trying to locate the source of their son's failures in emigration. Like this family, Zhang Yuan and her sister Zhang Wen busied themselves with the folding, sorting, and burning of stacks of spirit money and the transfer of life-size cardboard trunks filled with luxury goods in hopes of settling the old cosmic accounts of ancestors. Far from a village-wide event, this ritual was organized and performed mainly by the members of nine families. These families were all perceived as especially cursed with misfortune, and through this collective event of cosmic renewal, they were all trying to alter those perceptions. As part of the ritual, Zhang Wen was also abstaining from meat for a month in order to accumulate additional merit for her husband's case.

Though Zhang Yuan did not go as far as her sister in her ritual sacrifices, I found her again in an optimistic mood three days later on her way back from another temple. That morning, she had risen early and gone to the Agricultural Commercial Bank, where she had withdrawn $3,000 just wired to her by her niece in New York City. Following her niece's instructions, she had taken the money to the Jiangjun temple and handed it over to the caretaker for use in recently initiated renovations. Recounting her activities of that morning, Zhang Yuan proudly emphasized that this donation was one of the largest given for the renovations and that it was the result of divine efficacy in her niece's recent approval for political asylum in the United States. Even as the middleman of a spiritual transaction, Zhang Yuan took heart in the signs of success for her extended kin and in the positive transformation of her family's circumstances that this large public donation could suggest to others and—even more important—to herself. Perhaps through continued worship, Zhang Yuan could still find redemption for a reciprocal wager she had already made—the shedding of tears for the promise of dollars. However provisional this new confidence in the gods turned out to be, Zhang Yuan's return to ritual practice highlighted the durability of this cosmology amid conditions of radical uncertainty; at the same time, it also underscored the lingering inadequacies and vulnerabilities of the cosmology in accounting for the messy and disjunctive outcomes of migrant desires and prayers.

"Doing Superstition," or the Productivity of Blind Faith

In this chapter, we have followed the different trajectories of monies—spirit and market currencies, USD and RMB—as they were set into motion by Longyan residents, and we have traced their reverberations with other discursive and material forces. Through the circulation of divergent currencies, I have attempted to sketch the rough contours of a distinctive cosmology of credit—an encompassing spiritual economy—that did not oppose the cosmology of capitalism so much as it harnessed "the market" to its own normative project of value production. Ritual expenditures in Longyan did not suggest an economy of scarcity or surplus so much as one of generalized debt (Roitman 2003), which required constant management through ritual transactions. Ultimately, what seemed like the excesses of ritual expenditures might be better described as the necessity of sacrifice and loss for producing value through the credit-debt nexus of karmic regulation (Hubert and Mauss 1964; Simmel 1978). In the ritual burning of currency, value was not consumed and wasted so much as it was transformed in the act of exchange between the visible world of humans and the invisible one of spirits.

If the extreme reversals of fortune in the last century taught Longyan residents anything, it was that wealth made in this world was fleeting and ephemeral. Not only did the organizing symbols of prosperity shift dramatically over the years but the means for achieving and maintaining wealth were also constantly challenged by state policies, local discourses, and material realities. By the time dollars were flooding the local economy, villagers were already accustomed to making moral distinctions among kinds of wealth, including kinds of money wealth. Through the promotion of the efficacy of dollars, worshippers in Longyan tried to distinguish their project of money accumulation from that of state officials and urban elites in the contemporary context. But the maintenance and reproduction of boundaries among moral overseas Chinese and corrupt officials, deserving and undeserving wealth, and the "market" and the "ritual economy" were always subject to the contingencies of everyday life. In the erratic engagement of Zhang Yuan with local ritual life, it was clear that "doing superstition" also contained the possibility of its own undoing.

Popular religion in Longyan provided an idiom for grappling with the enchantments of the money form. At the same time, it enabled the disenchantment of both RMB and USD. While suspicions of RMB accumulation highlighted growing structural inequalities in the era of market liberalization, laments of "tears for dollars" also raised questions concerning the pragmatic and moral worth of going overseas. But having already made their wagers, how else could those left behind shape the invisible forces to their favor except by the doing of "superstition"? Whether objectified as divine spirits, Western capitalism, or the imaginary America of "Restaurant English," invisible transnational (and translocal) forces already made their presence felt in the flow of everyday life in Longyan. In presenting dollar wealth as a co-production of those laboring and those praying, ritual displays of divine efficacy provided the broadest and most inclusive frame for imagining the agents and beneficiaries of these invisible forces.

As a positive force of modernity, "doing superstition" could carry along not only those who emigrated in the quest for overseas prosperity but also those who were left behind. Though physically they might be separated from their overseas kin, through prayers and ritual sacrifices, villagers could still *do* something to support the forward momentum of their loved ones abroad. They could ensure the solvency of cosmic accounts. And they could dispatch the gods on their behalf to places they could not otherwise access, to accompany and protect travelers along human smuggling routes or to intervene in INS decisions or to watch over the grand opening of a new Chinese restaurant in New York. Gods, after all, knew no physical boundaries, and through the "doing of superstition" worshippers otherwise "stuck" in Longyan could make claims to the extension of their social world into a transnational sphere and to the fruits of transnational circulation—dollar wealth. Moreover, through ritual celebrations of overseas successes, they could translate their commitments to a seemingly incredible project of emigration against all odds into a credible project of efficacious, if cosmically contingent and often deferred, ends.

Ultimately, the Chinese term *mixin*, often translated as "superstition," might be more fruitfully understood in its literal parts: *mi*, meaning "to be lost" or "to be fascinated by," and *xin*, meaning "to believe" or "to trust." Together, these two characters speak to the powerful pull of blind faith, even for the most cynical participants like Zhang Yuan, who still kept "doing superstition" despite the indeterminacy of success and the concreteness of daily failures. Ritual practices promised the interweaving of visible and invisible spheres into an integrated social order in which prosperity was always hinged to the cosmic regulation of ontological debt and its repayment. This was an economy of blind faith in the maintenance of reciprocal social bonds across the great divides that separated the concrete daily realities of Longyan from the uncertain promises of its invisible outposts and allies. In the efficacy of dollars, worshippers could point to the productivity of blind faith against all odds. They could highlight the value of costly sacrifices made for returns from invisible yet ever-present worlds, worlds not only of divine spirits but also of laboring relatives abroad.

Partings and Returns

Gender, Kinship, and the Mediation of *Renqing*

Keeping faith in invisible forces was not an easy task for Longyan residents, as demonstrated by Zhang Yuan's critiques in chapter 5. But as it turned out, gods, ghosts, and ancestors were the least of the villagers' concerns when it came to maintaining reciprocal relations with unseen but ever-present subjects. In the invisible spheres of village life stretching beyond the phenomenological boundaries of its three mountains and one winding river, overseas relatives—those very human but spectral members of Longyan's transnational community—provoked even greater anxiety over blind faith in a moral economy of just rewards. How did one know, as Zhang Yuan wondered, that once separated by oceans and national borders, a wife's tears would be returned with dollars or that a husband's dollars could redeem his absence from loved ones? If, as Zhang Yuan noted elsewhere, "With money, one can do anything," how could one be certain that dollars earned abroad would necessarily feed back into the normative loop of value transformation from wage to remittance to divine credit (and then back again to more wage and collective prosperity)?

While ritual exchanges openly and explicitly sanctioned the project of money accumulation via mass emigration overseas, Zhang Yuan's personal lament of "tears for dollars, beloved village for dollars" pointed to an undercurrent of doubt about the maintenance and reproduction of village ties in the face of indefinite transnational separation and sacrifice. Though Zhang Yuan may have been unique in directing her doubts so openly and explicitly toward divine beings, she was not alone in questioning the moral worth of transnational migration from Longyan. Gods may have been difficult to blame for uncertain sacrifices and deferred dreams, but human fallibility and excesses were not. As most villagers readily acknowledged, human ties were more unpredictable and fragile across the threshold of visibility than relations with gods, ghosts, and ancestors.

This chapter revisits the questions of exchange, reciprocity, and indebtedness raised by the previous chapter on spirit money and ritual life. But while the last chapter sketched a hegemonic vision of reciprocal and fair circulation in an encompassing ritual economy, this chapter looks at how asymmetries of debt and desire disrupt the staging and enactment of this kind of distributional order. Specifically, here I trace the ways the continual outflow of villagers and inflow of remittances work to unsettle collective sensibilities of exchange, relatedness, and personhood in Longyan. Against the transnational imaginary of devout villagers and overseas laborers morally linked and united through ritual exchange, this chapter highlights the troubling boundaries resulting from two decades of mass emigration—boundaries based not only on geography, but also on gender, kin, and generational divides—that pose undeniable and continual challenges for Longyan's social reproduction.

In focusing on social reproduction in relation to exchange and following anthropologists like Annette Weiner, I aim to situate more functional and mechanistic considerations of "norms of reciprocity" within the broader dynamic interplay of "human life cycles and the life trajectories of material and immaterial resources" through which persons and collectives get made and remade (Weiner 1980, 72). Like Weiner (cf. 1976, 1980), I am also concerned with the problems of decay, degeneration, loss, and replacement to the maintenance and expansion of social relations over time. But instead of focusing on the concrete finality of death and its challenges to social reproduction, as Weiner does in her work, I examine the subtler questions raised by corporeal absence and indefinite transnational separation for dealing with such contingencies.

This is not to suggest, however, that transnational separation has a necessary destabilizing or dysfunctional effect on the social reproduction of gender and kinship relations in Longyan. As some scholars have shown (Chan 1997; Ong 1999; J. Watson 1975, 2004), transnational dispersal can be both a productive and a normative strategy for fortifying the interests of certain Chinese kinship networks, including the hegemonic continuity and expansion of a patrilineal order. Kwok Bun Chan, for instance, has observed that for both nineteenth-century Guangdong migrants and contemporary Hong Kong cosmopolitans, "dispersing the patrilineal Chinese family [was] paradoxically . . . a resourceful and resilient way of strengthening it: families split in order to be together translocally" (1997,

195). Looking at various rituals and everyday practices concerning partings and returns in Taiwan and northern China, Charles Stafford has even argued that processes of separation and reunion are foundational to Chinese sociality. At times, he has noted, "It seems that going away and coming back again are even *more* significant *vis-à-vis* certain kinds of relationships, than any fixed state of being together" (2000, 2; emphasis in original).

Such observations certainly ring true in Longyan, where the dynamics of partings and returns were crucial to the orchestration and valuation of both personhood and relatedness in everyday life. Partings and returns, in this case, refer not only to the physical movement of migrants in and out of China but also to the transactional flows between sacrifices made and gains anticipated in these village projects for transnational migration. As I will show, in a place like Longyan, from which most villagers emigrated via illicit channels and hence found themselves exiled once overseas, people came to expect "returns" less in the form of physical reunion and future resettlement in China than through the mediation of dollars continually flowing in from overseas. This chapter focuses on village efforts to direct these flows into local circuits of social reproduction through certain moral incitements of debt and reciprocity. Of particular interest here are the gendered and kin asymmetries regulating the dynamics of partings and returns—that is, who should emigrate, how to compensate for the absences of the migrants, and who should have claims to such compensation.

"Tears for dollars, beloved village for dollars" was precisely a comment about the nature of replacement in village sociality and specifically about the commensurability of departed residents and monetary returns for binding and sustaining human relations stretched indefinitely across long distances. While chapter 5 suggested that the material and affective dimensions of ritual exchange were inseparable, here I argue that when it came to relations among people themselves (as opposed to human-divine ties), there were clear anxieties over the alienability of human sentiment from the material calculus of exchange in contemporary Longyan life. As this chapter will show, at stake in laments like "tears for dollars" were concerns over the stress of massive and continual emigration on the reproduction of what villagers called *renqing*, the proper embodiment of human feeling, conduct, and loyalty to others.

Containing the Eighteen-Thousand Dollar Wives

The first time I was invited into a villager's home for a chat (*liaotian*), I was completely surprised by the blunt and dramatic fashion in which my hostess confessed what seemed like her deepest and darkest doubts about emigration. Not more than five minutes after I had met Chen Mingming and sat down in her kitchen, she heaved a slow, deep sigh and announced dolefully, "Actually, to go abroad . . . it's a very bitter situation. People over there can be so horrible [*kongbu*]. We're not afraid of hardship, but it's very difficult to withstand a boss's maltreatment [*shou laobande qi*]." Chen Mingming then went on to emphasize how equally tough it could be on the China side, particularly for wives like her, who had been left to raise two daughters while indefinitely separated from her undocumented husband for eleven years and counting. Like Zhang Yuan, Chen Mingming punctuated her story of family sacrifice and separation with the village by saying, "U.S. dollars may be good to use, but you secretly shed tears."

Outside of funeral rituals and opera performances for the gods, no one had ever shed actual tears in front of me for the absence of loved ones from the village. Nonetheless, by the time I left Longyan, I was thoroughly familiar with the metaphorical tears soaked through the personal narratives of those left behind, especially the wives like Zhang Yuan and Chen Mingming, whose husbands were gone indefinitely without the means to return or to send for them and their children. Admittedly, I anticipated hearing such narratives of sorrow over the course of my field research. But in my ethnographic imagination of rapport, I had not expected these stories to come so quickly and easily. Most people, like Chen Mingming, had no qualms about relaying their concerns without the necessity on my part for first establishing relations of familiarity and trust. If on the streets and at temples villagers gave no explicit signs of migrant yearnings, I found that they were often quite eager to dramatize the loneliness and hardship of separation and the fears of betrayal and abandonment while chatting with me in the intimacy of their own kitchens and sitting rooms.

Over the years, the cohort of women with husbands overseas had grown distinct enough in the Fuzhou countryside to garner a common nickname: the *wanbasao*, or "eighteen-thousand-dollar sisters-in-law." This nickname referenced the average cost in U.S. dollars per person that it took to smuggle the first wave of migrants abroad in the mid-1980s. Unlike traditional stereotypes of Chinese migrants as single male sojourners, Longyan's first wave of migrants consisted mostly of married men; as a result, it left wives with overseas connections in its wake. Though a good number of these wives were able to join their spouses abroad over the years, the persistent separation of many others continued to support the gendered impression of Longyan as a place of "no men," where only women, children, and old people still resided. While the feminization of village life reflected a demographic shifts in Longyan's population since the mid-1980s, more important, it highlighted a hegemonic notion of migration as a gendered extension of the patrilineal family order, in which husbands-fathers were expected to be productively mobile in a globalizing economy while patrilocally anchored wives managed the domestic affairs of caregiving and reproduction "at home."

By the time I was doing research in Longyan, regardless of whether spouses had emigrated in the 1980s or paid $18,000 for smuggling services (the current average is $60,000 per person), *wanbasao* had become the general term for all wives with husbands overseas and with plenty of dollar remittances at their disposal. This was less a growing constituency of the village population than a finite and even shrinking cohort of women, most of whom were in their thirties and forties. As I found out, few women in their twenties or younger remained behind to join the ranks of the *wanbasao*. Instead, as emigrant aspirations expanded from married men to all working-age adults in the 1990s, the younger generation now preferred to go abroad first and marry once established overseas. Meanwhile, many wives who had originally been left behind found ways to join their spouses abroad. Also, of those remaining in China, a good number left Longyan for their natal homes in lieu of remaining in traditional patrilocal residences apart from their husbands.

The attrition in numbers, however, did not diminish the centrality of the "sisters-in-law" as figures of moral discourse in Longyan. As the first group to come into overseas remittances, the "eighteen-thousand-dollar sisters-in-law" continued to be the focal points for intergenerational and gendered clashes over the morality of newfound wealth and emigration. Wives who stayed behind felt the disproportionate moral scrutiny of elderly parents, in-laws, and neighbors. In addition, they were subject to the critical judgment of younger generations eager to differentiate their modern sensibilities from what they saw as the more retrograde *habitus* of the first wave. Moreover, far from presenting a united front against such critiques, women identified as "sisters-in-law" were often strongly divided among themselves and equally disparaging of each other. Mostly the moral contestations revolved around these women's iconic role as the primary recipients and managers of the dollar wealth circulating through Longyan.

More than any other figure, the "sister-in-law" raised uncomfortable questions about the complementarity of family duty and sacrifice between those who emigrated and those who stayed behind. While most villagers, like Chen Mingming, were surprisingly forthcoming and even eager to relay the sufferings endured by both sides in transnational separation, it turned out to be much more difficult to get people to talk about the glaring inequalities created by the redistribution of new wealth among those in Longyan at the expense of those toiling away in ascetic and frequently exploitative conditions abroad. In contrast to people's openness on the topic of suffering, the discourse of pleasure took the more elusive registers of rumor and confession.[1] At the heart of such discourse were anxieties over the new mediating role of dollars and the women who possessed them. As a description, the "eighteen-thousand-dollar sisters-in-law" highlighted both the new wealth made possible by emigration and the problematic concentration of this wealth among those positioned at the most unstable margins of the kinship order. Marking these women as *sao*, or "sisters-in-law," rather than mothers, wives, or even daughters-in-law, was a way to emphasize their disloyal and destabilizing potentialities as the least incorporated members of the family from the perspective of agnatic subjects.

Over the course of my stay in Longyan, I met many women who belonged to the cohort of "sisters-in-law" and heard even more rumors about the exploits of others I did not know. While most of these women resented gossip about their own moral conduct, many were themselves the frequent sources of the rumors circulating about other wives. Mainly, the divulgence of others' pleasures—from excessive vanity and consumerism to gambling problems and secret trysts—provided a common means for the "sisters-in-law" to both generally acknowledge and personally disavow the perceived female transgressions made possible by their possession of new wealth. But while almost all of the "sisters-in-law" shared a propensity for emphasizing their own self-discipline and sacrifice against the unruly desires of other women in their cohort, they also drew quite different moral boundaries among themselves between the limits of permissible and transgressive personal pleasure.

The range of moral positioning among these women was nicely embodied by the four wives of the absent Lin brothers, three of whom were overseas while the eldest brother resided and worked in a neighboring county. While Lin Qing, the eldest sister-in-law, was not technically of the cohort, she was gaining equal footing with the other Lin wives after her second eldest daughter, a nineteen-year-old, had succeeded in reaching the United States less than a year before. These four sisters-in-law, ranging in age from early thirties to mid-forties, all resided with their children in the absence of husbands within the same modest two-story red-brick compound. The house sat at the end of a crammed row of mostly fancier concrete and tiled buildings along the south side of the Min River leading to the foot of the sacred Dragon Head Mountain. Built by their father-in-law, Lin Yong, in the early 1980s during the initial construction boom, this unassuming brick building had at one point been a spacious and comfortable space for the Lins and their five sons before the sons each married and began to subdivide the property into separate quarters for their own branch families. But there was so little property to allocate among the many sons that both the parents and the youngest son and his wife eventually moved out of this house into two smaller dwellings. The remaining four sons divided the house into four equal quarters, each consisting of one ground-floor and one second-floor room, with the two front units occupied by the two eldest brothers' families and the two back units by the younger ones.

Given the tendency of many "sisters-in-law" to move into their natal homes in the absence of husbands, the continual patrilocal residence of four Lin wives under the same roof made these women quite distinct collectively as representatives of a waning, if still hegemonic, Chinese ideal of patrilineal order.[2] This did not mean that the Lin women approached patrilocal residence in the same fashion after their husbands' departures. In fact, though one could not tell from the uniform brick veneer of their small house, these four sisters-in-law embodied very different styles of habitation in their respective quarters of the Lin family compound. From the relative comfort of the interiors alone, the entire house could be divided down the middle between the crammed and worn units on the west side versus the newly remodeled and extended units on the east side (figure 17).

On the west side, the front and back units, occupied by Lin Qing and Lin Mengya respectively, still had the original poured concrete floors laid

Front road facing Min River

	West Side	East Side	
Front Unit	Lin Qing Wife of eldest Lin brother Worn interiors	Lin Xuan Wife of 2nd Lin brother Newly remodeled	New Extension
Back Unit	Lin Mengya Wife of 4th Lin brother Worn interiors	Lin Junhua Wife of 3rd Lin brother Newly remodeled	New Extension
	West Side	East Side	

FIGURE 17 Layout of the Lin residence.

down by their father-in-law in the early 1980s, with simple plastic and fold-out furniture scattered about. Though each residence had a refrigerator and gas burners in the downstairs kitchens and sitting rooms and a small, antiquated television in the single sleeping room upstairs, neither one of these two units possessed the coveted technological markers of new comfort—air conditioners, VCD players, and (increasingly) microwaves and computers. In contrast, both units on the east side, belonging to the second and third sisters-in-law, Lin Xuan and Lin Junhua respectively, housed these various technological signs of modern living. Additionally, both residences had undergone extensive renovation with the installation of new tiled floors and freshly painted walls, as well as built additions grafted onto the upstairs and downstairs rooms to expand the floor space of both living quarters.

This division in living conditions, however, had less to do with the relative prosperity of the Lin women than with their particular approaches and moral positionings as the mediators of new dollar wealth in Longyan. Though the poorest of the four wives, Lin Qing, certainly lived in a unit that reflected her limited resources in the Lin clan, the other occupant of the shabby western quarters, Lin Mengya, turned out to be the most prosperous of the sisters-in-law. As I found out, Lin Mengya's immediate household was the only one that had managed to clear all smuggling debts since her husband's departure; moreover, her husband had successfully established immigration status in the United States. The two Lin wives who resided in the eastern units of the house both turned out to have lingering smuggling debts and husbands still undocumented overseas.

My entrance into the lives of the Lin women developed out of my friendship with Lin Mengya, the youngest of these four sisters-in-law, who happened to be the mother of one of the seventh-grade students I taught at
Longyan middle school. Lin Mengya's eldest child, thirteen-year-old Lin
Cheng, was an incredibly studious, high-achieving, and well-liked student
whom all teachers praised and many classmates admired. Her daughter's
reputation as an exceptional student reflected well on Lin Mengya's own
standing among the teachers at the school. While teachers generally lambasted most "sisters-in-law" for neglecting to oversee their children in
favor of personal indulgences—like gambling in twelve-hour mahjong
sessions or disappearing for adulterous affairs in the city—Lin Mengya
was by all accounts a model mother of model students. As I later found
out, her other two children, a twelve-year-old daughter and a ten-year-old
son, turned out to have equally sterling records at the elementary school
in Longyan.

It took me two tries to meet Lin Mengya. The first time Lin Cheng led
me on an impromptu visit after school to see her mother, only to find
the house empty. Lin Mengya was quite embarrassed about her absence
the next time I had the chance to visit her at her home. A petite and fair
woman with large striking eyes and a self-effacing smile, she greeted me
with much warmth and nervous energy when we finally met at the rear
side door leading into her crammed kitchen and sitting room. Before I had
a chance to settle onto a stool around the family's worn and dingy fold-
out dining table, Lin Mengya was already apologizing for the sorry state
of her home while pushing an elaborate array of seafood and other rich
fare in front of me for some lunch. When I thanked her for this generosity, she apologized yet again for the lack of comfort in her humble home.
Soon this initial apology segued into another one for her having failed to
host me the last time I had stopped by the house. "I really don't go out
much," she apologized more than once for her previous absence. Without
prompting, she then self-consciously explained that she had gone to her
mother's house in a neighboring village. Her mother had needed help
with some household errands, she stressed, and that was the only reason she had not been around. More than any other "sister-in-law" I met,
Lin Mengya felt the need to carefully guard her reputation from even the
slightest hint of wifely impropriety in the absence of her husband. It was
important for her to convey the moral transparency of her actions and particularly to cast her every move outside of the house as a logical extension

of her domestic and kinship duties as wife, mother, and daughter. These included her very visible role as a devout participant in local temple activities and other common religious practices (for example, daily offerings to her household god and the upkeep of ancestral graves and altars) and, by extension, her public designation as the de facto manager of spiritual transactions and cosmic debt for the entire Lin clan.

Like most villagers I knew, Lin Mengya introduced herself by relaying her own tale of sacrifice and suffering on the part of both spouses in the face of mass emigration and conjugal separation. Similar to other "sisters-in-law," she was quick to display detailed knowledge and deep empathy for her husband's struggles in search of overseas prosperity—from his harrowing experiences on three failed smuggling ventures in the late 1980s and early '90s (including an incident of near suffocation in a sealed shipping container) to the daily humiliations and hardships he had endured after finally arriving in the United States in 1993 to his climb up the Chinese restaurant ladder from a lowly, undocumented dishwasher to a respectable cook with refugee status. Alongside her husband's story, she sketched a complementary tale of her own self-sacrifice in Longyan, from the anxious vigils she had held while waiting for news of each of her husband's four smuggling attempts to her frantic efforts after he finally arrived overseas to secure the massive sums necessary to pay off his smugglers.

Shortly after our first meeting, Lin Mengya invited me on a stroll from her house to the newly constructed but still closed-off highway, where she proceeded to lay out her recent history of debt and repayment in even finer detail. On this peaceful stretch of road untreaded by cars and most villagers, she first described the many relatives, friends, and acquaintances who had entrusted her with the loans she desperately needed to secure her husband's release from his smugglers overseas, who held all new arrivals captive until they received full payment for their services. Lin Mengya was not the only "sister-in-law" to emphasize the central role she played in assuming financial debt on her husband's behalf. She was, however, the most explicit in directing me to the importance of a wife's reputation in forging relations of credit. While it was important for lenders to have confidence in the earning capacity and reliability of migrant men, Lin Mengya told me that they also assessed the moral capacity of wives for directing household resources toward the proper channels of reciprocity and repayment. Ultimately, Lin Mengya suggested that much of her husband's situation overseas depended on the credibility of her own word and name among their potential network of lenders. If her husband failed to earn money overseas, creditors needed to know, she said, that "I was the kind of person they could count on, that no matter what, I would look for ways to pay them back."

While it was common to interpret the "eighteen thousand dollars" referenced by *wanbasao* as the new wealth of women left behind, Lin Mengya pointed to an alternative reading of this sum as the necessary debt, not profit, incurred partly on the good names of wives for the sake of husbands' journeys abroad. Money sent back over the years was mostly distributed to others as repayment, Lin Mengya emphasized. For a long while, her family spent 4,000–5,000 RMB every month on interests for loans alone. It had been only two years, after seven hard years of sacrifice, that Lin Mengya and her husband had finally succeeded in paying back all the money they owed. Lin Mengya described how she had shared the burden of debt with her husband by maintaining a disciplined, austere lifestyle and "using only what we needed" with the hard-earned remittances she received from overseas. Such sacrifices could not be expected from all "sisters-in-law," she noted. In no specific terms, Lin Mengya complained of "some mothers" who set bad examples for their children by being "too pleasure-seeking" (*tai tanwan*) in the absence of husbands.

On this quiet stroll, Lin Mengya started to hint at some of the differences and tensions between herself and her three sisters-in-law. She and Lin Qing had similar living quarters, but according to Lin Mengya, they did not share the same habits of domesticity. In an indirect swipe at her eldest sister-in-law, Lin Mengya praised Lin Qing's thirteen-year-old daughter for often cooking and doing laundry for herself and her little brother. Lin Qing, she suggested, did not spend much time minding her children and even less time taking care of household chores. The other two Lin wives had even less to do at home since both of them conveniently sent their children to board at nearby schools. In contrast, Lin Mengya saw it as her duty to keep her children at home under her constant supervision. Out of respect for her husband's sacrifices overseas, Lin Mengya noted that she herself stayed home most of the time to set a moral example for her children. "If you yourself are never around," she argued, "then your kids also don't need to come home. They can just run wild."

As my friendship with Lin Mengya developed, I learned from others around Longyan that her reputation as a self-sacrificing and disciplined wife was indeed impeccable in the village. Zhang Yuan, who lived down the street from the Lins, echoed the general good impression of Lin Mengya when she described her as someone who was "very well-behaved (*hen guai*) and always at home." Lin Mengya did not take her good standing in the village for granted. For one thing, the consummate local wife turned out not to be a true "local" but someone who had relocated to Fuzhou from Sichuan as a young child. Acutely tuned to villagers' suspicions of her "outsider" origins, Lin Mengya by her own admission had worked harder than most to cultivate local respectability as a model wife and fend off the kind of unseemly gossip that swirled around other "sisters-in-law" in Longyan.

In contrast to Lin Mengya, the other three Lin wives had more varied and contentious reputations in the village. Lin Qing made her presence felt in front of the Lins' little brick building, where on a typical afternoon she sat and surveyed all who passed by while exchanging news and gossip with those around her. A stout and plain woman in her forties, Lin Qing was largely known as a busybody who never strayed far from her house and could always be found in hushed or heated conversations with neighbors on the street. Though she lived in humble circumstances and was the poorest of the four Lin wives, Lin Qing was not generally seen as a disciplined wife exempt from village scrutiny of unruly female pleasures. Even without the requisite signs of money wealth, Lin Qing's leisurely indulgence in gossip made her suspect to those around her, and they often criticized her for a sharp tongue and a lack of discretion.

The other two Lin wives fit the more typical profiles of "sisters-in-law" as morally ambiguous and questionable women with new money to squander on personal pleasures. Both Lin Xuan, the second sister-in-law, and Lin Junhua, the third, were known to spend their time and resources more freely on themselves than either Lin Mengya or Lin Qing. This propensity for personal indulgence was reflected not only by the greater luxury of their living quarters, but also by both Lin Xuan's and Lin Junhua's inclination to while away the afternoons playing mahjong.

As I learned, playing mahjong had become one of the more controversial activities for those grappling with new wealth and leisure in the village, not only because mahjong always involved money stakes but also because those who played it were notorious for becoming obsessed with the game to the neglect of their responsibilities. Not surprisingly, the most common critiques singled out "sisters-in-law" for being so consumed in mahjong sessions that they played late into the night and forgot to come home to take care of their children. While there were always villagers with a penchant for gambling, people agreed that as a result of unprecedented money and free time among those with overseas connections, mahjong had grown from a marginal vice to a widespread and routine pastime over the last decade and a half. This centrality of mahjong in people's daily lives was evident by the humorous way players often referred to their gambling sessions as "going to work" (*shangban*) or "going to school" (*shangke*).

On a typical afternoon in Longyan, when the streets quieted down after the green market closed and the morning bustle of shoppers subsided, one could commonly find many villagers, especially women, gathered in groups of four in front of houses or in someone's sitting room, shuffling mahjong tiles in games that often stretched into the evening hours. Lin Xuan and Lin Junhua were among those who enjoyed spending their afternoons in mahjong sessions, though they did not play with the same consistency or for the same stakes. In particular, Lin Xuan tried hard to distinguish her more moderate approach from the destructive extremes associated with the younger Lin Junhua, who was known to lose upwards of 7,000 RMB in one sitting. Like most women I knew who played the game, including Chen Mingming and Zhang Yuan, Lin Xuan tried to deemphasize the money aspect of mahjong in favor of the sociability of these afternoon sessions. Mahjong gave Lin Xuan an opportunity to gather with friends, she told me. "When I don't play," she noted, "I'm just one person alone at home."

On different occasions, the outgoing Lin Xuan spoke with visible pleasure about the nuances of mahjong. While mahjong was inconceivable without some money at risk, Lin Xuan told me that one could just as easily play with small change as with big stakes if the goal was simply to get together with friends rather than to gamble with abandon. She suggested that mahjong did not have to become the kind of destructive obsession critics often claimed it to be. Rather, it could remain a harmless pleasure given the right discipline and measured approach to the game. Lin Xuan pointed out that she neither gambled for big stakes nor gathered for these games daily, as more avid mahjong players were known to do in Longyan. Though she was less self-conscious about her moral positioning in the domestic sphere than the disciplined Lin Mengya, Lin Xuan also did not want to be perceived as someone who only pursued personal pleasures to the detriment of household responsibilities. Although Lin Xuan never disavowed her interest in playing mahjong, she stressed how infrequently she had a chance to play the game because of some domestic duties she had recently assumed. Though her two teenage children no longer required much oversight, Lin Xuan had taken in a seven-year-old nephew who, she told me, needed a lot of attention at home and made it difficult for her to frequent afternoon mahjong sessions as she had done before. Unlike the younger Lin Junhua, who rarely stayed at home, Lin Xuan tried harder to maintain some balance between the personal pursuit of pleasures and domestic expectations.

Of the four Lin wives, Lin Junhua best evoked the kinds of moral problems associated with the "sisters-in-law" as arbiters of new money in Longyan. A thin and fashionable woman in her mid-thirties, Lin Junhua flaunted many of the conservative expectations for the patrilineal containment of wives in the absence of husbands. Unlike the other Lin wives, who never strayed very far from the Lin residence, Lin Junhua circulated broadly in pursuit of leisure activities without much regard for village gossip. With her only daughter at boarding school and her husband overseas, Lin Junhua saw little reason to stay cooped up at home around the other Lin wives. As it turned out, she was not even on speaking terms with either the other three wives or her elderly in-laws anymore.

Lin Junhua's estrangement from the Lin clan mainly revolved around what was perceived as her disregard for the norms of reciprocity and filiality in the extended family. According to Lin Mengya, Lin Junhua used to be the favorite daughter-in-law of the elderly Lin Yong and his wife before her husband emigrated. In fact, because of the parents' fondness for this couple, they had diverted most of their savings—some 200,000 RMB—to the smuggling venture of Lin Junhua's husband in the early 1990s. The other Lin sons apparently had to rely much more on themselves to finance their own journeys overseas. Despite this favoritism, Lin Junhua never once gave money to her in-laws, even on customary occasions like birthdays and Lunar New Year, after her husband began to send remittances home. Not only did she never show proper appreciation to the inlaws, but she also got into heated disputes with them over the excessive sums she lost at mahjong. While Lin Qing responded to her in-laws' distaste for mahjong by spending more time at home, Lin Junhua simply repudiated these criticisms by cutting off all ties with the in-laws, apparently with the blessings of her husband, who took her side in this family conflict.

The other Lin wives all resented Lin Junhua for what they saw as her excessive selfishness in shirking her family obligations in pursuit of personal pleasures. Because Lin Junhua did not contribute any money or energy to support the elderly Lin parents, the other three wives had to shoulder a greater proportion of the burden. The different moral positioning of these four wives became especially clear in the weeks approaching Lunar New Year, when the elderly Lins made it known that they would like $1,500 as the annual money gift from their children. Needless to say, the estranged Lin Junhua continued to keep all her money to herself. Meanwhile, upon hearing her in-laws' request, the loquacious Lin Qing made a public lament of her financial woes as the last one to establish overseas connections among the Lin wives. Though Lin Qing's vocal complaints about money did not win her any popularity among the neighbors, they discouraged the other Lin wives from exerting pressure on her to contribute a fair share to their in-laws' New Year's gift. Nobody relished the idea of Lin Qing's airing any more private family tensions on the village streets.

Thus Lin Mengya and Lin Xuan were left to work out between themselves how to meet their in-laws' request. Eager as always to please her in-laws, Lin Mengya hoped that she and Lin Xuan could each contribute $750. Lin Xuan, however, balked at the amount and offered to give a more moderate $500 instead. Given that only two of them were contributing, Lin Xuan wanted to strike a compromise for a smaller offering to the Lin parents. Lin Xuan also suspected that the in-laws wanted such a large sum only so that they could divert most of it to their youngest son, who still resided in Longyan, although he and his wife were often criticized by the other family members as unemployed and ungrateful loafers living freely off their parents and other siblings. Lin Xuan did not want to contribute any more than necessary to her in-laws' support of these indulgent and unproductive relatives. In contrast, Lin Mengya did not think it was her role to second-guess how her in-laws used the money they received from their children. As Lin Mengya saw it, her only moral obligation as a filial wife was to honor her in-laws' requests, not to judge them. In the end, while Lin Xuan stuck firmly to her $500 limit, the ever-dutiful Lin Mengya felt compelled to give the remaining $1,000 to meet the in-laws' original wish for the Lunar New Year.

The Tastes of Money: From "Eating Loss" to "Eating Duck"

Lin Mengya did not shoulder the extra financial burden without some complaint. "They're all so selfish," she said resentfully about the other Lin wives when she recounted this family dispute to me shortly after the New Year. "They think only of themselves and spend big money on their own bodies—wearing pretty clothes, making themselves up, out everywhere gambling and indulging [*xiangshou*]," she griped. Lin Mengya went on to complain about how the other women all believed they got the better of her by getting her to pick up their slack in meeting filial duties. While Lin Mengya deferred her own pleasures to meet moral obligations, the rest of the wives, she suggested, only wanted to protect themselves and make sure that they were not the ones to "eat loss" (*chikui*) or be taken advantage of in the family. "They are all more cunning [*lihai*] than me," she grumbled. "And they all think that I'm just a fool [*shagua*]." Lin Mengya then added defiantly, "But I'd rather eat loss and do what ought to be done. I'd rather play the fool and do the right thing." After all, she pointed out, there is such a thing as *huibao*, or moral retribution, in the world (cf. H.-C. Chang and Holt 1994; Hsu 1971; L-s. Yang 1957).

Like other devout worshippers of popular religion in Longyan (see chapter 5), Lin Mengya had great confidence in the cosmic regulation of people's fortunes in the long term, including the eventual karmic comeuppance of indulgent and unfilial wives. She regularly enacted such convictions by assuming the ritual responsibilities for daily prayers and spiritual transactions as the manager of the Lin family's cosmic debt. Amid more calculating and self-interested others, Lin Mengya's willingness to "eat loss" and "play the fool" made sense to her as part of a regime of value premised on the social embeddedness of money and sentiment in relations of ongoing debt and exchange. Directing money to the in-laws might have detracted from Lin Mengya's own possibilities for personal consumption. But it enabled her to enact her moral superiority as someone with proper regard and loyalty to others, as opposed to her sisters-in-law, whom she accused of "not having *renqing* (human feeling)" in their personal relationships. As observed elsewhere in China (H.-C. Chang and Holt 1994; Hwang 1987; Kipnis 1996; Pieke 1995; L-s. Yang 1957; M. Yang 1994), Lin Mengya evoked "human feeling" as a moral discourse on the proper conduct of social relations based on a sense of indebtedness and loyalty toward others. Someone with "human feeling" was expected to nurture bonds of reciprocity and empathy over instrumental interests, to privilege mutual aid and sacrifice over personal material gain. In contrast, as Mayfair Yang has noted, "To accuse someone of 'lacking human feeling' (*meiyou renqing*) is tantamount to saying he or she does not exhibit the natural affect and feelings of attachment and obligation to other people. It questions whether a person is morally worthy of being called human" (1994, 68). The recognition of "human feeling" was crucial to the art of "making oneself a person" (*zuoren*). Commonly spoken of as an emotional debt that was "owed" (*qian renqing*), it normalized human relations as affective entanglements through which demands of return had to be negotiated, whether voluntarily through moral acts of sacrifice or through the cosmic mechanism of karmic retribution (*huibao*) (Chang and Holt 1994; Hsu 1971).

Lin Mengya's embrace of "eating loss" did not simply negate calculation and self-interest in the politics of redistribution. Rather, it was an embodiment of sacrifice as a kind of credit in its own right, of loss as a productive extension of the self in relation to others.[3] As Lin Mengya saw it, it was not only the possession of money per se but how one managed its circulation—both within this world and across the next—that indexed the relative fortunes and moral creditability of wives left behind. Village debates over the uses of dollars and the relative balance of sacrifice and pleasure in everyday life exemplified what Judith Farquhar has aptly described as "the broad social problem of excess and deficiency for modern China" (2002, 124). In particular, Farquhar has noted that "a rich vocabulary and logic of excess and deficiency" has long suffused many aspects of social life and discourse from Chinese medicine to the various economisms of the Maoist regime and its reformist successors. Recognizing that deprivation and shortages coexisted and directly contributed to pockets of overabundance and surplus, both Chinese medicine and Maoist egalitarian policies sought to regulate the interrelated processes of depletion and repletion by promoting an ideal of balanced circulation and redistribution. From the management of bodily flows of *qi* and blood in Chinese medicine to the reallocation of state grain, land, and labor under Mao's collectivist vision, the problems of excess and deficiency, Farquhar argues, "link political and carnal domains from the most elevated to the most mundane" (30).[4] This assessment rang true in Longyan as well, where concerns over the asymmetries of indulgences and deprivations commonly manifested at the level of the body.

The realm of eating, Farquhar showed, was an especially rich domain for understanding the micro-maneuvering and moral management of social selves and relations in contemporary China. In Longyan, I found that eating, as both metaphor and practice, also figured prominently in the debates over deficiency and excess. Lin Mengya's incitement of "eating loss" was just one example of the larger moral discourse on newfound wealth and embodied desire that privileged food—its consumption and transmission—as a pragmatic and symbolic anchor of valuation. Linkages between the ethics of eating and economics were widely cited by Longyan villagers across gender, generation, and status. In criticizing the new tastes for luxury among the younger generations, village seniors commonly juxtaposed their visceral memories of hunger and "eating bitterness" (chiku) during the Great Leap famine against what they saw as the blasé and wasteful eating habits of their reform-era children and grandchildren. Younger generations, in turn, often dismissed the food practices of many seniors, who were known to save and eat every last scrap of leftovers, even food that had turned bad, as unnecessarily ascetic and backward.

Lin Yuliang, the elderly mother of the Lin clan, was among the older residents who complained of young people by pointing to their carelessness with food. "Youths today just want to play around," she told me in Lin Mengya's kitchen after watching her grandchildren eat lunch and dash out of the house one afternoon. "They don't want to work and don't understand how difficult it is to earn money anymore." "You see," she pointed to the half-eaten food left by Lin Mengya's son, "they eat a mouthful and if they don't like it, they just toss it out." A lean and wiry woman with a dash of gray in her straight bob, Lin Yuliang contrasted young people today with her own youth under the Maoist regime, when she recalled plowing the fields and breaking rocks in the surrounding mountains all day just to earn a little bit of rice to eat. She cupped her hands together to show me the meager portion of rice she had to survive on during the worst years of the Great Leap famine between 1959 and 1961. At the peak of her family's difficulties, Lin Yuliang told me about how her mother divided up her own rice allotment among the other family members and tried to subsist only on wild vegetation that the family gathered in the hills. Sacrificing her own health for the sake of her children and husband, the mother eventually grew weak and died of poor nutrition before the food crisis ended in China. This ethos of personal sacrifice for the collective good was one that Lin Yuliang, like many other seniors around her, tried to impart to her children and grandchildren with mixed success.

Of the four Lin wives, Lin Mengya aligned herself most closely with her mother-in-law's ideals of self-sacrifice and frugal living in service of the family. For Lin Mengya, "eating loss" could be said to encompass a whole style of living premised on the deferral of more tangible personal pleasures for the extension of personal ties and one's good reputation. Lin Mengya exhibited her willingness to "eat loss" in the money dispute with her sisters-in-law over the Lunar New Year. She also embodied the productive virtues of self-effacement and sacrifice in the more mundane ways she conducted her everyday life, from her humble living quarters to all manners of food, dress, and sociality. In particular, when it came to food hospitality, Lin Mengya was quite proud that her in-laws, as well as others around her, favored eating in her shabby residence over the more luxurious quarters of the other Lin wives. More than anything, Lin Mengya saw her in-laws' preference to eat in her kitchen as affirmation of her moral conduct and reputation as someone with superior "human feeling" for others.

As in other places in China and elsewhere, to give food in Longyan constituted a basic form of generosity, an act of self-expansion rather than contraction in relation to others. In contrast, a calculative and greedy person was often pointedly described by villagers as a voracious consumer or, more specifically, as someone "who eats others" (*chi bieren*). This understanding resonates strongly with Nancy Munn's description of Gawan food exchanges in Papua New Guinea, in which she highlighted the embodied nature of value transformation: "Whereas consumption directs food 'immediately' into the body, reducing the duration of the food and destroying its potential for yielding anything in the future, the transaction of food away from the body can produce further positive value products that themselves transcend the body of the donor" (1986, 50). Feeding others, especially one's parents and children, nurtured the reproductive ties of "human feeling" and extended one's intersubjective horizons as a person of moral repute.

Longyan residents suspicious of the corrupting influence of new money and leisure on the "sisters-in-law" especially liked to cite food practices as indicators of people's moral dispositions. Offering food or drink was a fundamental aspect of hosting etiquette in Longyan; moreover, how, where, and what one offered marked important social distinctions and hierarchical positionings among those involved in the food exchanges. In Lin Mengya's case, her in-laws' preference for eating at her place was significant as a marker not only of her more generous and filial nature but also of her domestic reliability as a proper wife and mother who could routinely be found at home, cooking hearty meals for family and guests alike. To preside over the stove and family meals at home was one of the most basic expectations of wives in Longyan—one that the "sisters-in-law" were commonly accused of failing to meet in the absence of husbands. Anecdotes of neglected children cooking for themselves served as typical illustrations of the family disorder caused by derelict and pleasure-seeking wives with new money and leisure at their disposal.

In one vivid and extreme instance, I watched Deng Feiyan rail against her cousin, a "sister-in-law," for shamelessly expecting her mother-in-law to cook for her and take care of all household chores while she herself slept until noon and played mahjong the rest of the day. As the mother-in-law bustled around the kitchen to prepare lunch for us on that visit to Deng Feiyan's relatives, the cousin made her entrance by blithely sitting down at the mahjong table in the adjacent room without so much as a nod to anyone else in the house. This promptly sent Deng Feiyan into a flying rage about the corrupting influence of new money on her cousin's moral conduct. As the cousin stoically shuffled mahjong tiles by herself, Deng Feiyan jabbed an accusatory finger her cousin's way while addressing her loud and biting comments to me. "Look at her!" she pointed. "Ever since her old man started to send her money [from abroad], she won't lift a finger [bu dongshou]." She added indignantly, "Who ever heard of an old mother cooking for her daughter-in-law?"

In contrast, Lin Mengya not only cooked regularly for family and guests but also served the food in a way that affirmed the filial norms and proper social hierarchy. On the many occasions I dined with Lin Mengya's family, she made sure her guests and in-laws had the first taste of the dishes hot off the wok, followed by her children; she herself was last. The richest and most elaborate foods were similarly offered to elders and visitors first, with Lin Mengya often instructing her children to place these morsels on others' plates before they were allowed to eat. Typically, Lin Mengya busied herself at the stove for a good portion of the meal and sat down only after others had had their share of the best dishes at the table. She not only ate last but often reserved leftovers for herself while encouraging others to consume the freshest and most desirable foods. For example, Lin Mengya polished off the half-eaten meal her son had left when her mother-in-law used it to illustrate the wasteful habits of the younger generations. Lin Mengya also occasionally lectured her children in front of me about the hardships their father had endured overseas to ensure that there was food on their table. In this way, food became a medium both for concretizing the sacrifices of labor power abroad and for enacting one's complementary efforts in the containment of consumer excesses at home.

This stance did not mean that Lin Mengya felt compelled to eat poorly. If anything, the rich fare she ate and shared with others was one of the distinctive ways she embodied prosperity amid otherwise humble living conditions. Eating well, and particularly displaying a taste for seafood, was a key distinguishing factor between villagers with overseas connections and those still stuck with "peasant" standards of living. Zhang Yuan first pointed out the social significance of eating habits to me when she explained her own family's motivations to establish overseas connections. "When they all eat seafood every day," she told me, "you want to eat seafood as well." Zhang Yuan added that while she herself did not mind eating more humble fare, she could not bear seeing her children longing to taste the same treats as their overseas-connected friends and neighbors had. Similarly, though Lin Mengya stressed her own frugal eating habits, she did not spare any expense in cooking lavish meals for family and guests.

As I found out, some indulgence in luxury was not only permissible but even necessary to distinguish the social status of villagers with overseas connections from those without. As noted, a taste for seafood was one of the minimal markers of class distinction that even the most self-sacrificing "sister-in-law" (like Lin Mengya) embraced. Dressing oneself and one's children in reasonably new and stylish fashion was the other widely permissible luxury for demarcating the lifestyle of "sisters-in-law" and other transnational villagers from their "peasant" neighbors. These minimum standards of eating and dressing set the hard boundaries between cosmopolitan and provincial taste cultures in Longyan.[5] In addition, they marked the safe end of a larger spectrum of emergent and contested pleasures among the growing consumer class of "sisters-in-law" and others with new money and leisure at their disposal.

Over the great distance between the United States and China, the dollar was no doubt the most prominent token of value circulating between villagers and their overseas kin. Both as loans to finance journeys abroad and as remittances wired back to villagers, dollars became primary mediators for the reproduction of kin, marital, and other relations of "human feeling" across the transnational divide. What one did with dollars became an important way for assessing ongoing loyalty and sentiment between husbands and wives, parents and children, and friends and neighbors in close and far-flung places. Ideally, most villagers hoped that dollars accumulated abroad would circulate back into the channels of social reproduction in Longyan, from the extension of divine credit through temple donations (see chapter 5) to the affirmation of filial and domestic duties through customary money gifts and the generous feeding of others. But villagers also understood that the sacrifices made for obtaining dollars did not always result in just rewards, particularly with social bonds tested by the corporeal absence and indefinite separation of loved ones. There were plenty of tragic stories of husbands who stopped sending remittances, abandoning village wives and children for mistresses and new families abroad, and there were even more tales of "sisters-in-law" who squandered their husbands' hard-earned dollars on all sorts of personal indulgences. In the worse case scenario, villagers feared that the sacrifices made for dollars could lead to the commodification of interpersonal relations and by extension of persons themselves; whereby sentiment could be calculated in dollars and alienated from loved ones, who could themselves be exchanged or replaced. Fundamentally, local sayings like "tears for dollars, beloved village for dollars" spoke to these anxieties over new money and the "commodity potential of all things" (Appadurai 1986).

Nowhere were these anxieties more evident than in widespread rumors about the "sisters-in-law" and their propensity to "eat duck" (chiya) in their husbands' absence. As one might guess, insinuations about "eating duck" had very little to do with culinary tastes for a certain fatty bird, but they had everything to do with these women's voracious appetites. In this case, "duck," or yazi—the desired object of female consumption—was a clever neologism and male counterpart to the older, gender-specific slang term for prostitute (ji), the word for chicken.[6] "Ducks" were largely described as urban outsiders who targeted lonely but rich village wives on their excursions into Fuzhou City. Ranging in age from the late teens through the thirties, these men were known to prowl urban spaces where "sisters-in-law" from the countryside congregated for occasional fun in the city. A typical opening line from one of these men was the question, "Are you from Lianjiang?" in reference to one of the rural counties in

Fuzhou notorious for transnational migration. Commonly presenting themselves as wealthy city entrepreneurs, these male charmers purportedly lured "sisters-in-law" into sexual affairs and lavish spending by offering to serve as their sophisticated guides to city thrills and entertainment. After initially dining these women on their own tabs, "ducks" typically cited some temporary cash flow problem or recent downswings in a fictive business to begin bilking them out of their dollar remittances. According to village gossip, some wives, caught up in sex and infatuation, willingly indulged their ducks with loans, fine dining, new clothes, and even rent for city apartments for their secret trysts. Those who refused to comply with such money demands had to struggle with threats of extortion and even violence from these men.

Although I never encountered a "duck" in the flesh, these male escorts made their presence felt in Longyan, as much as absent husbands did, through everyday exchanges of village gossip and through periodic phone conversations with overseas relations. Like their foil, the sacrificial husband overseas, "ducks" were largely spectral subjects of village life who cast long shadows from afar and registered a pervasive social presence less through direct encounters than through such highly mediated forms as the circulation of rumors, the speculative trails of money, and the perceived bodily discipline and moral conduct of the "sisters-in-law" in and out of Longyan. Villagers did not need to see the women with "ducks" to raise the specter of adulterous and commodified relations. As figures not only of prostitution but also of urban indulgence in general, "ducks" were often implicated in the embodied and moral trajectory of certain wives, especially those who routinely displayed pretensions for urban lifestyles and strayed far beyond their village homes in search of personal pleasure in Fuzhou City.

In effect, people pointed to a correlation between the physical and moral containment of the "sisters-in-law" within the circuits of social reproduction in Longyan. Village wives who squandered money on "ducks" were routinely denounced as "fools who don't know how to obediently stay at home [guaiguaide zai jia]." The farther one wandered (and circulated money) beyond the normative domains of domestic duty—from the house, village temples, and the local green market—the more one became morally suspect. Thus Lin Junhua, the wayward Lin sister-in-law who rarely remained home, was subject to more intense speculation of "eating duck" than the other Lin wives, who exerted a stronger presence in the house. Beyond her routine indulgence in high-stakes mahjong games around Longyan, Lin Junhua also tended to venture beyond the gaze of fellow villagers into urban consumer centers, including the nearby Mawei district, the official economic development zone in the region, and especially Fuzhou City, the commercial capital of the province. While no direct accusations were made against Lin Junhua for her city excursions, "sisters-in-law" who drifted far from their homes in the absence of their husbands were widely assumed to be in pursuit of the most objectionable and transgressive pleasure of all: adulterous and commodified sex with distant strangers.

The association of female adultery with the allure of city life also functioned as a moral indictment of what some people saw as the corrupting influence of growing urban consumerism and self-indulgence on village mores and interpersonal relations. In Longyan, villagers in their teens and twenties were especially inclined to embrace urban trends of fashion and entertainment and to venture into the city to spend money on nightlife and other consumer pleasures to the disapproval of the older generations, especially seniors who had lived through famine and collectivization. "Sisters-in-law" and others in their thirties and forties were more divided among themselves about the uses of dollars for city pleasures than either the cohort of elders above them or the generation of teens and young adults below. Just as some, like Lin Mengya, aligned themselves with the social mores of their elders, others, like Lin Junhua, embraced the more youthful desires of the children of economic reform and new money wealth. Although Lin Mengya and Lin Junhua shared some basic standards of eating and dressing, Lin Junhua was more likely to display her taste for seafood in city restaurants than over her own stove at home and to make herself presentable by wearing not only fashionable clothes but also sophisticated makeup and hairstyles reflective of urban trends. In contrast, Lin Mengya shunned such additional enhancements as immodest signs of female vanity and seduction.

While people believed that women's dealings with "ducks" mainly took place in Fuzhou City as part of a slippery slope of urban excess, the most incriminating rumors pointed to the havoc caused when lovers showed up in the home villages of adulterous wives. Some rumors involved "ducks" making sudden village appearances to expose their secret affairs to the women's clueless family and neighbors. Others simply told of "sisters-in-law" who were so shameless that they carelessly brought their "ducks" back to their homes. Either way, the presence of "ducks" in the village often foreshadowed violent encounters and bad ends for at least some of the people involved. One of the most notorious tales concerned two lonely "sisters-in-law" who happened to literally be the wives of two brothers living under the same roof in Longyan's neighboring town. With husbands gone indefinitely in the United States and a steady flow of dollars coming in their absence, these two sisters-in-law reportedly began an unseemly affair with the same young, spry "duck" right in their own village home. Whatever the actual arrangement, this affair was apparently so excessive and all-consuming that one morning the women awoke in their house to find their "duck" completely spent and stone-cold dead in bed. In what should have been the place of an absent husband, the commodified body of the dead "duck" offered a dystopic vision of what could happen as a result of family dispersal and indefinite separation when co-residence and corporeal intimacy were sacrificed for the liquidity of dollars.

Amid the diverse and seductive temptations for personal gratification in the increasingly commodified world of post-Mao China, tales of "ducks" and "sisters-in-law" pointed to widespread anxieties over the moral reliability of women as the mediators of new family wealth and interpersonal relations in Longyan. If the disposition to "eat loss" occupied one end of a moral continuum for managing dollars and desires, "eating duck" exemplified the other extreme. The rumors of sexual transgression also seemed to echo earlier preoccupations with the moral management of selves, particularly the excessive appetites of bodies conceived as economies of finite resources (cf. Furth 1999). As the tale of the two consuming sisters-in-law and their fully consumed "duck" illustrated, bodies could not indulge indefinitely without draining their life energies and turning good credit into dangerous debt. Like all other resources, bodies, as cosmic leases on life, could also be squandered and used up without some restoration of balance between excess and deficiency. As the late Ming scholar and physician Yuan Huang eloquently inquired about unchecked desire and the dangers of sexual indulgence, "When the fire is blazing, who can restore the firewood?" (cited in Furth 1999, 202). This question and its possible answers were, of course, very gendered for Yuan Huang as well as for my subjects in contemporary Longyan.

Although the village wives known as "eighteen-thousand dollar sisters-in-law" were certainly not the only people who gossiped or gambled or engaged in sexual transgressions, their appetites for such indulgences were generally considered more unruly and problematic than those of others in these migrant-sending communities. Not only were these women the main subjects of stories about sex but they were also imagined as the primary producers and consumers of such gossip. Though villagers of varying age, gender, marital status, and overseas connections shared such stories with me, they also implied that only certain kinds of female subjects with too much leisure time, overseas wealth, and lack of male supervision would foment the idle pleasures and dangerous excesses of such talk. Moreover, though it was common knowledge that overseas husbands indulged their sexual appetites with prostitutes and that their elderly fathers in the village employed female domestic workers (*baomu*) to fulfill all household needs including sex, these activities were rarely narrated with the same kind of public fascination and self-conscious moral positioning as tales of "ducks" and "sisters-in-law."

Not only were the men's appetites for commodified sex seen as more natural than those of women, but they were also considered more entitled to such consumption as the primary producers of wealth made overseas. While people did not necessarily approve of men's indulgences in prostitution or other kinds of commodified sex, many villagers, including some "sisters-in-law," acknowledged that because overseas husbands earned the money, they also reserved the right to spend it the way they wanted. This logic also extended to elderly fathers, who, unlike the "sisters-in-law," were not expected to allocate the funds they received from overseas for the collective benefit of the household. This positioning of men as the producers of wealth and women as the consumers becomes significantly more complicated when we consider the "ducks"—this curious category of persons who, though not women, were also not quite "men" in villagers' understanding. As I will show in the next section, in many ways questions of "ducks," men, and masculine productivity get at the heart of villagers' entangled desires for continual mass emigration and social reproduction.

Much Ado about Nothing:
Problems of Masculinity and Productivity

People in Longyan most commonly told me two things: (1) "There are no men here," and (2) "There's nothing to do here." Typically these two claims spoke to critiques of rural unemployment in post-Mao China and underlined the necessity for mass emigration from the Fuzhou country-side in the past two decades. In more insidious and elusive form, these notions of "no men" and "nothing to do" reappeared as the moral refrain to gossip about lonely but rich village wives and their propensity for "eat-ing duck" in their husbands' absence. In this way, villagers directly linked the problems of female indulgence and family disorder with the disap-pearance of men and productive labor from village life.

Yet all around me in Longyan I constantly witnessed the daily bustle of male laborers manning fruit stands, laying bricks on new houses, pound-ing metal molds in the concrete factory, and conducting numerous other tasks that seemed to contradict the claims of "no men" and "nothing to do." I was even more puzzled to hear the former assertion consistently issued by a broad swath of male villagers. This perception was so wide-spread among male residents that I quickly developed the retort, "Then what about you?" Similarly, I learned to point to the male laborers all around whenever someone issued the joint complaint of "no men" and "nothing to do." While my retorts often drew initial double takes and awk-ward pauses from villagers not used to challenges to their assumptions, most people were able to smooth over the seeming contradictions of their claims in one of the following ways. Typically, when asked about the seeming contradiction between their own gender positioning and their claim of "no men," most male villagers simply tried to vacate the category of "men" altogether. Young single men, mostly in their early twenties or younger, would declare that they were "still children" (*haishi haizi*), while older men, starting with those in their late thirties and early forties, would explain that they were "already old" (*yijing laole*) and therefore exempt from the expectations of masculine productivity. When asked about the many male laborers on the streets of Longyan, most villagers responded that these workers were internal migrants from peripheral provinces like Sichuan. These productive male bodies also did not qualify as "men"—at least not local "men." As Chen Mingming explained when I pointed out some male construction workers at a village temple, "They are not like us. You can't count them because they are outsiders [*waidiren*]."

These three exemptions of male subjects from the category of "men"—as children, seniors, and outsiders—all pointed to a conflation of mas-culinity with bodily capacities and desires for transnational mobility and overseas wage labor. Over the years, as the first waves of men emigrated en masse and internal migrants took over menial jobs in Longyan, villagers came to see local productive labor as the devalued domain of outsiders. As village employment became associated with lower wages and living standards and the bodily capacities of internal migrants, it became increasingly untenable for Longyan men to remain "men" by staying put in the local labor force.

Although many young men expressed anxieties about the dangers of human smuggling and the hardships of long workdays and menial living conditions abroad, most also saw emigration as a necessary rite of passage into adulthood and particularly into manhood. This did not mean that village youths wholeheartedly embraced this rite of passage. If anything, many young men on the cusp of adulthood seemed reluctant to leave Longyan and often clung to their status as "children" even into their mid-twenties, for as long as they remained "children," they could still indulge in the pleasures of consumption while eschewing family demands on their productive capacities as laboring bodies overseas. A reluctance to emigrate was especially evident among the children of overseas migrants, who had both intimate knowledge of the hardships involved and personal experience of the luxuries afforded by remittances.

Cai Tingjian was one of the many teenage boys coming of age in Longyan who had grown accustomed to a life of leisure since his father had left for the United States when he was still a toddler. Like many other children with a parent overseas, he was largely criticized by his elders, including his teachers and his mother, for spending money carelessly— on junk food, trendy fashions, the video arcade, the pool hall, and other youthful entertainments—without due respect for the sacrifices that had been made to earn the money he squandered. At Cai Tingjian's house one afternoon, I listened to his mother launch into a long rant about her son's self-indulgence and apathy toward school and her fears for his future while he sat sullenly nearby. If he could not make it through the exam system into high school and keep open the prospects of college and placement in a state job, he had no chance of succeeding locally, she told me. While only fourteen years old, Cai Tingjian was already feeling pressure from his mother about going abroad after he finished middle school. "What else are you going to do?" his mother lectured him in front of me. "You want to be like those Sichuanese breaking rocks in these mountains to survive? You think some girl is going to want to spend a whole lifetime suffering with you?" Outside of the house that afternoon, I found

Cai Tingjian sitting by himself down the street while tossing a basketball lazily up and down. While embarrassed about my having witnessed his mother's scolding, Cai Tingjian was passively defiant about the social expectation to emigrate. "Why would I want to go abroad?" he shrugged. "I like being here. It's very relaxed [*qingsong*], very comfortable [*shufu*]. Over there, it just seems so hard [*xinku*]."

As teenage boys like Cai Tingjian entered their twenties, though, those who remained in Longyan increasingly found themselves displaced as liminal subjects awkwardly stalled between childhood and adulthood. The twenty-three-year-old Liu Ming was one of the many boys who had spent his teenage years resisting village expectations for emigration only to have caved in to pressure in the past year. When I first met him, Liu Ming had just begun the process for his first smuggling venture abroad. Like the younger Cai Tingjian, Liu Ming also dreaded the hardships of menial labor and poor living conditions overseas, about which he had learned from long-distance conversations with his two older siblings and other friends who were already in the United States. If only his group of friends were still around, he told me, then he would probably still be enjoying his leisure time in Longyan and not even thinking about emigration. But as his cohort had gradually dispersed abroad over the past few years, Liu Ming said he found himself increasingly isolated and bored in the village, not to mention under heightened scrutiny as one of the few remaining young men without clear prospects or aspirations for leaving Longyan. In particular, as Liu Ming outgrew his claim to childhood status, his continued lack of ambition for going abroad was especially damaging to his village standing. Though there were plenty of male villagers remaining, at least those who had tried but failed to leave Longyan had showed some mettle and moral disposition for productive labor overseas. They had a credible claim on the good faith of villagers. In contrast, Liu Ming's evasion of both emigration and wage labor into his mid-twenties largely cemented his bad reputation as a lazy lout, or *liumang*, in Longyan.

Commonly translated as "hooligan" and associated with male criminality, the term *liumang* was used by villagers to reference certain deviations from village norms of masculine productivity. Male residents who were designated as hooligans, like Liu Ming, were usually able-bodied youths with reputations for indolence and apathy who squandered their productive capacities by shamelessly lingering in Longyan and pursuing idle pleasures at others' expense. The emphasis here was on the broader associations of the term with "the idea of the outsider, the unsettled, and, by implication, the unreliable" (Dutton 1998, 62). As Michael Dutton has observed, "The term *liumang* goes beyond criminal activity to incorporate all those people who . . . are 'without a place'" (1998, 20). This sense of displacement, Dutton added, goes beyond the spatial to the *liumang*'s "exclusion from the norm and exclusion from an acceptable social position" (62).

In many ways, "hooligan" provided a village counterpart to the figure of the "duck" in the city. Like "ducks," "hooligans" were also male subjects of consumer excess who lived off others and occupied marginal spaces of indulgence outside of the productive and reproductive domains of Longyan life. While they were not urban strangers like "ducks," they were also known to wander aimlessly outside of Longyan to dance clubs, bars, and other sites of consumer pleasure in Mawei and Fuzhou City on a regular basis. Similar to the term "ducks," the term *liumang* also had a dehumanizing meaning as the homonym for a "type of biting insect" or horsefly (Dutton 1998, 63). Like "ducks," who were humorously described by villagers as useless males who "feed off the soft hands of women," they were also parasitic figures akin to the biting insect their nickname recalled. While in other Chinese contexts the term has been associated with the machismo of male thugs and mobsters, in this case it was more a term of emasculation and dehumanization that, like "duck," expunged certain male subjects from the category of "men" and in effect marked their social death as moral persons in Longyan.

Although a few local men in respectable occupations—like the two party secretaries and a handful of teachers—circumvented challenges to their productive capacities while remaining in Longyan, the majority of male residents who held peasant registration were not expected to have good prospects as laboring bodies in the village or even in other parts of China. Young men I knew in Longyan uniformly discounted the possibility of working alongside internal migrants at home as an endeavor that would be socially degrading. Yet as Liu Ming discovered, young men could not remain unemployed and live in leisure indefinitely without facing increasing pressures to emigrate or becoming infantilized, dehumanized, or generally effaced as "men." In this sense, "no men" and "nothing to do" were as much prescriptive statements as they were descriptive of the situation for male subjects in Longyan.

Of the various male residents who remained in Longyan, those who could not comfortably occupy the position of either "children" or "seniors" had the hardest time dodging labels like "hooligan" and rationalizing their continual presence as unproductive male subjects in the village. This was especially true for men in their twenties and thirties, who were too old to claim childhood status and yet not old enough to have grown children of their own who could support them and take their place as potential laboring bodies overseas. Unlike other young men who argued that they were "still children" because they were not yet married, Hong Jianyi had fulfilled enough village expectations of adulthood—by becoming a husband and father—to make his inability to emigrate even more conspicuous and awkward. The twenty-six-year-old had little shelter from village speculations of his failed capacities as a "man." Though he had already tried twice to leave the village and continued to look for routes abroad, Hong Jianyi's continual presence as an unemployed husband and father was clearly a social burden to both himself and his family. This was evident in the way Hong Jianyi carried himself in public. Though a physically large man with a talkative and confident presence in his own home, Hong Jianyi always seemed to shrink in public encounters, becoming self-effacing and painfully awkward among others, as if willing his social disappearance from Longyan itself. While villagers did not fault Hong Jianyi for lacking ambition, as they did Liu Ming, they suspected that there must be a physical or mental deficiency keeping men like Hong Jianyi unemployed and stuck in Longyan despite their multiple attempts and great desire to emigrate.

I better understood why Hong Jianyi might cower in public when I witnessed (and became complicit in) the heckling of another male villager while visiting the local green market with Lin Qing one summer morning. Lin Qing and I were walking with groceries toward her house when we came upon a man in his early to mid-thirties walking his bike along the road. Lin Qing beamed at the sight of this disheveled man and cheerfully greeted him by nudging him on the shoulder. "My son said to me the other day that you look Sichuanese," she jokingly teased the man. When the man huffed at this comment and briskly moved ten paces ahead of us, Lin Qing, known for her sharp tongue, turned to me and noted humorously, "You see his face—all dark and strange, like something's not quite right? Looks Sichuanese. But he's not happy because he knows it's an insult." In a voice loud enough for the man to hear, Lin Qing went on to explain that this man had always failed when he had tried to emigrate and that he was just living off overseas relatives who had taken pity on him and sent him a bit of money at Chinese New Year and other occasions. As she continued to relay his social humiliations and low standing in Longyan, the man finally stopped, twirled around, and eyed me unhappily as a passive participant in his torment. "Who's *she?*" he pointed at me. Lin Qing gladly took the opportunity to heap further shame on the man. "She's from America, a *PhD*," she noted, as if to contrast my social status and connection to her with his. Surprisingly, the man nodded respectfully and then asked me wistfully, "America is so much better than here, right?" When I told him that I thought it seemed more relaxing and comfortable in Longyan than working sixteen-hour days as an undocumented migrant in the United States, he grew agitated again. "You don't know how much harder it is to have nothing to do," he told me angrily. As he launched into an extended complaint about the humiliations of relying on the charity of others and not working for oneself, Lin Qing pulled me away and pointed dismissively at the ranting man. "He's not right in the head," she laughed lightly. "He's been relying on others too long." Stunned by her comment, the man recoiled with shame. "You think I want it this way?" he hissed. "You just don't know how hard it is to live this way, how hard to have not a thing to do." Looking defeated, the man continued to complain audibly to himself even as he gave up talking to us and lurched ahead again, this time putting as much distance as he could between us.

Perhaps more than most, Lin Qing should have understood the social humiliations suffered by this man since her own husband had never managed to go overseas and merely lived in obscurity as a factory foreman about an hour outside of Longyan. But perhaps because her daughter had recently succeeded in going abroad, Lin Qing felt no qualms about publicly taunting this man about his failures. Teasing him that he resembled a Sichuanese was one way Lin Qing could differentiate her own newly elevated position as someone with overseas connections from this man's persistent outsider status as a non-person and non-"man" in village life. When it came to desires for emigration, villagers adamantly told me that there was no such thing as "men" who wanted to stay behind in Longyan. "It's not possible," Zhang Yuan told me. "The only ones who remain here are those who are disabled [*canfei*] or have mental problems [*tounao you wenti*]." While teenagers like Cai Tingjian may at first be reluctant to consider going overseas, most villagers believed that all able-bodied young men eventually saw the necessity and embarked on this rite of passage, as had the older Liu Ming. As people told me, emigration was "the only road out" (*chulu weiyi*) of social oblivion for those in their prime productive years. Even if one did not succeed in multiple attempts, giving up was not an option for men like Hong Jianyi, who were caught between the proverbial rock and hard place of village expectations for "men." At minimum, one needed to exhibit a desire to go overseas even as one remained stuck in Longyan. This was certainly the lesson Liu Ming had learned under increasing criticism for his "hooligan" ways when he finally initiated the process to emigrate.

Male villagers who could no longer claim the safe haven of childhood could give up trying to go abroad only when they had children old enough to take their places. Deng Kongshang, the forty-one-year-old brother of Deng Feiyan, was one of the many men who had attempted to emigrate several times until his nineteen-year-old daughter managed to get smuggled into the United States. A thin and rumpled man with an easy smile and a perpetual cigarette in his hand, Deng Kongshang carried himself gingerly and wearily around his house, like a man much older than his years. Like many unemployed men who no longer relentlessly pursued a way out of Longyan, Deng Kongshang proclaimed that he was "already old" and therefore entitled to a life of rest and leisure. Though he still lived with his wife and teenage son in a dark and crumbling brick house that reflected his failures to emigrate, Deng Kongshang no longer felt the need to redeem himself as a laboring body since he could point to his maturing children, particularly his daughter overseas, as the heirs to his emigrant aspirations.

Though he had never made it permanently out of Longyan, over the years Deng Kongshang had actually spent quite a bit of time overseas— one month in Japan, eight months in Thailand, and one and a half years in Vietnam (among other stints abroad)—all in an effort to enter the United States. In total, he estimated having spent three years in different intermediate sites, the results of which were always arrest, deportation, and fines. And these three years did not take into account the other years he had intermittently spent in the village plotting new attempts. But far from regretting the failed efforts, Deng Kongshang proudly defended the times he had spent overseas. He pointed to the valuable experience and knowledge he had gained every time he "stepped into the larger society" (*zoudao shehuishang*). He described how he had broadened his horizons by learning about other people's customs. He had learned to "use his head" (*dong naojin*) and discriminate between trustworthy people and those who only "ate others" (*chi bieren*). "It's only in these kinds of situations overseas that we Fuzhounese can learn how to do business better and become bosses ourselves," Deng Kongshang explained. Even failed smuggling ventures, he argued, are "much better than never once having left [the village], where day in and day out you only know how to plant sweet potatoes." Whether one failed or not, the act of leaving Longyan alone was valuable as "a kind of training" (*yizhong xunlian*), he said.

Although Deng Kongshang's many short stints abroad enabled him to claim some social creditability and self-respect as someone with experience and knowledge beyond Longyan's provincial borders, he admitted that until his daughter arrived in the United States, he could not shake village speculations about his productive capacities. Like Hong Jianyi and the man heckled by Lin Qing, both of whom had tried and failed to leave Longyan multiple times, Deng Kongshang increasingly found himself in a double bind of desire and disgrace. The more he tried and failed to emigrate, the higher were the stakes on his subsequent attempts. It seemed that villagers were willing to chalk up only one or two failed attempts to knowledge learned and "training" gained. After the first two, it became exponentially more difficult to convert failures into the kind of cosmopolitan savvy that Deng Kongshang claimed for himself. Ultimately, as Deng Kongshang acknowledged, "It doesn't matter who you are here; if you just get to the United States, everyone will say, 'Wow! This person is very sharp [*hen lihai*], very capable [*hen you nengli*].' If you don't get there? Well, then people all think you must be lacking in ability [*mei nengli*]." The only escape for men like Deng Kongshang was to claim old age and the entitlements of parenthood by transferring social expectations to their children as emerging laboring bodies.

The common view of Longyan as a domain of women, children, and old people with "nothing to do" suggests that gender had become deeply entangled with questions of mobility, productivity, and personhood in the project of mass emigration. In this case, the significant gender divide that had emerged had less to do with a binary between men and women than between "men" and "non-men," with the latter encompassing not only female subjects but also children, seniors, and outsiders who could be male but never "men" as long as they stayed put in Longyan.[7]

While all able-bodied males faced certain social death as "men" if they did not try to emigrate, women's physical residence and mobility were more contingent on their specific kin positionality as daughters, wives, or mothers. For example, I found that young women with plans to leave were just as likely to cite their conjugal prospects as their employment opportunities as their reasons for emigration. Echoing the general view of masculine productivity, Zheng Hui told me that her female friends were all emigrating these days because "all young men with ability have left or are leaving too." As it became impossible for young male villagers to prove their masculine worth in Longyan, it also became increasingly difficult for young women to find suitable marriage partners by remaining at home. But while all male residents, regardless of marital status, felt compelled to emigrate, not all female villagers felt the same pressure to leave Longyan. The conspicuous presence of the "sisters-in-law" provided at least some validation for certain women to remain behind as the main caregivers of children, parents, and more distant relations, including the spirits entangled with the living in relations of ongoing cosmic debt.

In contrast to the abundance of "sisters-in-law," there were very few male villagers who had spouses overseas and even fewer who could justify living off their wives' remittances indefinitely. Unlike the "sisters-in-law," who typically assumed domestic duties, the few men with absent wives almost always delegated child care, housework, and the rituals of daily worship to other female relatives like mothers, sisters, or hired female domestics. Though they were as ambivalent about emigration as the "sisters-in-law," husbands with wives overseas simply did not have the same moral claims (or expectations) to stay behind and live in relative leisure off the overseas labor of others.

Above all, the conflation of masculinity with transnational mobility and productivity made leaving Longyan seem compulsory for young male villagers in a way that was not true for young women. While most young women in their twenties expected to emigrate as much as the males in their cohort, they also admitted that they had more social latitude to remain behind. Not only did female villagers typically leave at a later age than male villagers, but they could also stay on indefinitely without necessarily provoking social disdain as someone with "no face" (*mei mianzi*) whom others could no longer look upon (*kan buqi*). In contrast, corporeal absence became a necessary and defining feature of one's social presence and visibility as a "man" in Longyan. For all those who remained in the flesh, moral refuge could be found only through the feminized circuits of social reproduction, where one could stake claims as either someone who deserved to be fed (children, aged parents) or someone who generously nurtured and fed others (wives and mothers; for example, the "sisters-in-law").

Inter-Face: Renqing, Visibility, and the Making of Persons in Circulation

Like the other chapters in this book, this one has attempted to follow the imagined and material circulation of various bodies and objects in and out of Longyan as part of the phenomenon of mass emigration. But while previous chapters have mainly focused on single things-in-motion (for example, "peasant" subjects, spirit money), here I have tried to broaden the scope by considering the differential circulation of distinct bodies and their various valued substances—reproductive and labor power, money, and food (among other objects)—across the social divides produced by family dispersal and indefinite separation over the past two decades. These divides, as I have shown, have concerned not only the vicissitudes of geography but also the fragmentations of interpersonal relations among village subjects encountering new wealth and leisure in the era of economic reform. In particular, in examining the problem of social reproduction amid sustained emigration, this chapter has not only traced the normative transnational flows that direct all "men" abroad and remittances back to Longyan but has also elaborated on the many digressive translocal trails that could easily lead desiring bodies and their fungible dollars astray from the moral circuits of renqing (human feeling) and mutual sacrifice across the transnational divide.

The notion of the "person," Marcel Mauss once noted, has its roots partially in the Latin term persona, meaning "a mask, a tragic mask, a ritual mask, and the ancestral mask" (1985, 13). Chinese conceptions of "face" (lian or mianzi) have often been taken as exemplary incarnations of these masking aspects of personhood, albeit in the more pejorative sense of social pretense and dissimulation (Kipnis 1995a, 123–25). Within a Cartesian model of personhood, in which sincerity implies depth and interiority, a concept like "face" has typically been reinterpreted in a simple binary fashion as the superficial shield or top layer to a more substantive and authentic subject hidden behind or underneath the presumed surface of social life. In this kind of framework, one thinks of "face" as something one can gain or lose in social interaction, masking or exposing the authentic "hidden" person though never truly altering or compromising its stalwart composition.

Scholars attuned to emic understandings of "face" (C-y. Cheng 1986; H. Hu 1944; Kipnis 1995a; Zito 1994, 1997) have offered compelling critiques of this Eurocentric equation of depth with authenticity by sketching an alternative model of personhood imagined less through interiority than through infinite layers of social surface. In this framework of substantive surfaces, "face" resembles less the throwaway peel of an orange than the spiraling layers of an onion, which both constitute and exceed the whole in their unraveled twists and turns. In fact, the variegated complexities of "face" beyond superficial "mask" are evident by the distinctions made in Mandarin between the notion of *lian* and *mianzi*. While *lian* references the physiognomy or first-order layer of visibility basic to all human beings, *mianzi* highlights the second-order, expandable layer of social prestige and influence accrued by differentially positioned persons. As Andrew Kipnis has noted, "Everyone (except for social outcasts) can be said to have *lian*, while only those of some social standing have *mianzi*" (1995a, 127). Far from false appearance, such multilayered notions of "face" point to what Kipnis termed the "constitutive visibilities" of personhood (127). It is the site, as Angela Zito has noted, "where surface meets a gaze" (1997, 48) and "from which hierarchical communication is possible" (21). In other words, what "face" highlights is less the superficiality of a masking surface than the centrality of social mediation or *inter-face* to the making of persons.

Mediation or inter-face is particularly central to this discussion of sentiment and subject formation among a Longyan population dispersed and on the move. Despite villagers' widespread embrace of overseas status as an index of household prosperity and personal productivity, sustained emigration over the past two decades has largely troubled rather than smoothed over the fault lines of kinship, gender, and generation among differentially mobile villagers. But while this chapter has sketched the ruptures and disequilibrium entailed by family dispersal, I have also shown that those stuck and indefinitely separated by physical distance could still draw from other mediating substances—money, food, ritual blessings, and other materializations of caregiving—to sustain relations of "human feeling" stretched beyond their visible reach. Through the mediation of these various things-in-motion, people in Longyan could also concretize the pervasive if ever-elusive presence of loved ones overseas, absent in body though not in spirit or influence.

Nowhere did the discourse of "face" flourish more than around the issues of masculinity and productivity in Longyan, where to be socially visible and "looked upon" (*kandeqi*, or respected) as a "man," one necessarily had to become corporeally absent from China. As I have argued, among the bodies that moved in and out of Longyan, the most critical gender divide ultimately fell between men and non-men, with the latter category encompassing not only all women but also various male subjects lacking transnational mobility and reach. Not unlike the mobile gods, ghosts, and ancestors that populated village life, "men" were largely spectral subjects, more powerfully present as invisible, out-of-body forces than the remaining male inhabitants, who mostly shirked and shrank their physicality, their bodies infantilized (as children), infirmed (as elders), racialized (as outsiders), or simply declared unfit (as mentally or physically disabled).

If subjects became "men" by becoming invisible yet potent forces, their wives mainly became "sisters-in-law" by submitting to hypervisibility at home. As I have suggested, more than any other group, it was the distinctive cohort of women living under the shadow of absent husbands who felt the most pervasive and intensified moral scrutiny of other villagers around them. What they consumed and circulated, how they inhabited and strayed from the domestic sphere—these aspects were all subject to a penetrating patrilineal gaze because in the end, they not only refracted the surface of these women's basic *lian,* or social dignity, as proper "sister-in-laws" but also mediated the more prestigious and expandable layer of their husbands' *mianzi,* or masculine reputation, in absentia. If "face" was the multilayered site "where surface meets a gaze," the moral questioning of overseas-connected wives ultimately highlighted a decidedly panoptic gaze orchestrated to reflect the patrilineal honor and influence of invisible men overseas through the visible discipline of female desires in Longyan. While women who "ate duck" were said to have no *lian,* model "sisters-in-law," like Lin Mengya, were praised not only for having self-respect but more significantly for extending their absent husbands' *mianzi.*

As an intersubjective plane of social visibility and honor, "face" was a critical component for the spatial-temporal extension not only of those dispersed overseas but also of everyone struggling to sustain "human feeling" across a transnational social field. "Face" among Longyan villagers was not unlike fame among the kula-trading Gawans described by Nancy Munn (1986, 105–20). It was a social valuation of persons that accrued and expanded through the circulation of things-in-motion from migrant bodies themselves to their various extendable and convertible substances: labor power, dollar wages, overseas remittances, immigration documents, temple donations, holiday gifts, housing renovations, respectable clothing, lavish home-cooked meals, spirit money, ritual blessings, and so forth.

While I have gone to some lengths to highlight the various forms of mediation mentioned above, perhaps the one glaring omission is of conventional *electronic* mediums—forms we usually think of as "the media"—that help form the infrastructure for transnational circulation and linkages. There is much more to say about these mediations than can be accommodated in the conclusion of this chapter. However, in keeping with the theme of differentiated mobility at the crossroads of gender and kinship, let me end by briefly highlighting just two flows of electronic mediation here.

It is no secret among Longyan inhabitants that rumor and gossip are potent forces in the moral regulation of villagers, particularly the "sisters-in-law," because of their transnational extension through long-distance phone lines. The availability of cheap international calling cards has enabled news to flow freely and instantaneously between Longyan and its U.S. outposts so that cheating wives at home were rarely out of the punitive reach of absent husbands, while those embittered by terrible working and living conditions overseas had ready access to sympathetic ears, if not shoulders to cry on, at home. But what is most relevant to the discussion here is the directionality of phone mediation, which, because of the bargain rates of calling cards overseas, predominantly flowed from callers abroad to recipients in Longyan. Phone calls from overseas not only gave form to long-absent husbands but also personalized them largely as penetrating, disembodied voices able to survey and discipline wives whenever they wished to dial in from abroad. While certainly these constant calls from absent husbands could be seen as evidence of their care, as their wives often argued, other villagers were apt to interpret them as signs of either unhealthy spousal suspicion or skillful masculine domestication of female desires.

In tandem with the unidirectional flow of phone calls from abroad, visual media, especially photographs and home videos burned onto vcds, largely circulated in the opposite direction—from villagers to relatives overseas—as testaments to the appropriate distribution and conversion of hard-earned remittances to bolster the collective bonds of kinship, as well as the *mianzi* of spectral subjects toiling abroad. While photographs of growing children and changing village landscapes were largely sent to sustain the affective ties and reciprocal commitments with relatives overseas, pictures and videos of newly purchased prestige commodities, renovated houses, and elaborate rituals for temple gods and funerals were largely produced specifically as proof of proper expenditures, as approved and demanded by absent husbands from village wives. A whole industry of image-making, particularly in videography, had blossomed in Longyan and its vicinity in order to orchestrate village luxuries and comforts for the surveillance of absent men who through these mediated scenes could glimpse the returned image of their own panoptic gaze—their own expanded social visibility in circulation. Perhaps nothing captured the "face" of these spectral subjects better than the videos customarily made of the lavish rituals staged to celebrate and bless the completion of their new high-rise mansions. Though it was more than likely that the overseas relatives who financed these houses lived in humble, cramped places and even sites of squalor, these videos enabled Fuzhounese migrants to come face to face with a potent, visible incarnation of their own grand absence—the elaborate yet empty mansions they built and left in their wake.

When Fortune Flows

To calculate a risk is to master time, to discipline the future. . . . To provide for the future does not just mean not living from day to day and arming oneself against ill fortune, but also mathematizing one's commitments. Above all, it means no longer resigning oneself to the decrees of providence and the blows of fate, but instead transforming one's relationships with nature, the world and God so that, even in misfortune, one retains responsibility for one's affairs by possessing the means to repair its effects.
—François Ewald, "Insurance and Risk"

The more that life is regulated administratively, the more people must learn waiting. Games of chance have the great attraction of making people free from waiting.
—Walter Benjamin, *Das Passagen-Werk*

On any given afternoon, the clacking sound of mahjong tiles being quickly shuffled and dramatically flipped over on felt-covered tables could be heard from every sleepy street in Longyan. In sitting rooms and kitchens, behind temples and on sidewalks, villagers regularly gathered in clusters of four to test their fortunes in an ever-shifting and fast-paced field of play and to display their instincts for discerning patterns out of the jumbled signs before them. Mahjong, as mentioned in chapter 6, had become such a dominant pastime in Longyan that people commonly referred to their gambling sessions as "going to school" or "going to work." As I have argued, the blossoming of this game from a marginal vice to a widespread daily activity largely had to do with the new wealth and leisure among those with overseas connections. Two decades earlier in another emigrant village in rural Hong Kong, anthropologist James Watson had observed an uncannily similar mahjong obsession among those left behind:

> Emigration has raised the standard of living in San Tin and changed the
> community into a center of leisure and affluence. . . . Except for the Lunar

New Year festivities and rare celebrations like the temple renovation, the villagers seldom have any break in the daily routine of eating, gambling, gossiping, and napping. . . . A high percentage of villagers find diversion by spending all their spare time playing mahjong. . . . Gambling is undoubtedly the major pastime in the New Territories . . . but in San Tin it has become a way of life. Residents of all ages, including some of the adolescents, have no other form of recreation except gambling (1975, 167–68).

Watson went on to suggest that people flocked to mahjong tables not because of the money stakes involved, which were typically low, but because "the games are the only source of excitement in the village" (1975, 168). Mass emigration, he argued, brought not only great leisure and affluence into the home village but, as it turned out, also a good deal of boredom and ennui among those freed of labor time, especially the men, who wound up with "difficulties keeping themselves occupied" (168).

As I have shown, a sense that "there is nothing to do" also dominated village life in Longyan. "Nothing to do" not only anchored villagers' gender and class critiques of the local dearth of job opportunities but also framed their moral debates over the expansion of consumer indulgences, including mahjong. At the heart of these dual complaints over "nothing to do," there lay a central concern over temporality—the experience of its flow, rhythm, and directionality and the politics of its distribution and differentiation as labor or leisure time, commodified or "free" time. For most villagers, time teetered unsteadily between lagging and lurching forward. The quest of emigration proceeded in fits and starts, alternating between long bouts of interminable waiting and short bursts of chaotic rushing. Failure was a drawn-out and repetitive motion among aspiring migrants while success a rare, elusive breakthrough.

Quests for transnational mobility were temporalizing practices in more ways than one. They were also centrally about contested futures—what I have called "the politics of destination" for my Fuzhounese subjects. Immobilized as state-classified peasants under China's household registration system, Longyan villagers were precisely not the kinds of subjects authorized to chart moral careers abroad as cosmopolitan overseas Chinese. Yet despite legal prohibitions, staggering smuggling fees, daunting physical dangers, and known labor exploitation overseas, aspirations for emigration persisted among Longyan residents because the stakes involved more than the calculative "risks" of market rationality. Though people certainly touted the dollar-to-RMB exchange rate as a catalyst for ventures overseas, they also did not operate simply by the cost-benefit logics of some neoliberal cosmology. Time and again people continued to edge onward and outward regardless of multiple failures, deepening financial debt, and frayed personal relations because more than anything else, *immobility* in all senses of the word—physical, social, and economic—had become the ultimate form of displacement in a post-Mao world boasting of forward momentum and global openings. Situated on China's mercurial edge between rural backwardness and coastal cosmopolitanism, Longyan inhabitants were unabashedly modern(izing) subjects striving for spatial-temporal extension beyond their stagnant and delimiting positioning as "peasants" in a "peasant village."

Though I did not sense much nostalgia for past lifeways and lifeworlds among Longyan residents, this did not mean they wanted to or *could* discard extant schemas for sense- and subject-making in the contemporary context. Even if their goals for mobility were deeply entangled with the hegemonic state fantasies of a Chinese modernity, their largely illicit and divergent tactics for achieving those goals via illegal smugglers, traveling gods, and informal back doors also worked to insinuate unauthorized and devalued aspects of "peasantness" into the privileged category of the flexible Chinese cosmopolitan.

Among the many mediating forces that elude the conventional analytic boundaries of "the state" and "the market," ritual practices and the local gods they animate were integral to villagers' quests for wrangling some control over the ever-present but invisible flows structuring everyday life—for plotting moral careers in a world of differentiated mobility and regulating the smooth circulation of migrant bodies, immigration papers, dollar remittances, and sustained "human feeling" across an expanded, transnational social field. Overseas connections and new prosperity celebrated collectively through the building of temples and the orchestration of elaborate religious festivals highlighted the gods as productive forces, not cultural fetters, to villagers' embrace of modernity. As mobile subjects who knew no boundaries, the gods were exemplary vanguards of a cosmopolitan ideal, albeit one anchored by a nodal and multicentric appreciation of value production as the credit-able extension of persons inextricably tangled in moral-economic webs of generalized debt and repayment. Such webs did not oppose or replace the world conjured through China's project for market liberalization and "opening up." Rather they insinuated themselves into the density of existing global circuits and flows, translating village desires to emigrate against incredible odds into a credible project for producing value. Within villagers' pursuit of what I have termed a *discrepant* cosmopolitanism, creditability took forms both discernible (as money, capital, legal recognition, social connections, human feeling) and beyond human grasp (as cosmic accounts of ancestral and personal demerit, the vicissitudes of structural forces, chance encounters, and plain luck). Much of this book, with its focus on the paths and divergences of things-in-motion, has been concerned with villagers' struggles for practical mastery over those elusive yet powerfully pervasive forces of credit-making that exceed the visible threshold of their daily lives.

Over the past century, across disparate political regimes in China, extreme reversals of fortune, including dramatic shifts in the organizing symbols of wealth, kept Longyan villagers not only guessing about the appropriate calculative techniques for forging and sustaining prosperity in this world but also searching for the elusive secrets of value production through other-worldly means. In the post-Mao era, the revitalization of popular religion has certainly provided villagers with one of their central mediating technologies for intuiting the invisible patterns of credit and debt amid China's opening up to global capitalism. That such strategies were fundamentally speculative did not make them necessarily irrational or unique in the context of late modernity. As some anthropologists have pointed out in recent years (Comaroff and Comaroff 2000; B. Lee and LiPuma 2002; Maurer 1999; Strange 1986), the fortunes increasingly conjured by capitalism's vanguards through high finance—venture capital, stocks, bonds, and futures—were themselves celebrations of speculation as a technology for value production. The hedging in hedge funds was not altogether different from the gamble made by the Fuzhounese in "gambling their own bodies" on smuggling ventures overseas. At heart, both the high roller and the humble stowaway hoped to grasp the elusive signs of the times in order to bet on futures that would flow in their favor.

One of the key questions that dogged and spurred my research forward concerned the relative risks and rewards of Fuzhounese migration via illegal human smuggling. Over the past two decades, so much of what made the Fuzhounese phenomenon into a dramatic and sensational story for the international media revolved around the striking imbalance of odds and ends: the conditions of illicit travel were harrowing and the deaths gruesome; moreover, the debt of a half million RMB did not square well with the "reward" of menial and often exploitative labor for the smuggled migrants who managed to arrive overseas. The costs and benefits did not seem to add up in a rational, calculative model of "risk." The common explanation to smooth over the dysfunctions of "risk" has been to portray the Fuzhounese as either the grand dupes and overwhelming victims of a penetrating global capitalism or as minor dupes and mediocre players in a game of profit maximization.

As the end and departing point for this book, let me offer another game—the village pastime of mahjong—as a different model for and of Fuzhounese strategies for value production. As mentioned above, gambling as a valorized strategy and salient metaphor for mastering the flows of fortune was not unique to the Fuzhounese in an increasingly speculative world of "casino capitalism" (Strange 1986). This did not mean that the particular version of mahjong played daily by Longyan villagers merely reproduced or mimicked the cultural logics of international finance or other speculative enterprises for prosperity in distinct and far-flung sites. In fact, the way the Fuzhounese played mahjong did not even resemble the cutthroat, skillful, and highly individualizing version of the game as played by their Cantonese neighbors—those other coastal and outward-bound southern Chinese.

Not unlike gin rummy, the goal of mahjong is to order the tiles in one's hand into patterned sets by grouping them either by sequence or by resemblance. Tiles are divided into three basic suits—(1) the circle suit, (2) the bamboo suit, and (3) the "10,000" suit, indexed by the Chinese character for that number (*wan*). Suit tiles are numbered 1 through 9, and in any given suit, there are four of each number. A winning hand consists of tiles arranged into six ordered groupings—(1) a pair of identical tiles (in poker terms, two of a kind), and (2) five sets of three or four tiles with each set consisting of either three of a kind, four of a kind, or a run of three sequential tiles from the same suit (for example, tile numbers 2, 3, and 4 in the circle suit). Players maneuver for the right combinations by taking turns discarding and replacing tiles, each time tossing an unwanted piece face up on the table before either drawing a new tile from a blind collective stack or claiming the last discarded tile of the previous player. A game consists ideally and maximally of four players exchanging tiles in sequential

FIGURE 18 Looking for patterns in mahjong.

turn, with play typically moving counterclockwise from the designated dealer. The first person to complete all six sets wins the game by declaring "Mahjong!" and then flipping all of his or her tiles over to reveal the winning combination for inspection and scoring. Fundamentally, it is a game about circulation, speed, and pattern recognition (figure 18).

Within these basic parameters, mahjong can take on quite different inflections of skill and competition, depending on the way the game is scored and how additional tiles that are not part of the three suits (not unlike the joker in a deck of cards) are put into play. For instance, in the Cantonese and Taiwanese versions, one can make combinations of three and four of a kind with tiles symbolizing the winds (east, south, west, and north) and the dragons (red, green, and white). Additionally, the Cantonese version—the most complicated of the lot—uses two other kinds of tiles marking the seasons (spring, summer, autumn, and winter) and flowers (plum, orchid, chrysanthemum, and bamboo). In particular, in the Cantonese version these season and flower tiles link players' winning stakes to their actual seating arrangements, which are each designated with a particular flower, season, and direction corresponding to one of these mahjong tiles. In other words, players of the Cantonese version must consider not only what tiles they have in hand but also where they are sitting in each game and round of mahjong.

The emphasis on skill and maneuvering in the Cantonese game is also highlighted by the way this version rewards and punishes players. While there is only one winner possible in all forms of mahjong, the Cantonese version, unlike either the Taiwanese or Fuzhounese game, distinguishes between losers and non-losers. Specifically, while everyone must pay the winner when the victory is clinched with a self-drawn tile, the Cantonese version singles out a loser when the winning set is completed with a discarded tile. In this situation, only the player who gave up the winning tile pays for the loss. Making a distinction between winner, loser, and non-losers not only isolates and punishes unskillful play but also individualizes the stakes of each game much more than in versions of mahjong where loss is always a collective burden.

The complexities of the Cantonese game provide a striking contrast to the pared-down version of mahjong routinely played in Longyan. Unlike the Cantonese, the Fuzhounese version uses only the most basic suit tiles for making patterns, excluding the wind and dragon tiles. Additionally, the Fuzhounese eliminate the strategic importance of seating arrangements and make no distinction between losers and non-losers in any given game. All these simplifications have the virtue of expediting the flow of the game by minimizing the variables players must consider. Because no one is singled out and punished for making the losing move in the Fuzhounese version, mahjong players in Longyan do not have to worry about the consequences of every discarded tile. Though there is individual glory in winning, the Fuzhounese version ensures that the losers have company in misery.

All these simplified features enable villagers to play mahjong as a fast-paced game of circulation with tiles changing hands almost instantaneously and few tactical or strategic pauses between players. As villagers uniformly saw it, winning in mahjong mostly had to do with luck (*yunqi*) and only a little with the skill (*jishu*) of individual players. "It all depends on the luck of the draw (*shouqi*)," Lin Qing, along with others, told me.

The importance of the blind draw in the Fuzhounese game was enhanced by the addition of a wild card—a tile randomly selected and revealed by the dealer before the start of each game that became the floating equivalent for all other tiles, able to substitute for any missing piece needed to complete a particular set. In any given game, the designated wild cards—of which there were always three identical pieces in play—automatically became the most valuable tiles for their unparalleled flexibility and liquidity.

These wild-card tiles were so useful and dominant that if one drew all these pieces as part of one's initial hand at the start of a game, one could instantly declare "Mahjong!" even before play began and earn tenfold in winnings. The only other equally rewarding victories—drawing a complete winning set in one's initial hand, clinching a game by self-drawing a wild card or with two wild cards as the winning pair—all privileged the value of a random lucky draw and, secondarily, the liquidity of the wild card. It is interesting that these various ways of winning were all termed *qiangjin*, or "snatching/stealing the gold," and entitled the victor to the same instant tenfold jackpot.

As villagers played it, mahjong was more a game of the blind draw than of the calculation and management of chance. Rather than strategizing defensively against fellow players on every turn, people circulated their pieces briskly and freely without much thought to the maneuvers of others. Instead of weighing every move, they learned to simply bide their time for the right pieces to fall into their hands by pushing for a quick turnover of tiles. As a novice among seasoned mahjong players in Longyan, I quickly learned the importance of keeping up with the fast pace when I kept getting friendly advice to not think so much on my turns because it was disrupting the rhythm of the game. In a typical mahjong game, players' turns rotated almost instantly to the steady staccato of tiles pounded on and picked off the table in one fell swoop lasting less than a few seconds. This brisk pace meant that one's turn usually came every ten or so seconds. For an initially slow and ponderous player like me, this speedy turnover made it seem like it was perpetually my turn, and play would come to an embarrassing grinding halt while I agonized over what tile to exchange. In lieu of driving fellow players crazy with boredom, I quickly learned to give up on any careful play-by-play maneuvering in favor of a more knee-jerk, free flow of tiles around the table.

The brisk pace of circulation also ensured that victories and losses came quickly and often. Without the possibility of non-losers, one learned to expect and to weather long bouts of recurring loss in the hopes of an occasional big win or short string of small victories. While such wins and losses hinged more on the luck of the draw than on individual strategic maneuvering, villagers did not discount skill altogether in the way they played. Given the frequent turnover of tiles and games in play, this kind of mahjong rewarded those who were most quick on their feet and able to discern when luck was turning in their favor. After all, even the luckiest player could not win without the facility to recognize and seize the signs of good fortune if such signs ever surfaced temporarily in the ever-shifting and accelerated field of circulation. Above all, winning in mahjong among Longyan villagers required the skill to flexibly order the random flow of tiles into productive patterns and take advantage of the chanced alignment of structure, flow, and agency when fleeting opportunities happened to present themselves. The glory and drama in the game largely hinged on a quick flick of the wrist when, after many lightning rounds of uneventful exchange and recurring loss, a player could finally seize the moment to pounce on a long-awaited winning piece and declare a victorious hand.

These dynamics of play in mahjong resonated strongly with villagers' quests for emigration, particularly in the unpredictable shifts of temporality between stagnant states of waiting and ephemeral openings to rush forward. Fundamentally, success in both mahjong and emigration was premised on worlds in motion in which one expected to be at the mercy of circulatory flows beyond one's complete control. Unlike a depersonalized, statistical model of risk in which one hopes "to master time" and "discipline the future," as Ewald's opening epigraph to this chapter describes, mahjong offered villagers another model for weighing loss and reward based on one's fortune-in-hand.

Mahjong showed people that recurring defeat, though expected, did not need to be feared since there was always company in loss to share the burden of debt. Though winning always entailed personal reward and glory, losing did not necessarily spell individual failure and shame. Liability was par for the course; what was important was how it was managed. People commonly told me that the best way to counter a losing streak was to persist in the game and keep playing regularly, despite accumulating failure and debt. Sooner or later, villagers argued, the pendulum of luck would swing back in one's favor. The trick was to know when fortune was flowing one's way so that one could adeptly ride it for all it was worth before the ebb of luck set in once more.

Ultimately, people believed that one could not control the hand one was dealt, as the old cliché goes. Nonetheless, villagers were not merely complacent subjects blaming "fate" for all their ills, as state critiques of "superstitious peasants" would have it. Agents of fate—whether the gods, the "state," or other grand invisible forces—were never beyond approach and negotiation for Longyan residents. Unlike the predestined world of

Weberian Protestants, there was always a role for human agency in the Fuzhounese politics of destination. Just as one aimed to discern the patterns of good fortune so that one could seize fleeting opportunities in the fast-paced game of mahjong, one also hoped to visualize and grasp the elusive currents for enacting value in the general world of accelerated and expanded circulation.

In fact, mahjong itself provided villagers with a convenient barometer of their cosmic fortunes or karma on any given day. Sustained losing or winning streaks in mahjong enabled players to speculate on how their luck in other risky ventures, like human smuggling, might play out at a particular time. This was not unlike Ellen Oxfeld Basu's description of the speculative uses of gambling among the entrepreneurial Calcutta Chinese: "While Taiguo's story also recounted spates of hard work and study, there is no doubt that he believed luck was a significant factor in his success, and he described his gambling luck as a foreshadowing of his luck in business. One's fate in business, therefore, like one's fate in gambling, is viewed as beyond one's ultimate control" (1991, 248). Basu went on to argue that mahjong was particularly appealing to her Chinese subjects because of the sociability of play among the four known competitors, which heightened "ramifications in terms of one's social relations, prestige and face." This kind of setting, she argued, enabled players not only to accumulate economic capital by winning money stakes but also to publicly display wealth "through indifference to its loss" and, in turn, garner "symbolic capital" from others (1991, 250–51). Basu's focus on forms of capital ultimately led her back to the maximizing logic of economic rationality still operative at the heart of mahjong.[1] After all, she argues, "we must also remember that such symbolic gains [for example, of "face" via indifference to monetary loss] are intrinsically and fundamentally connected to real economic power" (251).

I do not want to dispute these economic aspects of mahjong so much as question their singularizing and reductive powers as the modi operandi of value production in the larger context of the game. For beyond the distribution of monetary wins and losses, these games were also occasions for other social transactions and redistributive practices—the exchange of the latest gossip of overseas failures and successes, the sharing of strategies and contacts for emigration and INS status, the mobilization of monetary loans, social commiseration from fellow players, and the like. In fact, play-by-play maneuvers were so marginal in the game in part because players were just as occupied with maintaining the easy flow of camaraderie and chit-chat as they were with the speedy circulation of tiles and money.

Certainly much of the controversy over mahjong as a dominant pastime in Longyan had to do with games played for huge money stakes. But while money—particularly in the form of dollar remittances—was a prerequisite for participation in mahjong, it was neither the only nor the central reward at stake in these games. Like Watson, I also noticed how much more common it was for villagers to play mahjong for small change just to have a reason to get together with others and pass an afternoon in gamely camaraderie. The great attraction of mahjong, however, was not that it made people "free from waiting," as Benjamin argues for games of chance in the epigraph to this chapter. Rather, its appeal came from enabling people to collectively wrangle with the vicissitudes of time itself, albeit on a smaller scale; to hone skills in the company of supportive others for coping with the unrelenting speed of circulation and the burdens of stagnation and waiting, and for recognizing timely patterns and taking timely action. Amid radical uncertainty about prosperity's mercurial shape and stabilizing sources, mahjong was less a site of respite than a training ground through which Longyan villagers hoped to grasp the elusive patterning and flow of life's fortune and, in turn, intuit a way forward in a world of increasing transnational circulation.

INTRODUCTION

1. I discuss these spatial-temporal processes in more detail in part I of this book; in particular see pp. 23–30.

2. Peter Kwong (1997, 2001) suggests that a distinct wave of illegal immigration from rural Fuzhou in Fujian Province began in the early 1970s, though it picked up only after 1986 with the passage of the U.S. Immigration Reform and Control Act (IRCA), which offered a blanket, one-time amnesty to all previously undocumented migrants and enabled subsequent and widespread chain migration among the Fuzhounese (cf. Chin 1999, 2001; Guest 2003; Kyle and Koslowski 2001). The extent of this new massive wave of emigration from Fuzhou has been documented by a number of researchers. For instance, Liang and Ye (2001) have noted that by 1995 Fujian Province ranked first in emigration flows out of China, with 66,200 people, or 28 percent, of China's total emigrant population. Paul Smith (1994) has suggested that between 1991 and 1994, an annual twenty-five thousand Fuzhounese entered illegally into the United States (cited in Kwong 2001, 37). Other estimates suggest that anywhere between ten thousand and one hundred thousand enter every year (P. J. Smith 1997a). New York has been a central destination of this flow. Einhorn (1994) has estimated that by 1994 as many as one hundred thousand Fujianese were living in New York, with an additional ten thousand entering each year (cf. Liang and Ye 2001).

3. *Sing Tao Daily*, December 2, 1996, 26; also cited in Chin (1999, 9).

4. I draw the notions of calculative logics from Callon (1998) and regimes of value from Appadurai (1986).

5. On the pragmatics of desire and its actualization as affect, see Deleuze and Guattari (1987) and Massumi (2003). For an ethnographic exploration, also see Stewart (2007).

6. On the productivity of friction, see Tsing (2005). Also see Callon (1998) on the inevitable "overflowing" coextensive with the framing of transactions as economic calculations.

7. In arguing for modernity in terms of an ontological politics of the one and many, I draw from the insights of various scholars working in the vein of "actor network theory," including Latour (1993), Law (2002), Mol (1999), and Verran (2001).

8. My thanks to John Osburg for pushing me to refine my usage of "modernity" and particularly for posing the question of the "master signifier," which I directly recast as an argument in this introduction.

9. For instance, see Appadurai (1997), Chatterjee (1998), Comaroff and Comaroff (1993), Gaonkar (2001), Knauft (2002), Larkin (2002), Latour (1993), Lichblau (1999), Piot (1999), Prakash (1999), and Rofel (1999).

10. Another way to think of the one and the many of modernity is in terms of what Massumi, by way of Deleuze, refers to as the ongoing processual and dynamic unity of "the virtual" and "the actual," the two being "mutually convertible modes of the same reality" that recursively feed back and feed forward into each other. The very unfolding of this relation activates the incorporeal yet material sense of the concept's "continuities under qualitative transformations" (2003, 5, 8).

11. In this piece, Sahlins offers a comparative sketch of the cosmologies of the imperial Qing court in China, the Hawaiian rulers of the Sandwich Islands, and the chiefly Kwakuitl on the northwest coast of North America—all connected by European trade routes around the late eighteenth century.

12. I thank Jeff Himpele and his "Capitalism" course in the Department of Anthropology at New York University for bringing Sahlins's article to my attention in the spring of 2003.

13. Sahlins's analytic preference for the formal elegance of sweeping cultural schemas over the messy nuances and excesses of inter- and intracultural processes has been noted by some anthropologists (cf. Marcus 1988; Mosko 1992; Ortner 1984; Webster 1987). He himself admitted the limitations of such broad analytic strokes in his sketch of the *longue durée* of "Western Cosmology" from Augustine through Adam Smith (Sahlins 1996, 395, 421–22).

14. Such an analytic focus on credit is itself indebted to a whole host of scholars from Karl Marx to Georg Simmel to Marcel Mauss to Annette Weiner and various other contemporary anthropologists, many of whom I discuss in more detail in part III of this book.

15. My use of the notion of boundary making draws inspiration from various works, including Mary Douglas's ethnographic classic, *Purity and Danger* (1966); Patricia Spyer's edited collection, *Border Fetishisms* (1998); and (outside of anthropology) Catherine Bell's arguments about ritualization (1992); Bruno Latour's insights on modern practices of purification amid hybridity (1993); and Timothy Mitchell's writings on enframing (1991). I also draw from ethnographies of contemporary China such as Ann Anagnost's analysis of state reappropriations of local religious space (1994) and Li Zhang's research on the privatization, state de-

molishment, and rebuilding of migrant residential compounds in Beijing (2001a, 2001b), not to mention the works of Dutton (1992, 1998) and Zito (1994, 1997). Angela Zito, in particular, explicitly points to the importance of ritual as a boundary-making practice in China (albeit in reference to the eighteenth-century imperial regime). As she notes, "People do not consist of divinely endowed or biologically fixed human nature. Instead they are exemplars of dynamically contingent positions both in space and social hierarchy. . . . They are boundary makers and breakers" (1997, 211).

16. The first three terms—liberation (*jiefang*), revolution (*wenge*), and reform (*gaige*)—these emic concepts widely used in state discourse and by mainland Chinese themselves, including people in Fuzhou, to mark three recent historical turning points. "Liberation" refers to the 1949 Communist Revolution and the initiation of state rule under Mao Zedong and the Chinese Communist Party (CCP). "Revolution" refers to the politically turbulent decade of the Cultural Revolution from 1966 to 1976. "Reform" refers to the contemporary era of economic policies initiated in 1978 under the leadership of Deng Xiaoping to move China from a centrally planned economy to a market-oriented one "opened" to global capital.

17. This emphasis is perhaps best exemplified by the transnational Chinese subjects of Aihwa Ong's book *Flexible Citizenship* (1999), though Ong herself has issued sharp critiques of hegemonic and homogenizing notions of cosmopolitan privilege and in turn has argued for attention to "splintering cosmopolitanism" among differentially mobile Asian migrants (2005; also see Ong and Nonini 1997). Other works that have noted the elite emphasis in Chinese transnational and cosmopolitan imaginaries include H. Liu (1997), Nonini (1997), and Sun (2002).

18. This politics of *pre*-destination, as Weber noted, led inadvertently to the collective valorization and channeling of human energies toward things like this-worldly asceticism; industriousness; and calculative, rational investments of wealth—in other words, the lethal combination necessary for massive capitalist expansion and development since Benjamin Franklin's time.

19. For instance, the concept of circulation, claimed Wolfgang Schivelbusch, "serves as a key to unlock the open triumphs as well as the hidden anxieties of the nineteenth century" (1986, 195), while at the end of the twentieth century, motion and mass migration, Arjun Appadurai has argued, are central to "a new order of instability in the production of modern subjectivities" (1997, 4). In between the beginning and end of these two centuries, Daniel Lerner (1958) would positively trumpet "the mobile personality"—persons eager to move, to change, and to invent—as the principal force of modernity, while Hannah Arendt (1975, 475) would decry the darker side of mobility—in terms of "uprootedness and superfluousness"—as "the curse of modern masses since the beginning of the industrial revolution" (cf. Asad 1993, 10–11).

20. For the contemporary research, see, for instance, Appadurai (1997), Bauman (2000), Clifford (1997), Cresswell (2006), Hannerz (1996), Hardt and Negri (2000), Jain (2002), Massumi (2003), Ong (1999), Sassen (1991), Thrift (1996), and Virilio (1986).

21. It is notable that contemporary officials are only too eager to embrace and conjure these existing foreign ties as part of a diplomatic narrative of long-standing solidarity and exchange in recent efforts to expand Chinese influence over parts of Africa and Latin America.

22. As Massumi describes it, "the sensible concept is a materialized idea embodied not so much in the perceiving or the perceived considered separately as in their between, in their felt conjunction" (2003, 95).

23. Such embodied forms include academic texts, as Callon (1998) has persuasively argued in regard to the contribution of economics to shaping "the economy." In turn, this book itself cannot help but produce its own embodied version(s) of mobility as a qualisign. In fact, the book's very organization around things-in-motion performs this qualisign in various guises.

24. This is an appropriation and inversion of Trinh's turn of phrase, "not foreigner, yet foreign" about minority positioning in the West (1995, 216).

PART I. *Edgy Dispositions*

1. These two neighboring provinces, with their long histories of foreign trade and overseas connections, even constitute what some scholars have described as a distinctive cultural and economic unit—a "Guangdong-Fujian culture" (White and Cheng 1993) or "lower-east-coast macroregion" (Spence 1999)—dividing China along a north-south axis between a more inward-oriented elite culture emanating from Beijing's imperial center and a more outward-bound and often renegade mercantile population along the empire's southeastern "frontier" (Pan 1990). Sociologist Zai Liang has noted that in 1982, Fujian represented less than 2 percent of China's emigrant population, while by 1990, it constituted more than 13 percent and ranked third among migrant-sending provinces. By 1995, Fujian had overtaken Guangdong to rank first as the home of Chinese emigrants, representing 28 percent of China's overseas population (Liang 2001, 682).

2. Fujian's proximity to Taiwan and general sea access to foreign intercourse has always stood in sharp contrast to its internal isolation from the rest of China. If not for the Min River cutting northwest to southeast across the province into the Taiwan Strait and into other tributaries flowing through China, inhabitants of Fujian would have few accessible routes via land to the rest of the country. Owing largely to its difficult mountainous landscape, which constitutes 87 percent of its terrain (less than 10 percent of Fujian is arable land), Fujian Province did not

have rail connections to other parts of China until the mid-1950s, when the southern city of Xiamen was finally linked into the national network of train transport (Yeung and Chu 2000). The network of paved roads connecting Fujian to other Chinese regions also remained underdeveloped for most of the province's history partly due to the same obstacles of its natural terrain.

3. Marco Polo himself took note of the high-profile presence of the Mongol Yuan armies that surrounded Fuzhou City to prevent potential uprisings during Kublai Khan's rule in the late 1200s (Polo and Latham 1958, 233). As noted, beyond its consistent history of outlaw trade and travel through successive dynasties into the present era, Fujian also famously served as the rebellious home base for the Ming loyalists under Zheng Chenggong making their last stand against the ascending Manchus in the mid-seventeenth century. As part of its effort to isolate and squelch the Ming rebels by cutting off their sea access to food, supplies, and mobility, the Qing government decreed that Fujian's entire coastal area be evacuated, with the population pushed several miles inland and all travel banned (Pan 1990).

4. Beyond this notion of the "edge," anthropologists have offered other spatial metaphors, including "ethnoscape" (Appadurai 1991, 1997), "transnational circuit" (Rouse 1991), the "transnational public sphere" (M. Yang 1997), and the "global ecumene" (Hannerz 1996), not to mention "borderlands" (Alvarez 1995; Kearney 1991) and "diaspora" (Brown 1998; Gopinath 1995; Kannabiran 1998) in conversation with scholars outside the discipline (e.g., see Anzaldúa 1987 and Clifford 1994 respectively). Collectively, these projects have challenged the conflations of people, territory, and culture by highlighting the disjunctive and unexpected links forged across national boundaries by people dispersed and on the move (also see Gupta and Ferguson 1992; 1997). I have chosen to privilege the notion of edge here because I think it better captures the particular volatile sense of positioning for a coastal area like Fuzhou that is both inwardly closed off and outwardly connected. The closest alternative, borderlands, which also suggests an indeterminate zone of hybridity and multiplicity, is less suitable here mainly because it tends to imply the kind of space that bisects contiguous terrain into separate like units—that is, nation-states. "Edge," I would argue, better illuminates coastal sites adjacent to a discontinuous and incommensurable terrain like the seas, which often are divided into more varied units (national, international, privatized waters, etc.) than contiguous land (territorial nation-states). While "borderlands" shares the implications of space as social interface and crisscrossing flows, it does not suggest the dual notion of a site either leading or being marginalized and potentially falling off altogether.

5. The figure of 85 percent was an estimate provided by the head of Longyan's (Peasant) Village Committee in an interview conducted on March 25, 2002. Most

recent data, from Longyan's 2008 village annals, report 2,917 residents along with 2,800 overseas villagers. Additionally there are more than 400 internal migrants currently in residence (H. Chen and Liu 2010).

6. Occasionally, Fuzhounese has also been identified as a Minbei (Northern Min) dialect. My choice of Mindong as Fuzhou's regional designation reflects the conventional understanding of residents in and around Fuzhou, as well as that of local scholars I met in the area.

7. Through analysis of Chinese census and survey data, Zai Liang also suggested that "the illegal emigration from Fujian probably did not start in significant numbers until the middle of the 1980s" (2001, 682).

ONE. *To be Emplaced*

1. Also see Schendel (2005) on scale-making in state regulations of borders and illicit flows.

2. The figures reported here were estimates provided by the head of Longyan's (Peasant) Village Committee in an interview conducted on March 25, 2002. Longyan's village annals for 2008 also note that since the 1990s, overseas remittances have comprised the majority of village income, becoming "village residents' main source of income" (H. Chen and Liu 2010). Although statistics in China are notorious for inaccuracies, they are still useful as normative, ideological constructs of empirical reality in Longyan and reflect both official self-promotion of the village as an overseas village and critiques of certain kinds of ritual and housing expenditures among "peasant" subjects (*nongmin*).

3. I borrow Raymond Williams's term "structures of feeling," which he defines as "social experiences *in solution*, as distinct from other social semantic formations which have been *precipitated* and are more evidently and more immediately available" (Williams 1977, 133–134; emphasis in original).

4. Pierre Bourdieu used the term *habitus* (via Mauss 1992 [1934]) to describe "systems of durable, transposable *dispositions*" (1977, 72) and to foreground the socially informed body as a nondiscursive and inert source for the encoding of social memory and for the maintenance, affirmation, and transformation of existing social orders. I am extending these meanings of *habitus* here to discuss particular social imaginations of embodied ways of being.

5. I do not want to suggest that somehow the structuring of domestic space *unilinearly* determined how people inhabited that space. For instance, during my 2001–2 fieldwork in China, installing shower stalls was all the craze as part of rising middle-class aspirations for a modernizing lifestyle—both among urbanites and wealthy Longyan residents. While most people had had indoor plumbing for at least a decade, it was common to wash with a water-filled basin, as was the

practice before people had access to running water. Functionally, one would think that having a new, separate space carved out for showering would lead its users to logically confine themselves to standing under the running nozzle for their regular ablutions. But as it turned out, people not only still brought their washbasin, small rag, and comb into the shower stall with them but moreover commonly transgressed the demarcated showering space itself by extending the nozzle for use into the general bathroom area, where they persisted in washing their hair, if not their bodies, with a water-filled basin set on a stool. New shampoo commercials from Taiwan with sultry pop stars lathering under the nozzle were certainly part of a developing pedagogical project that was beginning to link the desirability of this emerging domestic space with a certain style of hygienic practice. But as far as I could tell as a village resident and frequent guest in urban homes (and their shower-equipped bathrooms), this pedagogical project had not yet been fully realized at the time I left Fuzhou in August 2002.

6. It is interesting that the old caretaker of the Monkey King temple, who first told me this story on the bridge, basically reenacted the whole scene as he traced its unfolding, dramatizing different actors' performances on the stage and guiding me with the arcing movement of his index finger, as a witness might have, to the flight of the Monkey King from one side of the river to the other. Through his performative storytelling, he highlighted the very affective dimensions of the built environment and particularly the embodied form memories assumed as evoked by the actual temple standing before the old caretaker.

7. See the introduction for a discussion of Massey's notion of "differentiated mobility."

8. Although there were English instruction books published in China that also specialized in restaurant-related vocabulary and dialogue, people I knew in Longyan uniformly dismissed the Chinese versions as having little relevance to their preparations for going overseas. This was mainly because the books published domestically were all geared toward those working at hotel restaurants in China's urban centers, which served foreign tourists or businessmen and, as such, did not resemble the kind of work situations migrants faced overseas. Moreover, unlike the books shipped from the United States, these China-based texts offered little beyond basic vocabulary and dialogue exercises for dealing with the restaurant customer in China.

TWO. *Stepping Out*

1. A number of terms have been used to designate overseas Chinese: *huaqiao* (overseas Chinese), *haiwai huaren* (Chinese residing overseas), and recently *xin yimin* (new migrant) and *xin huaqiao* (new overseas Chinese). Although some have

argued for meaningful distinctions among these terms, particularly between the more China-bound *huaqiao* and diasporic *huaren* (G. Wang 1991, 2000; L. Wang 1991), I found that these terms were used interchangeably among local residents in Longyan. Perhaps the one significant distinction villagers made was between the "new" and "old" *huaqiao*, referring to those who emigrated since the 1980s and those who emigrated earlier respectively. This resonates with the distinction Nyíri highlights in the post-Mao discourse on the "new immigrant" (2002, 221–26; also see Thunø 2001; Biao 2003). However, because people in Longyan typically call all Chinese residing overseas *huaqiao*, I privilege this term here as an emic short-hand, though I recognize that it does not capture the more complicated position-ings around overseas Chinese status elaborated at the national level via state poli-cies and public discourse.

2. In addition to Cohen, Andrew Kipnis (1995b) also offers a nuanced analysis of the deployment of the peasant and peasantness from the Republican Era to the contemporary period of economic reform. In particular, he points to the contra-dictory uses under Mao of *nongmin*, which was both celebrated as a revolutionary force righteous in poverty and linked to notions of "feudal superstition" and "back-wardness." Kipnis argues that after the Cultural Revolution, *nongmin* devolved into a singular sign of backwardness. See also Guldin (2001) and Ruf (1998) for discussions of the state category of "peasant" in China.

3. Specifically, following the disasters of the Great Leap Forward, state poli-cies effectively sought to prevent those with peasant registration from flooding the cities. This was accomplished by both the physical deportation of 50 million rural migrants from the cities between 1961 and 1963 and the institutionalization of a strict rationing and job-allocation system in urban areas that prevented those with rural registrations from purchasing basic staples such as grain, cooking oil, and cloth in city markets or obtaining placement in urban work units (*danwei*), through which nearly all city employment and housing were assigned. From 1958 forward, those classified as peasants under the registration system were structur-ally bound to their rural land and made responsible for producing the food supply for feeding both themselves and the industrializing urban population (T. Cheng and Selden 1997; Ma 1994; MacKenzie 2002; Solinger 1999; F. Wang 1997). Dur-ing the Mao years, it became nearly impossible to change a peasant registration to an urban one, with the exception of the few who were officially recruited by urban labor departments for specific state projects. By 1977, even rural inhabitants who married urban dwellers were barred from moving to cities. Furthermore, the same 1977 policy made household registration hereditary through mothers and barred children with rural status from residing with city-registered fathers (MacKenzie 2002).

4. As Dorothy Solinger has noted, "Not only the quality of goods supplied, but the transportation conditions, the range of cultural entertainment, the nature of

education offered, and the type of health care one received depended upon where one resided. And it was not just these more tangible goods that were allocated by the rank of residents, but the wages people were paid, the prices they were charged, and the subsidies and welfare benefits they received were so fixed as well (1999, 36).

5. Many scholars have noted that the resulting "floating population" of unregistered rural migrants in the cities has so far maintained rather than challenged the existing spatial hierarchy of the registration system, only this time reinscribing the inequalities directly onto the urban landscape in the form of ghettoized migrant "villages" cut off from the rest of the city, its resources, and infrastructure (MacKenzie 2002; Solinger 1999; Zhang 2001a; 2001b).

6. Longyan is sufficiently large and diverse enough to have two village committees, one overseeing "non-peasants," who are basically nonagricultural personnel like cadres, factory workers, and teachers attached to work units, and another overseeing "peasants," who were (theoretically) allocated agricultural land by households during decollectivization in the early 1980s. In 2003, Longyan's village committee in charge of peasant administration (*cun weiyuanhui*) reported 3,620 residents, compared to 1,358 reported by the committee for non-peasant administration (*shequ juweihui*) (H. Chen and Liu 2010).

7. Secretary Lin's description of Longyan as "hundred surname" is meant to distinguish the diverse roots of the village population from single-lineage or single-surname villages common in China.

8. My interactions with teachers at Longyan Middle School support an argument made by Andrew Kipnis that "schools were thoroughly non-peasant institutions" (1995, 130). While he was making an argument for an institutional culture that fueled ambitions to escape peasanthood through educational achievement, my work additionally points to the urban background and identification of teachers as part of the non-peasant nature of Longyan Middle School.

9. Pál Nyíri (2002) describes how after Mao's death and the beginning of reforms, the government set out to court overseas Chinese for investments and donations to China. Proactive moves to strengthen ties with overseas Chinese included the 1977 establishment of overseas organizations, a 1985 policy for loosening travel restrictions, and 1993 declarations of the rights of overseas Chinese. Together these policies marked a shift from an expectation of return to an encouragement of patriotism from overseas without the expectation of return. In Fuzhou, an official organization to support and court overseas Chinese was initiated in August 1981 (Ji 1999). See also Barabantseva (2005); Biao (2003); Thunø (2001); Thunø and Pieke (2005); G. Wang (1985); and Woon (1990) on China's post-Mao policy toward the overseas Chinese. On the emigration front, since the 1980s the central government has worked to reform and simplify its passport system and make it more possible for people to travel and emigrate overseas. In 2001, the Ministry of

Public Security began experimenting with streamlining the administrative procedures for passport issuance in select locations in Guangdong Province so that residents in these sites could apply for passports with only their national ID card and receive their travel documents in as little as three working days. The central government has also acknowledged the widespread institutionalization of emigration service agencies all across China through its efforts since 2000 to regulate this industry of migration consultants and exit-entry facilitators (Biao 2003). Such efforts, Xiang Biao (2003) has noted, are part of the central government's stipulated goal over the past two decades to recast emigration management as an area of "service" rather than "control."

10. "Stowaway" is also termed *touduzhe,* with *zhe* referring to a "person" engaging in a referenced action (stowing away), as opposed to *touduke,* with *ke* referring to a "customer" of *toudu* as a service.

11. Post-Mao policies courting overseas Chinese, particularly the category of new immigrants (*xin yimin*), who have ventured abroad since the 1980s, have focused predominantly on the highly skilled and educated (Biao 2003, 37; Thunø 2001, 923). My characterization of the term *huaqiao* as evoking a kind of elite cosmopolitanism also draws from precedents like Aihwa Ong's work on transnational Chinese and flexible citizenship (1999, 1997). Additionally, my impressions are based on circulating media images of celebrated overseas Chinese and conflations of elite student and entrepreneurial status in villagers' use of the term *huaqiao.* Last, my understanding is also refracted through people's imagination of me as a model *huaqiao* who can come and go at will. See also footnote 1 above for clarification of terminologies for overseas Chinese.

12. Michael Dutton (1995) offers a much more nuanced discussion of political campaigns across the Maoist/post-Mao divide than I can elaborate in my argument here. In particular, in arguing for continuity and change in policing strategies as a matter of "repetition with a difference," Dutton highlights how Maoist campaigns in the 1960s and '70s tended to be disciplinary and transformational—to "touch people to their very souls"—as opposed to current ones, which are more "overtly punitive and semiotechnical" with aims "not to transform but to frighten" (437).

13. Much has been written in China scholarship about the informal ties of affective and material exchange commonly referenced as *guanxi* (Bian 1994; Gold 1985; Guthrie 1998; Hsing 1997; Kipnis 1996, 1997; W. Myers 1997; Smart 1993; Vogel 1965; Wank 1996; Y. Yan 1996; M. Yang 1989, 1994). I address the concept more specifically in subsequent chapters, particularly in chapter 3, on emigration strategies. For now, my aim is to point out the centrality of informal networks to people's conception of household registration status and their potentiality as state subjects.

14. This argument resonates and supports points made by Friedman et al. (1991) regarding the centrality and flexible continuity of informal networks in

structuring inequalities across the Republican/Maoist/Reform era divides and by Dutton (1992) about the persistence of a collective form of subjectivity in China as opposed to a more individualizing, discrete sense of the disciplinary subject à la Michel Foucault (1979), which Dutton argues never materialized. As a synthesis of these two arguments, I am proposing a collectivist sense of subjectivity anchored more by expansive, informal networks than official, state-delineated social units like rural commune, peasant village, work unit, or household registration. Such networks do not necessarily oppose state units but can often support them, as in the case of urbanites whose ties are intimately bound up with their work units.

15. Nyíri (2002) and Thunø (2001) have both noted a categorical shift between the 1980s and 1990s in CCP policies toward Chinese abroad, from the narrow courtship of long-settled overseas Chinese through their dependents (*qiaojuan*) to a broader embrace of new migrants who emigrated in the post-Mao era. While the CCP agenda for the new immigrants was ideally imagined by officials as an effort for "mak[ing] friends with [ethnic Chinese] professionals and business people . . . and other famous persons" (Thunø 2001, 923), it is interesting that non-elite and often illicit migrants like the Fuzhounese are being interpellated into this privileged state category through official courtship at different levels of government (as evident by the banquet attendees in the introduction of this chapter) and that as a result, they are reworking the very terms of state subjectification. For another discussion of the impact of different levels of government involvement in the promotion of overseas Chinese ties and Chinese emigration in Fuzhou, see Thunø and Pieke (2005).

PART II. *Exits and Entrances*

1. A number of scholars have noted that legislative changes in U.S. immigration policy over the last two decades have eased migrant flows from Fuzhou (Chin 1999; Guest 2003; Kwong 2001; P. J. Smith 1997a). Most agree that the Immigration Reform and Control Act of 1986 was a watershed for Fuzhounese in allowing the few who were here without the wherewithal for gaining legal status to become a viable seed population for bringing others over, both through legal channels under the family reunification provisions of the 1965 Immigration and Nationality Act and through the growth of human smuggling networks. Subsequent expansion of political asylum opportunities for Chinese migrants has made it increasingly appealing and possible for the Fuzhounese to look for paper routes out of China. In particular, many who arrived via smuggling prior to 1990 were able to legalize their status through two key executive orders signed by President George H. W. Bush. The first, following the 1989 Tiananmen Square protests, enabled Chinese students overseas to attain political asylum, and the second, in 1990, gave privileged consideration to asylum applicants on the basis of forced abortion and

sterilization as a result of China's one-child policy. Recently media coverage of religious persecution, particularly of the Falun Gong and underground evangelical
Christian churches, has also eased the way for Chinese migrants to claim asylum
on this basis. My sources suggest that claiming persecution on the basis of the
one-child policy has been the most prevalent strategy among Longyan residents
seeking political asylum.

2. Latour is referring to the making of scientific facts. I am appropriating his
terms to talk about practices of inscription deployed by state bureaucracies to so-
lidify classifications of persons as "facts" of identity.

THREE. *Snakeheads and Paper Trails*

1. Early on in my research, I had decided not to seek out the known snakeheads in the area in hopes of avoiding direct involvement and, in turn, problems
of complicity, with the most dicey aspects of the illicit in Fuzhounese migration.
Since other scholars had already mapped out the various strategies and organizational structures of smugglers and their transnational networks (Chin 1999; 2001;
Kwong 1997; P. J. Smith 1997b), my goal had been to focus more on the everyday
lives of aspiring migrants and to deal with issues of illegality only as they cropped
up in people's stories of migration successes or failures. Little did I know that I
would also be spending part of my time grappling with villagers' requests for my
help with reading various immigration documents that came their way. I limited
my assistance to the most straightforward tasks, such as direct translation of immigration forms and letters. On occasion, I also helped fill in simple application
forms in English with personal data like name, birth date, and gender, for legal
applicants.

2. See chapter 1 for an elaboration of this notion of mobility as qualisign.

3. The gender implications of such behavior are discussed in chapter 6.

4. Kellee Tsai also notes the gendered nature of boat smuggling in Fuzhou's
Changle county, where over 90 percent of stowaways were male (2002, 77).

5. Fuzhounese understandings of boat smuggling as a masculine mode of
transport stands in sharp contrast with most international media and policy representations of global smuggling and trafficking networks, which predominantly
fixate on women and, to a lesser extent, children involved in sex work as "trafficking victims" (Agustin 2006; Chapkis 2003; A. Murray 1998).

6. For other ethnographic analyses of the materiality and technologies of gendered mobility, see Jain (2002) and Ong (2003).

7. Such associations of waste and illicit migration may not be unique to the
Chinese smuggled from Fuzhou. Representations of undocumented Latino migration also feature images of garbage and human waste, particularly in photographs
of trash strewn along the U.S.-Mexico border as the remnant material traces of ab-

sconding "illegal aliens" (Davis 2006; Fitzsimmons 2006; Johnson 2006; Robbins 2006). In addition to recurring representations of garbage and human waste in *Inside* ICE, the ICE's official newsletter, ICE spokesperson Virginia Kice also appeared in numerous newspapers in 2006 describing the olfactory markers of stowaways who were apprehended along the West Coast in separate incidents. "By the time they reach the West Coast, they are just reeking," Kice said in one article. "One of the recent ones, there was effluence seeping out of the container. You're confined in that space with 30 or 40 people with nothing but coffee cans for waste" (cited in Grossberg 2006).

8. Interestingly, Aihwa Ong has noted that in the *Facts of Life in the United States* guide issued to refugee adults, "the focus on inadvertently offensive bodies dwells on odor." As the guide explains, "Americans are very sensitive to personal body odors" (2003, 97), and in fact, as Ong observes, "So much is made of the masking of smell, this 'most animal' of our senses, that it seems as if poor newcomers were being urged to stock up on Listerine and Right Guard. Other instructions include ventilating the home so that strong cooking smells will not offend the neighbors" (97). Ong concludes that "The focus on offensive smells, those 'invasive' and invisible forces, highlights anxiety over regulating refugee bodies in social space" (97). Also see Manalansan (2006) on the linkages of smells and immigrant alterity.

9. The technical, as Bruno Latour (1999) has argued, occupies a peculiar ontological status as a set of practices, people, and objects that is at once subordinate, underappreciated, and yet indispensable within programs of action. Often it is only through the occasional "technical" glitch or snag that the crucial yet invisible role of technicians and technicalities comes into focus in everyday life. Here I also draw from Kimberly Coles's discussion of *techne* of elections in Bosnia-Herzegovina, as well as Ong (2003) on what she describes as the "technologies of government." Also see Hull (2003) and Harper (1998).

10. Here I draw from scholarship working to shift the analytic focus from the law as a status attribute of certain migrants to the social and historical *processes* for legalizing and illegalizing movements (Coutin 2000; De Genova 2002; Heyman 1999; Peutz 2006; Schendel and Abraham 2005).

11. This list of required documents and the language describing it is taken mostly from the Guangzhou consulate's Web site but also from my encounters with the actual application materials via informants, though I have modified some of the descriptions of individual documents on the original list to better capture the process involved in obtaining such paperwork.

12. In fact, in the revised edition of *Imagined Communities* (1991), Anderson briefly highlights the significance of personal identification documents in his musings on the institutions of census, map, and museum in the imaginings of the colonial state: "The photograph, the fine child of the age of mechanical

reproduction, is only the peremptory of a huge modern accumulation of documentary evidence (birth certificates, diaries, report cards, letters, medical records, and the like) which simultaneously records a certain apparent continuity and emphasizes its loss from memory. Out of this estrangement comes the conception of personhood, *identity* . . . which, because it cannot be 'remembered,' must be narrated" (204).

13. Sociologist John Torpey (2000) noted that standardization of such travel documents in an "international passport system" only came into being after the Second World War, though histories of nationalism and the emergence of nation-states certainly date further back. In particular, the postwar emergence of global nongovernmental organizations (NGOs) like the International Standards Organization (ISO) and the International Civil Aviation Organization (ICAO) has been instrumental in the international standardization of passports. Since 9/11, both the ISO and ICAO have been crucial as coordinating bodies in promoting the development of new "smart" passports with biometric, digital, and radio frequency features. For another perspective on passport standardization, Horng-luen Wang (2004) provides an interesting case study of the legal aesthetics of the Taiwanese passport as an anomaly in the international passport system and therefore as a diagnostic of the power asymmetries and inequalities in the current regime of mobility. Yngvesson and Coutin (2006) also point to the standardizing "pull" of IDs on persons to national "origins." Also see Amoore (2006) and Chalfin (2004, 2006) on post-9/11 realignments of customs and border regimes.

14. See McKeown (2003) on the introduction of procedural regulations on Chinese emigration under the Chinese Exclusion Act. In particular, I draw here on McKeown's discussion of the ritualization of bureaucratic protocols as one of the key outcomes of that act. Ferme (2004), Jeganathan (2004), and Das (2004) have also provided rich ethnographic analyses of checkpoints and crossings that inform my argument.

15. The most common forms of sponsorship for legal status were through a spouse, parent, or adult child, with either citizenship or political asylum.

16. Longyan villagers tell me that high interest loans typically demand 1 to 1.5 percent interest per month, though they can cost up to 3 percent per month.

17. My observations resonate with Andrew Kipnis's (1997) analysis of *guanxi* and sentiment in rural northern China. The importance of such connections as a resource and as a renewed post-Mao practice is also described by Mayfair Yang (1994) and Yan Yunxiang (1996). Also see Smart (1993) and Hsing (1997).

18. Since my field research in 2000–2002, the INS has been completely reorganized, with its functions divided among several different administrative units, including the ICE and Customs and Immigration Services (CIS)—both of which are now housed under the new post-9/11 Department of Homeland Security. I refer to

"INS" here because it was still the extant administrative unit for U.S. immigration at the time of my research.

19. See chapter 5 for elaborations on cosmic accounting and debt relations with gods.

FOUR. *Bad Subjects*

1. The most famous case of "bad subjects" described by Torpey (2000) concerns Louis XVI's attempt to sneak out of Versailles while dressed as a nondescript servant with a valet's passport during the French Revolution.

2. It is interesting that this kind of specialized language training was also central to the socialization of new INS inspectors at the U.S.-Mexican border, though in this case it was Spanish that they needed to master in anticipation of encounters with mostly Mexican migrants. As Josiah Heyman has described in his research on the INS, the Spanish textbook used in INS training included a series of dialogues involving "defiant behavior by immigrants . . . or [describing] humility, remorse and desire to seek entry through proper channels" (1995, 268). Not unlike the Travel English studied by Longyan residents, these were texts meant to set up expectations of interactions at ports of entry, albeit from the perspective of state agents. Aihwa Ong has also noted that English training in refugee camps helped socialize Cambodians as "viable migrants" by offering lessons about American social hierarchies and other aspects necessary for becoming "good citizens" once overseas (2003, 59–60).

3. This is not to diminish the marginalizing effects that deportation commonly has on those subjected to forced removal (see Ferme 2004; Peutz 2006; Yngvesson and Coutin 2006). My aim here is merely to point out the generative dimensions of state power in terms of reshaping people and their social landscape. In chapter 6, I elaborate on the limits of deportees' claims to training and knowledge by analyzing the gendered dimensions of stigma attached to male migrants who had failed to reach their destinations one too many times.

4. On the other side, the attention of immigration inspectors to the physical signs of suspicion, as well as to racial and class markers of illegality, has also been noted by Heyman: "Above all, the inspector examines the physical demeanor of the people being inspected: are they self-confident or nervous, forthcoming, evasive or defiant? Is a downcast look a matter of humility and a bit of fright before governmental authorities or a nonverbal signal of deception? These cues are real, but by no means certain or devoid of social and cultural interpretation" (2004, 309; also see Heyman 1995; Gilboy 1991, 1992). Aihwa Ong (2003) has also noted the importance of embodied cultural signs to the adjudication of Cambodian refugee claims. In particular, she has observed that "social differences such as

the refugees' body language—smiling even under stress, reporting deaths of relatives with a dispassionate expression—made them Khmer Rouge suspects in the eyes of INS officers" (2003, 58). Attention to the physical signs of migrant legality or illegality has been reinforced by such post-9/11 inspecting programs as SPOT (Screening Passengers by Observation Techniques), which promises to identify suspicious travelers through their physical gestures and behavior.

5. As mentioned in chapter 3, consistency of personal narratives was one of the basic standards for determining "legal credibility" (cf. McKinnon 2009; Melloy 2007; Sweeney 2009).

6. The United States is one of only a few countries to distinguish between refugee and asylee status in immigration policy. The term "refugee" designates those recognized as having a well-founded fear of persecution before their admission into the United States, while "asylee" refers to those who request protection from within the United States only after their entry into the country. Once they are granted legal status, the rights and privileges of refugees and asylees are virtually the same.

7. Since the passage of the Illegal Immigration Reform and Immigrant Responsibility Act (IIRIRA) in 1996, the United States can immediately deport individuals trying to enter the country with invalid, fraudulent, or missing travel documents if they do not indicate to INS officers on the spot a "credible fear" of persecution in their own country. But even if they claim asylum, IIRIRA has severely eroded due process for migrants by giving INS officers the discretion to determine whether the asylum seekers have a strong possibility for establishing eligibility for their claims and, if not, to give deportation orders for immediate removal. At this point, migrants may appeal the determination to an immigration judge, who is expected to render a decision within one week. The rise of immediate deportation orders due to these legislative changes has no doubt increased the concern of aspiring migrants in Longyan because IIRIRA has raised the stakes even higher for migrants to produce persuasive narratives for entrance immediately upon arrival and interaction with the INS.

8. Recent news articles have pointed to immigration officers' familiarity with certain kinds of coached asylum claims from Chinese migrants from Fujian Province (Amon 2002; Gee 2001; Guo 2003; Zhao 2001). This phenomenon was also noted by Mahler (1992) for Latino immigrants in the New York area.

9. Sarah Mahler (1992, 182–83) has also observed the reluctance of Salvadoran migrants in Long Island to apply for political asylum despite the legitimacy of their claims, while Aihwa Ong has noted that, like the Fuzhounese, Cambodian survivors seeking refugee status often did not see officials as "people to whom one could tell the complex truths of one's situation." As a result, even those with legitimate claims often failed because they routinely saw officials and their questions

as challenges around which to navigate via strategies of "silence, dissembling and faked life stories" (2003, 58–59).

10. There have been some journalistic reports about exploitative lawyers linked to smugglers and fraudulent immigration agencies in Chinese communities in the United States who file shoddy and/or fake claims for clients or simply swindle migrants out of money without providing any services at all (see Zhao 2001 and Amon 2002). Mahler (1992) has also observed a similar phenomenon among her Salvadoran subjects in Long Island. Because my fieldwork took place mostly in China, I do not have adequate evidence to support these observations. However, people's views of the lawyer-client relationship certainly suggest easy opportunities for exploitation.

11. As Ong has aptly noted, "The individual is never totally objectified or rationalized by state agencies and civic associations, nor can the individual totally escape the power effects of their regulatory schemes" (2003, 17).

12. In fact, in her subsequent research on Cambodian refugees in the United States, Ong adds much nuance to this kind of economic analysis by examining, for instance, "the tension between the American stress on individualism, pragmatism, and materialism on the one hand, and the Khmer-Buddhist ethos of compassionate hierarchy, collectivism, and otherworldliness on the other . . . in the ethical project of becoming citizens" (2003, 7; also see ch. 8, pp. 195–228). This line of analysis certainly resonates more with my work and particularly with the argument I am making here about the centrality of religiosity to the Fuzhounese project for legality and prosperity overseas.

13. Since 1956, when Chinese party leaders began promoting cremation as a "civilized" and "rational" alternative to the "superstitious" excesses of traditional funeral and burial practices (Cheater 1991; Whyte 1990), illegible or unmarked graves have often cropped up in obscure corners of communities, particularly in rural areas, in quiet defiance of state campaigns for funeral reform (cf. Teather 1999, 414–15). Yet aside from the ten-year period of the Cultural Revolution, when all popular religious practices, including death rituals, came under intense scrutiny and attack (Bruun 1996; Whyte 1990), state mandates for cremation rarely inspired sustained and uniform enforcement at the local level until after 1997, when mandatory cremation gained both the force of law with the State Council's issuance of "Regulations on Funeral and Interment Control" and new symbolic weight with the exemplary death of party leader and reform-era icon Deng Xiaoping, who had his remains cremated and scattered across land and sea (Faison 1997). In Longyan, more vigilant enforcement of mandatory cremation began in 1999.

14. Not only did the demand for sending the newly dead to state crematoriums disrupt the customary sequence of ritual practices necessary for securing the

newly dead from the threat of ghosts and other obstacles as they made their way to the afterlife, but there was also widespread fear among seniors that cremation itself would "feel like dying twice" by doing violence to bodies not quite purged of the spirit of the newly dead. Moreover, there were rumors of state negligence and improper handling of ashes involving not only mix-ups of human remains but also the contamination of the ashes of loved ones with animal remains and other nonhuman debris—all of which had dislocating and disturbing effects on the spirits of the dead.

PART III. *Debts and Diversions*

1. I cannot possibly do justice in an endnote to the vast range of scholarship engaged with Mauss's *The Gift*. A small sample of works, from which I draw in developing my analysis, includes the following: Akin and Robbins (1999), Bloch and Parry (1989), Callon (1998), Cliggett (2003), Derrida (1992), Godelier (1999), Graeber (2001), Gregory (1997), Hart (2001), Maurer (2005), Miller (1998), Sahlins (1972), Strathern (1988, 1992), Thomas (1991), Weiner (1976, 1992), and Wilk and Cliggett (2007).

2. "The evolution of economic law has not been from barter to sale, and from cash sale to credit sale," Mauss argued (1967, 36). Rather, it was the logic of the gift that enabled disparate items to change hands in the first place and in turn underwrote ongoing exchange relations through the constant deferral of returns and the unsettling of balances. As Mauss continues, "On the one hand, barter has arisen through a system of presents given and reciprocated according to a time limit. . . . On the other hand, buying and selling arose in the same way, with the latter according to a fixed time limit, or by cash, as well as by lending" (36).

3. For a critique of barter as the origin of monetary exchange and modern capitalism, see Humphrey and Hugh-Jones (1992).

4. Additionally, some interlocutors of Mauss have usefully reexamined the gift for its analytic and empirical contingencies as a claim to social recognition of debt and credit through exchange (e.g., Derrida 1992; Graeber 2001; Strathern 1988; Thomas 1991). Such works have persuasively argued that the gift can be better understood as a "tropic hook" (Guyer 2004), rather than a pre-given social domain, in the formation of transactional orders. Here the emphasis on the semiotic and performative aspects of exchange offers a way out of the analytic rut tethered to binary assumptions of gifts versus commodities and of personalizing debts versus alienating money in social life.

5. Among the various theories of money's origin, there is even one genealogy that posits credit-debt as foundational to money's development and ultimate extension as circulating capital in social life (Ingham 1996, 2001; Kintzele 1988; Skaggs 1997; Théret 1999). This argument has been traced to the British eco-

nomic thinker Henry Dunning Macleod (1882), to proponents of state theories of money such as A. Mitchell Innes (1913) and Goerg Friedrich Knapp (1928), and to German sociologist Georg Simmel (1978).

6. As Marx notes in *Capital*, Vol. I, "In all cases, therefore, the use-value of the labour-power is advanced to the capitalist: the labourer allows the buyer to consume it before he receives payment of the price; he everywhere gives credit to the capitalist. That his credit is no mere fiction, is shown not only by the occasional loss of wages on the bankruptcy of the capitalist, but also by a series of more enduring consequences" (2003, 170–71). Also see Hart on this point (2001, 200–202).

FIVE. *For Use in Heaven or Hell*

1. Passing observations of spirit money in scholarship on Chinese popular religion are so prevalent that there are in fact too many citations to list. For more detailed studies see de Groot (1972), Doolittle (1865), Doré and Kennelly (1967), Gates (1987), Hou (1975), McCreery (1990), Seaman (1982), A. Wolf (1978), and M. Yang (2000).

2. *Feng shui*, which literally translates as "wind-water," is the traditional Chinese practice of geomancy, or the art of spatial arrangement aimed at achieving maximum harmony between the flow of energy (*qi*) in all things.

3. For other works on currency distinctions, see Akin and Robbins (1999), Dickinson (2007), Maurer (2005), Moodie (2007), Notar (2002), Pederson (2002), Rogers (2005), and Truitt (2007).

4. In his monograph on spirit money in China, Ching-Lang Hou (1975) suggests that the notion of an other-worldly economy organized around a central bank was consolidated only during the Southern Sung (1127–1279), alongside a rising urban merchant class and the institutionalization of a banking economy (cf. Gates 1987; Seidel 1978).

5. This set of categories is perhaps best captured by Arthur Wolf's brief yet succinct sketch of spirit money in his classic essay on gods, ghosts, and ancestors (1978, 180–81). However, I want to stress that these are rough distinctions, as most analysts of spirit money point to some exceptions to these rules of exchange. Gary Seaman (1982, 88), for instance, notes that gold spirit money is sometimes offered to ancestors in Taiwan during certain key rituals involving a change in the social status of an individual member of a lineage or in the status of the lineage as a whole. Stephan Feuchtwang (1974, 2001), on the other hand, suggests that the crucial divide is between gods, who typically receive gold offerings, and ancestors and ghosts, who both receive silver (also see Harrell 1974; Weller 1987). John McCreery also observes that "small silver" was being "routinely offered to both ancestors and ghosts" in Taiwan (1990, 11). Funeral processions in particular

are common occasions in which ghosts are offered more valuable forms of spirit money, like silver notes, than the typical small change they get. My main aim here is to sketch the general categories of monies that scholars have described in the Chinese ritual economy. Notably absent here is the form of spirit money that is the focal point of the above scholarship.

6. Reverend Justus Doolittle, for instance, observed "a kind of mock-money, called foreign cash [with] rude impressions . . . of a Spanish dollar" in the Fuzhou region during the mid-nineteenth century (1865, 541).

7. Among the few scholars who mention state currencies in their work on Chinese spirit money (e.g., Hou 1975; Gates 1987), none have moved beyond passing observations to shed light on local understandings and uses of this particular kind of money in ritual practices. One possible reason for this analytic neglect may be that Taiwan has been a focal point for a good deal of the field research and analysis of Chinese spirit money. For instance, Hou, who wrote one of the only full-length monographs on spirit money based on research in Taiwan, has suggested that though "occidental-style" spirit money was available on the island (introduced via Shanghai merchants in the nineteenth century), the traditionally minded Taiwanese continued to prefer using the more long-standing forms of paper money (e.g., gold, silver, cash) that could be traced back to the Sung period (1975, 17). Or perhaps following the critiques of Stephen Murray and Keelung Hong (1991) regarding ethnographies of Taiwan, one could conjecture that such a "Western"-style artifact might have easily fallen out of the purview of specialists mainly interested in aspects of religion reflecting Chinese "tradition." USD spirit money, however, has been the focus of ethnographic analysis in Vietnam (see Kwon 2007). While Kwon's work highlights how the USD circulated as a general currency to destabilize the traditional hierarchies of monies and spheres of exchange in the afterlife, my work points to a very different scenario in Fuzhou and hence departs from his arguments regarding the social effects of dollarization.

8. Note that it is the design from the 1990 series of the USD that is under discussion here. This may reflect a time lag in local familiarity and hence incorporation of the redesigned 1996 version of the USD into Chinese spirit money.

9. Two classic ethnographic accounts of the bureaucratic nature of the afterlife in Chinese communities are A. Wolf (1978) and Ahern (1982). Also see Doré and Kennelly (1967), Eberhard (1967), Feuchtwang (1977, 1993), Gates (1987), Rawski and Watson (1988), Teiser (1988, 1993), and Weller (1987).

10. While the character *mi* (blind or confused) had been used as early as medieval China to describe confusions or deviations from particular ceremonial rites or doctrinal teachings (Campany 2003), it was only through the neologism of *mixin*—with its emphasis on *xin*, or belief—that critics could convey not only disapproval of particular practices but also a more total condemnation of "the superstitious" as an entire backward way of being.

11. In fact, teachers at Longyan middle school not only uniformly complained to me about "superstition" among villagers but they also built such critiques into the school's curriculum, especially in politics classes and around the Lunar New Year, which featured an annual anti-superstition film screening. Also see Kipnis (1995a, 129–30) on critiques of "feudal superstition" in schools.

12. Robert Weller has also noted that ghosts "receive certain offerings that are not appropriate to either gods or ancestors, but that emphasize their pitiful need for alms, just like living persons with no kin" (1995, 49).

13. Some of my subjects told me that this difference in days had to do with the number of children the deceased possessed, while others suggested it reflected the relative wealth of the family. In both cases, people noted that the more children or more money the deceased had, the more likely mortuary rituals and the period of mourning would be prolonged for the entire forty-nine-day period. In this sense, a shorter journey would not reflect better fortune but rather the opposite.

14. As discussed above, "liberation" here refers to the 1949 Communist Revolution, which ushered in state socialism under the CCP, lead by Mao Zedong.

15. Between February and May 2002, I surveyed all the stores operating in Longyan and in a larger adjacent town that sold only paper goods and items like incense and vessels used for religious purposes. This survey consisted of open-ended interviews with the owners of these specialty stores—four in Longyan and four in the neighboring town.

16. I draw this notion of "nested hierarchies" from other scholarly works on Chinese cosmology and social structure, particularly from those who, with some inspiration from Louis Dumont (1980), have forwarded "encompassment" as a means for understanding hegemony in yin-yang conceptualizations of complementarity (Furth 1999; Sangren 1987; Taylor 1989; Zito 1997).

17. These figures are from an interview with Longyan's party secretary of peasant administration on July 13, 2000. I was unable, however, to determine how local officials arrived at these estimates. Hence, they are useful here as indicative not only of empirical "reality" but also of elite discourse of the wastefulness (*langfei*) of religious activity.

18. This figure was cited in a local scholar's unpublished report and corroborated by my own survey of these temples.

19. The gendered asymmetries of karmic debt and particularly of mother figures in Chinese popular religion have been examined by a number of scholars, including Cole (1998), Gernet (1995), Sangren (1983, 2000), and Teiser (1988).

20. The gods receiving regular offerings ranged from domestic gods, such as the kitchen god and others worshipped on personal alters in the home, to local temple gods, to the divine spirit of "heaven" (*tian*).

21. Divination blocks consist of two wooden crescent-shaped pieces, each with a curved top and a flat bottom. To communicate with the gods, worshippers ask a

yes-or-no question and then toss the two pieces for the response. If the blocks land with one curved and one flat side up, the answer is yes. If they land with any other combination (two flat sides, two curved sides), the response is interpreted as no or, more intimately, as inconclusive laughter by the gods.

22. Fuzhounese opera was similar to Peking opera but sung in the local dialect.

23. I use the terms "purely economic" and "capitalistic" crudely here to denote a particular narrow understanding of "economy" that anthropologists from Mauss (1967) and Malinowski (1961) to Sahlins (1994), Appadurai (1986), Bloch and Parry (1989), Miller (1998), F. Myers (2002), Wilk and Cliggett (2007), and countless others have critiqued and complicated through the years and whose efforts I join through my analysis in this chapter.

24. I agree here with Andrew Kipnis's critique of economism in his analysis of *guanxi* and ritualized exchange. As he argues, "Feeling and instrumentality are a totality, unifying what Western bourgeois relationships separate: material exchange and affectionate feelings" (1997, 23). I elaborate on this argument by examining the concept of sentiment (*renqing*) in chapter 6.

25. It is interesting that transfers of funds to ancestors were much less routine than those to both gods and ghosts. For ghosts, offerings of small change and basic provisions were commonly made on the second and sixteenth day of each lunar month, following the payments to gods on the lunar first and fifteenth (as noted). Typically, these regular ghostly sacrifices were more casual than those for gods and involved fewer participants. Unlike the lunar first and fifteenth, when people ventured out to specific sites of worship early in the morning, offerings for ghosts took place casually behind the back door of one's own house whenever it was convenient to do so on the second and sixteenth. There was neither the same kind of moral imperative nor formal public space for ghostly offerings as there was for making offerings to gods. Still, ancestral offerings appeared even more infrequently. Beyond funeral rituals and the annual tomb-sweeping day, the only other common occasion for making offerings to deceased kin was on ancestral birthdays. It could be that because Longyan was a "hundred-surname village," the cult of ancestor worship was simply not as well elaborated or central to local ritual life as in ethnographic accounts of single-surname villages in China (e.g., Jing 1996).

26. This emphasis on "the doing" of superstition is not unique among the Fuzhounese in China. My argument here also draws inspiration from a number of key works on praxis in Chinese popular religion; chief among them are James Watson's insights on orthopraxy in funeral rites and temple cults (1985, 1988, 1993); Sangren's emphasis on ritual as productive action (2000); and Marcel Granet's observations of agnostic calculation as "superstitious positivism" among

worshippers (1975). See also Feuchtwang (2007) on ritual as communicative performance and Chau (2006) on the modes of producing or "doing" Chinese popular religion.

27. In a 1926 report on currency diversity in China, the U.S. Department of Commerce noted the lack of uniformity of money as a sign of China's failure to achieve modernity. These problems of currency disarray, the report said, were "bound up to a considerable extent with the 4,000 years or more of the history of the Chinese people" (F. Lee 1926, 18). The report went on to highlight Fuzhou as case in point, noting that it was "an excellent example of some of the currency problems with which the foreign business man in China is confronted" (28). The diversity of currency in Fuzhou included "two kinds of Mexican dollars, one kind acceptable in Shanghai and the other not, Yuan Shih Kai dollar, Hong Kong dollar, Japanese silver yen, Philippine peso, Spanish pillar dollar, United States trade dollar, French Indo-China dollar, Chinese dragon dollar, and the Straits Settlements dollar" (28). Beyond that, "What might be called the real currency of Foochow is native bank paper notes used by Chinese business men generally" (29). These native paper notes were distinguished as "big money, small money" and formed the apex of the chaotic currency system: "When the Westerner begins to talk of 'big-money, small money" it seems that he has reached the limit in the complexities of Chinese currency systems" (21).

28. Tiejun Cheng and Mark Selden argue that rationing provided "one crucial mechanism for defining and restructuring social and economic position within a clearly defined hierarchy," which they describe as a "permanent *spatial* hierarchy of positions that were transmitted across generations" (1997, 36, 45; my emphasis).

29. See the discussion of state and local discourses of overseas Chinese in chapters 1–4 above.

30. I draw the term "value transformation" from Munn (1986) to foreground action (or the performative aspect) in the analysis of value (cf. Graeber 2001).

31. While metaphorically all wealth spent on popular religion has been considered money "burned" by Chinese officials and modernizing elites since the Republican era (Anagnost 1987; Dorfman 1996; Duara 1991; Feuchtwang and Wang 1991; M. Yang 2000), the fact that worshippers have incinerated spirit money while claiming its value has long proved to be good materialist fodder for those arguing against the irrationality and futility of Chinese popular religion. As Doolittle scoffed about ritual exchange in Fuzhou more than a century ago, "No intelligent person, either in this or the ghost-world, would ever take ashes for money" (1865, 121).

32. In her analysis of "filial finance" Angela Zito suggests that money might be more fruitfully seen as a "thing-in-motion" or "thing-as-connector" in the context of seventeenth-century China: "The things of the world, including money, could be mobilized in their potentiality to make the invisible visible, to bring hidden

propensities to light. It was their function and not necessarily cause for metaphysical anxiety" (n.d., 10).

33. I draw here from a number of Marxist-inspired analyses of commodity fetishism that argue that it is the very immateriality of exchange value (e.g., as monetary price), not its materialization via some object, that is the locus of fetishization in capitalist transactions (Graeber 2001; Pietz 1993; Stallybrass 1998; Taussig 1980). In turn, highlighting the boundary of money's im/materiality in ritual acts of burning can be seen as a way for grappling with fetishisms in the plural—that is, as alienated power objectified both in the thing (religious fetish) and in the intangible abstraction of the exchange relation (commodity price). In fact, following David Graeber's observations (2001, 248), one could argue that given their emphasis on money's immateriality in ritual transactions, Longyan worshippers actually approach an unfetishized understanding of the value produced through the very object we think of as a "fetish."

34. Two roughly opposing arguments have been made about spirit money's relation to the logic of capitalism. On the one hand, Hill Gates has offered a Marxist analysis of spirit money transactions as the superstructural reflection of "the extreme capitalist penetration of Chinese culture" among worshippers in Taiwan (1987, 266). On the other, Mayfair Yang (2000), by way of George Bataille (1991), has argued for understanding ritual exchanges in Wenzhou as manifestations of a more deep-seated urge among worshippers for the exuberant destruction of capital. In the case of Longyan, I argue that such contrasting claims to the significance of spirit money do not need to be so exclusive.

35. In Fuzhounese, this saying makes the poetic rhyme *Miging zing ho lai, ang ang lau mëük zai*. In Mandarin, it can be translated as *Meijin zhen haoyong, an an liu yanlei*.

36. According to villagers, the case of Zhang Wen's husband was complicated by his possession of counterfeit documents during his detention.

SIX. *Partings and Returns*

1. My attentiveness to discursive "registers" on suffering versus pleasure owes a debt to Foucault's work on sexuality (1980).

2. Despite decades of Maoist proclamations and efforts to revolutionize the terms of kinship and gender (e.g., via collectivization), Longyan understandings and enactments of relatedness were still being shaped by a hegemonic patrilineal order. In anthropological scholarship on China, much has been written about the patrilineal form of kinship and social organization, from the work of Maurice Freedman to his subsequent interlocutors and critics (Ahern 1973, 1976; Cohen 1969, 1976; Crissman 1967; Freedman 1958, 1966, 1970; Pasternak 1972; J. Watson

1975, 1982; R. Watson 1985; A. Wolf and Huang 1980; M. Wolf 1968, 1972). Many of these works have focused on the importance of descent and inheritance as a structural principle, emphasizing the corporate, communal holdings of property and other material resources organized and distributed by patrilineal ties. Patrilineage has offered an explanatory framework for understanding social organization and conflict, especially over resource distribution within and between single-surname villages. Some, however, have critiqued the economistic bent of this analysis and have instead emphasized the ritual responsibilities associated with patrilineal organization, particularly around the maintenance and extension of ancestral cults (Chun 1996). Feminist interventions and gender analysis have also significantly challenged and refined the dominant assumptions of the lineage paradigm, particularly since Margery Wolf's influential work (1968, 1972, 1985) on women's consolidation of the "uterine family" (consisting of a mother and her children) as an alternative base of kinship for securing women's influence, as well as their future security vis-à-vis their marginalization in the patrilineal order. Writing about gender differentiation and the maintenance of strong natal relations among rural Chinese women, Judd (1989) also argued for making a distinction between patriliny as social structure and as ideology of normative moral order (also see Judd 1994; Strauch 1983). In this chapter, I also approach the patriline as both hegemonic discourse and practice rather than as a totalizing principle for organizing kinship.

3. I am reminded here particularly of Georg Simmel's argument for the fundamental importance of sacrifice in exchange relations. As Simmel argues, "Moral merit is attained only by the sacrifice of lower and yet very tempting goods, and it is the greater the more inviting the temptations and the more comprehensive and difficult the sacrifice" (1978, 88). Later he observes the following of the relation between sacrifice and sentiment: "One not only makes sacrifices for what one loves, but also one loves that for which one has made sacrifices. If motherly love is the source of innumerable sacrifices for the children, then so too the trouble and worries that the mother endures for the child form an ever closer bond with the child" (372).

4. *Qi* is the term for vital energy or life force believed to be inherent in all things. It is often depicted in traditional Chinese medicine as the life energy circulating through the body in meridians.

5. This discussion of "taste cultures" is in many ways inspired by Pierre Bourdieu's (1984) attentiveness to the socially informed body and the class stratification of taste in contemporary France, although I emphasize the dynamic and transitional processes for forging these embodied distinctions over Bourdieu's more stolid and immobile vision of class difference.

6. The character for chicken is a homonym of the character for prostitute (*ji*).

7. This argument joins anti-essentialist critiques of gender/sex systems coming out of feminist historical and anthropological research; these are too many to cite adequately here. However, I want to single out two sources to whom I owe a special debt: within feminist scholarship on China, Tani Barlow (1994), whose genealogical analysis of the category of *funu*, or "Chinese women," focuses attention on the kin positionality of gendered subjects; and, in a very different context of *travestis*, or Brazilian transgendered prostitutes, Don Kulick (1998), whose argument for a different gendered binary beyond men/women strongly resonates with my own observations of the divide between men/non-men in Longyan.

CONCLUSION. *When Fortune Flows*

1. As I have argued in the introduction, this is one of the weaknesses of arguments deploying Bourdieu's (1986) "forms of capital" schema (i.e., economic, social, cultural), which always seems to lead back to a utilitarian logic of economic maximization. This seems to be where Basu ends up in her argument despite her various astute observations of the "complex interplay of intention and fate" in mahjong (1991, 249).

Abu-Lughod, Janet L. 1989. *Before European Hegemony: The World System A.D. 1250–1350*. New York: Oxford University Press.

Agamben, Giorgio. 1998. *Homo Sacer: Sovereign Power and Bare Life*. Stanford, Calif.: Stanford University Press.

———. 2005. *State of Exception*. Chicago: University of Chicago Press.

Agustin, Laura. 2006. "The Disappearance of a Migrant Category: Migrants Who Sell Sex." *Journal of Ethnic and Migration Studies* 32 (1): 29–47.

Ahern, Emily M. 1973. *The Cult of the Dead in a Chinese Village*. Stanford, Calif.: Stanford University Press.

———. 1976. "Segmentation in Chinese Lineages: A View through Written Genealogies." *American Ethnologist* 3:1–16.

———. 1982. *Chinese Ritual and Politics*. Cambridge: Cambridge University Press.

Akin, David, and Joel Robbins. 1999. *Money and Modernity: State and Local Currencies in Melanesia*. Pittsburgh: University of Pittsburgh Press.

Alvarez, Robert. 1995. "The Mexican-U.S. Border: The Marking of an Anthropology of Borderlands." *Annual Review of Anthropology* 24:447–70.

Amon, Elizabeth. 2002. "The Snakehead Lawyers." *National Law Journal* 24 (43): A1.

Amoore, Louise. 2006. "Biometric Borders: Governing Mobilities in the War on Terror." *Political Geography* 25:336–51.

Anagnost, Ann. 1987. "Politics and Magic in Contemporary China." *Modern China* 13 (1): 40–61.

———. 1989. "Prosperity and Counter-Prosperity: The Moral Discourse of Wealth in Post-Mao China." In *Marxism and the Chinese Experience*. Edited by Arif Dirlik and Maurice Meisner, 210–34. Armonk, N.Y.: M. E. Sharpe.

———. 1994. "The Politics of Ritual Displacement." In Keyes, Kendall, and Hardacre, *Asian Visions of Authority*, 221–54.

———. 1995. "A Surfeit of Bodies: Population and the Rationality of the State in Post-Mao China." In *Conceiving the New World Order: The Global Politics of Reproduction*. Edited by Faye D. Ginsburg and Rayna Rapp, 22–41. Berkeley: University of California Press.

———. 2004. "The Corporeal Politics of Quality (Suzhi)." *Public Culture* 16 (2): 189–208.

Anderson, Benedict. 1991 [1983]. *Imagined Communities: Reflections on the Origin and Spread of Nationalism*. Revised edn. London: Verso.

Andrade, Tonio. 2005. "The Company's Chinese Pirates: How the Dutch East India Company Tried to Lead a Coalition of Pirates to War against China, 1621–1662." *Journal of World History* 15 (4): 415–44.

Ang, Ien. 1994. "On Not Speaking Chinese: Postmodern Ethnicity and the Politics of Diaspora." *New Formations* 24 (Winter): 1–18.

Anzaldúa, Gloria. 1987. *Borderlands/La Frontera: The New Mestiza*. San Francisco: Aunt Lute.

Appadurai, Arjun, ed. 1986. *The Social Life of Things: Commodities in Cultural Perspective*. Cambridge: Cambridge University Press.

———. 1990. "Disjuncture and Difference in the Global Cultural Economy." *Public Culture* 2 (2): 1–23.

———. 1991. "Global Ethnoscapes: Notes and Queries for a Transnational Anthropology." In *Recapturing Anthropology: Working in the Present*. Edited by R. G. Fox, 191–209. Santa Fe, N.M.: School of American Research Press.

———. 1997. *Modernity at Large: Cultural Dimensions of Globalization*. Minneapolis: University of Minnesota Press.

Apter, E. and W. Pietz, eds. 1993. *Fetishism as Cultural Discourse*. Ithaca, N.Y.: Cornell University Press.

Arendt, Hannah. 1975. *The Origins of Totalitarianism*. New York: Harcourt Brace Jovanovich.

Asad, Talal. 1993. *Genealogies of Religion: Discipline and Reasons of Power in Christianity and Islam*. Baltimore: Johns Hopkins University Press.

Barabantseva, Elena. 2005. "Trans-nationalising Chineseness: Overseas Chinese Policies of the PRC's Central Government." ASIEN 96 (July): 7–28.

Barlow, Tani E. 1994. "Theorizing Woman: *Funu, Guojia, Jiating*." In Zito and Barlow, *Body, Subject, and Power in China*, 253–90.

Basch, Linda G., Nina Glick Schiller, and Cristina Szanton Blanc. 1994. *Nations Unbound: Transnational Projects, Postcolonial Predicaments, and Deterritorialized Nation-States*. Langhorne, Pa.: Gordon and Breach.

Basu, Ellen Oxfeld. 1991. "Profit, Loss, and Fate: The Entrepreneurial Ethic and the Practice of Gambling in an Overseas Chinese Community." *Modern China* 17 (2): 227–59.

Bataille, Georges. 1991. *The Accursed Share: An Essay on General Economy*, vol. 1. Translated by R. Hurley. New York: Zone Books.

Bauman, Zygmunt. 2000. *Liquid Modernity*. Cambridge: Polity Press.

Bell, Catherine M. 1992. *Ritual Theory, Ritual Practice*. New York: Oxford University Press.

Berman, Marshall. 1982. *All That Is Solid Melts into Air: The Experience of Modernity*. New York: Simon and Schuster.

Bian, Yanjie. 1994. "*Guanxi* and the Allocation of Urban Jobs in China." *China Quarterly*, 971–99.

Biao, Xiang. 2003. "Emigration from China: A Sending Country Perspective." *International Migration* 41 (3): 21–46.

Biehl, João. 2001. "Vita: Life in a Zone of Abandonment." *Social Text* 19 (3 68): 131–49.

Bloch, Maurice, and Jonathan P. Parry, eds. 1989. *Money and the Morality of Exchange*. Cambridge: Cambridge University Press.

Bohannon, Paul. 1959. "The Impact of Money on an African Subsistence Economy." *Journal of Economic History* 19 (4): 491–503.

Bosco, Joseph. 2003. "The Supernatural in Hong Kong Young People's Ghost Stories." *Anthropological Forum* 13 (2): 141–49.

Bourdieu, Pierre. 1977. *Outline of a Theory of Practice*. Cambridge: Cambridge University Press.

———. 1984. *Distinction: A Social Critique of the Judgement of Taste*. Cambridge, Mass.: Harvard University Press.

———. 1986. "The Forms of Capital." In *Handbook of Theory and Research for the Sociology of Education*. Edited by J. G. Richardson, 241–58. New York: Greenwood Press.

Brecher, Jeremy, Tim Costello, and Brendan Smith. 2000. *Globalization from Below: The Power of Solidarity*. Cambridge, Mass.: South End Press.

Brendon, Piers. 1991. *Thomas Cook: 150 Years of Popular Tourism*. London: Secker and Warburg.

Brokaw, Cynthia Joanne. 1991. *The Ledgers of Merit and Demerit: Social Change and Moral Order in Late Imperial China*. Princeton, N.J.: Princeton University Press.

Brown, Jacqueline Nassy. 1998. "Black Liverpool, Black America, and the Gendering of Diasporic Space." *Cultural Anthropology* 13 (3): 291–325.

Bruun, Ole. 1996. "The Fengshui Resurgence in China: Conflicting Cosmologies between State and Peasantry." *China Journal* 36 (July): 47–65.

Buck-Morss, Susan. 1991. *The Dialectics of Seeing: Walter Benjamin and the Arcades Project*. Cambridge, Mass.: MIT Press.

Callon, Michel. 1998. "Introduction: The Embeddedness of Economic Markets in Economics." In *The Laws of the Markets*. Edited by M. Callon, 1–57. Oxford: Blackwell Publishers.

Campany, Robert Ford. 2003. "On the Very Idea of Religions (in the Modern West and in Early Medieval China)." *History of Religions* 42:287–309.

Certeau, Michel de. 1984. *The Practice of Everyday Life*. Berkeley: University of California Press.

Chalfin, Brenda. 2004. "Border Scans: Sovereignty, Surveillance and the Customs Service in Ghana." *Identities* 11:397–416.

———. 2006. "Global Customs Regimes and the Traffic in Sovereignty: Enlarging the Anthropology of the State." *Current Anthropology* 47 (2): 243–76.

Chan, Kwok Bun. 1997. "A Family Affair: Migration, Dispersal and the Emergent Identity of the Chinese Cosmopolitan." *Diaspora* 6 (2): 195–213.

Chang, Chak-yan. 2000. "The Overseas Chinese." In Yeung and Chu, *Fujian.*

Chang, Hui-Ching, and G. Richard Holt. 1994. "Debt-Repaying Mechanism in Chinese Relationships: An Exploration of the Folk Concepts of *Pao* and Human Emotional Debt." *Research on Language and Social Interaction* 27 (4): 351–87.

Chao, Emily. 1999. "The Maoist Shaman and the Madman: Ritual Bricolage, Failed Ritual, and Failed Ritual Theory." *Cultural Anthropology* 14 (4): 505–34.

Chapkis, Wendy. 2003. "Trafficking, Migration, and the Law: Protecting Innocents, Punishing Immigrants." *Gender and Society* 17 (6): 923–37.

Chatterjee, Partha. 1998. "Talking about Our Modernity in Two Languages." In *A Possible India: Essays in Political Criticism*, 263–85. Calcutta: Oxford University Press.

Chatterji, Roma. 1998. "An Ethnography of Dementia: A Case Study of an Alzheimer's Disease Patient in the Netherlands." *Culture, Medicine and Psychiatry* 22:355–82.

Chau, Adam Yuet. 2006. *Miraculous Response: Doing Popular Religion in Contemporary China.* Stanford, Calif.: Stanford University Press.

Chavez, Leo. 1992. *Shadowed Lives: Undocumented Immigrants in American Society.* Ft. Worth: Harcourt Brace Jovanovich College Publishers.

Cheater, A. P. 1991. "Death Ritual as Political Trickster in the People's Republic of China." *Australian Journal of Chinese Affairs* 26:67–97.

Chen, Heping, and Renai Liu. 2010. *A Famed Cultural-Historical Village of Fujian Province: Longyan Town Annals (Fujian sheng lishi wenhua mingeun: Longyan zhen zhi).* Fuzhou, China: Longyan Village Committee.

Chen, Jie. 1984. *Longyan Town Annals (Longyan zhen zhi).* Fuzhou, China: Self-published.

Cheng, Chung-ying. 1986. "The Concept of Face and Its Confucian Roots." *Journal of Chinese Philosophy* 13 (3): 329–48.

Cheng, Tiejun, and Mark Selden. 1997. "The Construction of Spatial Hierarchies: China's Hukou and Danwei Systems." In *New Perspectives on State Socialism in China.* Edited by Timothy Cheek and Tony Saich, 23–50. Armonk, N.Y.: M. E. Sharpe.

Chin, Ko-Lin. 1999. *Smuggled Chinese: Clandestine Immigration to the United States.* Philadelphia: Temple University Press.

———. 2001. "The Social Organization of Chinese Human Smuggling." In

Global Human Smuggling: Comparative Perspectives. Edited by D. Kyle and R. Koslowski, 216–35. Baltimore: Johns Hopkins University Press.

Chun, Allen. 1996. "The Linage-Village Complex in Southeastern China: A Long Footnote in the Anthropology of Kinship." *Current Anthropology* 37 (3): 429–50.

Clark, Hugh R. 1990. "Settlement, Trade and Economy in Fukien to the Thirteenth Century." In *Development and Decline of Fukien Province in the 17th and 18th Centuries*. Edited by E. B. Vermeer, 35–61. Leiden: E. J. Brill.

Clifford, James. 1994. "Diasporas." *Cultural Anthropology* 9 (3): 302–38.

———. 1997. *Routes: Travel and Translation in the Late Twentieth Century*. Cambridge, Mass.: Harvard University Press.

Cliggett, Lisa. 2003. "Gift Remitting and Alliance Building in Zambian Modernity: Old Answers to Modern Problems." *American Anthropologist* 105 (3): 543–52.

Cohen, Myron L. 1969. "Agnatic Kinship in South Taiwan." *Ethnology* 8:167–89.

———. 1976. *House United, House Divided: The Chinese Family in Taiwan*. New York: Columbia University Press.

———. 1993. "Cultural and Political Inventions in Modern China: The Case of the Chinese 'Peasants.'" *Daedalus* 122 (2): 151–70.

Cole, Alan. 1998. *Mothers and Sons in Chinese Buddhism*. Stanford, Calif.: Stanford University Press.

Coles, Kimberley A. 2004. "Election Day: The Construction of Democracy through Technique." *Cultural Anthropology* 19 (4): 551–80.

Collier, Jane Fishburne, and Sylvia Junko Yanagisako. 1987. *Gender and Kinship: Essays toward a Unified Analysis*. Stanford, Calif.: Stanford University Press.

Comaroff, Jean, and John L. Comaroff. 2000. "Millennial Capitalism: First Thoughts on a Second Coming." *Public Culture* 12 (2): 291–343.

Comaroff, John L., and Jean Comaroff, eds. 1993. *Modernity and Its Malcontents: Ritual and Power in Postcolonial Africa*. Chicago: University of Chicago Press.

Coronil, Fernando. 1997. *The Magical State: Nature, Money, and Modernity in Venezuela*. Chicago: University of Chicago Press.

Coutin, Susan B. 2000. *Legalizing Moves: Salvadoran Immigrants' Struggle for U.S. Residency*. Ann Arbor: University of Michigan Press.

Cresswell, Tim. 2006. *On the Move: Mobility in the Modern Western World*. New York: Routledge.

Crissman, Lawrence. 1967. "The Segmentary Structure of Urban Overseas Chinese Communities." *Man* 2 (2): 185–204.

Croll, Elizabeth. 1994. *From Heaven to Earth: Images and Experiences of Development in China*. New York: Routledge.

Cunningham, Hilary. 2004. "Nations Rebound?: Crossing Borders in a Gated Globe." *Identities* 11:329–50.

Cunningham, Hilary, and Josiah M. Heyman. 2004. "Introduction: Mobilities and Enclosures at Borders." *Identities* 11:289–302.

Dai, Yifeng. 1996. "Overseas Migration and the Economic Modernization of Xiamen City during the Twentieth Century." In *South China: State, Culture and Social change during the 20th Century*. Edited by Leo M. Douw and Peter Post, 159–68. Amsterdam: Royal Netherlands Academy of Arts and Sciences.

Dai, Yuan. 1995, 1996. *Practical English for People Working in Chinese Restaurants.* Elmhurst, NY.: GBE Publishing.

Das, Veena. 2004. "The Signature of the State: The Paradox of Illegibility." In Das and Poole, *Anthropology in the Margins of the State,* 225–52.

Das, Veena, and Deborah Poole, eds. 2004. *Anthropology in the Margins of the State.* Santa Fe, N.M.: School of American Research Press.

Davis, Tony. 2006. "Crossers Burying Border in Garbage." *Arizona Daily Star* (Tucson), July 30: A1.

Dean, Kenneth. 1993. *Taoist Ritual and Popular Cults of Southeast China.* Princeton, N.J.: Princeton University Press.

———. 1998. *Lord of the Three in One: The Spread of a Cult in Southeast China.* Princeton, N.J.: Princeton University Press.

De Genova, Nicholas. 2002. "Migrant 'Illegality' and Deportability in Everyday Life." *Annual Review of Anthropology* 31:419–47.

de Groot, J. J. M. 1972. *The Religious System of China.* 6 vols. Taipei: Ch'eng Wen Publishing.

Deleuze, Gilles, and Felix Guattari. 1987. *A Thousand Plateaus: Capitalism and Schizophrenia.* Minneapolis: University of Minnesota Press.

Derrida, Jacques. 1992. *Given Time: I. Counterfeit Money.* Translated by P. Kamuf. Chicago: University of Chicago Press.

Dickinson, J. A. 2007. "Changing Money in Post-Soviet Ukraine." In Senders and Truitt, *Money,* 27–42.

Dirlik, Arif. 1996. "Reversals, Ironies, Hegemonies." *Modern China* 22 (3): 243–84.

Dittmer, Lowell, and Samuel S. Kim, eds. 1993. *China's Quest for National Identity.* Ithaca, N.Y.: Cornell University Press.

Doolittle, Justus. 1865. *Social Life of the Chinese: With Some Account of Their Religious, Governmental, Educational, and Business Customs and Opinions: With Special but Not Exclusive Reference to Fuhchau.* New York: Harper and Brothers.

Doré, Henri, and M. Kennelly. 1967. *Researches into Chinese Superstitions.* Translated from the French with notes, historical and explanatory, by M. Kennelly. New York: Paragon Book Gallery.

Dorfman, Diane. 1996. "The Spirits of Reform: The Power of Belief in Northern China." *positions* 4 (2): 253–89.

Douglas, Mary. 1966. *Purity and Danger: An Analysis of Concepts of Pollution and Taboo.* New York: Praeger.

Duara, Prasenjit. 1991. "Knowledge and Power in the Discourse of Modernity: The Campaigns against Popular Religion in Early Twentieth-Century China." *Journal of Asian Studies* 50 (1): 67–83.

———. 1995. "The Campaign against Religion and the Return of the Repressed." In *Rescuing History from the Nation: Questioning Narratives of Modern China*, 85–114. Chicago: University of Chicago Press.

Dumont, Louis. 1980. *Homo Hierarchicus: The Caste System and Its Implications*. Chicago: University of Chicago Press.

Dutton, Michael. 1992. *Policing and Punishment in China: From Patriarchy to "the People."* Cambridge: Cambridge University Press.

———. 1995. "Dreaming of Better Times: Repetition with a Difference." *positions* 3 (2): 415–47.

———. 1998. *Streetlife China*. Cambridge: Cambridge University Press.

Eberhard, Wolfram. 1967. *Guilt and Sin in Traditional China*. Berkeley: University of California Press.

Einhorn, Bruce. 1994. "Send Your Huddled Masses, and a Hot and Sour Soup." *Business Week*, November 14.

Elyachar, Julia. 2005. *Markets of Dispossession: NGOs, Economic Development, and the State in Cairo*. Durham, N.C.: Duke University Press.

Eng, Kuah-Pearce Khun. 2006. "The Worship of Qingshui Zushi and Religious Revivalism in South China." In Tan, *Southern Fujian*, 121–44.

Ewald, François. 1991. "Insurance and Risk." In *The Foucault Effect: Studies in Governmentality*. Edited by G. Burchell, C. Gordon, and P. Miller, 197–210. Chicago: University of Chicago Press.

Fairbank, John King. 1969. *Trade and Diplomacy on the China Coast: The Opening of the Treaty Ports, 1842–1854*. Stanford, Calif.: Stanford University Press.

Faison, Seth. 1997. "Donation of Organs Is Unusual in China." *New York Times*, February 23.

Farquhar, Judith. 2002. *Appetites: Food and Sex in Postsocialist China*. Durham, N.C.: Duke University Press.

Ferme, Mariane C. 2004. "Deterritorialized Citizenship and the Resonances of the Sierra Leonean State." In Das and Poole, *Anthropology in the Margins of the State*, 81–115.

Feuchtwang, Stephan. 1974. "Domestic and Communal Worship in Taiwan." In A. Wolf, *Religion and Ritual in Chinese Society*, 105–30.

———. 1977. "School Temple and City God." In *The City in Late Imperial China*. Edited by G. W. Skinner, 581–608. Stanford, Calif.: Stanford University Press.

———. 1993. "Historical Metaphor: A Study of Religious Representation and the Recognition of Authority." *Man* 28 (1): 35–49.

———. 2001. *Popular Religion in China: The Imperial Metaphor*. Richmond, Surrey: Curzon Press.

————. 2007. "On Religious Ritual as Deference and Communicative Excess." *Journal of the Royal Anthropological Institute* 13:57–72.

Feuchtwang, Stephan, and Ming-ming Wang. 1991. "The Politics of Culture or a Contest of Histories: Representations of Chinese Popular Religion." *Dialectical Anthropology* 16:251–72.

Fitzgerald, Stephen. 1972. *China and the Overseas Chinese: A Study of Peking's Changing Policy, 1949–1970.* Cambridge: Cambridge University Press.

Fitzsimmons, Elizabeth. 2006. "The Environmental Cost of Illegal Immigration." *San Diego Union Tribune*, August 6.

Fong, Vanessa L. 2004. *Only Hope: Coming of Age under China's One-Child Policy.* Stanford, Calif.: Stanford University Press.

————. 2007. "Morality, Cosmopolitanism or Academic Attainment? Discourses on 'Quality' and Urban Chinese-Only-Children's Claims to Ideal Personhood." *City and Society* 19 (1): 86–113.

Foster, Robert J. 1998. "Your Money, Our Money, the Government's Money: Finance and Fetishism in Melanesia." In Spyer, *Border Fetishisms*, 60–90.

Foucault, Michel. 1979. *Discipline and Punish: The Birth of the Prison.* New York: Vintage Books.

————. 1980. *The History of Sexuality, Volume 1: An Introduction.* New York: Vintage Books.

Frank, Andre Gunder. 1998. *Reorient: Global Economy in the Asian Age.* Berkeley: University of California Press.

Freedman, Maurice. 1958. *Lineage Organization in Southeastern China.* London: University of London, Athlone Press.

————. 1966. *Chinese Lineage and Society: Fukien and Kwangtung.* London: Athlone Press.

————. 1970. *Family and Kinship in Chinese Society.* Stanford, Calif.: Stanford University Press.

Fried, Morton. 1953. *The Fabric of Chinese Society.* New York: Praeger.

Friedman, Edward, Mark Selden, and Paul Pickowicz. 1991. *Chinese Village, Socialist State.* New Haven: Yale University Press.

Furth, Charlotte. 1999. *A Flourishing Yin: Gender in China's Medical History, 960–1665.* Berkeley: University of California Press.

Gaonkar, Dilip Parameshwar, ed. 2001. *Alternative Modernities.* Durham, N.C.: Duke University Press.

Gates, Hill. 1987. "Money for the Gods." *Modern China* 13 (2): 259–77.

Gee, Jack. 2001. "Human Traffic Gang Snared." *The Express* (Paris), June 23.

Gernet, Jacques. 1995. *Buddhism in Chinese Society: An Economic History from the Fifth to the Tenth Centuries.* New York: Columbia University Press.

Gilbert, Emily. 2005. "Common Cents: Situating Money in Time and Place." *Economy and Society* 34 (3): 357–88.

Gilboy, Janet A. 1991. "Deciding Who Gets In: Decisionmaking by Immigration Inspectors." *Law and Society Review* 25 (3): 571–99.

———. 1992. "Penetrability of Administrative Systems: Political 'Casework' and Immigration Inspections." *Law and Society Review* 26 (2): 273–314.

Gilroy, Paul. 1991. "It Ain't Where You're From, It's Where You're At . . . : The Dialectics of Diasporic Identification." *Third Text* 13:3–16.

———. 1993. *The Black Atlantic: Modernity and Double Consciousness*. Cambridge, Mass.: Harvard University Press.

Gladney, Dru. 1994. "Salman Rushdie in China: Religion, Ethnicity, and State Definition in the People's Republic." In Keyes, Kendall, and Hardacre, *Asian Visions of Authority*, 255–78.

Godelier, Maurice. 1999. *The Enigma of the Gift*. Chicago: University of Chicago Press.

Goffman, Erving. 1962. *Asylums: Essays on the Social Situation of Mental Patients and Other Inmates*. Chicago: Aldine.

———. 1986. *Stigma: Notes on the Management of Spoiled Identity*. New York: Simon and Schuster.

Gold, Thomas B. 1985. "After Comradeship: Personal Relations in China since the Cultural Revolution." *China Quarterly*, 657–75.

Gopinath, Gayatri. 1995. " 'Bombay, U.K., Yuba City': Bhangra Music and the Engendering of Diaspora." *Diaspora* 4 (3): 303–22.

Gordillo, Gaston. 2006. "The Crucible of Citizenship: ID-Paper Fetishism in the Argentinean Chaco." *American Ethnologist* 33 (2): 162–76.

Graeber, David. 2001. *Toward an Anthropological Theory of Value: The False Coin of Our Own Dreams*. New York: Palgrave.

Granet, Marcel. 1975 [1922]. *The Religion of the Chinese People*. New York: Harper Torchbooks.

Greenhalgh, Susan. 1994. "Controlling Births and Bodies in Village China." *American Ethnologist* 21 (1): 3–30.

———. 1995. *Situating Fertility: Anthropology and Demographic Inquiry*. Cambridge: Cambridge University Press.

———. 2003. "Planned Births, Unplanned Persons: 'Population' in the Making of Chinese Modernity." *American Ethnologist* 30 (2): 196–215.

Gregory, C. A. 1997. *Savage Money: The Anthropology and Politics of Commodity Exchange*. Amsterdam: Harwood Academic.

Grossberg, Josh. 2006. "Container Stowaways Reported Easy to Find." *Daily Breeze* (Torrance, Calif.), April 19.

Guest, Kenneth J. 2003. *God in Chinatown: Religion and Survival in New York's Evolving Immigrant Community*. New York: New York University Press.

Guldin, Gregory Eliyu. 2001. *What's a Peasant to Do? Village Becoming Town in Southern China*. Boulder, Colo.: Westview Press.

Guo, Nei. 2003. "21 People Smugglers on Trial." *China Daily* (Beijing), April 24.

Gupta, Akhil, and James Ferguson. 1992. "Beyond 'Culture': Space, Identity, and the Politics of Difference." *Cultural Anthropology* 7 (1): 6–23.

———, eds. 1997. *Anthropological Locations: Boundaries and Grounds of a Field Science.* Berkeley: University of California Press.

Guthrie, Douglas. 1998. "The Declining Significance of *Guanxi* in China's Economic Transition." *China Quarterly*, 254–82.

Guyer, Jane I. 2004. *Marginal Gains: Monetary Transactions in Atlantic Africa.* Chicago: University of Chicago Press.

Hall, Stuart. 1991. "The Local and the Global: Globalization and Ethnicity." In *Culture, Globalization, and the World System.* Edited by A. King, 18–39. Minneapolis: University of Minnesota Press.

Hall, Stuart, David Morley, and Kuan-Hsing Chen. 1996. *Stuart Hall: Critical Dialogues in Cultural Studies.* London: Routledge.

Hannerz, Ulf. 1996. *Transnational Connections: Culture, People, Places.* London: Routledge.

Haraway, Donna. 1992. "The Promises of Monsters: A Regenerative Politics for Inappropriate/d Others." In *Cultural Studies.* Edited by L. Grossberg, C. Nelson, and P. A. Treichler, 295–337. New York: Routledge.

Hardt, Michael, and Antonio Negri. 2000. *Empire.* Cambridge, Mass.: Harvard University Press.

Harper, Richard H. R. 1998. *Inside the IMF: An Ethnography of Documents, Technology and Organisational Action.* San Diego: Academic Press.

Harrell, C. Stevan. 1974. "When a Ghost Becomes a God." In A. Wolf, *Religion and Ritual in Chinese Society,* 193–206.

Hart, Keith. 2001. *Money in an Unequal World: Keith Hart and His Memory Bank.* New York: Textere.

Harvey, David. 1989. *The Condition of Postmodernity: An Enquiry into the Origins of Cultural Change.* Oxford: Blackwell.

Herzfeld, Michael. 2005. *Cultural Intimacy: Social Poetics in the Nation-State.* 2nd edn. New York: Routledge.

Heyman, Josiah M. 1995. "Putting Power in the Anthropology of Bureaucracy: The Immigration and Naturalization Service at the Mexico-United States Border." *Current Anthropology* 36 (2): 261–88.

———, ed. 1999. *States and Illegal Practices.* Oxford: Berg.

———. 2004. "Ports of Entry as Nodes in the World System." *Identities* 11:303–27.

Ho, Engseng. 2006. *The Graves of Tarim: Genealogy and Mobility across the Indian Ocean.* Berkeley: University of California Press.

Holmes, Douglas, and George Marcus. 2006. "Fast Capitalism: Para-Ethnography and the Rise of the Symbolic Analyst." In *Frontiers of Capital: Ethnographic Re-*

flections on the New Economy. Edited by M. S. Fisher and G. Downey, 33–57. Durham, N.C.: Duke University Press.

Hood, Marlowe. 1997. "Sourcing the Problem: Why Fuzhou?" In P. J. Smith, *Human Smuggling*, 76–92.

Hou, Ching-lang. 1975. *Monnaies d'offrande et la notion de trésoserie dans la religion chinoise.* Paris: Collège de France.

Hsing, You-tien. 1997. "Building *Guanxi* across the Straits: Taiwanese Capital and Local Chinese Bureaucrats." In Ong and Nonini, *Ungrounded Empires.*

Hsu, Francis L. K. 1971. "Eros, Affect, and Pao." In *Kinship and Culture.* Edited by F. L. K. Hsu, 439–75. Chicago: Aldine.

Hu, Hsien Chin. 1944. "The Chinese Concept of Face." *American Anthropologist* 46:45–64.

Hu, Xuwei, and Tianxin Hu. 2000. "Trends and Patterns of Foreign Direct Investment." In Yeung and Chu, *Fujian*, 212–30.

Hubert, Henri, and Marcel Mauss. 1964. *Sacrifice: Its Nature and Function.* Chicago: University of Chicago Press.

Hull, Matthew S. 2003. "The File: Agency, Authority, and Autography in an Islamabad Bureaucracy." *Language and Communication* 23:287–314.

Humphrey, Caroline, and Stephen Hugh-Jones, eds. 1992. *Barter, Exchange and Value: An Anthropological Approach.* Cambridge: Cambridge University Press.

Hwang, Kwang-kuo. 1987. "Face and Favor: The Chinese Power Game." *American Journal of Sociology* 92 (4): 944–74.

"ICE Fighting Chinese Human Smugglers." 2005. In *Inside ICE*, 2:2. Washington, D.C.: ICE Office of Public Affairs.

Ikels, Charlotte. 1996. *The Return of the God of Wealth: The Transition to a Market Economy in Urban China.* Stanford, Calif.: Stanford University Press.

Ingham, Geoffrey. 1996. "Money Is a Social Relation." *Review of Social Economy* 54 (4): 507–29.

———. 2001. "Fundamentals of a Theory of Money: Untangling Fine, Lapavitsas and Zelizer." *Economy and Society* 30 (3): 304–23.

Innes, A. Mitchell. 1913. "What is Money?" *Banking Law Journal* (May): 377–408.

Jain, Sarah S. Lochlann. 2002. "Urban Errands: The Means of Mobility." *Journal of Consumer Culture* 2 (3): 419–38.

Jeganathan, Pradeep. 2004. "Checkpoint: Anthropology, Identity, and the State." In Das and Poole, *Anthropology in the Margins of the State*, 67–80.

Ji, Chen, ed. 1999. *Fuzhou shi jiaoqu zhi* (Annals of Fuzhou City suburban districts). Fuzhou, China: Fuzhou Jiaoyu Chuban.

Jing, Jun. 1996. *The Temple of Memories: History, Power, and Morality in a Chinese Village.* Stanford, Calif.: Stanford University Press.

Johnson, Bridget. 2006. "Trashing the Border." *USA Today*, July 11.

Judd, Ellen. 1989. "Niangjia: Chinese Women and Their Natal Families." *Journal of Asian Studies* 48 (3): 525–44.

———. 1994. *Gender and Power in Rural North China.* Stanford, Calif.: Stanford University Press.

Kannabiran, Kalpana. 1998. "Mapping Migration, Gender, Culture and Politics in the Indian Diaspora: Commemorating Indian Arrival in Trinidad." *Economic and Political Weekly,* 53–57.

Keane, Webb. 1997. *Signs of Recognition: Powers and Hazards of Representation in an Indonesian Society.* Berkeley: University of California Press.

———. 2002. "Money Is No Object: Materiality, Desire, and Modernity in an Indonesian Society." In Myers, *The Empire of Things,* 65–90.

———. 2003. "Semiotics and the Social Analysis of Material Things." *Language and Communication* 23:409–25.

Kearney, Michael. 1991. "Borders and Boundaries of State and Self at the End of the Empire." *Journal of Historical Sociology* 4 (1): 52–74.

———. 2000. "Transnational Oaxacan Indigenous Identity: The Case of Mixtecs and Zapotecs." *Identities* 7 (2): 173–96.

Keyes, Charles F., Laurel Kendall, and Helen Hardacre, eds. 1994. *Asian Visions of Authority: Religion and the Modern States of East and Southeast Asia.* Honolulu: University of Hawaii Press.

Kim, Eleana. N.d. "This Is All There Is: Legibility and Illegibility in the Adoption File." Unpublished manuscript.

Kintzele, Jeff. 1988. "Man, Money, and Time: Logic of Credit—Logic of Modernity?" *Design Issues* 4 (1–2): 131–40.

Kipnis, Andrew B. 1995a. "'Face': An Adaptable Discourse of Social Surfaces." *positions* 3 (1): 119–48.

———. 1995b. "Within and Against Peasantness: Backwardness and Filiality in Rural China." *Comparative Studies in Society and History* 37 (1): 110–35.

———. 1996. "The Language of Gifts: Managing Guanxi in a North China Village." *Modern China* 22 (3): 285–314.

———. 1997. *Producing Guanxi: Sentiment, Self, and Subculture in a North China Village.* Durham, N.C.: Duke University Press.

———. 2001. "The Flourishing of Religion in Post-Mao China and the Anthropological Category of Religion." *Australian Journal of Anthropology* 12 (1): 32–46.

———. 2006. "*Suzhi:* A Keyword Approach." *China Quarterly* 186:298–313.

Klima, Alan. 2002. *The Funeral Casino: Meditation, Massacre, and Exchange with the Dead in Thailand.* Princeton, N.J.: Princeton University Press.

Knapp, Georg Friedrich. 1928. *The State Theory of Money.* London: MacMillan.

Knauft, Bruce M., ed. 2002. *Critically Modern: Alternatives, Alterities, Anthropologies.* Bloomington: Indiana University Press.

Kulick, Don. 1998. *Travesti : Sex, Gender, and Culture among Brazilian Transgendered Prostitutes*. Chicago: University of Chicago Press.

Kumar, Amitava. 2000. *Passport Photos*. Berkeley: University of California Press.

Kwon, Heonik. 2007. "The Dollarization of Vietnamese Ghost Money." *Journal of the Royal Anthropological Institute* 13:93–90.

Kwong, Peter. 1997. *Forbidden Workers: Illegal Chinese Immigrants and American Labor*. New York: New Press.

———. 2001. "Impact of Chinese Human Smuggling on the American Labor Market." In Kyle and Koslowski, *Global Human Smuggling*, 235–56.

Kyle, David, and Rey Koslowski, eds. 2001. *Global Human Smuggling: Comparative Perspectives*. Baltimore: Johns Hopkins University Press.

Larkin, Brian. 2002. "Indian Films and Nigerian Lovers: Media and the Creation of Parallel Modernities. In *The Anthropology of Globalization: A Reader*. Edited by J. X. Inda and R. Rosaldo, 350–80. Malden, Mass.: Blackwell Publishing.

Latour, Bruno. 1986. "Visualization and Cognition: Thinking with Eyes and Hands." *Knowledge and Society* 6:1–40.

———. 1993. *We Have Never Been Modern*. Cambridge, Mass.: Harvard University Press.

———. 1999. *Pandora's Hope: Essays on the Reality of Science Studies*. Cambridge, Mass.: Harvard University Press.

Lau, Yee-cheung, and Kam-keung Lee. 2000. "An Economic and Political History." In Yeung and Chu, *Fujian*, 25–56.

Law, John. 2002. *Aircraft Stories: Decentering the Object in Technoscience*. Durham, N.C.: Duke University Press.

Lee, Ben, and Edward LiPuma. 2002. "Cultures of Circulation: The Imaginations of Modernity." *Public Culture* 14 (1): 191–213.

Lee, Frederic Edward. 1926. *Currency, Banking, and Finance in China*. Washington, D.C.: Government Printing Office.

Lemon, Alaina. 1998. "'Your Eyes Are Green Like Dollars': Counterfeit Cash, National Substance, and Currency Apartheid in 1990s Russia." *Cultural Anthropology* 13 (1): 22–55.

Lerner, Daniel. 1958. *The Passing of Traditional Society: Modernizing the Middle East*. Glencoe, Ill.: Free Press.

Levitt, Peggy. 2001. *The Transnational Villagers*. Berkeley: University of California Press.

Li, Hongren. 1987. *Remembering Longyan, the Old Town (Huainian Longyan guzhen)*. Taiwan: Self-Published.

Liang, Zai. 2001. "Demography of Illicit Emigration from China: A Sending Country's Perspective." *Sociological Forum* 16 (4): 677–701.

Liang, Zai, and Wenzhen Ye. 2001. "From Fujian to New York: Understanding the New Chinese Immigration." In Kyle and Koslowski, *Global Human Smuggling*, 187–216.

Lichtblau, Klaus. 1999. "Differentiations of Modernity." *Theory, Culture and Society* 16 (3): 1–30.

Lin, Guoping. 1993. *Fujian Popular Beliefs (Fujian minjian xinyang)*.

Lin, Guozhi, and Huangdu Lin. 1982. "Looking at the Problem of Overseas Capital Utilization through Fujian's Particular History of Overseas Chinese Investment" (*Cong Fujian huaqiao touzi de lishi tedian kan liyong qiaozi wenti*). In *The Population, Nation, Overseas Chinese and Taiwanese Ties of Fujian (Fujian de renkou, minzu, huaqiao ji mintai guanxi)*. Fuzhou, China: Fujian People's Press (*Fujian renmin chubanshe*).

Liu, Hong. 1998. "Old Linkages, New Networks: The Globalization of Chinese Voluntary Associations and Its Implications." *China Quarterly* 155 (September): 582–609.

Liu, Xin. 1997. "Space, Mobility, and Flexibility: Chinese Villagers and Scholars Negotiate Power at Home and Abroad." In Ong and Nonini, *Ungrounded Empires*, 91–114.

Louie, Andrea. 2004. *Chineseness across Borders: Renegotiating Chinese Identities in China and the United States*. Durham, N.C.: Duke University Press.

Lü, Hsiao-po, and Elizabeth J. Perry. 1997. *Danwei: The Changing Chinese Workplace in Historical and Comparative Perspective*. Armonk, N.Y.: M. E. Sharpe.

Lyons, Thomas P. 1998. "Intraprovincial Disparities in China: Fujian Province, 1978–1995." *Economic Geography* 74 (4): 405–32.

———. 1999. "Rural Welfare in Fujian, 1976–1978: The Maoist Legacy." *China Quarterly* 160 (December): 953–76.

Ma, Xia. 1994. "Changes in the Pattern of Migration in Urban China." In *Migration and Urbanization in China*. Edited by L. H. Day and X. Ma, 193–216. Armonk, N.Y.: M. E. Sharpe.

MacKenzie, Peter W. 2002. "Strangers in the City: The Hukou and Urban Citizenship in China." *Journal of International Affairs* 56 (1): 305–19.

Macleod, Henry Dunning. 1882. *Lecture on Credit and Banking*. London: Longman, Green, Reader, and Dyer.

MacNair, Harley. 1924. *The Chinese Abroad*. Shanghai: Commercial Press.

Madancy, Joyce. 2001. "Unearthing Popular Attitudes toward the Opium Trade and Opium Suppression in Late Qing and Early Republican Fujian." *Modern China* 27 (4): 436–83.

Mahler, Sarah. 1992. *American Dreaming: Immigrant Life on the Margins*. Princeton, N.J.: Princeton University Press.

Malinowski, Bronislaw. 1961 [1922]. *Argonauts of the Western Pacific*. Prospect Heights, Ill.: Waveland Press.

Malkki, Liisa. 1995. "Refugees and Exile: From 'Refugee Studies' to the National Order of Things." *Annual Review of Anthropology* 24:495–523.

Manalansan, Martin F. 2006. "Immigrant Lives and the Politics of Olfaction in the Global City." In *The Smell Culture Reader.* Edited by J. Drobnick, 41–52. Oxford: Berg.

Marcus, George. 1988. "Parody and the Parodic in Polynesian Cultural History." *Cultural Anthropology* 3 (1): 68–76.

Marx, Karl. 2003. *Capital,* Vol. 1. Edited by Frederick Engels. New York: International Publishers.

Massey, Doreen. 1993. "Power-Geometry and a Progressive Sense of Place." In *Mapping the Futures: Local Cultures, Global Change.* Edited by John Bird, Barry Curtis, Tim Putnam, and Lisa Tickner, 59–69. New York: Routledge.

Massumi, Brian. 2003. *Parables for the Virtual: Movement, Affect, Sensation.* Durham, N.C.: Duke University Press.

Maurer, Bill. 1999. "Forget Locke? From Proprietor to Risk-Bearer in New Logics of Finance." *Public Culture* 11 (2): 365–85.

———. 2005. *Mutual Life, Limited: Islamic Banking, Alternative Currencies, and Lateral Reason.* Princeton, N.J.: Princeton University Press.

Mauss, Marcel. 1967. *The Gift: Forms and Functions of Exchange in Archaic Societies.* New York: Norton.

———. 1985. "A Category of the Human Mind: The Notion of the Person; the Notion of Self." In *The Category of the Person: Anthropology, Philosophy, History.* Edited by M. Carrithers, S. Collins, and S. Lukes, 1–25. Cambridge: Cambridge University Press.

———. 1992 [1934]. "Techniques of the Body." In *Incorporations.* Edited by J. Crary and S. Kwinter, 455–77. New York: Zone.

McCreery, John L. 1990. "Why Don't We See Some Real Money Here? Offerings in Chinese Religion." *Journal of Chinese Religions* 18 (Fall): 1–24.

McKeown, Adam. 2003. "Ritualization of Regulation: The Enforcement of Chinese Exclusion in the United States and China." *American Historical Review* 108 (2): 377–403.

McKinnon, Sara L. 2009. "Citizenship and the Performance of Credibility: Audiencing Gender-based Asylum Seekers in U.S. Immigration Courts." *Text and Performance Quarterly* 29 (3): 205–21.

Melloy, Katherine E. 2007. "Telling Truths: How the REAL ID Act's Credibility Provisions Affect Women Asylum Seekers." *Iowa Law Review* 92:637–76.

Meyer, Birgit, and Peter Pels, eds. 2003. *Magic and Modernity: Interfaces of Revelation and Concealment.* Stanford, Calif.: Stanford University Press.

Miller, Daniel. 1998. *A Theory of Shopping.* Ithaca, N.Y.: Cornell University Press.

Mintz, Sidney. 1998. "The Localization of Anthropological Practice: From Area Studies to Transnationalism." *Critique of Anthropology* 18 (2): 117–33.

Mitchell, Timothy. 1991. *Colonizing Egypt.* Berkeley: University of California Press.

———. 2000. *Questions of Modernity.* Minneapolis: University of Minnesota Press.

———. 2002. *Rule of Experts: Egypt, Techno-Politics, Modernity.* Berkeley: University of California Press.

Mol, Annemarie. 1999. "Ontological Politics: A Word and Some Questions." In *Actor Network Theory and After.* Edited by J. Law and J. Hassard, 74–89. Oxford: Blackwell and the Sociological Review.

Moodie, Ellen. 2007. "Dollars and *Dolores* in Postwar El Salvador." In Senders and Truitt, *Money,* 43–56.

Mosko, Mark S. 1992. "Other Messages, Other Missions; or Sahlins among the Melanesians." *Oceania* 63 (2): 97–113.

Mueggler, Erik. 2001. *The Age of Wild Ghosts: Memory, Violence, and Place in Southwest China.* Berkeley: University of California Press.

Munn, Nancy D. 1986. *The Fame of Gawa: A Symbolic Study of Value Transformation in a Massim (Papua New Guinea) Society.* Cambridge: Cambridge University Press.

Murray, Allison. 1998. "Debt-Bondage and Trafficking: Don't Believe the Hype." In *Global Sex Workers: Rights, Resistance, and Redefinition.* Edited by K. Kempadoo and J. Doezema, 51–68. London: Routledge.

Murray, Stephen O., and Keelung Hong. 1991. "American Anthropologists Looking through Taiwanese Culture." *Dialectical Anthropology* 16:273–299.

Myerhoff, Barbara. 1978. *Number Our Days.* New York: Simon and Schuster.

Myers, Fred R., ed. 2002. *The Empire of Things: Regimes of Value and Material Culture.* Santa Fe, N.M.: School of American Research Press.

———. 2004. "Ontologies of the Image and Economies of Exchange." *American Ethnologist* 31 (1): 5–20.

Myers, Willard H. III. 1997. "Of Qinqing, Qinshu, Guanxi, and Shetou: The Dynamic Elements of Chinese Irregular Population Movement." In P. J. Smith, *Human Smuggling,* 93–133.

Nonini, Donald. 1997. "Shifting Identities, Positioned Imaginaries: Transnational Traversals and Reversals by Malaysian Chinese." In Ong and Nonini, *Ungrounded Empires,* 203–27.

Notar, Beth. 2002. "Viewing Currency Chaos: Paper Money for Advertising, Ideology, and Resistance in Republican China." In *Defining Modernity: Guomingdang Rhetorics of a New China, 1920–1970.* Edited by T. D. Bodenhorn, 123–49. Ann Arbor: University of Michigan Press.

Nyers, Peter. 2003. "Abject Cosmopolitanism: The Politics of Protection in the Anti-Deportation Movement." *Third World Quarterly* 24 (6): 1069–93.

Nyíri, Pál. 2002. "From Class Enemies to Patriots: Overseas Chinese and Emigration Policy and Discourse in the People's Republic of China." In *Global Chinese Migration: Trends in Europe and Asia.* Edited by P. Nyíri and I. R. Saveliev, 208–41. Aldershot, Hampshire, England: Ashgate.

Ong, Aihwa. 1987. *Spirits of Resistance and Capitalist Discipline: Factory Women in Malaysia.* Albany: State University of New York Press.

———. 1997. "'A Momentary Glow of Fraternity': Narratives of Chinese Nationalism and Capitalism." *Identities* 3 (3): 331–66.

———. 1999. *Flexible Citizenship: The Cultural Logics of Transnationality.* Durham, N.C.: Duke University Press.

———. 2003. *Buddha Is Hiding: Refugees, Citizenship, the New America.* Berkeley: University of California Press.

———. 2005. "Splintering Cosmopolitanism: Asian Immigrants and Zones of Autonomy in the American West." In *Sovereign Bodies: Citizens, Migrants, and States in the Postcolonial World.* Edited by T. B. Hansen and F. Stepputat, 257–75. Princeton, N.J.: Princeton University Press.

Ong, Aihwa, and Stephen J. Collier, eds. 2005. *Global Assemblages: Technology, Politics, and Ethics as Anthropology Problems.* Malden, Mass.: Blackwell.

Ong, Aihwa, and Donald Nonini, eds. 1997. *Ungrounded Empires: The Cultural Politics of Modern Chinese Transnationalism.* New York: Routledge.

Ortner, Sherry. 1984. "Theory in Anthropology since the Sixties." *Comparative Studies in Society and History* 26:126–66.

Orzech, Charles D. 1994. "Mechanisms of Violent Retribution in Chinese Hell Narratives." *Contagion: Journal of Violence, Mimesis, and Culture* 1 (Spring): 111–26.

Ownby, David. 1996. *Brotherhoods and Secret Societies in Early and Mid-Qing China: The Formation of a Tradition.* Stanford, Calif.: Stanford University Press.

Oxfeld, Ellen. 1992. "Individualism, Holism and the Market Mentality." *Cultural Anthropology* 7 (3): 267–300.

Painter, Joe. 2006. "Prosaic Geographies of Stateness." *Political Geography* 25:752–74.

Pan, Lynn. 1990. *Sons of the Yellow Emperor: A History of the Chinese Diaspora.* New York: Kodansha International.

Pasternak, Burton. 1972. *Kinship and Community in Two Chinese Villages.* Stanford, Calif.: Stanford University Press.

Pederson, David. 2002. "The Storm We Call Dollars: Determining Value and Belief in El Salvador and the United States." *Cultural Anthropology* 17 (3): 431–59.

Peirce, C. S. 1998. *The Essential Peirce: Selected Philosophical Writings, Vol. 2 (1893–1913).* Edited by the Peirce Edition Project. Bloomington: Indiana University Press.

Perry, Elizabeth J. 1997. "From Native Place to Workplace: Labor Origins and Outcomes of China's Danwei System." In Lü and Perry, *Danwei*, 42–59.

Peutz, Nathalie. 2006. "Embarking on an Anthropology of Removal." *Current Anthropology* 47 (2): 217–41.

Pieke, Frank N. 1995. "Bureaucracy, Friends, and Money: The Growth of Capital Socialism in China." *Comparative Studies in Society and History* 37 (3): 494–518.

Pieke, Frank N., Pál Nyíri, Mette Thunø, and Antonella Ceccagno. 2004. *Transnational Chinese: Fujianese Migrants in Europe.* Stanford, Calif.: Stanford University Press.

Pietz, William. 1993. "Fetishism and Materialism: The Limits of Theory in Marx." In Apter and Pietz, *Fetishism as Cultural Discourse*, 119–51.

Piot, Charles. 1999. *Remotely Global: Village Modernity in West Africa.* Chicago: University of Chicago Press.

Polo, Marco, and R. E. Latham. 1958. *The Travels of Marco Polo.* Baltimore: Penguin.

Potter, Sulamith Heins, and Jack M. Potter. 1990a. "A Caste-Like System of Social Stratification: The Position of Peasants in Modern China's Social Order." In Potter and Potter, *China's Peasants*, 296–326.

———. 1990b. *China's Peasants: The Anthropology of a Revolution.* Cambridge: Cambridge University Press.

Prakash, Gyan. 1999. *Another Reason: Science and the Imagination of Modern India.* Princeton, N.J.: Princeton University Press.

Pun, Ngai. 2003. "Subsumption or Consumption? The Phantom of Consumer Revolution in 'Globalizing' China." *Cultural Anthropology* 18 (4): 469–92.

Rawski, Evelyn Sakakida, and James L. Watson. 1988. *Death Ritual in Late Imperial and Modern China.* Berkeley: University of California Press.

Robbins, Ted. 2006. "Environmentalists: Nature in Crossfire of Border War." On *All Things Considered*, National Public Radio, April 19.

Rofel, Lisa. 1994. "Liberation Nostalgia and a Yearning for Modernity." In *Engendering China: Women, Culture, and the State.* Edited by Christina K. Gilmartin, Gail Hershatter, Lisa Rofel, and Tyrene White, 226–49. Cambridge, Mass.: Harvard University Press.

———. 1999. *Other Modernities: Gendered Yearnings in China after Socialism.* Berkeley: University of California Press.

Rogers, Douglas. 2005. "Moonshine, Money, and the Politics of Liquidity in Rural Russia." *American Ethnologist* 32 (1): 63–81.

Roitman, Janet. 2003. "Unsanctioned Wealth: Or, The Productivity of Debt in Northern Cameroon." *Public Culture* 15 (2): 211–37.

———. 2005. *Fiscal Disobedience: An Anthropology of Economic Regulation in Central Africa.* Princeton, N.J.: Princeton University Press.

Rouse, Roger. 1991. "Mexican Migration and the Social Space of Postmodernism." *Diaspora* (Spring): 8–23.

Ruf, Gregory A. 1998. *Cadres and Kin: Making a Socialist Village in West China, 1921–1991.* Stanford, Calif.: Stanford University Press.

Safran, William. 1991. "Diasporas in Modern Societies: Myths of Homeland and Return." *Diaspora* 1 (1): 83–99.

Sahlins, Marshall. 1972. *Stone Age Economics.* Chicago: Aldine.

———. 1994. "Cosmologies of Capitalism: The Trans-Pacific Sector of 'the World System.'" In *Culture/Power/History: A Reader in Contemporary Social Theory.* Edited by Nicholas B. Dirks, Geoff Eley, and Sherry B. Ortner, 412–55. Princeton, N.J.: Princeton University Press.

———. 1996. "The Sadness of Sweetness: The Native Anthropology of Western Cosmology." *Current Anthropology* 37 (3): 395–428.

Sangren, P. Steven. 1983. "Female Gender in Chinese Religious Symbols: Kuan Yin, Ma Tsu, and the Eternal Mother." *Signs* 9:4–25.

———. 1987. "Orthodoxy, Heterodoxy and the Structure of Value in Chinese Rituals." *Modern China* 13 (1): 63–89.

———. 2000. *Chinese Sociologics: An Anthropological Account of the Role of Alienation in Social Reproduction.* London: Athlone Press.

Sassen, Saskia. 1991. *The Global City: New York, London, Tokyo.* Princeton, N.J.: Princeton University Press.

Schendel, Willem Van. 2005. "Spaces of Engagement: How Borderlands, Illicit Flows, and Territorial States Interlock. In Schendel and Abraham, *Illicit Flows and Criminal Things,* 69–100.

Schendel, Willem Van, and Itty Abraham, eds. 2005. *Illicit Flows and Criminal Things: States, Borders, and the Other Side of Globalization.* Bloomington: Indiana University Press.

Schivelbusch, Wolfgang. 1986. *The Railway Journey: The Industrialization of Time and Space in the 19th Century.* Berkeley: University of California Press.

Schmitt, Carl. 2005 [1922]. *Political Theology: Four Chapters on the Concept of Sovereignty.* Chicago: University of Chicago Press.

Scott, James C. 1998. *Seeing like a State: How Certain Schemes to Improve the Human Condition Have Failed.* New Haven, Conn.: Yale University Press.

Seaman, Gary. 1982. "Spirit Money: An Interpretation." *Journal of Chinese Religions* 10:82–87.

Seidel, Anna. 1978. "Review: Buying One's Way to Heaven: The Celestial Treasury in Chinese Religions." *History of Religions* 17 (3–4): 419–32.

Senders, Stefan, and Allison Truitt, eds. 2007. *Money: Ethnographic Encounters.* Oxford: Berg.

Shi, Tie-sheng. 2001. "Fate." In The *Vintage Book of Contemporary Chinese Fiction.* Edited by C. Choa and D. S. Li-qun, 22–41. New York: Vintage Books.

Shieh, Shawn. 2000. "Centre, Province and Locality in Fujian's Reforms." In Yeung and Chu, *Fujian.*

Shryock, Andrew, ed. 2004. *Off Stage/On Display: Intimacy and Ethnography in the Age of Public Culture.* Stanford, Calif.: Stanford University Press.

Simmel, Georg. 1978. *The Philosophy of Money*. London: Routledge and Keegan Paul.

Siu, Helen. 1990. "Recycling Tradition: Culture, History and Political Economy in the Chrysanthemum Festivals of South China." *Comparative Studies in Society and History* 32 (4): 765–94.

Skaggs, Neil T. 1997. "Henry Dunning Macleod and the Credit Theory of Money." In *Money, Financial Institutions and Macroeconomics*. Edited by A. J. Cohen, H. Hagemann, and J. Smithin, 109–23. Boston: Kluwer Academic Publishers.

Smart, Alan. 1993. "Gifts, Bribes, and *Guanxi*: A Reconsideration of Bourdieu's Social Capital." *Cultural Anthropology* 8 (3): 388–408.

Smith, Adam. 1999 [1776]. *The Wealth of Nations*. Books I–III. London: Penguin.

Smith, Michael Peter. 1994. "Transnational Migration and the Globalization of Grassroots Politics." *Social Text* 39:15–33.

Smith, Paul J. 1994. "The Strategic Implications of Chinese Emigration." *Survival* 36 (2): 60–77.

———. 1997a. "Chinese Migrant Trafficking: A Global Challenge." In P. J. Smith, *Human Smuggling*, 1–22.

———, ed. 1997b. *Human Smuggling: Chinese Migrant Trafficking and the Challenge to America's Immigration Tradition*. Washington, D.C.: Center for Strategic and International Studies.

Snow, Philip. 1988. *The Star Raft: China's Encounter with Africa*. London: Weidenfeld and Nicolson.

Solinger, Dorothy J. 1999. *Contesting Citizenship in Urban China: Peasant Migrants, the State, and the Logic of the Market*. Berkeley: University of California Press.

"Some Problems and Suggestions on the Aging of China's Population" (*Wo guo renkou laolinghua de luogan wenti he jianyi*). 2002. *Bulletin of the Chinese Academy of Sciences* 17 (5).

Spence, Jonathan D. 1999. *The Search for Modern China*. New York: W. W. Norton.

Spyer, Patricia, ed. 1998. *Border Fetishisms: Material Objects in Unstable Spaces*. New York: Routledge.

Stafford, Charles. 2000. *Separation and Reunion in Modern China*. Cambridge: Cambridge University Press.

Stallybrass, Peter. 1998. "Marx's Coat." In Spyer, *Border Fetishisms*, 183–207.

Staples, Edward J. 2004. "Safeguarding ports with chemical profiling." *The Industrial Physicist* (Jun/July): 22–26.

Stewart, Kathleen. 2007. *Ordinary Affects*. Durham, N.C.: Duke University Press.

Strange, Susan. 1986. *Casino Capitalism*. Oxford: Blackwell.

Strathern, Marilyn. 1988. *The Gender of the Gift: Problems with Women and Problems with Society in Melanesia*. Berkeley: University of California Press.

———. 1992. "Qualified Value: The Perspective of Gift Exchange." In Humphrey and Hugh-Jones, *Barter, Exchange and Value*, 169–91.

Strauch, Judith. 1983. "Community and Kinship in Southeastern China: The View from the Multilineage Villages of Hong Kong." *Journal of Asian Studies* 43 (1): 21–50.

Sun, Wanning. 2002. *Leaving China: Media, Migration, and Transnational Imagination.* Lanham, Md.: Rowman and Littlefield.

Sweeney, James A. 2009. "Credibility, Proof and Refugee Law." *International Journal of Refugee Law* 21 (4): 700–726.

Tan, Chee-Beng, ed. 2006. *Southern Fujian: Reproduction of Traditions in Post-Mao China.* Hong Kong: Chinese University Press.

Taussig, Michael T. 1980. *The Devil and Commodity Fetishism in South America.* Chapel Hill: University of North Carolina Press.

———. 1993. "Maleficium: State Fetishism." In Apter and Pietz, *Fetishism as Cultural Discourse,* 217–50.

———. 1997. *The Magic of the State.* New York: Routledge.

Taylor, Romeyn. 1989. "Chinese Hierarchy in Comparative Perspective." *Journal of Asian Studies* 48 (3): 490–511.

Teather, Elizabeth K. 1999. "High-Rise Homes for the Ancestors: Cremation in Hong Kong." *Geographical Review* 89 (3): 409–30.

Teiser, Stephen F. 1988. *The Ghost Festival in Medieval China.* Princeton, N.J.: Princeton University Press.

———. 1993. "The Growth of Purgatory." In *Religion and Society in T'ang and Sung China.* Edited by P. Ebrey and P. N. Gregory, 115–46. Honolulu: University of Hawaii Press.

Théret, Bruno. 1999. "The Socio-Political Dimensions of the Currency: Implications for the Transition to the Euro." *Journal of Consumer Policy* 22 (1–2): 51–79.

Thomas, Nicholas. 1991. *Entangled Objects: Exchange, Material Culture, and Colonialism in the Pacific.* Cambridge, Mass.: Harvard University Press.

Thrift, Nigel. 1996. *Spatial Formations.* London: Sage.

Thunø, Mette. 2001. "Reaching Out and Incorporating Chinese Overseas: The Trans-Territorial Scope of the PRC by the End of the 20th Century." *China Quarterly* 168 (December): 910–29.

Thunø, Mette, and Frank N. Pieke. 2005. "Institutionalizing Recent Rural Emigration from China to Europe: New Transnational Villages in Fujian." *International Migration Review* 39 (2): 485–514.

Torpey, John. 1997. "Revolutions and Freedom of Movement: An Analysis of Passport Controls in the French, Russian, and Chinese Revolutions." *Theory and Society* 26 (6): 837–68.

———. 2000. *The Invention of the Passport: Surveillance, Citizenship and the State.* Cambridge: Cambridge University Press.

Trinh, T. Minh-ha. 1995. "No Master Territories." In *The Post-Colonial Studies*

Reader. Edited by B. Ashcroft, G. Griffiths, and H. Tiffin, 215–18. New York: Routledge.

Trouillot, Michel-Rolph. 2001. "The Anthropology of the State in the Age of Globalization: Close Encounters of the Deceptive Kind. *Current Anthropology* 42:125–38.

Truitt, Allison. 2007. "Hot Loans and Cold Cash in Saigon." In Senders and Truitt, *Money*, 57–68.

Tsai, Kellee S. 2002. *Back-Alley Banking: Private Entrepreneurs in China*. Ithaca, N.Y.: Cornell University Press.

Tsing, Anna. 2005. *Friction: An Ethnography of Global Connection*. Princeton, N.J.: Princeton University Press.

Urry, John. 2007. *Mobilities*. Cambridge: Polity Press.

Verdery, Katherine. 1998. "Transnationalism, Nationalism, Citizenship, and Property: Eastern Europe since 1989." *American Ethnologist* 25 (2): 291–306.

Verran, Helen. 2001. *Science and an African Logic*. Chicago: University of Chicago Press.

Virilio, Paul. 1986. *Speed and Politics*. New York: Semiotext(e).

Vogel, Ezra F. 1965. "From Friendship to Comradeship: The Change in Personal Relations in Communist China." *China Quarterly* 21 (January/March): 46–60.

Von Glahn, Richard. 1996. *Fountain of Fortune: Money and Monetary Policy in China, 1000–1700*. Berkeley: University of California Press.

Wang, Feng. 1997. "The Breakdown of a Great Wall: Recent Changes in the Household Registration System of China." In *Floating Population and Migration in China*. Edited by T. Scharping, 149–65. Hamburg: Institut fur Asienkunde.

Wang, Gungwu. 1985. External China as a New Policy Area. Pacific Affairs 58 (1): 28–43.

———. 1991. *China and the Chinese Overseas*. Singapore: Times Academic Press.

———. 2000. *The Chinese Overseas: From Earthbound China to the Quest for Autonomy*. Cambridge, Mass.: Harvard University Press.

Wang, Horng-luen. 2004. "Regulating Transnational Flows of People: An Institutional Analysis of Passports and Visas as a Regime of Mobility." *Identities* 11 (3): 351–76.

Wang, L. Ling-chi. 1991. "Roots and Changing Identity of the Chinese in the United States." *Daedalus* 120 (2): 181–206.

Wank, David L. 1996. "The Institutional Practice of Market Clientism: *Guanxi* and Private Business in a South China City." *China Quarterly* 147 (September): 820–38.

Watson, James L. 1975. *Emigration and the Chinese Lineage: The "Mans" in Hong Kong and London*. Berkeley: University of California Press.

———. 1982. "Chinese Kinship Reconsidered: Anthropological Perspectives on Historical Research." *China Quarterly* 92 (December): 589–622.

————. 1985. "Standardizing the Gods: The Promotion of T'ien Hou ('Empress of Heaven') along the South China Coast 960–1960." In *Popular Culture in Late Imperial China*. Edited by David Johnson, Andrew J. Nathan, and Evelyn Rawski, 292–324. Berkeley: University of California Press.

————. 1988. "The Structure of Chinese Funerary Rites: Elementary Forms, Ritual Sequence, and the Primacy of Performance." In Rawski and Watson, *Death Ritual in Late Imperial and Modern China*, 3–19.

————. 1993. "Rites or Beliefs? The Construction of a Unified Culture in Late Imperial China." In Dittmer and Kim, *China's Quest for National Identity*, 80–103.

————. 2004. "Presidential Address: Virtual Kinship, Real Estate, and Diaspora Formation—The Man Lineage Revisited." *Journal of Asian Studies* 63 (4): 893–910.

Watson, Rubie S. 1985. *Inequality among Brothers: Class and Kinship in South China.* Cambridge: Cambridge University Press.

Weber, Max. 1992 [1930]. *The Protestant Ethic and the Spirit of Capitalism.* New York: Routledge.

Webster, Steven. 1987. "Structuralist Historicism and the History of Structuralism: Sahlins, the Hanson's *Counterpoint in Maori Culture*, and Postmodernist Ethnographic Form." *Journal of Polynesian Society* 96 (1): 27–65.

Weiner, Annette B., ed. 1976. *Women of Value, Men of Renown: New Perspectives in Trobriand Exchange.* Austin: University of Texas Press.

————. 1980. "Reproduction: A Replacement for Reciprocity." *American Ethnologist* 7 (1): 71–85.

————. 1992. *Inalienable Possessions: The Paradox of Keeping-While-Giving.* Berkeley: University of California Press.

Weller, Robert P. 1987. *Unities and Diversities in Chinese Religion.* Seattle: University of Washington Press.

————. 1995. "Bandits, Beggars and Ghosts: The Failure of State Control over Religious Interpretation in Taiwan." *American Ethnologist* 12 (1): 46–61.

————. 1998. "Divided Market Cultures in China: Gender, Enterprises, and Religion." In *Market Cultures: Society and Morality in the New Asian Capitalisms.* Edited by R. W. Hefner, 78–103. Boulder, Colo.: Westview Press.

————. 2000. "Living at the Edge: Religion, Capitalism, and the End of the Nation-State in Taiwan." *Public Culture* 12 (2): 477–98.

White, Lynn, and Li Cheng. 1993. "China's Coastal Identities: Regional, National and Global." *In* Dittmer and Kim, *China's Quest for National Identity*, 154–93.

Whyte, Martin K. 1990. "Death in the People's Republic of China." In Rawski and Watson, *Death Ritual in Late Imperial and Modern China*, 289–316.

Wilk, Richard, and Lisa Cliggett. 2007. *Economies and Cultures: Foundations of Economic Anthropology.* Boulder, Colo.: Westview Press.

Williams, Raymond. 1977. *Marxism and Literature.* Oxford: Oxford University Press.

Wolf, Arthur P., ed. 1974. *Religion and Ritual in Chinese Society*. Stanford, Calif.: Stanford University Press.

———. 1978. "Gods, Ghosts, and Ancestors." In *Studies in Chinese Society*. Edited by A. P. Wolf and E. M. Ahern, 103–30. Stanford, Calif.: Stanford University Press.

Wolf, Arthur P., and Chieh-shan Huang. 1980. *Marriage and Adoption in China, 1854–1945*. Stanford, Calif.: Stanford University Press.

Wolf, Margery. 1968. *The House of Lim: A Study of a Chinese Farm Family*. Englewood Cliffs, N.J.: Prentice-Hall.

———. 1972. *Women and the Family in Rural Taiwan*. Stanford, Calif.: Stanford University Press.

———. 1985. *Revolution Postponed: Women in Contemporary China*. Stanford, Calif.: Stanford University Press.

Woon, Yuen-Fong. 1990. "International Links and the Socioeconomic Development of Rural China: An Emigrant Community in Guangdong." *Modern China* 16 (2): 139–72.

Wu, Chun-hsi. 1967. *Dollars, Dependents, and Dogma: Overseas Chinese Remittances to Communist China*. Stanford, Calif.: Hoover Institution on War, Revolution and Peace.

Yan, Hairong. 2003. "Neoliberal Governmentality and Neohumanism: Organizing *Suzhi*/Value Flow through Labor Recruitment Networks." *Cultural Anthropology* 18 (4): 493–523.

———. 2008. *New Masters, New Servants: Migration, Development, and Women Workers*. Durham, N.C.: Duke University Press.

Yan, Yunxiang. 1996. *The Flow of Gifts: Reciprocity and Social Networks in a Chinese Village*. Stanford, Calif.: Stanford University Press.

Yang, Andy, and Ann Lincoln. N.d. *The Most Practical (Eat-In, Take-Out) Restaurant English (Zui shiyong, tangchi wamai, cangyuan yingyu)*. New York: AEP (Meiguo Qingzhi Chubanshe).

Yang, Lien-sheng. 1952. *Money and Credit in China: A Short History*. Cambridge, Mass.: Harvard University Press.

———. 1957. "The Concept of 'Pao' as a Basis for Social Relations in China." In *Chinese Thought and Institutions*. Edited by J. K. Fairbanks, 291–309. Chicago: University of Chicago Press.

Yang, Mayfair Mei-hui. 1989. "The Gift Economy and State Power in China." *Comparative Studies in Society and History* 31:25–54.

———. 1994. *Gifts, Favors, and Banquets: The Art of Social Relationships in China*. Ithaca, N.Y.: Cornell University Press.

———. 1997. "Mass Media and Transnational Subjectivity." In Ong and Nonini, *Ungrounded Empires*, 287–322.

————. 2000. "Putting Global Capitalism in Its Place." *Current Anthropology* 41 (4): 477–509.

Yeung, Y. M., and David K. Y. Chu, eds. 2000. *Fujian: A Coastal Province in Transition and Transformation*. Hong Kong: Chinese University Press.

Yngvesson, Barbara, and Susan B. Coutin. 2006. "Backed by Papers: Undoing Persons, Histories, and Return." *American Ethnologist* 33 (2): 177–90.

Zelizer, Viviana A. Rotman. 1994. *The Social Meaning of Money*. New York: Basic Books.

Zhang, Li. 2001a. "Migration and Privatization of Space and Power in Late Socialist China." *American Ethnologist* 28 (1): 179–205.

————. 2001b. *Strangers in the City: Reconfigurations of Space, Power, and Social Networks within China's Floating Population*. Stanford, Calif.: Stanford University Press.

Zhao, Yilu. 2001. "For Immigrant Chinese, a Hard Lesson in an Old Ruse." *New York Times*, June 17.

Zheng, Gong. 1983. *My Hometown Longyan (Wuxiang Longyan zhen)*. Taiwan: Self-Published.

Zhou, Kate Xiao. 1996. *How the Farmers Changed China: Power of the People*. Boulder, Colo.: Westview Press.

Zito, Angela. 1994. "Silk and Skin: Significant Boundaries." In Zito and Barlow, *Body, Subject, and Power in China*, 103–30.

————. 1997. *Of Body and Brush: Grand Sacrifice as Text/Performance in Eighteenth-Century China*. Chicago: University of Chicago Press.

————. N.d. "Filial Finance: Purchasing Parents in Seventeenth-Century China." Unpublished manuscript.

Zito, Angela, and Tani E. Barlow, eds. 1994. *Body, Subject, and Power in China*. Chicago: University of Chicago Press.

Italicized page numbers indicate illustrations.

boundary-making/breaking effects (*cont.*) 70, 72, 201, 218, 252; legality of travel and, 118–19; money and, 166, 174, 203–4, 206, 214–15; moral career and, 8, 118–19, 259, 270n15; state regulations/policies and, 118–19

Bourdieu, Pierre, 7, 83, 148, 179, 274n4, 293n5, 294n11

built environment, 21, 35, 38–39, 42–46, 49–51, 161, 274n2. *See also* house renovations/construction; temple renovations/construction

burial rights/rites, 162–64, *164*, 285nn13–14

burning spirit money: criticism of, 173; description of, 188; exchange between visible and invisible worlds through, 169, 207, 214–17, 291n32; market currencies vs. ashes from, 206–7, 291n31; state regulations/policies and, 88; for temple gods, 175–78, *176*, 180–81, 186–89, *189*, 206; value/value production and, 206, 260, 292n33

cadres: class status and, 19, 35, 66–67, 80–81; divine efficacy and, 197–99; on Longyan as overseas village, 68–69; on Longyan villagers' emigration, 71–72; Monkey King god temple and, 49; research and living among village, 18–20; on transitions and peasants as overseas-connected population, 97; on transitions and peasants as overseas-connected subjects, 69–74

capitalism (*zibenzhuyi*), 7, 12, 168, 193, 207–8, 260, 287n6, 290n23, 292n34

CCP (Chinese Communist Party). *See* Communist Revolution; Mao era

Chan, Kwok Bun, 218–19

China: cremation policy mandated in, 162–64, *164*, 285nn13–14; Cultural Revolution and, 48–49, 89, 182, 208, 271n16, 285n13; Great Leap Forward famine and, 64, 66, 85, 87, 95, 234, 276n3; Guangdong Province and, 24–25, 27–28, 218, 272n11, 277n9; national ID card and, 277n9; population problem in, 10–11, 67, 69, 78–80, 87–95, 90–92, 97, 277n5, 279n11; Qing dynasty and, 6, 24, 28–29, 36, 181, 270n11, 273n3; Republican Era and, 36, 47, 52, 181–82, 200–201, 276n2; state regulatory/policy powers and, 160, 285n11; Yuan dynasty and, 24, 200. *See also* Communist Revolution; Fujian Province; household registration system (*hukou*); post-Mao era; religion/superstition (*mixin*); state identification

Chinese American. *See* overseas Chinese (*huaqiao*)

Chinese Communist Party (CCP). *See* Communist Revolution

Chinese RMB: ancestors and, 187; class status asymmetries and flows of, 166, 167, 174, 191, 203–4; debt and, 169; exchange act between visible and invisible worlds and, 167, 169, 214–16; as generalized vs. specialized currency, 201; market currencies vs. circulation of spirit, 174–75, 205–6, 213–14, 291n31; materiality of, 167, 174–75, 199–200, 201–2, 291n27; as modernity marker, 174, 215; morality of wealth and accumulation of, 201–6; multicentric economy and, 21, 205–6; as remittances, 202; as spirit money, 174–75, 187–88, 203, 205–6, 213–14, 291n31; transnational connection with, 190; U.S. dollar and exchange rate with, 166; U.S. dollar and incommensurability with, 199; as wealth, 174, 204, 214. *See also* gambling; mahjong; spirit money

chulu weiyi ("only road out") of social oblivion, 77, 249

class status: boat smuggling and, 104; cadres and, 19, 35, 66–67, 80–81; Chinese RMB flows and asymmetries of, 166, 167, 174, 191, 203–4; cosmopolitanism and, 11, 259; cross-class resentments and, 8, 18–19, 63, 66, 75, 81, 86–87, 161–62; culture/education and, 35, 68, 75, 80, 82–84, 98; gender/kinship relation and, 222, 226, 230–31, 235–36, 254–55; household registration system and, 64; internal migrants and, 67, 78–79, 243–44, 277n5; teacher, 18, 19, 37, 66; travel hierarchies and, 105–6, 108, 114–15, 117, 125; U.S. dollar flows and asymmetries of, 174, 214; work unit and, 66–67, 85–86, 276n3, 278n14. *See also* class tensions; peasant (*nongmin*)

class tensions: house renovations/construction and, 35, 38–42, *40*, 223–24, *224*; between non-peasant elites and peasants, 19, 74, 81–85, 182; overseas Chinese status and, 11, 61–62, 217, 259, 275n1; peasant and teacher, 18, 19, 37, 66, 80–81, 182, 289n11; Restaurant English classes and, 58. *See also* class status

Clifford, James, 10–11, 51

Cohen, Myron, 63, 67, 68, 276n2

Collier, Jane, 7–8

commodification: of "ducks"/male charmers, 232, 238–43, 246; of

female bodies, 241–42, 293n6; of relations, 122, 167, 169, 238–42, 256, 292n33, 293n6; of time, 258

communism (*gongchanzhuyi*), 8, 87, 166

Communist Revolution: description/history of, 271n16; Fujian history and, 25–26, 65–66; Guangzhou history and, 27; historical transformations after, 8–13, 271n16, 289n14; Longyan village and effects of, 36, 52, 70, 197, 200–201; Mao Zedong and, 13–14, 63–64, 71, 272n21, 276n2; peasants and, 63–64, 66, 276n2. *See also* Mao era; post-Mao era

consular interview challenges, 126–27, 130–33, 134

consumption: in relation to gender, 232, 238, 242, 244

Cook, Thomas, 13

cosmic accounting, 136, 176, 194–95, 198–99, 287n4

cosmic credit: ancestors and, 204–5; capitalism vs., 7, 168, 193, 260, 287n6, 290n23; cosmic debt vs., 195–96; gods/goddesses as creditors and, 191, 195, 259; green card IDs in relation to, 163; karmic relations of de/merit and, 12, 194–95, 204–5, 266–67; mahjong and, 191–99, 205, 207, 214, 232–33; mobility and types of, 12–13, 161; morality of wealth and, 204; retribution in relation to, 204–5, 233; as sociality, 124, 167–68, 286n2, 286nn4–5; spirit money vs. market currencies and, 174–75, 205–6, 213–14, 259, 260, 291n31; U.S. dollar as, 204–6. *See also* gods/goddesses

cosmic debt: ancestors and, 163, 175, 193, 195, 212–13, 260, 290n25; capitalism vs., 7, 168, 287n6; cosmic

cosmic debt (*cont.*)
accounting and, 136, 176, 194–95, 198–99, 287n4; cosmic credit vs., 195–96; credit-able practices and, 7, 289n19; divine efficacy and, 191–99, 195, 215; gods/goddesses as creditors and, 191, 195, 259; mahjong and, 7, 191–98, 207–9, 212–14, 232–33; retribution in relation to, 233; rituals for paying off, 212–13; "sister-in-law" and, 251

cosmology/cosmologies: of capitalism, 7, 207; of credit, 7; of heaven and hell, 163, 176–77, 189; immobility and neoliberal, 259; intercultural encounters and, 6–7, 270n11, 270n13; nested hierarchies in, 189, 280n16; of value and value transformation, 12, 205–7, 260, 291n30

cosmopolitanism: boundary-making/breaking effects between provincial peasants status and, 166, 174, 203–4, 214, 237, 259, 293n5; human smuggling and desires for, 38, 259; Longyan village and, 36, 68, 72–74, 201; Longyan villagers and desires for, 21, 37–38, 201, 259; moral career and, 9–11, 259; post-Mao era and aspirations of, 11, 25–26, 73–74; temple renovations/construction and aspirations for, 50–51, 192–93, 259

courage/nerve (*danzi*), 76–78

court hearings: political asylum pleas, 144, 153–58

Coutin, Susan, 104, 282n13

credit: cosmology/cosmologies of, 7; "face" and, 124; "human feeling"/bonds and, 12, 206, 238, 286n4; sacrifices as, 233, 293n3; "sister-in-law," and relation to, 226–27, 230, 232–

33; as sociality, 124, 167–69, 286n2, 286nn4–5. *See also* cosmic credit

creditability (*xinyong*), 122–26, 132–34, 169, 193, 282n16

credit-able practices, 7, 259–60

cremation policy, 162–64, 164, 285nn13–14

Cultural Revolution, 48–49, 89, 182, 208, 271n16, 285n13

culture/education (*wenhua*), 35, 68, 75–78, 80, 82–84, 93, 98

Dai, Yuan: *Practical English for People Working in Chinese Restaurants*, 31, 54, 55

dangdiren (local person), 31, 36–37

danwei (work unit), 66–67, 85–86, 276n3, 278n14

danzi (courage/nerve), 76–78

Das, Veena, 118, 121

debt: borrowing methods and, 123–24, 168–69, 203–4, 212, 226–27, 237–39, 282n16; Chinese RMB and, 169; creditability and, 126, 169; distributional order and, 218–19, 233; diversions and, 5, 21, 169, 241, 258; "face" and, 124; "human feeling" and, 169, 218–19, 232–33, 237–38, 286n4; human smuggling financial cost and, 3, 109–10, 123–24, 169, 209, 220–21, 224–27, 261; mahjong in relation to loss and, 265–66; mobility limitations and repayment of, 258–59; money as generalized, 167, 214, 259–60; money in relation to, 167–69, 286n5; post-Mao era and, 259–60; remittances and, 212, 226–27; "sister-in-law" and relation to, 226–27, 230, 232–33; for smuggling services, 123–24, 169, 209, 224–27,

261; as sociality, 124, 167–69, 286n2, 286nn4–5; value production and stabilization of, 169, 173–74, 214, 259–60. *See also* cosmic debt; financial costs

De Certeau, Michel, 94

Deleuze, Gilles, 158–59, 270n10

deportation: entrance process failures and, 142; legal knowledge and, 147–48, 283n3; marginalization and, 283n3; overseas Chinese and possibility of, 139; paper/paperless routes overseas and, 136, 155, 284n7; snakehead travel arrangements and possibility of, 114–15; as training for emigration attempts, 146–48, 283n3; U.S. policies and, 284n7. *See also* political asylum

detention centers, 106, 136–37, 142, 152, 210

diaspora vs. transnationalism, 11, 13, 33–35

differentiated mobility, 10, 51, 110, 163, 255, 259, 285n14

diversions: debt and, 5, 21, 169, 241, 258; "ducks"/male charmers and, 232, 238–43, 246; transgressive personal pleasures and, 222, 225–26, 228–32, 238–41, 254–55, 293n6

divine authority, 94–95. *See also* gods/ goddesses

divine efficacy (*ling*): cadres and, 197–99; cosmic debt and repayments for, 191–99, 195, 215; description of, 188, 196–97; entrance processes and, 158–59, 198; luck and, 208–13, 292n36; migrant fortunes in relation to, 208–13, 214–16; money in relation to, 191–93, 208–16; morality of wealth in relation to, 203, 211–12; non-peasant

elites and, 197–99; remittances and, 197–98; ritual expenditures and, 191; state regulations/policies and, 195–96, 208; wealth in relation to, 191–93, 208–16. *See also* gods/goddesses

Dorfman, Diane, 204

"ducks"/male charmers, 232, 238–43, 246

Dutton, Michael, 85–86, 246, 278n12, 278n14

eating/eat(ing) loss: as moral management of selves and promotion of "human feeling," 232–36, 238–39, 241, 293n6

edgy dispositions, 21, 25–30, 26, 52–53, 273nn4–5. *See also* Fuzhounese; moral career

educational opportunities, 66–67, 69, 73, 78, 144, 202, 276n4, 277n8

education/culture (*wenhua*), 35, 68, 75–78, 80, 82–84, 93, 98

$18,000 "sister-in-law" (*wanbasao*). *See* "sister-in-law" (*wanbasao*)

electronic mediums: multidirectional flow of "human feeling"/bonds (*renqing*) and, 255–56

elites, village. *See* non-peasant (*jumin*) elites

emigrants/emigration: gambling as metaphor for, 133–34, 161, 260–61; *habitus* of, 221; internal migrants in relation to, 243–44; labor markets and, 162; mahjong as model for, 21, 135–36, 161, 261, 265, 266–67; as "only road out" of social oblivion, 77, 249; patrilineal family order and, 218, 220–21. *See also* deportation; entrance processes; exit processes; failure in migration

emigration flows, 4, 13, 28–29, 32–33, 78, 269n2, 271n19, 272n1, 274nn6–7, 284n8

energy (qi) flows, 173, 233, 287n2, 293n4

English language: overseas relatives as translators and scribes in, 127–28; Restaurant English for employment and, 31–32, 32, 54–58, 275n8; Travel English lessons for migration and, 144–46, 147, 151, 283n2

entitlement of subjects, 105, 108, 144, 150–52

entrance processes: airport habitus and, 144, 146, 148–53; allies vs. state as coherent/monolithic regulator of, 144, 157–58; bad subjects and, 141–44, 147–50, 153–54, 283n1; detention centers and, 106, 136–37, 142, 152, 210; differentiated mobility and, 10, 51, 110, 163, 255, 259; divine efficacy as component of, 158–59, 198; embodied performances/encounters during, 143, 144, 149–53, 283n4; failures and, 142, 145–46; files-selves as legible and complete vs. paperless routes for, 21, 103–4; Fuzhou notoriety and, 141–43; gods/goddesses and, 5, 11, 157–59, 161; human agency and, 158–59, 198, 265–66; karma and, 161; kinship relations and, 105, 144, 280n2; legality and, 105–6, 136–39, 144, 280n2; legal knowledge about, 108, 133, 146–48, 249–50, 283n3; narratives and coordination with paperwork for, 151–52, 155–56, 284n5, 284nn7–8; nation-state experience and, 159–61, 281–82nn12–14, 285n11; paper/paperless routes and, 21, 102–4, 114; paperwork and claims of entitlement in, 144, 150–52; per-

sonal relationships/network vs. entitlement of subjects and, 105; reciprocal effects during act of travel and, 15, 105, 217–18, 256; religious practices and, 145, 149, 161–62; self-making practices and, 105, 143–44; state agents' decisions vs. state as monolithic regulator of, 144, 152–53, 158–59, 162, 285n11; state regulatory/policy powers and, 158–62, 285n11; Travel English lessons for migration and, 144–46, 147, 151, 283n2; travel hierarchy and, 105–6. See also deportation; exit processes; political asylum

exchange act: the gift as, 167–68, 286n2, 286n4; "human feeling" and collective sensibilites in, 169, 218, 232; paperwork in bureaucratic, 107–8, 121–22, 125, 138; between visible and invisible worlds, 167, 169, 184–88, 185, 206–7, 214–16, 291–92n32–33

exit processes: competence/potential for success overseas and, 108, 133, 247–50; failures and, 108, 133, 247–50; gods/goddesses and, 2, 11, 135–36, 209; kinship relations and, 124–25; legality and, 98, 117–22; legal knowledge about, 108, 133, 146–48, 249–50, 283n3; luck and, 134–36; personal relationships/network vs. entitlement of subjects and, 108

"face" (lian), 252–54

"face" (mianzi), 124, 191, 251–56

failure in migration: entrance processes, 142, 145–46; exit processes and, 108–10, 133, 247–50; financial setbacks from, 109–10; as measure of competence and potential for success overseas, 108, 133, 247–50; multiple attempts and, 108, 109, 133,

135, 145, 247, 249–50, 259, 283n3; personhood for male subject and, 247–50; skills and knowledge gains from, 108, 133, 146–48, 249–50, 283n3

fake-marriage (*jia jiehun*) arrangements: as alternative paper route, 107, 110; legality vs., 114, 117, 122, 137; luck calculations and, 134; paperwork preparedness and, 132; personal relationships and, 124–25; travel hierarchies and, 117, 125

Farquhar, Judith, 233–34

fate (*yuanfen*), 12, 50, 157, 265–66, 294n1

female subject: commodification of body of, 241–42, 293n6; consumption and, 232, 238–43, 246; gender categorization and, 232, 238–43, 246; mobility and transnationalism of, 251; personhood for, 113–14, 251, 254; plane routes and, 113–14; productive actions of rituals and, 169, 174, 204–5, 214; ritual offerings as household duty of, 193–94, 204, 208; social reproduction and, 251–52; as trafficking victim, 112–14, 280n5. *See also* "sister-in-law" (*wanbasao*)

feminization: of villages, 220–21

Feuchtwang, Stephan, 181, 287n5

file-selves, 21, 103–4, 126–27, 131–34

financial costs: of human smuggling, 3, 109–10, 123–24, 169, 209, 220–21, 224–27, 261; of paperwork for plane routes, 112, 144; of political asylum, 156–57, 285n10. *See also* debt

"floating population" of internal migrants, 10–11, 37, 42, 67, 78–79, 243–44, 277n5

food and eating: eat(ing) loss, 232–36, 238–39, 241, 293n6; peasant memories of, 65–66, 234–35

foreign fiancé(e) visa (K-1), 119–21, 137

foreign student status, 69, 102–3, 212

Foucault, Michel, 147, 278n14

Friedman, Edward, 89, 278n14

"front door" strategies, 122, 131

Fujian Province: administration of, 28, 49; emigration flows from, 28–29, 269n2, 272n1, 274n7, 284n8; history of, 25–28, 65–66, 272n1, 273n3; Taiwan in relation with, 25, 272n2, 275n5. *See also* Fuzhou area/countryside; Fuzhou City; Fuzhounese; Longyan village; Longyan villagers

Fuzhou area/countryside: economic transformations during Mao/post-Mao eras, 25–26, 41; emigration flows from, 4, 28–29, 32–33, 269n2, 274nn6–7; history of, 24, 200–201, 272–73nn1–3; human smuggling notoriety of, 75, 79, 134, 141–43, 147; internal migrant flow to, 37, 42, 78; materiality of money in, 200, 291n27; "opening up" policy and, 25–27, 143; remittance statistics, 28–29; value production and, 260; work unit and, 86

Fuzhou City: domestic space structure and, 45; English translators and scribes industry in, 127–28; history of, 27, 29–30; housing construction industry in, 41; Longyan village compared with, 44–45, 73–74, 178; "opening up" policy and, 44; overseas Chinese status and, 74–75, 277n9; urban opportunities for Longyan villagers in, 41, 67–68; U.S. dollar familiarity in, 178; work unit and, 86. *See also* non-peasant (*jumin*) elites; urbanites

Fuzhounese: edginess tensions and, 21, 25, 26; gods/goddesses as mobile/timely and, 5, 11; as Inappropriate/d

Fuzhounese (*cont.*)

Other, 15–21; mobility and, 11–12, 32–35, 38, 53–54, 259; overseas Chinese history of, 24–29, 34, 42, 273n5; privileged Same and, 16. *See also* built environment; Fuzhou area/countryside; Fuzhou City

gambling: fate and, 265–66; as leisure vs. as vice, 229, 257; as metaphor for emigration, 133–34, 161, 260–61; as metaphor for participation in human smuggling, 76–77, 79–80, 110–11, 134. *See also* mahjong

gender: categorization by, 232, 238–43, 246; consumption in relation to, 232, 238, 242, 244; distributional order and asymmetries of, 6, 169, 219, 220–21, 241–42; "human feeling" and, 221, 234, 243, 250, 253–55; human smuggling channels and, 112–14, 280nn4–5; kinship relation to, 222, 226, 230–31, 235–36, 254–55; morality of transnationalism and, 221; morality of wealth clashes and, 221; patrilineal family order and, 218, 221, 223, 230, 254, 292n2; retribution and regulation of relations between, 232; transnationalism and alienability of human sentiment/bodies and, 21, 169, 219, 238. *See also* female subject; male subject; personhood for female subject; personhood for male subject

generational divides: "human feeling"/bonds, 218, 221, 234, 253; intergenerational ties vs., 95–96, 193, 292n2

geographic boundaries, 70, 72, 201, 218, 252

ghost money, 184–86, 189, 289n13

ghosts, 175, 184–86, 188, 196, 206, 287n5, 289n12, 290n25

gift exchange, 167–68, 286n2, 286n4

Gilroy, Paul, 11, 34, 54

gods/goddesses: bureaucracy in life and afterlife of, 175–77, *176*, *179*; burning spirit money for temple gods, 175–78, *176*, 180–81, 186–89, *189*, 206; counter-hegemonic actions and, 94–95, 259; as creditors, 191, 195, 259; divination from, 2–3, 5–6, 188, 192, 289n21; entrance processes and, 5, 11, 157–59, 161, 209; exit processes and, 2, 11, 135–36, 209; Guanyin god, 46–48, *47*, 51, 275n6; household, 45, 161, 192, 289n20; Hua Guang Dadi god, 49, 50; Mazu goddess, 2–3; mobility and timeliness of, 5, 11, 50, 94–95, 215; modernity and, 49–50, 94–95, 161; as modern vanguards, 49–50, 94–95, 161; Monkey King god, 20, 46–51, *47*, 198, 275n6; offerings to temple, 20, 192, *193*, 289n20; politics of destination and, 12, 265–66; repayment for specific request fulfillment by, 192, 289n21; state regulations/policies vs. divine authority of, 12, 94–95; temple districts and territorial gods, 20, 48–50, 177, 188; Tour of the Gods ritual, 196–98, 208. *See also* cosmic credit; divine efficacy (*ling*); temple districts; temple renovations/construction; temples

Goffman, Erving, 62, 96, 137

"going to court" (*shang ting*) for political asylum pleas, 144, 153–58

gongchanzhuyi (communism), 8, 87, 166

Great Leap Forward famine, 64, 66, 85, 87, 95, 234, 276n3

green card IDS, 129–30, *130*, 137, 147, 162–64, *164*, 285nn13–14

Greenhalgh, Susan, 92

Guangdong Province, 24–25, 27–28, 218, 272n1, 277n9

Guangzhou: U.S. Consulate in, 119, 126–27, 130–33, 150

guanxi (personal relationships/ network). *See* personal relationships/network (*guanxi*)

Guanyin goddess/temple, 46–48, *47*, 51, 275n6

habitus: airport, 144, 146, 148–53; of housing renovations/constructions, 41; of immigrants, 221; of state identification and legibility, 104, 128–29, 162; use of term, 174, 274n4

Hall, Stuart, 33–34

heaven, 163, 176–77, 189

hegemony: and counter-hegemonic actions, 94–95, 259

hell, 163, 172–73, 175–77, 189

Herzfeld, Michael, 173

Heyman, Josiah, 283n2, 283n4

Holmes, Douglas, 56

home sites, 11–12, 33–34, 53–54, 249

hooligan (*liumang*), 245–46

household registration system (*hukou*): class status and, 64; description of, 64; inscription and performance restrictions due to, 105, 127–29, 280n2; internal migrants and, 10–11, 37, 42, 67, 78–79, 243–44, 277n5; as internal passport system, 64; legality/morality delinking of, 70–73, 90–94, 98–99; Longyan villager peasant classification under, 73; mobility and divergent futures enabled by, 62, 70–71, 89–95, 97–98, 259; non-peasant elites classification and, 66–67, 74, 81–83, 89–90, 93, 277n8; peasant classification and, 37–38, 42, 62, 66–69, 82–83, 89–90, 93, 98–99, 161; urbanites classification and, 37, 63–68, 81–82. *See also* state identification

house renovations/construction: "American guest," 38–46, *39*, *40*, *42*, 50–51; class tensions and moral positionings reflected in, 35, 38–42, *40*, 223–24, *224*; description of, 38–43, *39*, *40*, *42*; domestic space structure and, 45, 223–24, *224*, 274n5; *habitus* of, 41; locality production as structure of feeling from, 35, 42–46, 73; marginalization and, 46; mobility vs. stuck and, 40–41, 43–44, 51; remittances and, 21, 35, 40, 190, 274n2, 289n17; ritual celebrating and, 59–62, *60*; spatial-temporal processes and prosperity represented in, 41–42, *42*, 73, 223–24, *224*; tradition/modernity shifts and, 21, 45–46. *See also* "American guests"

Hua Guang Dadi god/temple, 49, *50*

huaqiao (overseas Chinese). *See* overseas Chinese (*huaqiao*)

huibao (retribution), 204–5, 232–33

hukou (household registration system). *See* household registration system (*hukou*)

"human feeling"/bonds (*renqing*): alienability of human sentiment/bodies and, 21, 169, 219, 238; asymmetries of gender and, 6, 169, 219, 220–21, 241–42; asymmetries of kinship and, 219, 256, 292n1; commodification of

jumin (non-peasant) elites. *See* non-peasant (*jumin*) elites

kaifang ("opening up") policy. *See* "opening up" (*kaifang*) policy
karma: cosmic debt and, 289n19; de/merit and, 12, 194–95, 204–5, 266–67; entrance processes and, 161; mahjong as barometer of, 266–67; social recognition of "human feeling" and, 12, 232–33
Keane, Webb, 15, 108
kinship relations: distributional order and asymmetries of, 219, 256, 292n1; entrance processes and, 105, 144, 280n2; exit processes and, 124–25; gender and, 222, 226, 230–31, 235–36, 254–55; "human feeling"/bonds and, 218, 230, 235–36, 253; personhood for female subject validation and, 251, 254; retribution and regulation of, 232
Kipnis, Andrew, 252, 253, 276n2, 277n8, 282n17, 290n24
к-1 (foreign fiancé(e) visa), 119–21, 137
Kumar, Amitava: *Passport Photos*, 141

land reforms, 87
land smuggling routes, 103, 104, 111–12
Latour, Bruno, 105, 108, 109, 120, 158, 280n2, 281n9
legality: boundary making effect and, 118–19; court hearings for asylum and, 144, 153–58; detention centers and, 106, 136–37, 142, 152, 210; entrance processes and, 105–6, 136–39, 144, 280n2; exit processes and, 98, 117–22, 118; fake-marriage arrangements vs., 114, 117, 122, 137; household registration system and, 70–73, 90–94, 98–99; identity/legal status

in China and, 103–6, 279n1; inscription and performance in search for, 105, 144, 280n2; of paperwork, 110, 121; political asylum as last chance for, 144, 153–58; of travel, 69, 102–3, 112, 114–15, 117–18, 212, 281n10; travel hierarchy and, 105–6
legal knowledge about entrance/exit processes, 108, 133, 146–48, 249–50, 283n3
Lemon, Alaina, 174, 200
Lerner, Daniel, 271n19
lian ("face"), 252–54
ling (divine efficacy). *See* divine efficacy (*ling*)
Liu, Xin, 10
liumang (hooligan), 245–46
locality/locality production, 8, 11–12, 35–38, 42–46, 51, 73
local person (*dangdiren*), 31, 36–37
Longyan village (pseud.): "American guests" status in, 187; big vs. small money in, 200–202, 203, 291n27; Communist Revolution and, 36, 52, 70, 197, 200–201; cosmopolitanism and, 36, 68, 72–74, 201; domestic space structure and, 45, 274n5; "ducks"/male charmers and, 232, 238–43, 246; edgy dispositions and, 52–53; Fuzhou City compared with, 44–45, 73–74, 178; hooligan and, 245–46; mahjong as pastime in, 229, 257–58; non-peasant village committee in, 69–70, 277n6; as overseas village, 36–37, 46, 68–69, 273n5, 274n2; patrilineal family order in, 218, 221, 223, 230, 254, 292n2; peasants village committee for, 60–62, 69–70, 273n5, 274n2, 277n6; remittance statistics, 35, 178; as research site, 16–20; social reproduction in,

Longyan village (pseud.) (*cont.*)
217–19, 237–38, 242, 251–52; transnationalism and feminization of, 220–21. *See also* built environment; house renovations/construction; money; religion/superstition (*mixin*); "sister-in-law" (*wanbasao*); spirit money; temple renovations/construction; U.S. dollar

Longyan villagers (pseud.): adultery and, 238–42, 293n6; cosmopolitan desires of, 21, 37–38, 201, 259; "ducks"/male charmers and gender categorization by, 232, 238–43, 246; "face" and status for, 124, 191, 251–56; Fuzhou City and, 41, 67–68; household registration system classification as peasants for, 73; identity/legal status for, 103–6, 279n1; Inappropriate/d Other status and, 15; locality production for, 35–38; materiality of money for, 200–201; potentiality of mobility vs. ontology of state identification and, 37, 96, 99, 278n13; "stepping out" and, 70–72; transitions and overseas-connected, 69–74, 97; undocumented subject's life compared with life of, 248; urbanites compared with, 70. *See also* cadres; moral career; non-peasant (*jumin*) elites; peasant (*nongmin*); personhood for female subject; personhood for male subject; "sister-in-law" (*wanbasao*); teacher/s (fz. *sinnang*)

luck (*yunqi*), 134–36, 208–13, 263–65, 292n36

Lyons, Thomas, 65–66

mahjong: cosmic credit and, 191–99, 205, 207, 214, 232–33; cosmic debt

and, 7, 191–98, 207–9, 212–14, 232–33; debt/loss relation to, 265–66; as emigration model, 21, 135–36, 161, 261, 265, 266–67; fate and, 265–66, 294n1; karmic de/merit and, 12, 194–95, 266–67; luck vs. skill and, 263–65; money circulation and, 228–29, 258, 266–67; moral positioning of class tension with, 222, 225, 228–29, 232, 241–42; obsession with, 229, 257–58; rules for, 261–64, *262*; sociality of, 229, 266–67; styles of playing, 229, 261–63; temporality and, 258; value production and, 266–67, 294n1; as village pastime, 229, 257–58

Mahler, Sarah, 284nn8–9

male subject: adultery and, 242; boat smuggling and, 112, 280n4; body and productivity of, 241, 254; construction workers as outsider, 243; consumption and, 242, 244; "ducks"/male charmers and, 232, 238–43, 246; "face" and, 251; gender categorization and, 232, 238–43, 246; patrilineal family order and, 218, 221, 223, 230, 254, 292n2; social reproduction by, 251–52; with status of "sister-in-law," 242, 251; as trafficking victim, 112–14, 280nn4–5

Malkki, Liisa, 33

Mao era: land reforms during and after, 87; mobility during era of, 13–14, 71; money as taboo and, 201; non-Western world and, 13, 272n21; overseas Chinese and transnationalism during, 60–62, 69, 279n15; religion/superstition during, 48–49, 87–88, 181–82; rural commune system during, 65, 97; state regulations/policies as disciplinary and transformational during, 278n12. *See also* household registration system (*hukou*)

Mao Zedong, 13–14, 63–64, 71, 272n21, 276n2

Marcus, George, 56

marginalization: deportation and, 283n3; "ducks"/male charmers and spaces of, 232, 238–43, 246; edgy dispositions and, 52–53; English language proficiency and, 57, 58, 146; hooligan and spaces of, 245–46; house renovations/construction and, 46; Monkey King god displacement and, 51; of undocumented subjects, 137, 160

market currencies vs. spirit money, 174–75, 205–7, 213–14, 259–60, 291n31

marriages: adultery and, 238–42, 293n6; foreign fiancé(e) visa paperwork for, 119–21, 137. *See also* fake-marriage (*jia jiehun*) arrangements; "sister-in-law" (*wanbasao*)

Marx, Karl, 83, 168, 200, 205, 287n6, 292nn33–34

Massey, Doreen, 10, 51, 110

Massumi, Brian, 14–15, 270n10, 272n22

materiality of money, 167, 174–75, 199–203, 291n27

Mauss, Marcel, 148, 167, 252, 286n2, 286n4

Mazu goddess of the sea, 2–3

mediation/inter-face, 253–56

Meiguoke ("American guests"). *See* "American guests" (*Meiguoke*)

mianzi ("face"), 124, 191, 251–56

Mitchell, Timothy, 6, 118, 270n15

mixin (religion/superstition). *See* religion/superstition (*mixin*)

mobility: cosmic credit types and, 12–13, 161; debt repayments and limitations on, 258–59; description of, 10; de-

sires for, 10–12; differentiated, 10, 51, 110, 163, 255, 259, 285n14; divergent futures enabled by household registration system and, 62, 70–71, 89–95, 97–98, 259; embodied experience of, 15, 111–12, 114–16, 143, 280n7, 282n8; emplacement in relation to, 32–35; of ghosts, 186; of gods/goddesses, 5, 11, 50, 94–95, 215; house renovations/construction and elevators as reflection of, 40–41; of humans, 5, 10–11, 13–14, 33, 64, 219; immobility vs., 3, 5, 11–12, 34, 102, 201, 259; during Mao era, 13–14, 71; modernity in relation to, 3–6, 13–14, 259; ontology of state identification vs. potentiality of, 37, 96, 99, 278n13; passports and, 15, 116; past used for claims for, 9–10, 70–71, 277n6; as qualisign, 14–15, 21, 73, 108–9, 272n23; as sensible concept, 14–15, 272n22; stuck vs., 12, 34, 38, 43–44, 51, 62, 249, 251, 267; surplus births outside one-child policy and, 79–80, 90–92, 161; transnationalism of female subject and, 113–14

modernity/modernities: Chinese RMB, as marker for, 174, 215; emigration flows and transnational circulation, 13, 271n19; gods/goddesses as vanguards of, 49–50, 94–95, 161; house renovations/construction shifts in tradition and, 21, 45–46; mobility as trope for, 3–6, 13–14, 120, 259; oscillations between, 6, 270n10

money: ambiguity of, 166–67, 195; big vs. small, 200–202, 203, 291n27; boundary-making/breaking effects of, 174, 206, 214–15; commodification relations of, 167, 238–42, 256, 292n33; debt in relation to, 167–69, money (*cont.*)

286n5; divine efficacy in relation to, 191–93, 208–16; equivalence relations of, 167–68, 174, 199; exit processes and creditability of, 122–26; as generalized debt, 167, 214, 259–60; ghost, 184–86, 189, 289n13; mahjong and circulation of, 228–29, 258, 266–67; Mao era and taboo status of, 201; materiality of, 167, 174–75, 199–203, 291n27; overseas Chinese as source of new, 21, 83, 228–30, 235–37, 240; as specialized vs. generalized currency, 206. *See also* Chinese RMB; U.S. dollar

Monkey King (Qitian Dasheng) god, 20, 46–51, 47, 198, 275n6

moral career: boat smuggling acceptance and, 109–10; boundary-making/breaking and, 8, 118–19, 259, 270n15; cosmopolitanism and claims for, 9–11, 259; as counter-hegemonic, 94; cross-class resentments and, 8, 18–19, 63, 66, 75, 81, 86–87, 161–62; description of, 62, 96, 161; legality/morality delinking of household registration system and, 70–73, 90–94, 98–99; "opening up" policy and, 4, 10, 13, 30, 33, 59, 78, 97, 259–60; past used for claims for, 9–10, 70–71, 277n6; peasant vs. overseas Chinese and contested, 21, 61–62, 69, 72, 75–76, 98, 278n11, 279n15; pervasive sense of momentum and transnational desires of, 1–3, 9; potentiality of mobility vs. ontology of state identification and, 37, 63, 96, 99, 278n13. *See also* Goffman, Erving; peasant (*nongmin*)

morality: digressions from moral circuits of "human feeling"/bonds

and, 222, 225–26, 228–32, 238–41, 252, 293n6; "human feeling"/bonds and transnational, 221–22, 238; legality and, 70–73, 90–94, 98–99; of transnationalism, 208–13, 215, 217, 219–22, 238

morality of wealth: Chinese RMB accumulation and, 201–6; cosmic credit and, 204; divine efficacy in relation to, 203, 211–12; gender and, 221; "sister-in-law" divisions over, 221–22, 227, 233, 240–41; spirit money and, 183, 214; U.S. dollar and, 204–6

Munn, Nancy, 5, 14, 95, 235, 255, 291n30

Myerhoff, Barbara, 162

narratives and paperwork coordination during exit processes, 121, 127

national ID card, 277n9

nation-state experience, 119–21, 159–61, 281–82nn12–14, 285n11

networked body, 95–96, 161

9/11: and effects on emigration, 9, 136, 138–39, 159–60, 282n13

nongmin (peasant). *See* peasant (*nongmin*)

non-peasant (*jumin*) elites: built environment and conflicts between local peasants and, 35; class status for, 19, 35, 66, 80–81; class tensions between peasant and, 19, 74, 81–85, 182; critiques of peasant emigration aspirations and strategies by, 74, 80–81; Cultural Revolution and, 89; divine efficacy and, 197–99; educational advantages for, 73, 202, 277n8; household registration system and, 66–67, 74, 81–83, 89–90, 93, 277n8; house renovations/construction and conflicts between peasants and, 35,

paper/paperless routes (*cont.*)
files-selves as legible and complete and, 21, 103–4, 126–27, 131–34; paperwork and claims of entitlement in, 144, 150–52

paperwork: in bureaucratic exchange, 107–8, 121–22, 125, 138; creditability claims of conscientiousness during exit processes through, 132–34; fake-marriage arrangements and, 132; foreign fiancé(e) visa, 119–21, 137; INS, 107; legality of, 110, 121; narratives and, 121, 127, 151–52, 155–56, 284n5, 284nn7–8; non-peasant elites and, 102–3; plane routes and financial costs of, 112, 144; religious practices and, 135–37, 157–59, 162; religious ritual burial rights/rites and, 162–64, *164*; signatures on, 128–29, 162; snakehead and, 127, 133, 147; state identification and, 104, 128–29, 162; "work" in, 126–34, 162

para-ethnography, 56

passports: fetishization of, 162; household registration system as internal system of, 64; international system of, 282n13; material dispossession, 103; mobility and, 15, 116; paper routes and counterfeit, 114, 147; personal relations and, 124; personal skill and revaluation of, 105; post-Mao policies and, 277n9; as state-authorized sign of entitlement, 150; U.S. policies and, 138, 282n13

patrilineal family order, 218, 221, 223, 230, 254, 292n2

peasant (*nongmin*): as administrative identity, 62, 63–64, 66–67, 276nn2–3; aspirations for overseas Chinese status by, 17, 74–75, 80–81, 161, 258, 277n9; baggage for plane travel as markers and, 148–49; boundary-making/breaking effects between cosmopolitanism and provincial, 117, 214, 237, 259, 293n5; built environment and conflicts between elites and, 35; class status for, 19, 35, 66, 80–81; class tension between non-peasant elites and, 19, 74, 81–85, 182; Communist Revolution and, 63–64, 66, 276n2; courage/nerve and correlation with education of, 76–78; critiques of emigration aspirations and strategies of, 74; culture/education and, 35, 68, 75–77, 80, 82–84, 93, 98; educational disadvantages of, 66–67, 69, 70–73, 80, 84–85, 145, 212, 276n4; educational opportunities for, 66–67, 69, 73, 78, 144, 202, 276n4, 277n8; food and eating memories for, 65–66, 234–35; Great Leap Forward famine and, 64, 66, 85, 87, 95, 276n3; household registration system and, 37–38, 42, 62, 66–69, 82–83, 89–90, 93, 98–99, 161; land reforms and, 87; mobility vs. stuck and, 12, 34, 38, 43–44, 51, 62, 237, 249, 267; moral careers of, 68; movement restrictions for, 64–65, 89–90, 201, 276n3; multiple children as moral legacy/networked body, 95–96, 161; overseas Chinese and transformation of, 21, 61–62, 69, 72, 75–76, 98, 278n11; past used for claims for mobility and moral careers for, 9–10, 70–71, 277n6; as pejorative term, 63, 66, 68; policing and punishment critiques by, 88–89; potentiality of mobility vs. ontology of state identification for, 37, 96, 99, 278n13; quantity over quality dispositions of, 79–

80, 82–83; religious ritual burial rights/rites and aspirations for foreign state identification for, 162–64, 284n13, 285n14; self-descriptions of, 84–96; teacher class tension with, 18, 19, 37, 66, 80–81, 182, 289n11; transitions and overseas-connected, 69–74, 97; urbanites and disparities with life of, 64, 65–66, 276n4; U.S. dollar circulation and boundaries between non-peasant elites and, 174, 214; village committee for, 60–62, 69–70, 273n5, 274n2, 277n6; village life/history of, 64–66, 70, 277n6; work unit and, 66–67, 85–87, 89, 92, 276n3. *See also* household registration system (*hukou*); moral career; overseas Chinese (*huaqiao*); religion/superstition (*mixin*)

Peirce, C. S., 14

personal pleasures: for "sister-in-laws," 222, 225–26, 228–32, 237–41, 254–55, 293nn5–6

personal relationships/network (*guanxi*): creditability for borrowing funds and, 124–25, 282n17; description of, 161–62; entitlement of subjects vs., 105, 108; fake-marriage arrangements and, 124–25; household registration system registration status vs., 89–95, 278n14; smuggling services in relation to, 121–22, 124–26; state registration status vs., 278n13; surplus births outside one-child policy and, 90–94

personhood for female subject, 113–14, 251, 254. *See also* "sister-in-law" (*wanbasao*)

personhood for male subject: "child/children" position and, 243–44, 247, 249, 251–52; collective sensibilities

of villagers, 218, 243–52, 254, 294n7; dislocating effects of being stuck and, 249; "elderly" position for, 247, 249–50, 251–52; "face" and, 251–52, 254; failure in migration and, 145–46, 247–50, 283n3; hooligan and, 245–46; internal migrants in relation to, 243–44; men/non-men binary, 250, 254, 294n7; mobility vs. stuck and, 249; production and, 204, 243–46, 251; reticent public behavior of men and, 109, 136, 247–48, 254; wives as overseas Chinese and, 251

plane routes: embodied experience of mobility and, 114–15, 143; as female gendered form of transit, 113–14; financial costs of paperwork for, 112, 144; legality and use of, 103, 112, 114–15, 117–18, 281n10; snakehead/smuggler and document assistance for, 112, 114–15; technicalities and challenges of using, 117–18, 281n9; travel hierarchies and, 114–15

political asylum, 144; asylee status described, 153, 284n6; bad subject status legitimized when seeking, 153–54; financial costs and, 156–57, 285n10; as juridical performance, 153; as last resort, 156, 284n9; lawyers and, 155, 156–57, 159, 285n10; under "one-child" policy, 69, 279n1; refugee status described, 139, 284n6; religious grounds for, 155–56; religious practices and divine intervention for, 157–59, 192; unidirectional flow of migrants and, 154; U.S. policies and, 155, 284n7. *See also* deportation

politics of destination, 12, 54, 258, 266

politics of pre-destination, 12, 271n18

politics of return, 11, 53–54

Poole, Deborah, 118, 121

population problem (*renkou wenti*), 10–11, 67, 69, 78–80, 87–95, 97, 277n5, 279n1

post-Mao era: capitalist commodification during, 207, 214; cosmopolitan aspirations during, 11, 25–26, 73–74; credit-able practices during, 7, 259–60; economic reforms during, 9–10, 33; personal relationship sentiments during, 282n17; rural unemployment during, 242–43; state regulations/policies as punitive during, 278n12; transnationalism during, 4–5, 30, 37, 275n1, 277n9, 278n11, 279n15. *See also* China; money; religion/superstition (*mixin*); U.S. dollar

Practical English for People Working in Chinese Restaurants (Yuan Dai), 31–32, *32*, 54, 55

production: "human feeling"/bonds and frictions that unsettle distributional order and, 5, 169, 218, 246; locality/locality, 8, 11–12, 35–38, 42–46, 51, 73; mobilization of resources for exit and, 21, 107–8; personhood for male subject and, 204, 243–46, 251; productivity of male subject and, 241, 254; religion/superstition and actions of rituals as, 169, 174, 204–5, 214; social reproduction and, 217–19, 237–38, 242, 251–52

qi (energy) flows, 173, 233, 287n2, 293n4

Qing dynasty, 6, 24, 28–29, 36, 181, 270n11, 273n3

Qitian Dasheng (Monkey King) god, 20, 46–51, *47*, 198, 275n6

reciprocal effects, 15, 105, 108–9, 116–17, 217–18, 256

religion/superstition (*mixin*): beliefs and practice of, 193–94, 290n26; boat smuggling and protection through, 2–3; bureaucratic logic of afterlife, 175–77, *176*, *179*; burial rights/rites and, 162–64, *164*, 285nn13–14; Chinese RMB for ritual activities and, 187–88, 203; criticisms of, 80–81, 173, 182–83, 289n11; Cultural Revolution and, 48–49, 208, 285n13; disavowal of, 173–74; divine efficacy and role in ritual expenditures and, 191; "doing" of, 173, 180, 182–84, 205, 214–17; entrance processes and, 145, 149, 161–62; etymology of, 215, 288n10; exit processes and, 135–37, 162; "face" ritual expenditures in, 191, 256; fate and, 12, 50, 157, 266; hell and, 172–73, 175–77, 189; history/genealogy of, 48, 181–84; Mao era and, 48–49, 87–88, 181–82; material understanding of invisible world and, 177–78; *mixin* as pejorative term, 182; non-peasant elite ritual offerings and, 193–94; peasants' alignment with gods/goddesses for access to modernity and, 49–50, 94–95, 161; productive actions of rituals and, 169, 174, 204–5, 214; revivalism and, 46–48, *47*, 68, 182–83, 260, 275n6; state regulations/policies against, 48–49, 87–89, 181–83, 186, 196, 208. *See also* ancestors; cosmic credit; cosmic debt; cosmology/cosmologies; gods/goddesses; spirit money; spirits of the dead; temple districts

remittances: debt and, 212, 226–27; divine efficacy as component of, 197–98; house renovations/construction and, 21, 35, 40, 190, 274n2,

289n17; human agency as component of, 197–98; as new money from overseas Chinese, 21, 83, 228–30, 235–37, 240; road construction and, 35; statistics, 28–29, 35, 178; Tour of the Gods ritual and, 197–98

renkou wenti (population problem). *See* population problem (*renkou wenti*)

Renminbi (RMB). *See* Chinese RMB

renqing ("human feeling"/bonds). *See* "human feeling"/bonds (*renqing*)

Republican Era, 36, 47, 52, 181–82, 200–201, 276n2

research: immigration/immigration document involvements and, 107, 127, 280n11; Inappropriate/d Other position during, 16–17, 107, 272n24; kinship positionality and, 17–18; living among cadres and, 18–20; location for, 1–2, 17–19; reverse anthropology and, 16

Restaurant English, 31–32, *32*, 54–58, 275n8

retribution (*huibao*), 204–5, 232–33

rhythms of waiting/activity, 134–35, 258, 267

road construction, 35, 51–53, *52*

Rofel, Lisa, 9

Roitman, Janet, 168, 169, 214

rural commune system, 65, 97

sacrifices, 69, 103–4, 137, 208, 226, 233–35, 237, 293n3

Sahlins, Marshall, 6–7, 270n11, 270n13

Sangren, Steven, 290n26

Schivelbusch, Wolfgang, 271n19

Schmitt, Carl, 160

Scott, James, 121

self-making practices, 105, 143–44

shang ting ("going to court") for political asylum pleas, 144, 153–58

shenfen (identity/legal status), 103–6, 279n11

shetou (snakehead/smuggler), 15, 111–12, 114–15, 121–24, 127, 133, 147

Shi, Tie-sheng, "Fate," 102–3

Sichuanese as internal migrants, 10–11, 67, 78–79, 243–44, 277n5

Simmel, Georg, 293n3

sinnang (teacher/s). *See* teacher/s (fz. *sinnang*)

"sister-in-law" (*wanbasao*): adultery and, 238–42, 293n6; cosmic debt and, 251; credit/debt relations and, 226–27, 230, 232–33; domestic space structure and, 223–24, *224*; electronic mediums and husbands' care for/control of, 255; "face" and, 254; kinship order and, 222, 226, 230–31, 235–36, 254–55; male subjects with status of, 242, 251; morality of wealth from transnationalism and, 221–22, 227, 233, 240–41; permissible personal pleasures and, 237, 255, 293n5; sacrifices of, 226–68, 235; transgressive personal pleasures and, 222, 225–26, 228–32, 238–41, 254–55, 293n6; transnationalism and disruption in lives of women nicknamed, 220–21, 238–40

snakehead/smuggler (*shetou*), 15, 111–12, 114–15, 121–24, 127, 133, 147

sociality: credit-debt and, 124, 167–69, 286n2, 286nn4–5; debt as, 124, 167–69, 286n2, 286nn4–5; "human feeling"/bonds and, 169, 232; of mahjong, 229, 266–67

social reproduction, 217–19, 237–38, 242, 251–52

spatial-temporal processes: American child and, 95–96; ancestor relations and, 95, 217; commodification of

spatial-temporal processes (*cont.*)
time and, 258; cosmopolitan desires
realized and, 38, 50–51, 192–93, 259;
"face" and, 254–55; housing transformations as representation of
prosperity in, 41–42, *42*; mobility/
timeliness of gods/goddesses and, 5,
11, 50, 94–95, 215; mobility vs. stuck
and, 12, 34, 38, 43–44, 51, 62, 249,
267; multiple children as moral
legacy/networked body and, 95; of
persons and collectivities, 4–5, 11–12;
prosperity represented in, 41–42, *42*,
73, 223–24, *224*; rhythms of waiting/
activity and, 7–8, 134–35, 258, 267;
temple renovations and, 51
spirit money: ancestor repayments and
circulation of, 173, 175, 186–89, 193,
195–96, 206, 212–13, 260, 287n5,
290n25; capitalism in relation to,
207–8, 292n34; Chinese RMB as,
174–75, 177, 179, 187–88, 203, 205–6,
213–14, 291n31; Cultural Revolution
and, 182; denominations of, *176*,
177–81, *179*, *180*, 187, 199; funeral
processions and, 171–72; ghost money
in exchange rituals and, 184–88, *185*;
for ghosts, 175, 188, 196, 206, 287n5,
289n12, 290n25; gold standard for,
188–91, *189*, 287n5, 288n7; hierarchical ranking of, 175, 185–86, 287n5;
market currencies vs., 174–75, 205–7,
213–14, 259–60, 291n31; morality of,
183, 214; sociality of, 169, 183; state
currencies as, 175, 288nn6–7; state
regulation of, 182–83; U.S.-Chinese
exchange rate and, 166; U.S. dollar
overseas remittances as, 172–78, *176*,
180–81, *180*, 186–89, 203–6, 288n8;
Yama and, 177

spirits of the dead, as ghosts, 175, 184–
86, 188, 196, 206, 287n5, 289n12,
290n25. *See also* ancestors
Stafford Charles, 219
state identification: *habitus* of legi-
bility/paperwork and, 104, 128–29,
162; identity/legal status and, 103–6,
279n11; labor market participation
and, 162, 285n12
state regulations/policies: allies in entrance processes vs., 144, 157–58;
boundary making effect and, 118–19;
as disciplinary and transformational
during Mao era, 278n12; divine authority vs., 12, 94–95; divine efficacy
vs., 195–96, 208; entrance processes
and, 158–62, 285n11; for legal emigration, 69, 74–75; new immigrants
and, 278n11; overseas Chinese status
and, 10–11, 74–75, 271n17, 277n9;
power and, 160, 285n11; religion/
superstition and, 48–49, 87–89, 181–
83, 186, 196, 208; religious ritual
burial rights/rites and aspirations
for foreign, 162–64, 285nn13–14;
state agents' decisions vs., 144, 152–
53, 158–59, 162, 285n11; undocumented subjects and, 69, 103. *See
also* household registration system
(*hukou*)
"stepping out" (*zou chuqu*), 70–72. *See
also* "opening up" (*kaifang*) policy
stowaway (*touduke*), 74–76, 97, 278n10
structures of feeling, 35, 36, 274n3
surplus births outside one-child policy
(*toushen*), 79–80, 90–92

Taiwan: currencies and, 199; edgy dispositions and, 26; Fujian Province
in relation with, 25, 272n2, 275n5;

history of, 24–26, 200; mahjong style in, 262–63; passport as anomaly and, 282n13; separation/reunion processes and, 219; spirit currencies, 189, 287n5, 292n34

teacher/s (fz. *sinnang*): class status for, 18, 19, 37, 66; class tensions between peasants and, 18, 19, 37, 66, 80–81, 182, 289n11; household registration system category of nonpeasant elites for, 74, 81, 277n8; on human smuggling, 74; as outsiders in Longyan village, 74–75; overseas Chinese aspirations for, 74–75; peasant class tension with, 18, 19, 37, 66, 80–81, 182, 289n11; on religion/superstition, 182, 289n11; ritual offerings and, 193–94; work unit and, 66, 277n6

temple districts: description of, 20, 48; Monkey King god and, 20, 46–51, 47, 198, 275n6; territorial gods and, 20, 48–50, 177, 188. *See also* gods/goddesses

temple renovations/construction: cosmopolitan desires realized through, 50–51, 192–93, 259; divine space for, 47, 48, 51; Guanyin temple and, 46–48, 47, 51, 275n6; locality production and, 35; remittances and, 21, 35, 40, 48, 80–81, 190, 213, 274n2, 289n17; state regulations/policies against, 48–49, 208; tradition/modernity shifts and, 49–50. *See also* gods/goddesses

temples: "American guests" contributions to, 190; Cultural Revolution and, 48–49, 208, 285n13; displacement and marginalization of, 51; districts and territorial god in, 20;

Guanyin temple, 46–48, 47, 51, 275n6; history/role of, 20, 48–49; Hua Guang Dadi temple, 49, 50; Monkey King god and, 20, 46–51, 47, 198, 275n6; offerings to gods/goddesses in, 192, 193, 289n20; religious revivalism and, 46–48, 47, 275n6; temple renovations and divine space for, 20, 48, 49–51; Tour of the Gods ritual and, 198. *See also* gods/goddesses

territorial gods, 20, 48–50, 177, 188

things-in-motion circulation, 206, 232–36, 238–39, 241, 254–56, 259–60, 266–67, 291n32, 293n6. *See also* "human feeling"/bonds (*renqing*); money; peasant (*nongmin*); personhood for male subject; spirit money

Torpey, John, 89–90, 143, 282n13, 283n1

toudu (human smuggling). *See* human smuggling (*toudu*)

touduke (stowaway), 74–76, 97, 278n10

Tour of the Gods (*Youshen*) ritual, 196–98, 208

toushen (surplus births outside one-child policy), 79–80, 90–92

transitions: and peasants as overseas-connected subjects, 69–74, 97

transnationalism: afterlife and, 162–64, *164*; alienability of human sentiment/bodies and, 21, 169, 219, 238; American child and networked, 95–96; Chinese RMB and connection, 190; described, 10–11, 271n17; diaspora vs., 11, 13, 33–35; feminization of Longyan village and, 220–21; gender and morality of, 221; map of New York City and, 31–32, *32*; moral/pragmatic worth of, 208–13, 215, 217,

transnationalism (*cont.*)
219–22, 238; overseas connections/
sponsorship and, 129–30, *130*; patrilineal family order and role in,
218, 221, 223, 230, 254, 292n2; unidirectional flow of migrants and, 154
travel and road construction, 35, 51–
53, *52*
Travel English, 57, 144–46, 147, 151,
283n2
travel hierarchies, 105–6, 108, 114–15,
117, 125
Trinh, T. Minh-ha, 15, 16, 272n24
Tsai, Kellee, 280n4

undocumented/documented routes.
See boat smuggling; human smuggling (*toudu*); plane routes; snake-
head/smuggler (*shetou*)
undocumented subjects: asylum plea
denials and permanent status as,
153–54, 159–60; deportation possibilities for, 139; files-selves as legible
and complete vs. paperless routes
for, 21, 103–4; illegal status/life of,
94, 220, 224, 248; internal migrants
as, 79; marginalization of, 137, 160;
moral career and maneuver from,
226; paper/paperless routes and,
79; state identification and, 69, 103
United States: American child from,
95–96; deportation policies and,
284n7; detention centers in, 106,
136–37, 142, 152, 210; Fujian-U.S.
government office and, 61, 68, 74;
green card IDS, 129–30, *130*, 137, 147,
162–64, *164*, 284n13, 285n14; Guangzhou consulate for, 119, 126–27, 130–
31; imaginaries of place and emplacement and, 31–32, *32*; Immigration

and Customs Enforcement, 116,
280n7, 282n18; Immigration and
Naturalization Service, 107, 126,
282n18, 283n2; immigration policies of, 104, 279n11; practices and
aspirations for citizenship in, 64, 96,
161; state regulatory/policy powers
and, 159–61, 285n11. *See also* "American guests"; English language; overseas Chinese (*huaqiao*)
urbanites: cultural capital and, 83;
household registration system and,
37, 63–68, 81–82; on human smuggling conflation with rural emigration, 74, 79–80; Longyan villagers
compared with, 70; overseas Chinese status and, 74–75, 277n9; on
past and peasants as unfavorable
characters, 74–83, 97; on religion/
superstition, 80–81, 173. *See also*
non-peasant (*jumin*) elites; outsiders
(*waidiren*); teacher/s (fz. *sinnang*)
Urry, John, 13
U.S. dollar: "American guests" and
circulation of spirit, 180; ancestors
and circulation of spirit, 175, 186–
89, 196, 206; Chinese RMB exchange
rate with, 166; Chinese RMB incommensurability with, 199; class status
asymmetries and flows of, 174, 214;
as cosmic credit, 204–6; ghosts and
circulation of spirit, 185, 196; gods/
goddesses and circulation of spirit,
175–78, *176*, 180–81, 186–87, 189, 196;
as market currency vs. spirit money,
174, 205–6; materiality of, 202–3;
morality of wealth and, 204–6;
nested hierarchies in cosmologies
and position of spirit, 189, 204–5;
social reproduction and, 237–38; as

spirit money, 172–78, *176*, 180–81, *180*, 186–89, 196, 203–6, 288n8; temple restorations and value of, 189–90; transnational connection with, 190

value/value production: burning spirit money and, 206, 260, 292n33; cosmology role in value transformation and, 12, 205–7, 260, 291n30; as credit-able practices, 259–60; debt stabilization and, 169, 173–74, 214, 259–60; Fuzhou area/countryside and, 260; mahjong and, 266–67, 294n1; ritual and mundane monetary transactions for stabilization of, 169, 173–74, 214, 259–60
village, use of term, 27, 36
visible and invisible worlds: burning spirit money and exchange act between, 184–88, *185*, 206–7, 214–16, 291n32, 292n33; religion/superstition and material understanding of invisible world, 177–78

waidiren (outsiders). *See* outsiders (*waidiren*)
wanbasao ("sister-in-law"). *See* "sister-in-law" (*wanbasao*)
Watson, James, 257–58, 267
Weber, Max, 12, 271n18

Weiner, Annette, 218
Weller, Robert, 26, 89n12
wenhua (culture/education), 35, 68, 75–78, 80, 82–84, 93, 98
"work" in paperwork, 126–34, 162
work unit (*danwei*), 66–67, 85–86, 276n3, 278n14

xinyong (creditability), 122–26, 132–34, 169, 193, 282n16

Yama (King of Hell), 177
Yanagisako, Sylvia, 7–8
Yang, Mayfair, 233, 282n17, 292n34
Yngvesson, Barbara, 282n13
Youshen (Tour of the Gods) ritual, 196–98, 208
Yuan dynasty, 24, 200
yuanfen (fate), 12, 50, 157, 265–66, 294n1
yunqi (luck), 134–36, 208–13, 263–65, 292n36

zibenzhuyi (capitalism), 7, 12, 168, 193, 207–8, 260, 287n6, 290n23, 292n34
Zito, Angela, 206, 253, 271n15, 291n32
zones of departure, 138
zou chuqu ("stepping out"), 70–72. *See also* "opening up" (*kaifang*) policy
zou houmen (back door) strategies, 121–22, 124–25, 131, 137, 161, 259

JULIE Y. CHU is an assistant professor of
anthropology at the University of Chicago.

Library of Congress Cataloging-in-Publication Data

Chu, Julie Y., 1974–

Cosmologies of credit : transnational mobility and the
politics of destination in China / Julie Y. Chu.

p. cm.

Includes bibliographical references and index.

ISBN 978-0-8223-4792-7 (cloth : alk. paper)

ISBN 978-0-8223-4806-1 (pbk. : alk. paper)

1. Fujian Sheng (China)—Emigration and
immigration. 2. Fujian Sheng (China)—Rural
conditions. I. Title. JV8709.F8C48 2010

304.80951'245—dc22

2010022933